The best

of the

light ales

is a

WHITBREAD

LTD

The Cash Jewellers for over 100 Years.

Chief Store: **KINGS CROSS, N.1**

(Kings Cross Store is open all day on Saturdays)

75, FLEET STREET, E.C. 4

22, ORCHARD STREET, W.1

189, BROMPTON ROAD, S.W.3

"RENOWN"
Silver Plated

3" high	5" high
£1 · 3 · 6	£2 · 7 · 6
6" high	**7" high**
£3 · 12.6	£5 . 5 . 0

Sunday Chronicle Cricket and Golf Annual, 1953

(Incorporating the Athletic News Cricket Annual)

56th Year of Publication

General Index

TEST CRICKET

GOLF

KEMSLEY NEWSPAPERS LTD., MANCHESTER: Kemsley House, 4.
LONDON: Kemsley House, W.C.1

Fast Bowling Battles of 1953

AUSTRALIA'S NEW CHECK TO BUMPERS

by W. E. (BILL) BOWES

Yorkshire & England

SINCE 1933 the Australians have had cricket very much as they liked it. In pre-war years, batsman Bradman and bowler O'Reilly, more than any other players, gave them superiority. In post-war cricket, fast bowlers Lindwall and Miller have blasted the hopes of all opponents.

So, for 20 years, Australia have not been beaten in a Test series. Mostly the matches have been a challenge for supremacy in name only.

This canter to victory after victory began to pall rather than please the spectators, and Australian officialdom became smug. Even the players have grinned when some silly mistake cost them their wicket.

Grinned ! They knew someone in the side would make good their error. If Lindwall and Miller turned on the heat, they knew the best blooms in the opposition would wilt. And unfortunately they were right.

For the good of cricket the world over, a change was needed. Dare we hope that it's now arriving ?

Freddie Brown and his men gave the Australians several severe jolts during the 1950-51 tour and actually won the last Test match by a handsome margin.

" INEXCUSABLE " BUMPERS

ALTHOUGH the West Indians, on tour there in 1951-52, did not produce any of the expected fireworks, they did prove the Australians were vulnerable. A last-wicket stand of 38 runs between Johnston and Ring in the fourth Test of the series, which gave Australia a one-wicket victory, made the rubber score 3–1 instead of 2–2 . . . that's what it might have been.

This shook the Australian players from their complacency. In the fifth and final Test an attack of bumpers was launched by Lindwall which the Press described as " inexcusable."

Trueman as Answer to Miller and Lindwall

The law which states that "the persistent and systematic bowling of fast, short-pitched balls at the batsman standing clear of his wicket is unfair play" was not violated. It was not violated for the simple reason that few batsmen do stand clear of their stumps.

Australian officials smugly sought to have those words "standing clear of his wicket" struck out of the law, thereby making systematic bowling of short-pitched deliveries unfair. They sought to put a responsibility on the umpires which they should have accepted themselves.

If they really thought that Lindwall had infringed the spirit of cricket, which to me is far more important than breaking the laws, why did they not have a word with the player? The Australian selectors or the captain could have stopped it in an instant.

Instead, they suggested a rule whereby an umpire may stop a fast bowler bowling short of length at a batsman who may have a tendency to "nibble" at the ball. They suggested a rule whereby the bouncer—part of the stock-in-trade of any fast bowler—may be penalised.

The South African cricketers who were in Australia last winter were easily persuaded to give this change a trial. They had no fast bowler of their own and, though the law was to be interpreted by Australian umpires, it could only limit Lindwall and Miller. Fortunately, at the time of writing this article, M.C.C. had not been asked to approve this experimental rule.

I CANNOT FAULT THEM

I HAVE seen every Test match in which Lindwall and Miller have bowled against this country, and I cannot fault them. I think cricketers in England have only envied their ability, or been influenced by the fact that we had only cruisers to return the fire of their battleships.

I don't think that limiting the fast bowlers was the reason why South Africa shared the honours of last winter's Tests. I believe the tide of cricket supremacy is changing. So what's ahead this summer?

More than for many years, there is widespread optimism that England will be successful. With the retirement of Don Bradman and the decision of Sid. Barnes to report rather than play cricket, Australia's batting lost much of its steel. *(Continued overleaf)*

DON'T SHOUT TOO SOON!

Hassett, one of the most reliable players in an emergency, is now in the veteran class, and left-hander Neil Harvey, who made such a magnificent maiden Test century at Leeds in 1948 and record breaking scores last winter, quite often fails unaccountably. Likewise Arthur Morris.

There appear to be gaps in the Australian batting which the youngsters—De Courcy, Craig, Hole, McDonald—have not yet filled. There doesn't seem to be another Bradman, Ponsford, Woodfull or McCabe.

On the other hand, in England last summer we saw three outstanding batsmen in Peter May, Tom Graveney and David Sheppard. May, in particular, seemed to be the ready-made Test player and there are also many promising youngsters.

TRUEMAN'S YEAR?

NOW let us look at the attack—at the fast-bowling battles brewing in England in 1953.

Lindwall and Miller—good as they are—approach the veteran stage. This means, at least, they will not have the same powers of recovery.

Douglas Ring, at 34, is the best leg-break-googly bowler in Australia, and he came to England with the 1948 Tourists and only played in one Test match. Off-spinner Johnson has been dropped by the selectors and only fast-medium left-hander Bill Johnston seems to have retained all his skill.

In the newcomers—fast left-hander Alan Davidson, fast-medium Archer, leg-breaker Hill or all-rounders Hole and Benaud—there is no threat of another Grimmett, O'Reilly or Macdonald.

In Yorkshire, however, we have unearthed a fast bowler, in Fred Trueman, who promises to be another Larwood. He came into cricket against the Indians last year like a gale. He tore up stumps by the roots.

The English war-horse, Alec Bedser, and his team-mates Laker and Lock won the County Championship for Surrey last year, and proved that they can supply steady, predictable bowling support for Trueman in the Tests. Moreover, Lancashire's fast bowler, Statham, is a useful reserve.

EASIER FOR SCORES

HERE, then, are reasons for optimism. But let me recommend caution. Remember that, although we found three batsmen last year, we had three stars, Compton, Washbrook and Simpson, in decline.

Remember that Trueman is only 22 and not fully mature and, above all, let us admit the Australian batsmen are likely to find our slower English pitches easier for making scores.

We have in Trueman the likely answer to Lindwall and Miller. In Hutton we have the greatest batsman in the world. We have, yes, good grounds for cautious optimism, in a season which promises magnificent cricket.

Not Like 1948 Side

STARS' VIEWS ON TOUR TEAM

HERE is the list of players in Australia's touring team :

A. L. HASSETT (Victoria) (captain)
A. R. MORRIS (New South Wales), vice-captain
R. ARCHER (Queensland)
R. BENAUD (New South Wales)
C. McDONALD (Victoria)
W. A. JOHNSTON (Victoria)
G. LANGLEY (South Australia)
I. CRAIG (New South Wales)
D. RING (Victoria)
K. MILLER (New South Wales)
N. HARVEY (Victoria)
D. TALLON (Queensland)
R. R. LINDWALL (New South Wales)
G. HOLE (South Australia)
J. DE COURCY (New South Wales)
A. DAVIDSON (New South Wales)
J. HILL (Victoria)

VIEWS OF LEADERS

And this is what leading cricket personalities think about this 1953 combination :

LEN HUTTON takes the view that Bradman was worth two or three players and the team are sure to miss him, as was shown in the recent series of Tests with South Africa.

He regards the batting as below the average of Australian touring teams and the bowling as depending on whether Miller and Lindwall are as powerful as of yore.

" If they are, there's very little the matter with the attack. There are two excellent supporters in Davidson and Johnston.

" Davidson resembles Yorkshire's Abe Waddington—left-arm fast-medium. In this country he should be able to make the ball move a great deal.

" I'm looking forward to the tour and feel confident England will show up well and, I hope, win the rubber."

F. R. BROWN OPTIMISTIC

F. R. BROWN, England's last captain :

" I'm certain Australia must have been shaken by their second defeat by South Africa and I feel our prospects of regaining the Ashes are brighter than at any time since the war.

" In my opinion, Miller and Lindwall are still the two best fast bowlers in the world, but Australia are definitely suspect if anything happens to either bowler through injury or loss of form.

" Obviously Australia will have a good batting side, especially if our groundsmen prepare easy-paced pitches but whether they'll score enough runs to give their bowlers a reasonable chance is another matter.

Sir Don Says—

'MUCH DEPENDS ON MORRIS'

" The series just ended has shown that Australia's batting is not as strong as it was.

"Above all, England's fielding should give us an advantage, especially close to the wicket. In this phase I feel that our attacking powers were rather lacking until that memorable exhibition against India at Manchester last summer.

" The only surprise to me is the inclusion of Hill, who I remember slightly for his steady bowling in one match for Victoria against M.C.C. He could be a good bowler in this country, where the pitches will help him more. I presume he's been chosen to do much of the stock work in county games."

" EVEN STRUGGLE," SAYS BRADMAN

SIR DONALD BRADMAN : The Tests will be an even struggle, much depending on the opening batsman, Arthur Morris.

Should Australia's openers fail, Hassett will have to shoulder the heavy responsibility of facing the new-ball attack in order to pave the way for Harvey, who is now at the peak of his form. Hole, Craig and de Courcy should make many runs.

Australia's attack again depends on Miller and Lindwall, but their recent injuries necessitate Hassett nursing them carefully.

CYRIL WASHBROOK : England's chances are the best since 1946. The Australian side is nothing like so strong as that led by Bradman.

We have been told that their bowling is going down the hill but it is far stronger than ours. Where the Australian bowling may fall down is on soft wickets.

NOT LIKE 1948

JACK FINGLETON (Australia) thinks the only surprise in the Australian selections is the inclusion of Hill, the 29-year-old leg-spinner who has been in and out of the Victoria XI these last four years.

This decision he attributes to panic because Ring and Benaud did not go through South Africa on a wearing wicket on the sixth day of the last Test.

Fingleton adds that young Craig is a brilliant fieldsman, and Davidson, the medium-pace left-arm bowler, might be suited by English pitches.

But he considers the 1953 team is " nothing like so good as Bradman's side in 1948."

W. A. OLDFIELD, former Australian Test wicket-keeper, says: It would have been impossible to choose a better side from the material available.

W. J. O'REILLY, " Tiger " of earlier Australian teams, calls the inclusion of Hill a " here's hoping " effort to tighten up the " depressing state of the spin section of our attack."

'THE SECOND BRADMAN'

Tall Talk about Youngster of 17

By IVAN SHARPE

LINDSAY HASSETT (Victoria), smiling skipper of the 1953 team, led the Australian Services' side in England and India in 1945-46, acted as Australian vice-captain from 1946 to 1948, and took charge after Bradman in 1949.

In his first Test tour in England in 1938 he scored 220 not out against Cambridge University in his opening match, and he is now one of Australia's best batsmen—sound, yet a stroke-maker. Against South Africa he scored 163 in the fourth Test last winter and, during the season, set an individual record for Victoria Sheffield Shield cricket by totalling 6,915 runs (average 65).

Australian skippers are shrinking in size. Warwick Armstrong was a mountainous man—and not so merry. Woodfull was just as inconspicuous. Bradman was short, alert, efficient. Hassett is the smallest man . . . with the biggest smile. Age 39.

ARTHUR MORRIS (New South Wales). The vice-captain is the left-hand opening bat who starred here in 1948. But he has since slumped and was out of form last winter against South Africa.

He scored six centuries in his first ten Tests against England, including one in each innings at Adelaide in 1946-47, and led the Australian Test batting averages on the 1948 tour in England, with 696 runs (average 87).

In 1940 he set a world record by scoring two centuries (148 and 111) in his first-class debut for his State against Queensland.

He has kept his place in the 1953 tour team because, in the absence of Barnes, he is only opening bat with experience of English conditions. Age 31.

RON ARCHER (Queensland). Here's a young all-rounder still in his 'teens—a strong bat and new-ball bowler.

Taking a short run, he gets the ball through at a fast pace, and uses his height (6ft. 1in.) to advantage. Age 19.

THE NEW BOY

IAN CRAIG (New South Wales). Fancy playing for Australia at the age of only 17 ! Craig is the youngest cricketer to do so. He made an impressive debut, too; in the final Test against South Africa at Melbourne, he scored 53.

Craig has been named as the second Bradman, and according to former Test bowler W. J. O'Reilly, he is more mature than Bradman was at the same age. And O'Reilly should know, as he met Bradman on the field in youth. But "a second Bradman"—that's a very tall order.

Craig, at 16, played for New South Wales against South Australia, scoring 91, and so was the youngest player to represent his State.

Yet he scored 213 not out for New South Wales off South

Over-Many "IF" Men

MUCH DEPENDS ON OLD GUARD

Africa's attack last winter and so became the youngest batsman to make a double-century against an international team. Like The Don, he is cool and assured, and shows deep concentration. Build : slight. Appearance : freckled. Business : assistant in chemist's shop.

RITCHIE BENAUD (New South Wales). Another young all-rounder—good bat, useful leg-spin bowler and sound fieldsman.

His Test debut in the fifth match against the West Indies was by no means impressive, and in the South African series his best effort was four wickets for 118 in the fourth Test. Not startling, but he's only 22.

JAMES DE COURCY (New South Wales). Here's a right-hand bat who can control his game when needed but likes to attack. He was 12th man in the third Test against South Africa. Age 25.

ALAN DAVIDSON (New South Wales) is a left-arm fast-medium bowler, who has done well for his State this season, but has yet to play in Test cricket. He is also a forceful left-hand bat and a brilliant field.

He has really been given a place in the team as understudy for established pace-attack. Age 23.

JACK HILL (Victoria) deals in slow-medium top-spinners and leg breaks, but has been overshadowed by Ring and was the surprise selection. He has a good control of flight and keeps a steady length. Age 29.

GRAEME HOLE (South Australia), another fine fieldsman, could not get going with the bat against South Africa—played in the first four Tests and then lost his place to Craig.

Tall, slim and a stylist, he is also a useful slow-medium off-spinner. Age 22.

HOPE OF HIS SIDE

NEIL HARVEY (Victoria). The "boy star" of 1948 here is now the great batting hope of 1953. One of five cricketing brothers, he entered Test cricket in 1947 against India, and scored 112 in his first Test against England at Leeds a year later.

Then he starred in South Africa in 1949-50, obtaining four Test centuries. These he followed with four against South Africa last season.

In fact, in the final Test Harvey scored 205, highest innings of his career and, with an aggregate of 827 runs, broke Sir Donald Bradman's record of 806 against South Africa in one series. Age 24.

BILL JOHNSTON (Victoria). Left-arm fast-medium swing bowler who can turn to slower stuff on demand. Another important bit of Australia's backbone.

He took 22 England wickets out there two years ago and 23 against

FROM BASEBALL TO CRICKET

West Indies in 1951-52. This after being the only Australian to claim 100 wickets on their last tour in England.

Started out as a pitcher at baseball. Failed. Turned to cricket. Triumph. Age 30.

GIL LANGLEY (South Australia). Succeeded Don Tallon—then out of cricket through illness—as wicket-keeper and captured 21 West Indies wickets, to equal the record of Strudwick for a Test series.

THE BROTHERS THUNDERBOLT

RAY LINDWALL (New South Wales) has lost some of the fire that broke Bedser's middle stump at Melbourne in 1951.

Like Miller, he missed the final Test last winter because of injury—wear and tear—and the question is: Can the Brothers Thunderbolt now stay the distance?

Ray led Australia's bowling averages against England in the 1946-47 series and again in 1948 over here, and is also a useful bat.

In the last Test at the Oval five years ago he scattered the English batsmen like chaff but when he came to Nelson last summer, in the Lancashire League, some of the fury seemed to have faded.

Probably Lindwall and Miller will turn on the tap in the Tests but, if the pair are reserved in this way, the Australians may lose other matches. Age 32.

KEITH MILLER (New South Wales) is the world's most dangerous all-round cricketer. More spectacular than India's Mankad.

Has played against England since 1946. Brilliant bat with terrific power; tearaway fast bowler, and exceptional fieldsman. In matches against England Miller and Lindwall have brought about the bumper controversy discussed by Bill Bowes elsewhere in this issue.

Miller's all action. Fortunate Australia to produce such a successor to J. M. Gregory. Age 34.

COLIN McDONALD (Victoria) is one of Australia's few good opening batsmen. He obtained his maiden Test century (154) against South Africa in the fourth match at Adelaide. In these Tests he was more consistent than his senior partner, Morris. Age 24.

DOUGLAS RING (Victoria) is the outstanding spin bowler in Australia. Leg-breaks a speciality.

Toured England with Bradman's team in 1948, taking 69 wickets (average 21), and against South Africa last December had six for 72 at Brisbane—but you know what Brisbane is! Age 34.

And last but not least—

DON TALLON (Queensland), now described as No. 2 wicket-keeper for tour. Why? Because he only reappeared in first-class cricket last winter after a long absence through illness.

Like Lindwall a good, upright, front-of-the-wicket batsman.

"Kept" marvellously in England in 1948. Quiet in action; orchestral in appeal.

TRUEMAN, MAY, SHEPPARD

Snapshots of England's New Hopes

by H. L. V. DAY

THREE young cricketers upon whom Englishmen rest high hopes in the forthcoming battle to regain the Ashes are **D. S. Sheppard, P. B. H. May** and **Fred Trueman.**

Averages and statistics are not always reliable as an indication of worth on the cricket field, especially in these days when there is no "gold standard." Style is the only true guide. Still, the figures are incontrovertible.

Sheppard, by his consistently sound batting for Cambridge University and Sussex, finished at the top of the batting averages for 1952 with 64, following the example of **May** in 1951 who averaged 68. And **May** was second this year with 62. Astonishing figures.

Trueman took 29 wickets in the four Tests for just over 13 runs apiece. It is worth while remembering that in the third Test he had 8 for 31 in India's first innings. No England bowler has obtained as many as 8 wickets in any innings since Verity bowled out Australia at Lord's in 1938 on a turning wicket.

Making reservations for supine and suicidal strokes, the fact remains that at long last England has a bowler of REAL pace. It would be ludicrous to hail Trueman as another Larwood yet awhile ; but if he continues to improve in his direction and length as he did during 1952, and has the good sense to conserve his energy by variations of pace, he may be a trenchant answer to Lindwall and Miller.

TRUEMAN'S STAMINA

After some doubt had been expressed about his stamina I noted that he bowled with two short breaks for upwards of three hours in the second Test, with no observable diminution of pace or spirit. He is built on strong lines.

His ability to produce the occasional yorker is a very considerable asset, for such a delivery is almost unstoppable, as Lindwall, Larwood and G. O. Allen have shown.

Trueman was in trouble at times with his tendency to drag his right foot at the moment of delivery. One over in the fourth Test lasted nine balls, of which there were three no-balls in a row.

He is in the development stage, but Yorkshire can be relied upon to bring the best out of him and no doubt Bill Bowes will do a bit of plain speaking to him. His run-up obviously needs adjustment.

There must be no wasting of the new ball, or of his energy, by bowling wide of the stumps. If he keeps the Australian batsmen playing at the ball which is going away, without giving them any respite, he will enhance his value as a shock trooper, a fast bowler's correct role.

Continued on next page.

Australians' Tour

Fixtures of 1953 Visit

(Three-day matches, unless otherwise stated)

APRIL
29 Worcestershire (Worcester)

MAY
2 Leicestershire (Leicester)
6 Yorkshire (Bradford)
9 Surrey (The Oval)
13 Cambridge Univ. (Cambridge)
16 M.C.C. (Lord's)
20 Oxford University (Oxford)
23 Minor Counties (Stoke)
27 Lancashire (Manchester)
30 Notts (Nottingham)

JUNE
3 Sussex (Hove)
6 Hampshire (Southampton)
11 **ENGLAND (First Test Match) (5 days) at NOTTINGHAM**
17 Derbyshire (Chesterfield)
20 Yorkshire (Sheffield)
25 **ENGLAND (Second Test Match) (5 days) at LORD'S**

JULY
1 Gloucestershire (Bristol)
4 Northants (Northampton)
9 **ENGLAND (Third Test Match) (5 days) at MANCHESTER**
18 Middlesex (Lord's)
23 **ENGLAND (Fourth Test Match) (5 days) at LEEDS**
29 Surrey (The Oval)

AUGUST
1 Glamorgan (Swansea)
5 Warwickshire (Birmingham)
8 Lancashire (Manchester)
12 Essex (Southend)
15 **ENGLAND (Fifth Test Match) (6 days) at THE OVAL**
22 Somerset (Taunton)
26 Gentlemen (Lord's)
29 Kent (Canterbury)

SEPTEMBER
2 An England XI (Hastings)
5 Combined Services (Kingston)
9 T. N. Pearce's XI (Scarborough)
12 Scotland Tour
16 Scotland Tour
19 Scotland Tour

Much of the success of **May** is due to the excellence of the coaching he received at Charterhouse from George Geary, the Leicester and England bowler who once wheeled up 84 overs to Bradman, Woodfull and company.

For Surrey and Cambridge University May has accumulated runs with impressive ease. All the shots are in his bag. Perhaps his one failing is a reluctance to use his feet to the slow spinners. He seems to prefer to play them from the confines of the crease.

In 1951 he followed a brilliant 119 not out for the Gentlemen by making 138 in his Test debut against South Africa at Leeds.

COOL SHEPPARD

Watching **Sheppard** not only in Test but in county cricket, I have been impressed by his imperturbable temperament, so important for the big occasion.

In the final Test, for example, when Divecha or Mankad deceived and beat him without upsetting his stumps he prepared for the next delivery with the same nonchalance that Philip Mead and Herbert Sutcliffe used to show. He had the satisfaction of hitting his first Test hundred (119), aided by some great good fortune. But he took nearly six hours over it.

At 23 he has more than 20 hundreds to his credit, and in 1950 shared in first-wicket stands of 349 v. Sussex and 343 v. West Indies.

England v. Australia

SUMMARY OF WINS

	England Won	Australia Won	Drawn	Totals
In England	21	20	30	71
In Australia	35	48	4	87
	56	68	34	158

RESULTS AT VARIOUS GROUNDS

Venue	England Won	Australia Won	Drawn
Birmingham	1	0	1
Leeds	0	4	5
Lord's	5	6	6
Manchester	3	2	10
Nottingham	2	3	3
The Oval	10	4	5
Sheffield	0	1	0

Venue	England Won	Australia Won	Drawn
Adelaide	5	9	1
Melbourne	13	18	3
Sydney	14	19	0
Brisbane	3	2	0

IN ENGLAND

Highest English innings, 903 (7 wickets dec.) The Oval, 1938
Highest Australian innings, 729 for 6 wickets: Lord's, 1930
Lowest English innings, 52: The Oval, 1948
Lowest Australian innings, 36: Edgbaston, 1902
Highest scorer, England, 364: L. Hutton, The Oval, 1938
Highest scorer, Australia, 334: D. G. Bradman, Leeds, 1930
Highest aggregate: 1,723 for 31 wickets, Leeds, 1948
Lowest aggregate: 291 for 40 wickets, Lord's, 1888

IN AUSTRALIA

Highest English innings, 636: Sydney, 1928-29
Highest Australian innings, 659 (8 wickets): Sydney, 1946-47
Lowest English innings, 45: Sydney, 1886-87
Lowest Australian innings, 42: Sydney, 1887-88
Highest scorer, England, 287: R. E. Foster, Sydney, 1903-04
Highest Australian scorer, 270: D. G. Bradman, Adelaide, 1936-37
Highest aggregate: 1,753 for 40 wickets, Adelaide, 1920-21
Lowest aggregate: 374 for 40, Sydney, 1887-88

RECORD PARTNERSHIPS—(A.) For England

1st wicket—323, Hobbs and Rhodes, at Melbourne ... 1911-12
2nd wicket—382, Hutton and Leyland, at The Oval ... 1938
3rd wicket—262, Hammond and D. R. Jardine, at Adelaide ... 1928-29
4th wicket—222, W. R. Hammond and Paynter, at Lord's ... 1938
5th wicket—206, Paynter and Compton, at Nottingham ... 1938
6th wicket—215, Hutton and Hardstaff, at The Oval ... 1938
7th wicket—143, Vine and Woolley, at Sydney ... 1911-12
8th wicket—124, Hendren and Larwood, at Brisbane ... 1928-29
9th wicket—151, W. W. Read and Scotton, at The Oval ... 1884
10th wicket—130, R. E. Foster and Rhodes, at Sydney ... 1903-04

(B.)—For Australia

1st wicket—180, W. Bardsley and S. E. Gregory, at The Oval... 1909
2nd wicket—451, W. H. Ponsford and D. G. Bradman, at The Oval 1934
3rd wicket—276, D. G. Bradman and A. L. Hassett, Brisbane ... 1946-47
4th wicket—388, W. H. Ponsford and D. G. Bradman, Leeds... 1934
5th wicket—405, D. G. Bradman and S. G. Barnes, Sydney ... 1946-47
6th wicket—346, D. G. Bradman and J. H. W. Fingleton, at Melbourne ... 1936-37
7th wicket—165, C. Hill and H. Trumble, at Melbourne ... 1897-98
8th wicket—243, R. J. Hartigan and C. Hill, at Adelaide ... 1907-08
9th wicket—154, J. McC Blackham and S. E. Gregory, at Sydney 1894-95
10th wicket—127, A. A. Mailey and J. M. Taylor, at Sydney ... 1924-25

See how thick—how extra thick—is the covering of full-cream milk chocolate in these delicious **Milk Tray** Chocolates.

made by Cadburys

Test Match Records

ENGLAND v. AUSTRALIA

	Won by E.	Won by A.	Drawn
1876-77	1	1	0
1878-79	0	1	0
1880	1	0	0
1881-82	0	2	2
1882	0	1	0
1882-83	2	2	0
1884	1	0	2
1884-85	3	2	0
1886	3	0	0
1886-87	2	0	0
1887-88	1	0	0
1888	2	1	0
1890	2	0	1*
1891-92	1	2	0
1893	1	0	2
1894-95	3	2	0
1896	2	1	0
1897-98	1	4	0
1899	0	1	4
1901-02	1	4	0
1902	1	2	2
1903-04	3	2	0
1905	2	0	3
1907-08	1	4	0
1909	1	2	2
1911-12	4	1	0
1912	1	0	2
1920-21	0	5	0
1921	0	3	2
1924-25	1	4	0
1926	1	0	4
1928-29	4	1	0
1930	1	2	2
1932-33	4	1	0
1934	1	2	2
1936-37	2	3	0
1938	1	1	3*
1946-47	0	3	2
1948	0	4	1
1950-51	1	4	0

* Includes one match abandoned without a ball being bowled.

ENGLAND v. INDIA

	Won by E.	Won by I.	Drawn
1932	1	0	0
1933-34	2	0	1
1936	2	0	1
1946	1	0	2
1951-52	1	1	3
1952	3	0	1

ENGLAND v. SOUTH AFRICA

	Won by E.	Won by S.A.	Drawn
1888-89	2	0	0
1891-92	1	0	0
1895-96	3	0	0
1898-99	2	0	0
1905-6	1	4	0
1907	1	0	2
1909-10	2	3	0
1912	3	0	0
1913-14	4	0	1
1922-23	2	1	2
1924	3	0	2
1927-28	2	2	1
1929	2	0	3
1930-31	0	1	4
1935	0	1	4
1938-39	1	0	4
1947	3	0	2
1948-49	2	0	3
1951	3	1	1

ENGLAND v. NEW ZEALAND

	Won by E.	Won by N.Z.	Drawn
1929-30	1	0	3
1931	1	0	2
1932-33	0	0	2
1937	1	0	2
1946-47	0	0	1
1949	0	0	5
1950-51	1	0	1

ENGLAND v. WEST INDIES

	Won by E.	Won by W.I.	Drawn
1928	3	0	0
1929-30	1	1	2
1933	2	0	1
1934-35	1	2	1
1939	1	0	2
1947-48	0	2	2
1950	1	3	0

PRINCIPAL TEST PLAYERS

ENGLAND v. AUSTRALIA, 1877-1951

Batsmen (who have scored 600 runs)

ENGLAND.	Runs	Average
Hutton	1765	67.88
Sutcliffe	2741	66.85
Leyland	1705	56.83
Hobbs	3636	54.26
Hammond, W. R.	2852	51.85
Jackson, Sir F. S.	1412	48.68
Ranjitsinhji, K. S.	985	44.77
Compton (D.)	1288	42.93
Gunn (G.)	844	42.20
Hendren	1740	39.54
Barnett (C. J.)	614	38.37
Hayward	1747	35.65
Chapman, A. P. F.	784	35.63
Stoddart, A. E.	996	35.57
Shrewsbury	1277	35.47
Steel, A. G.	600	35.29
MacLaren, A. C.	1931	33.87
Wyatt, R. E. S.	633	33.31
Woolley (F. E.)	1664	33.28
Washbrook	892	33.03
Edrich, W. J.	848	32.53
Grace, W. G.	1098	32.29
Fry, C. B.	825	31.73
Rhodes	1706	31.01
Tyldesley (J. T.)	1389	30.86
Douglas, J. W. H. T.	696	27.76
Bates (W.)	656	27.33
Read, W. W.	680	27.20
Ames	679	27.16
Braund	834	25.27
Ulyett	901	25.02
Hirst	746	24.86
Barnes (W.)	725	23.38
Lilley (A. A.)	800	20.00
Briggs	809	18.81

AUSTRALIA.	Runs	Average
Bradman, D. G.	5028	88.78
Barnes, S. G.	846	70.57
Morris, A. R.	1520	63.33
McCabe, S. J.	1931	48.27
Ponsford, W. H.	1558	47.21
Miller, K. R.	918	45.90
Ryder, J.	1060	44.16
Woodfull, W. M.	1675	44.07
Macartney, C. G.	1640	43.15
Brown, W. A.	980	42.60
Hassett, A. L.	1207	38.93
Collins, H. L.	1012	38.92
Ransford, V. S.	893	38.82
Taylor, J. M.	957	38.28
Iredale, F. A.	807	36.68
Hill, C.	2660	35.46
Armstrong, W. W.	2172	35.03
Gregory, J. M.	941	34.85
Kippax, A. F.	753	34.22
Bardsley W.	1487	33.04
Trumper, V. T.	2263	32.79
Duff, R. A.	1079	32.69
Fingleton, J. H.	671	32.42
Murdoch, W. L.	896	32.00
Kelleway, C.	874	31.21
Darling, J.	1632	30.79
Noble, M. A.	1905	30.72
Bruce, W.	702	29.25
McDonnell, P. S.	958	29.03
Lyons, J. J.	731	27.07
Gregory, S. E.	2193	25.80
Carter, H.	776	25.03
Richardson, V. Y.	622	24.88
Giffen, G.	1238	23.35
Oldfield, W. A.	1116	23.25
Trott, G. H. S.	921	21.92
Trumble, H.	838	19.95
Kelly, J. J.	613	17.51
Blackham, J. McC.	800	15.68

Bowlers (who have taken 30 wickets)

ENGLAND.	Wickets	Avge.
Lohmann	77	13.01
Barnes (W.)	51	15.54
Bates (W.)	49	16.75
Peel	102	16.81
Ulyett	49	20.06
Briggs	97	20.54
Lockwood (W. H.)	43	20.55
Blythe	41	21.39
Barnes (S. F.)	106	21.58
Foster, F. R.	34	21.82
Barlow	35	21.91
Peate	31	22.00
Hearne (J. T.)	48	22.29
Rhodes	109	24.00
Bowes	30	24.70
Crawford, J. N.	30	24.73
Richardson	88	25.22
Farnes,	38	27.50
Voce	41	27.51
Verity	59	28.06
Larwood	64	29.93
Tate (M. W.)	83	30.55
Bedser, (A. V.)	64	31.96
Hirst	49	32.34
White, J. C.	31	33.32
Parkin	32	34.06
Douglas, J. W. H. T.	35	35.05
Woolley (F. E.)	43	36.16
Allen, G. O.	43	37.27
Braund	46	38.45
Wright, (D. V. P.)	48	42.47
Hammond, W. R.	36	44.72

Continued at foot of next page

BORING TO WATCH AND TO TEAMS

—Says F. R. BROWN

F. R. BROWN, Northants and former England captain, says that easy-paced pitches all over the country, with Northampton as the worst, have done a great deal of harm to cricket.

Although Northants scored more runs than any county last season—12,343—that did not mean much in relation to winning matches, taking into consideration the easy-paced pitches.

The big scoring matches that resulted were not only boring to watch but boring to the players.

A side could score too many runs and so reduce the time available for the bowlers to get the other team out. To determine the value of runs the rate at which they were made had to be considered.

It had amazed him how a team could score anything from 80 to 100 runs an hour in the fourth innings when usually their first innings rate was below 60 an hour.

ENGLAND v. AUSTRALIA—BOWLERS—Continued from previous page

AUSTRALIA.	Wickets	Avge.
Ferris, J. J.	48	14.25
Turner, C. T. B.	101	16.53
Spofforth, F. R.	94	18.41
Boyle, H. F.	32	20.03
Lindwall, R. R.	60	20.68
Trumble, H.	141	20.88
Johnston, W. A.	49	21.46
Palmer, G. E.	78	21.51
Miller, K. R.	46	22.26
Hordern, H. V.	32	24.37
Noble, M. A.	115	24.78
Saunders, J. V.	64	25.32
O'Reilly, W. J.	102	25.36
Laver, F. J.	37	25.97
Garrett, T. W.	36	27.00
Giffen, G.	103	27.00
Macartney, C. G.	33	27.51
Cotter, A.	67	28.59
Jones, E.	60	29.28
Armstrong, W. W.	74	30.91
Kelleway, C.	37	31.21
McDonald, E. A.	33	32.12
Grimmett, C. V.	106	32.44
Gregory, J. M.	70	33.77
Mailey, A. A.	86	34.12
Howell, W. P.	35	35.57
Fleetwood-Smith, L. O'B.	33	36.06
Wall, T. W.	43	39.03
McLeod, C. E.	33	40.15

Sunday Chronicle Hits:

NORMAN YARDLEY'S

Cricket Bureau

HELPS ALL CLUBS AND PLAYERS

J. L. MANNING'S

Last Word on Sport

STARS OF THE . . .

Batsmen With 1,000 Runs in All Tests

(Up to the end of the 1952-53 Tests in Australia)

	No. of Tests	Runs	100's	High't inns.	Average
D G Bradman (A.)	52	6996	29	334	99.94
F M Worrell (W.I.)	14	1403	5	261	70.15
R N Harvey (A.)	24	2416	10	205	65.29
G Headley (W.I.)	21	2173	10	270*	63.91
S G Barnes (A.)	13	1072	3	234	63.05
H Sutcliffe (E.)	54	4555	16	194	60.73
L Hutton (E.)	60	5545	16	364	59.62
E Paynter (E.)	20	1540	4	243	59.23
W R Hammond (E.)	85	7249	22	336*	58.46
J B Hobbs (E.)	61	5410	15	211	56.94
V S Hazare (Ind.)	25	1998	7	164*	55.50
A D Nourse, jun. (S.A.)	34	2960	9	231	53.81
E Weekes (W.I.)	20	1715	6	194	53.59
D. Compton (E.)	49	3718	14	208	51.63
J Ryder (A.)	20	1394	3	201*	51.62
A R Morris (A.)	33	2707	10	206	51.07
C P Mead (E.)	17	1184	4	182*	49.33
B Mitchell (S.A.)	42	3471	8	189*	48.88
Sir F S Jackson (E.)	20	1412	5	144*	48.68
A. L. Hassett (A.)	38	2708	8	198*	48.35
S J McCabe (A.)	39	2756	6	232	48.35
W H Ponsford (A.)	29	2122	7	266	48.22
D R Jardine (E.)	22	1296	1	127	48.00
E Hendren (E.)	51	3525	7	205*	47.63
W A Brown (A.)	22	1592	4	206*	46.82
J Hardstaff, jun (E.)	23	1636	4	205*	46.74
M Leyland (E.)	41	2764	9	187	46.06
W M Woodfull (A.)	35	2291	7	161	45.82
J B Stollmeyer (W.I.)	20	1460	3	160	45.62
H L Collins (A.)	19	1352	4	203	45.06
W J Edrich (E.)	31	2100	6	219	43.75
E A B Rowan (S.A.)	26	1965	3	236	43.66
C Washbrook (E.)	34	2465	6	195	43.24
J H Fingleton (A.)	18	1189	5	136	42.46
C G Macartney (A.)	35	2132	7	170	41.80
G A Faulkner (S.A.)	25	1754	4	204	40.79
H W Taylor (S.A.)	42	2936	7	176	40.77
C L Walcott (W.I.)	18	1100	4	168*	40.74
L E G Ames (E.)	47	2438	8	149	40.63
W Bardsley (A.)	41	2469	6	193*	40.47
K R Miller (A.)	35	1894	3	145*	40.29
G Gunn (E.)	15	1120	2	122*	40.00
C Hill (A.)	49	3402	7	191	39.10
V T Trumper (A.)	48	3163	8	214*	39.04
W W Armstrong (A.)	50	2873	6	159*	38.82
R H Catterall (S.A.)	24	1555	3	120	37.92
V S Ransford (A.)	20	1211	1	143*	37.81
C Kelleway (A.)	26	1422	3	147	37.42
J M Gregory (A.)	24	1146	2	119	36.96
R T Simpson (E.)	18	1102	3	156*	36.73
A F Kippax (A.)	22	1192	2	146	36.12
F E Woolley (E.)	64	3283	5	154	36.07
A Shrewsbury (E.)	23	1277	3	164	35.47
R A Duff (A.)	22	1307	2	146	35.32
G E Gomez (W.I.)	21	1055	1	101	35.16
C J Barnett (E.)	20	1088	2	129	35.09

. . . WORLD'S TESTS

Batsmen With 1,000 Runs—*continued*

	No. of Tests	Runs	100's	High't inns.	Average
T Hayward (E.)	35	1999	3	137	34.44
A C MacLaren (E.)	35	1931	5	140	33.87
W G Grace (E.)	22	1089	2	170	32.29
C B Fry (E.)	26	1223	2	144	32.18
R E S Wyatt (E.)	40	1839	2	149	31.70
J T Tyldesley (E.)	31	1661	4	138	30.75
M A Noble (A.)	42	1997	1	133	30.25
W Rhodes (E.)	58	2325	2	179	30.19
V. Mankad (Ind.)	25	1196	3	184	29.90
A D Nourse, sen. (S.A.)	45	2234	1	111	29.78
K G Viljoen (S.A.)	27	1365	2	124	29.67
J Darling (A.)	34	1657	3	178	28.56
H B Cameron (S.A.)	26	1073	—	90	26.17
M W Tate (E.)	39	1198	1	100*	25.48
S E Gregory (A.)	58	2282	4	201	24.53
T G Evans (E.)	44	1395	2	104	24.05
G Giffen (A.)	31	1238	1	161	23.35
J H Sinclair (S.A.)	25	1069	3	106	23.23
A C Bannerman (A.)	28	1108	—	94	23.08
W A Oldfield (A.)	54	1427	—	65*	22.65
S J Snooke (S.A.)	26	1008	1	103	22.40

Bowlers With 50 Wickets

(Up to the end of the 1952-53 Tests in Australia)

	No. of Tests	Wkts.	Aver.
G A Lohmann (E.)	18	112	10.75
J J Ferris (A.)	8	61	12.70
W Barnes (E.)	21	51	15.54
S F Barnes (E.)	27	189	16.43
C T B Turner (A.)	17	101	16.53
R Peel (E.)	20	102	16.81
J Briggs (E.)	33	118	17.74
H Ironmonger (A.)	14	74	17.97
F R Spofforth (A.)	18	94	18.41
C Blythe (E.)	19	100	18.63
G Ulyett (E.)	23	51	19.80
K R Miller (A.)	35	107	20.31
R R Lindwall (A.)	33	132	20.37
W J Whitty (A.)	14	65	21.12
G E Palmer (A.)	17	78	21.51
W A Johnston (A.)	29	132	21.75
H Trumble (A.)	32	141	21.78
W E Bowes (E.)	15	68	22.33
W J O'Reilly (A.)	27	144	22.59
J V Saunders (A.)	14	79	22.74
A E Vogler (S.A.)	15	64	22.75
A L Valentine (W.I.)	11	65	23.35
C V Grimmett (A.)	37	216	24.21
H Verity (E.)	40	144	24.37
M A Noble (A.)	42	121	24.91
T Richardson (E.)	14	88	25.22
G A Faulkner (S.A.)	25	82	25.36
A P Freeman (E.)	12	66	25.84
R Tattersall (E.)	14	54	25.97
A V Bedser (E.)	42	182	26.10
M W Tate (E.)	39	155	26.13
W Voce (E.)	27	98	26.24
R O Schwarz (S.A.)	20	53	26.73
W Rhodes (E.)	58	127	26.96
G Giffen (A.)	31	103	27.09
R W V Robins (E.)	18	64	27.46
V Mankad (Ind.)	25	108	28.12
R.T. Ramadhin (WI)	11	52	28.17
H Larwood (E.)	18	78	28.41
K Farnes (E.)	15	60	28.63
A Cotter (A.)	21	89	28.64
V Mankad (Ind.)	18	74	28.87
E Jones (A.)	19	64	29.01
G O Allen (E.)	25	81	29.37
J C Laker (E.)	15	54	29.51
I W Johnson (A.)	28	70	29.74
G H Hirst (E.)	24	59	30.00
L N Constantine (W.I.)	18	58	30.10
J M Blanckenberg (S.A.)	17	60	30.26
C L Vincent (S.A.)	25	84	30.95
J M Gregory (A.)	24	85	31.15
J H Sinclair (S.A.)	25	63	31.18
C Kelleway (A.)	26	52	32.26
N B F Mann (S.A.)	19	58	33.10
W W Armstrong (A.)	50	87	33.59
A A Mailey (A.)	21	99	33.91
F E Woolley (E.)	64	83	33.91
E P Nupen (S.A.)	17	50	35.76
T W Wall (A.)	18	56	35.89
W R Hammond (E.)	85	83	37.67
A M B Rowan (S.A)	15	54	38.58
D V P Wright (E.)	34	108	39.09

HISTORIC 100's . . .

ENGLAND v. AUSTRALIA—For England

*** Denotes not out**

Year	Ground, Batsman	Score
1880	The Oval, W. G. Grace...	152
1882	Melbourne, G. Ulyett.....	149
1883	Sydney, A. G. Steel......	*135
1884	Lord's, A. G. Steel.......	148
1884	The Oval, W W Read...	117
1884	Adelaide, W. Barnes.....	134
1885	Melbourne, J. Briggs.....	121
1885	Melbourne, A. Shrewsbury	*105
1886	The Oval, W. G. Grace...	170
1886	Lord's, A. Shrewsbury....	164
1892	Sydney, R. Abel.........	*132
1892	Adelaide, A. E. Stoddart..	134
1893	Lord's, A. Shrewsbury....	106
1893	The Oval, Hon. F. S. Jackson	103
1893	Manchester, W. Gunn....	*102
1894	Sydney A. Ward.........	117
1895	Melbourne, A. E. Stoddart	173
1895	Melbourne, A. C. MacLaren	120
1895	Melbourne, J. T. Brown...	140
1896	Manchester, K. S. Ranjitsinhji..	*154
1897	Sydney, K. S. Ranjitsinhji	175
1897	Sydney, A. C. MacLaren..	109
1898	Adelaide, A. C. MacLaren.	124
1899	Manchester, T. Hayward.	130
1899	The Oval, T. Hayward....	137
1899	The Oval. Hon. F. S. Jackson	118
1901	Sydney, A. C. MacLaren..	116
1902	Adelaide, L. C. Braund...	*103
1902	Birmingham, J. T. Tyldesley	138
1902	Manchester, Hon. F. S. Jackson..	128
1902	The Oval, G. L. Jessop...	104
1903	Sydney, R. E. Foster.....	287
1903	Sydney, L. C. Braund....	102
1905	Nottingham, A. C. MacLaren	140
1905	Leeds, J. T. Tyldesley....	100
1905	The Oval, J. T. Tyldesley.	*112
1905	Leeds, Hon. F. S. Jackson.	*144
1905	The Oval, C. B. Fry......	144
1905	Manchester, Hon. F. S. Jackson..	113
1907	Sydney, G. Gunn........	119
1908	Melbourne, K. L. Hutchings	126
1908	Sydney, G. Gunn.........	*122
1909	The Oval, J. Sharp.......	105
1912	Melbourne, J. W. Hearne.	114
1912‡	Melbourne, J. B. Hobbs..	*126
1912‡	Adelaide, J. B. Hobbs....	187
1912‡	Melbourne, J. B. Hobbs...	178
1912	Melbourne, W. Rhodes...	179
1912	Sydney, F. E. Woolley...	*133
1912	Lord's, J. B. Hobbs......	107
1921	Melbourne, J. B. Hobbs...	122
1921	Adelaide, J. B. Hobbs....	123
1921	Melbourne, H. Makepeace.	117
1921	Adelaide, A. C. Russell...	*135
1921	Manchester, A. C. Russell.	101
1921	The Oval, C. P. Mead....	*182
1921	The Oval, A. C. Russell...	*102
1924	Sydney, J. B. Hobbs.....	115
1924	Sydney, F. E. Woolley....	123
1924§	Sydney, H. Sutcliffe......	115
1925§†	Melbourne, H. Sutcliffe..	176
1925§†	Melbourne, H. Sutcliffe..	127
1925	Melbourne, J. B. Hobbs..	154
1925	Adelaide, J. B. Hobbs....	119
1925	Melbourne, H. Sutcliffe...	143
1926	Lord's, J. B. Hobbs......	119
1926	Lord's, E. Hendren......	*127
1926	Oval, J. B. Hobbs........	100
1926	Oval, H. Sutcliffe........	161
1928	Brisbane, E. Hendren....	169
1928	Sydney, W. R. Hammond.	251
1929	Melbourne, W. R. Hammond	200
1929	Melbourne, H. Sutcliffe...	135
1929†	Adelaide, W. R. Hammond	*119
1929†	Adelaide W. R Hammond	177
1929	Melbourne, J. B. Hobbs..	142
1929	Melbourne, M. Leyland...	137
1930	Lord's, K. S. Duleepsinhji	173
1930	Lord's, A. P. F. Chapman.	121
1930	Leeds, W. R. Hammond..	113
1930	Oval, H. Sutcliffe........	161
1932	Sydney, H. Sutcliffe......	194
1932	Sydney W. R. Hammond.	112
1932	Sydney, Nawab of Pataudi	102
1933	Sydney, W. R. Hammond.	101
1934	Lord's, M. Leyland.......	109
1934	Lord's, L. Ames..........	120
1934	Manchester, E. Hendren..	132
1934	Manchester, M. Leyland..	153
1934	Oval, M. Leyland........	110
1936	Brisbane, M. Leyland....	126
1936	Sydney, W. R. Hammond.	*231
1937	Melbourne, M. Leyland...	*111
1937	Adelaide, C. Barnett.....	129
1938	Nottingham, L. Hutton...	100
1938	Nottingham, C. Barnett..	126
1938	Nottingham, D. Compton.	102
1938	Nottingham, E. Paynter..	*216
1938	Lord's, W. R. Hammond.	240
1938‖	Oval, L. Hutton..........	364
1938	Oval, M. Leyland.........	187
1938	Oval, J. Hardstaff.......	*169
1946	Sydney, W. J. Edrich....	119
1947	Melbourne, C. Washbrook.	112
1947†	Adelaide, D. Compton....	147
1947†	Adelaide, D. Compton....	*103
1947¶	Sydney, L. Hutton.......	122
1948	Nottingham, D. Compton.	184
1948	Manchester, D. Compton.	*145
1948	Leeds, C. Washbrook.....	143
1948	Leeds, W. J. Edrich......	111
1951	Adelaide, L. Hutton.....	*156
1951	Melbourne, R. T. Simpson	*156

§ In three successive inns. † Same match. ‡ In three successive matches.
‖ Record Individual Score in Test Cricket. ¶ Retired ill.

1953 Lords L. Hutton 145
1953 Leeds W. Watson 109

. . . IN THE TESTS

For Australia

1877 Melbourne, C. Bannerman. 165
1880 The Oval, W. L. Murdoch.*153
1882 Melbourne, T. Horan..... 124
1882 Sydney, P. S. MacDonnell. 147
1884 The Oval, W. L. Murdoch. 211
1884 The Oval, P. S. MacDonnell 103
1884 The Oval, H. J. H. Scott.. 102
1884 Adelaide, P. S. MacDonnell 124
1885 Sydney, G. J. Bonnor.... 128
1892 Sydney, J J Lyons...... 134
1893 Lord's, H. Graham....... 107
1894 Sydney, S. E. Gregory.... 201
1894 Sydney, G. Giffen........ 161
1895 Adelaide, F. A. Iredale.... 140
1895 Sydney, H. Graham....... 105
1896 Lord's, G. H. S. Trott..... 143
1896 Lord's, S. E. Gregory..... 103
1896 Manchester, F. A. Iredale. 108
1897 Sydney, J. Darling........ 101
1898 Melbourne, C. E. McLeod. 112
1898 Adelaide, J. Darling....... 178
1898 Melbourne, C. Hill........ 188
1898 Sydney, J. Darling........ 160
1899 Lord's, C. Hill........... 135
1899 Lord's, V. Trumper......*135
1899 The Oval, S. E. Gregory.. 117
1902 Melbourne, R. A. Duff.... 104
1902 Sheffield, C. Hill......... 119
1902 Manchester, V. Trumper.. 104
1903 Sydney, V. Trumper.....*185
1903 Sydney, M. A. Noble...... 133
1904 Adelaide, V. Trumper..... 113
1904 Adelaide, S. E. Gregory... 112
1905 The Oval, R. A. Duff..... 146
1908 Adelaide, C. Hill......... 160
1908 Adelaide, R. Hartigan.... 116
1908 Melbourne, W W Armstrong*133
1908 Sydney, V. Trumper..... 166
1909 Lord's, V. S. Ransford...*143
1909†The Oval, W. Bardsley... 136
1909†The Oval, W. Bardsley... 130
1911 Sydney, V. Trumper...... 113
1921 Sydney, W. W. Armstrong 158
1921 Melbourne, J. M. Gregory. 100
1921 Melbourne, C. E. Pellew.. 116
1921 Sydney, H. L. Collins..... 104
1921 Adelaide, W. W. Armstrong 121
1921 Melbourne, W W Armstrong*123
1921 Adelaide, H. L. Collins... 162
1921 Adelaide, C. E. Pellew.... 104
1921 Adelaide, C. Kelleway.... 147
1921 Sydney, C. G. Macartney.. 170
1921 Leeds, C. G. Macartney... 115
1924 Sydney, H. L. Collins..... 114
1924 Sydney, W. H. Ponsford.. 110
1924 Sydney, J. M. Taylor..... 108
1925 Melbourne, W. H. Ponsford 128
1925 Melbourne, V. Richardson. 138
1925 Adelaide, J. Ryder.......*201
1926 Lord's, W. Bardsley......*193
1926§Lord's, C. G. Macartney..*133
1926§Leeds, C. G. Macartney... 151
1926 Leeds, W. M. Woodfull... 141
1926 Leeds, A. J. Richardson.. 100
1926§Manchester, C G Macartney 109
1926 Manchester, W. M. Woodfull 117
1928 Sydney, H. L. Hendry.... 112
1928 Sydney, W. M. Woodfull.. 111
1928 Melbourne, A. F. Kippax. 100
1929 Melbourne, J. Ryder...... 112
1929 Melbourne, W. M. Woodfull 107
1929 Melbourne, D. G. Bradman 112
1929 Melbourne, W. M. Woodfull 102
1929 Melbourne, D. G. Bradman 123
1929 Adelaide, A. Jackson..... 164
1930 Nottingham, D. G. Bradman 131
1930 Lord's, D. G. Bradman... 254
1930 Lord's, W. M. Woodfull... 155
1930 Leeds, D. G. Bradman.... 334
1930 Oval, D. G. Bradman.... 232
1930 Oval, W. H. Ponsford.... 110
1932 Sydney, S. J. McCabe....*187
1933 Melbourne, D. G. Bradman*103
1934 Lord's, W. A. Brown..... 105
1934 Manchester, S. J. McCabe. 137
1934 Leeds, W. H. Ponsford... 181
1934 Leeds, D. G. Bradman.... 304
1934 Oval, W. H. Ponsford.... 266
1934 Oval, D. G. Bradman..... 244
1936 Brisbane, J. H. Fingleton. 100
1937 Melbourne, J. H. Fingleton 139
1937 Melbourne, D. G. Bradman 270
1937 Adelaide, D. G. Bradman. 212
1937 Melb'ne (2), D. G. Bradman 169
1937 Melbourne (2), S. J. McCabe 112
1937 Melb'ne (2), C. L. Badcock 118
1938 Nottingham, S. J. McCabe 232
1938 Nottingham, W. A. Brown 133
1938 Nottingham, D. G. Bradman*144
1938 Lord's, W. A. Brown.....*206
1938 Lord's, D. G. Bradman...*102
1938 Leeds, D. G. Bradman... 103
1946 Brisbane, A. L. Hassett... 128
1946 Brisbane, D. G. Bradman. 187
1946 Sydney, S. Barnes........ 234
1946 Sydney, D. G. Bradman.. 234
1947 Melbourne, C. McCool.....*104
1947 Melbourne A. Morris..... 155
1947 Melbourne, R. Lindwall... 100
1947†Adelaide, A. Morris........ 122
1947†Adelaide, A. Morris.......*124
1947 Adelaide, K. R. Miller....*141
1948 Nottingham, D. G. Bradman 138
1948 Nottingham, A. L. Hassett 137
1948 Lord's, A. Morris......... 105
1948 Lord's, S. G. Barnes....... 141
1948 Leeds, R. N. Harvey...... 112
1948 Leeds, A. Morris.......... 182
1948 Leeds, D. G. Bradman...*173
1948 Oval, A. Morris.......... 196
1951 Sydney, K. R. Miller.....*145
1951 Adelaide, A. Morris....... 206
1951 Adelaide, J. Burke *101

† Same match. § In three successive inns.

ENGLAND v. SOUTH AFRICA.—For England

1889 Capetown, R. Abel....... 120
1892 Capetown, H. Wood......*134
1896 Capetown, A. J. L. Hill... 124
1896 Johannesburg, T. Hayward 122
1899 Johannesburg, P.F. Warner*132
1899 Capetown, J. T. Tyldesley. 112
1906 Johannesburg, F. L. Fane. 143
1907 Oval, C. B. Fry.......... 129
1907 Lord's, L. C. Braund..... 104
1910 Capetown, J. B. Hobbs... 187
1910 Johannesburg, D. Denton. 104
1912 Lord's, R. H. Spooner.... 119
1913 Durban, J. W. H. T. Douglas 119
1913 Johannesburg, W. Rhodes 152
1913 Johannesburg, C. P. Mead 102
1914 Port Elizabeth, C. P. Mead 117
1923 Durban, C. P. Mead...... 181
1923 Johannesb'g, F. E. Woolley*115
1923†Durban, A. C. Russell.... 140
1923†Durban, A. C. Russell.... 111
1924 Lord's, J. B. Hobbs...... 211
1924 Lord's, H. Sutcliffe....... 122
1924 Lord's, F. E. Woolley....*134
1924 Leeds, E. Hendren....... 132
1924 Oval, E. Hendren........ 142
1927 Johannesburg, H. Sutcliffe 102
1927 Johannesburg, E. Tyldesley 122
1928 Durban, E. Tyldesley..... 100
1929 Birmingham, H. Sutcliffe.. 114
1929 Birmingham, W. R. Hammond..*138
1929 Lord's, H. Sutcliffe....... 100
1929 Lord's, M. Leyland....... 102
1929 Lord's, M. W. Tate.......*100
1929 Manchester, R. E. S. Wyatt 113
1929 Manchester, F. E. Woolley 154
1929†Oval, H. Sutcliffe........ 104
1929†Oval, H. Sutcliffe........*109
1929 Oval, W. R. Hammond...*101
1931 Durban, W. R. Hammond*136
1935 Nottingham, R. E. S. Wyatt 149
1935 Manchester R. W. V. Robins 108
1935 Oval, M. Leyland........ 161
1935 Oval, L. Ames...........*148
1938†Johannesburg, E. Paynter. 117
1938†Johannesburg, E. Paynter. 100
1938 Johannesburg, P. A. Gibb. 106
1939 Capetown, W. R. Hammond 181
1939 Capetown, L. Ames...... 115
1939 Capetown, B. H. Valentine 112
1939 Durban, E. Paynter...... 243
1939 Durban, W. R. Hammond. 120
1939 Durban, P. A. Gibb...... 120
1939 Durban W. J. Edrich.... 219
1939 Durban, W. R. Hammond. 140
1947 Nottingham, D. Compton. 163
1947 Lord's, W. J. Edrich..... 189
1947 Lord's, D. Compton...... 208
1947 Manchester, W. J. Edrich. 191
1947 Manchester, D. Compton. 115
1947 Leeds, L. Hutton........ 100
1947 Oval, D. Compton........ 113
1948 Johannesburg, L. Hutton. 158
1948 Johannesb'g, C. Washbrook 195
1948 Johannesb'g, D. Compton. 114
1949 Johannesburg, A. Watkins 111
1949 Johannesburg, L. Hutton. 123
1949 Pt. Elizabeth, F. G. Mann*136
1951 Nottingham, R. T. Simpson 137
1951 Nottingham, D. Compton. 112
1951 Leeds, L. Hutton........ 100
1951 Leeds, P. B. H. May..... 138

† The same match.

For South Africa

1899 Capetown, J. H. Sinclair.. 106
1906 Johannesburg, M. Hathorn 102
1906 Johannesburg, G. C. White 147
1907 Lord's, P. W. Sherwell.... 115
1910 Johannesb'g, G. A. Faulkner 123
1910 Durban, G. C. White..... 118
1913 Durban, H. W. Taylor.... 109
1922 Johannesburg, H. W. Taylor 176
1923 Johannesburg, H. W. Taylor 101
1923 Durban, H. W. Taylor.... 102
1924 Birmingham, R. H. Catterall 120
1924 Lord's, R. H. Catterall.... 120
1928 Johannesburg, H. W. Taylor 101
1928 Durban, R. H. Catterall... 119
1929 Leeds, H. G. Owen-Smith. 129
1929 Oval, H. W. Taylor...... 121
1931 Capetown, B. Mitchell.... 123
1931 Capetown, I. J. Siedle.... 141
1931 Capetown, H. W. Taylor.. 117
1935 Lord's, B. Mitchell.......*164
1935 Manchester, K. G. Viljoen. 124
1935 Oval, B. Mitchell........ 128
1935 Oval, E. L. Dalton....... 117
1938 Johannesburg, E. L. Dalton 102
1939 Capet'n, A. D. Nourse, jun. 120
1939 Durban, B. Mitchell...... 109
1939 Durban, P. G. Van der Byl 125
1939 Durban, A. D. Nourse, jun 103
1939 Durban, A. Melville...... 103
1947 Nott'gh'm, A. D. Nourse, jun 149
1947†Nottingham, A. Melville... 189
1947†Nottingham, A. Melville...*104
1947 Lord's, A. Melville....... 117
1947 Manch'r, A. D. Nourse, jun 115
1947†Oval, B. Mitchell......... 120
1947†Oval, B. Mitchell.........*189
1948 Joh'nn'b'g, E. A. B. Rowan*156
1949 Capetown, B. Mitchell.... 120
1949 Capetown, A. D. Nourse, jun 112
1949 Joh'nn'b'g, A. D. Nourse, jun 129
1949 Port Elizabeth, W. Wade 125
1951 Nottingham, A. D. Nourse. 208
1951 Leeds, E. A. B. Rowan... 236

† The same match.

ENGLAND v. WEST INDIES.—For England

1928 Lord's, E. Tyldesley...... 122
1928 The Oval, J. B. Hobbs... 159
1930 Barbados, A. Sandham... 152
1930 P't of Spain E. H. Hendren *205
1930 Port of Spain, L. Ames... 105
1930 Georgetown, E. H. Hendren 123
1930 Kingston, A Sandham... 325
1930 Kingston, L. Ames....... 146
1933 Manchester, D. R. Jardine 127
1933 The Oval, A. H. Bakewell. 107
1935 Kingston, L. Ames....... 126
1939 Lord's, L. Hutton........ 196
1939 Lord's, D. Compton....... 120
1939 The Oval, L. Hutton..... *165
1939 The Oval, W. R. Hammond 138
1948 Port of Spain, S. C. Griffith 140
1948 Pt of Spain, J. D. Robertson 133
1948 Kingston, W. Place....... 107
1950 Manchester, T. G. Evans.. 104
1950 Lord's, C. Washbrook.... 114
1950 Nottingham, C. Washbrook 102
1950 Oval, L Hutton......... *202

For West Indies

1930 Barbados, C. A. Roach.... 122
1930 Barbados, G. Headley.... 176
1930 Georgetown, C. A. Roach. 209
1930†Georgetown, G. Headley.. 114
1930†Georgetown, G. Headley.. 112
1930 Kingston, G. Headley..... 223
1933 Manchester, G. Headley.. *169
1933 Manchester, I. Barrow.... 105
1935 Kingston, G Headley *270
1939†Lord's, G. Headley....... 106
1939†Lord's, G. Headley....... 107
1939 The Oval. K. H. Weekes. 137
1948 Port of Spain, G. Carew... 107
1948 Port of Spain, A. Ganteaume.. 112
1948 Georgetown, F. Worrell... *131
1948 Kingston, E. Weekes..... 141
1950 Lord's, A. F. Rae........ 106
1950 Lord's, C. L. Walcott.... *168
1950 Nottingham, F. M. Worrell 261
1950 Nottingham, E. Weekes.. 129
1950 Oval, A. F. Rae.......... 109
1950 Oval, F. M. Worrell...... 138

† Same match

ENGLAND v. NEW ZEALAND.—For England

1930 Auckland, E. H. Bowley.. 109
1930 Auckl'd, K. S. Duleepsinhji 117
1930 Auckland, G. B. Legge.... 196
1931 Lord's, L. Ames.......... 137
1931 Lord's, G. O. Allen....... 122
1931 Oval, H. Sutcliffe........ 117
1931 Oval, K. S. Duleepsinhji.. 109
1931 Oval, W. R. Hammond... *100
1931 Manchester, H. Sutcliffe.. *109
1933 Christchurch, W. R. Hammond.. 227
1933 Christchurch, L. Ames.... 103
1933 Auckland, W R. Hammond 336
1937 Lord's, J. Hardstaff...... 114
1937 Lord's, W. R. Hammond. 140
1937 Manchester, L. Hutton... 100
1937 Oval, J. Hardstaff........ 103
1949 Leeds, D. Compton...... 114
1949 Leeds, L. Hutton........ 101
1949 Leeds, C. Washbrook..... *103
1949 Lord's, D. Compton...... 116
1949 Lord's, J. D. Robertson.. 121
1949 Manchester, R. T. Simpson 103
1949 Oval, L. Hutton......... 206
1949 Oval, W. J. Edrich....... 100
1951 Christchurch, T. E. Bailey. *134

For New Zealand

1930 Wellington, J. E. Mills.... 117
1930 Wellington, C. S. Dempster 136
1931 Lord's, C. S. Dempster... 120
1931 Lord's. M. L. Page....... 101
1947 Christchurch, W. A. Hadlee 116
1949 Lord's, M. P. Donnelly... 206
1949 Manchester. B. Sutcliffe.. 101
1951 Christchurch, B. Sutcliffe . 116

ENGLAND v. INDIA.—For England

1933 Bombay, B. H. Valentine. 136
1934 Madras, C. F. Walters.... 102
1936 M'chester, W. R. Hammond 167
1936 Oval, W. R. Hammond... 217
1936 Oval, T. S. Worthington.. 128
1946 Lord's, J. Hardstaff...... *205
1951 N. Delhi, A. J. Watkins.. *138
1951 Bombay, T. W. Graveney. 175
1952 Lord's, L. Hutton........ 150
1952 Lord's, T. G. Evans...... 104
1952 Manchester, L. Hutton... 104
1952 Oval, D. S. Sheppard..... 119

For India

1933 Bombay, Amar Nath..... 118
1936 Manchester, Mushtaq Ali. 112
1936 Manchester, V. M. Merchant 114
1946 Oval. V. M. Merchant.... 128
1951 N. Delhi, V. M. Merchant. 154
1951 N. Delhi, V. S. Hazare ... *164
1951 Bombay, P. Roy........ 140
1951 Bombay, V. S. Hazare... 155
1952 Calcutta, D. G. Phadkar. 115
1952 Madras, P. Roy......... 111
1952 Madras, P. Umrigar..... *130
1952 Leeds, V. L. Manjrekar... 133
1952 Lord's, V. Mankad....... 184

2

AUSTRALIA v. WEST INDIES.—For Australia

1930 Adelaide, A. F. Kippax... 146
1931 Sydney, W. H. Ponsford.. 183
1931 Brisbane, W. H. Ponsford. 109
1931 Brisbane, D. G. Bradman. 223
1931 Melbourne, D. G. Bradman 152
1951 Sydney, A. L. Hassett... 132
1951 Sydney, K. R. Miller..... 129
1952 Melbourne, A. L. Hassett. 102

For West Indies

1931 Brisbane, G. Headley.....*102
1931 Sydney, F. R. Martin....*123
1931 Sydney, G. Headley...... 105
1951 Melbourne, F. Worrell... 108
1952 Sydney, J. Stollmeyer... 104

AUSTRALIA v. INDIA.—For Australia

1947 Brisbane, D. G. Bradman. 185
1948†Melbourne (1) D. G. Bradman.. 132
1948†Melbourne (1) D. G. Bradman..*127
1948 Melbourne (1) A. Morris..*100
1948 Adelaide, D. G. Bradman. 201
1948 Adelaide, A. L. Hassett...*198
1948 Adelaide, S. Barnes...... 112
1948 Melbourne (2) N. Harvey. 153

For India

1948 Melbourne (1) V. Mankad. 116
1948 Adelaide, D. Phadkar.... 123
1948†Adelaide, V. S. Hazare... 116
1948†Adelaide, V. S. Hazare.... 145
1948 Melbourne (2) V. Mankad. 111
(† Same match)

INDIA v. PAKISTAN.—For India

1952 Bombay, V. Hazare......*146
1952 Bombay, P. Umrigar..... 102
1952 Calcutta, Deepak Shoda.. ‡110
(‡ First Test innings)

For Pakistan

1952 Lucknow, N. Mohammed.*124

AUSTRALIA v. SOUTH AFRICA.— For Australia

1902-03 Johannesburg, C. Hill. 142
1902-03 Johannesburg, W. W. Armstrong*159
1910-11 Melbourne, W. W. Armstrong 132
1910-11 Melbourne, C. Hill..... 100
1910-11 Melbourne, V. Trumper 159
1910-11 Sydney, W. Bardsley.. 132
1910-11 Sydney, C. Hill........ 191
1910-11 Sydney, C.G. Macartney 137
1910-11 Adelaide, V. Trumper..*214
1912 Manchester, W. Bardsley 121
1912 Manchester, C. Kelleway 114
1912 Lord's, W. Bardsley... 164
1912 Lord's, C. Kelleway.... 102
1921-22 Johannesburg, H. L. Collins 203
1921-22 Johannesburg, J. M. Gregory 119
1921-22 Durban, C.G. Macartney 116
1921-22 Capetown, J. Ryder... 142
1931-32 Brisbane, D. G. Bradman 226
1931-32 Sydney, K. E. Rigg... 127
1931-32 Sydney, D. G. Bradman 112
1931-32 Melbourne, W. M. Woodfull 161
1931-32 Melbourne, D. G. Bradman 167
1931-32 Adelaide, D. G. Bradman*299
1935-36 Capetown, W.A. Brown 121
1935-36 Capetown, J. H. W. Fingleton 112
1935-36 Durban, A. G. Chipperfield 109
1935-36 Durban, J. H. W. Fingleton 118
1935-36 Durban, S. J. McCabe. 149
1935-36 Johannesburg, J. H. W. Fingleton 108
1935-36 Johannesburg, S. J. McCabe*189
1949-50 Jo'burg, A. L. Hassett. 112
1949-50 Jo'burg, S. Loxton.... 101
1949-50 Capetown, N. Harvey. 178
1949-50 Durban, N. Harvey...*151
1949-50 Jo'burg, A. Morris.... 111
1949-50†Jo'burg, J. Moroney... 118
1949-50†Jo'burg, J. Moroney...*101
1949-50 Jo'burg, N. Harvey.... 100
1949-50 P. Elizabeth, A. Morris 157
1949-50 P. Elizabeth, N. Harvey 116
1949-50 P. Elizabeth, A. Hassett 167
1952-53 Brisbane, N. Harvey... 109
1952-53 Sydney, N. Harvey.... 190
1952-53 Adelaide, C McDonald. 154
1952-53 Adelaide, A. L. Hassett 163
1952-53 Adelaide, N. Harvey... 116
1952-53 Melbourne (2) N. Harvey 205
(† Same match)

For South Africa

1902-03 Johannesburg, J. H. Sinclair 101
1902-03 Capetown, J. H. Sinclair 104
1910-11 Melbourne, G. A. Faulkner 204
1910-11 Adelaide, G. A. Faulkner 115
1910-11 Adelaide, S. J. Snooke. 103
1910-11 Adelaide, J. W. Zulch. 105
1910-11 Sydney J. W. Zulch... 150
1912 Manchester, G. A. Faulkner*122
1921-22 Johannesburg, C. N. Frank 152
1921-22 Johannesburg, A. D. Nourse, sen. 111
1931-32 Melbourne, K. G. Viljoen 111
1935-36 Johannesburg, A. D. Nourse, jun. 231
1949-50 C'town, A. Nourse, jun 114
1949-50 Durban, E. Rowan.... 143
1952-53 Melbourne (1) W. R. Endean*162

SOUTH AFRICA v. NEW ZEALAND.

For South Africa

1931-32 Christchurch, J. A. Christy.. 103
1931-32 Christchurch, B. Mitchell.. 113
1931-32 Wellington, X. Balaskas..*122

For New Zealand

1931-32 Wellington, H. G. Vivian 10[illegible]

THE INTER-UNIVERSITY MATCH

Rivals' Records:

Played 107. Cambridge won 47. Oxford won 42, drawn 18.

Hundreds for Oxford University

1876 W. H. Game.......... 109
1877 F. M. Buckland..........*117
1881 W. H. Patterson..........*107
1886 K. J. Key.......... 143
1886 W. Rashleigh.......... 107
1887 Lord G. Scott.......... 100
1892 M. R. Jardine.......... 140
1892 V. T. Hill.......... 114
1894 C. B. Fry..........*100
1895 H. K. Foster.......... 121
1896 G. O. Smith.......... 132
1898 A. Eccles.......... 109
1900 R. E. Foster.......... 171
1901 C. H. B. Marsham.......*100
1903 J. E. Raphael.......... 130
1910 P. R. Le Couteur.......... 160
1919 M. Howell.......... 170
1923 C. H. Taylor.......... 114
1927 E. R. T. Holmes.......... 113
1929 Nawab of Pataudi.......... 106
1931 Nawab of Pataudi..........*238
1932 B. W. Hone.......... 167
1934 D. C. H. Townsend.......... 193
1934 F. G. H. Chalk.......... 108
1937 J. N. Grover.......... 121
1946 M. P. Donnelly.......... 142
1947 H. A. Pawson.......... 135
1948 H. E. Webb..........*145

For Cambridge University

1870 W. Yardley.......... 100
1872 W. Yardley.......... 130
1876 W. S. Patterson..........*105
1882 G. B. Studd.......... 120
1883 C. W. Wright.......... 102
1885 H. W. Bainbridge.......... 101
1887 E. Crawley..........*103
1889 H. J. Mordaunt.......... 127
1892 E. C. Streatfeild.......... 116
1898 C. E. M. Wilson.......... 115
1901 E. R. Wilson.......... 118
1902 S. H. Day..........*117
1904 J. F. Marsh..........*172
1905 L. G. Colbeck.......... 107
1906 R. A. Young.......... 150
1921 H. Ashton.......... 118
1922 A. P. F. Chapman..........*102
1924 H. J. Enthoven.......... 140
1925 H. J. Enthoven.......... 129
1927 A. Judd.......... 124
1928 R. W. V. Robins..........*101
1929 J. T. Morgan.......... 149
1930 E. T. Killick.......... 136
1931 A. Ratcliffe..........*201
1932 D. R. Wilcox.......... 157
1932 A. Ratcliffe.......... 124
1934 A. W. Allen.......... 115
1937 N. W. D Yardley.......... 101
1938 P. A. Gibb.......... 122
1939 P. J. Dickinson.......... 100
1952 D. S. Sheppard.......... 127

GENTLEMEN v. PLAYERS AT LORD'S

Year	Player	Score
1821	Beagley	*113
1825	W. Ward	*102
1827	Saunders	100
1860	Hayward	132
1863	Hayward, T.	*112
1866	Hearne, T.	*122
1868	W. G. Grace	*134
1870	W. G. Grace	109
1872	W. G. Grace	112
1872	Daft, R.	102
1873	W. G. Grace	163
1875	W. G. Grace	152
1876	W. G. Grace	169
1876	A. W. Ridley	103
1882	A. P. Lucas	107
1882	C. T. Studd	100
1883	E. F. S. Tylecote	107
1887	Shrewsbury, A.	111
1889	Barnes, W.	*130
1892	Gunn, W.	103
1895	W. G. Grace	118
1896	Hayward, T.	*116
1897	Shrewsbury, A.	125
1898	Gunn, W.	139
1899	C. B. Fry	104
1900	R. E. Foster	*102
1900	R. E. Foster	136
1900	Brown, J. T.	163
1900	Hayward, T.	111
1901	Tyldesley, J. T.	140
1901	C. B. Fry	126
1902	Braund, L. C.	141
1902	Lockwood, W. H.	100
1903	C. B. Fry	*232
1903	A. C. MacLaren	*168
1903	Knight, A. E.	139
1904	K. S. Ranjitsinhji	121
1904	King, J. H.	104
1904	King, J. H.	*109
1905	Hayward, T.	*123
1906	R. H. Spooner	114
1907	Hayward, T.	*146
1911	Hobbs, J. B.	*154
1919	D. J. Knight	124
1919	Hobbs, J. B.	113
1921	P. G. H. Fender	101
1921	Mead, C. P.	108
1922	A. P. F. Chapman	160
1922	Hobbs, J. B.	140
1922	Russell, A. C.	162
1923	G. T. S. Stevens	122
1923	M. D. Lyon	120
1924	Hobbs, J. B.	118
1924	Kilner, R.	113
1925	Hobbs, J. B.	140
1925	G. T. S. Stevens	129
1926	Hobbs, J. B.	163
1926	Sutcliffe, H.	107
1926	Tyldesley, E.	131
1926	A. P. F. Chapman	108
1927	D. R. Jardine	123
1930	K. S. Duleepsinhji	125
1930	K. S. Duleepsinhji	*103
1932	K. S. Duleepsinhji	132
1932	Nawab of Pataudi	165
1932	Hammond, W. R.	110
1932	Hobbs, J. B.	*161
1934	Mitchell, A.	120
1934	R. E. S. Wyatt	*104
1938	H. T. Bartlett	*175
1946	Washbrook, C.	105
1947	M. P. Donnelly	*162
1947	Washbrook, C.	101
1948	Hutton, L.	*132
1950	F. R. Brown	122
1950	Dollery, H. E.	123
1951	Compton, D. C. S.	150
1951	P. B. H. May	119
1952	C. H. Palmer	127

TEST MATCH PRICES INCREASED

Increased Entertainment Tax results in increased charges for the England v. Australia Tests and other Australian matches this summer. Minimum admission to Tests up to 5s. at all grounds. Prices in 1952 were 4s. 6d. London, 4s. provinces. Minimum for counties versus Australians is up to 3s. Old price 2s. 6d. England Test players' fee of £75 is unchanged.

ACKNOWLEDGMENT OF ILLUSTRATIONS

Photographs of Duke of Edinburgh by *Associated Press;* G. Langley, H. Tayfield, G. Hole, A. L. Hassett, Ian Craig, R. Lindwall, P. B. H. May, F. Trueman's field, A. V. Bedser by *Central Press;* Henry Cotton, W. Johnston, J. Panton, F. Daly, A. D. Locke by *Kemsley Newspapers Ltd., Manchester;* T. W. Graveney, R. N. Harvey, D. S. Sheppard by *Sport and General Press Agency;* Miss A. Phillips, K. R. Miller by *Graphic Photo Union;* J. T. Ikin by *P.A. Reuter;* Harvie Ward by *Daily Record, Glasgow;* Miss M. Paterson by *A. C. Cowper, Perth;* M. F. Bonallack by *Press Photographic Agency, Southport.*

COUNTY CRICKET PROSPECTS

SECRETARIES

MARYLEBONE C.C.: R. Aird, Lord's Cricket Ground, St. John's Wood, London, N.W.8.

DERBYSHIRE: W. T. Taylor, 18, St. James's Chambers, Derby.
ESSEX: Hon. Secretary, H. G. Clark, 3, Crane Court, High Street, Chelmsford.
GLAMORGAN: Hon. Secretary, J. C. Clay, 6, High Street, Cardiff.
GLOUCESTERSHIRE: Lt.-Col. H. A. Henson, County Ground, Bristol 7.
HAMPSHIRE: Colonel R. A. W. Binny, County Cricket Ground, Southampton.
KENT: N. Christopherson, St. Lawrence Ground, Canterbury.
LANCASHIRE: C. G. Howard, County Cricket Ground, Old Trafford, Manchester 16.
LEICESTERSHIRE: C. H. Palmer, Spencer Chambers, 4, Market Place, Leicester.
MIDDLESEX: F. G. Mann, Lord's Cricket Ground. London, N.W. 8.
NORTHAMPTONSHIRE: Lt.-Col. A. St. G. Coldwell, County Cricket Ground, Wantage Road, Northampton.
NOTTINGHAMSHIRE: H. A. Brown, County Cricket Ground, Nottingham.
SOMERSET: Air Vice-Marshal M. L. Taylor, County Cricket Ground, St. James's Street, Taunton.
SURREY: B. C. Castor, Kennington Oval, London, S.E.11.
SUSSEX: Lt.-Col. G. S. Grimston, County Ground, Eaton Road, Hove 3.
WARWICKSHIRE: L. T. Deakins, County Ground, Birmingham 5.
WORCESTERSHIRE: Brigadier M. A. Green, County Ground, Worcester.
YORKSHIRE: J. H. Nash, Old Bank Chambers, 9, Park Row, Leeds. 1.

DERBY PROSPECTS BRIGHTER

MUCH good work behind the scenes of **DERBYSHIRE** cricket results in the Peak county facing this summer in as happy a position as they have enjoyed for many years.

Not only has the whole of the 1952 playing staff been retained under the successful captain, Guy Willatt, but the activities of the newly-formed Supporters' Club have resulted in a steady income for the county throughout the winter, which will do much to remove Derbyshire's financial problems.

In addition, the first steps have been taken to improve the Derby ground by laying a new centre square before moving the pavilion to the old racecourse grandstand.

Derbyshire's attack this summer will depend chiefly on the well-tried opening pace and swing pair, Jackson and Gladwin, with the much improved Morgan in support. Rhodes and Carr, and the younger professionals Edwin Smith and B. H. Richardson, provide a fair assortment of spin bowling, without calling on the off-spin of Yorkshire-born opening bat Hamer.

The other opener will be C. S. Elliott, while the captain, Guy Willatt, who last season was one of the most successful left-handed batsmen in the country, will go in No. 3 again.

The side's fielding was much improved last summer, and with Dawkes behind the wicket and with Willatt's inspiration, the 1952 standard should be maintained this summer when the side should be strong enough to keep the county in the top six.

Notts Enter New Era

CAN Australian Test player Bruce Dooland accomplish for **NOTTINGHAMSHIRE** what George Tribe achieved for neighbouring Northamptonshire last summer ?

Having swept away the old tradition of Nottinghamshire players only, the Trent Bridge club enters a new era, one which, it is hoped, will bring success for importations.

Dooland, highly successful in Lancashire League cricket both as a right-arm leg spinner and a batsman, has served his qualification period and Test batsman R. T. Simpson is likely to have at his command a stronger team than the old club has put in the field since the war.

There is another importation, also a right-arm leg spinner and batsman, now qualified, in a former airman stationed near Nottingham, Gamini Goonesena, a Cingalese.

Departures from Trent Bridge are veteran Walter Keeton and coach Bill Voce who, between them, gave over 50 years' of great service. Voce's successor is former Sussex all-rounder Jim Parks.

Nottinghamshire may not be so strong in their opening attack for pace bowlers Harold Butler and Arthur Jepson are in the veteran stage as pre-war players, but with Dooland available much of the burden can be lifted from their shoulders, and they can be better nursed.

The only other seam bowler of real promise is a local youngster, Colin Matthews, who did very well and made fairly regular appearances last year, bowling better than his figures suggested.

Nottinghamshire, as in former years, will be a strong batting side with Simpson and Joe Hardstaff, Cyril Poole and Freddy Stocks, a run-making quartet of established reputation.

In this department, too, Dooland will surely stiffen a middle which frequently " folded up " in strange and unexpected fashion last summer.

The much-publicised treatment of the Trent Bridge wickets last season was not successful in its immediate results ; further measures were taken during the past winter, and the club hopes to achieve the aim of converting the " square " into faster pitches.

NEW SUSSEX SKIPPER

NOT for years has the **SUSSEX** outlook been so bright. The county's financial position has improved, membership has steadily increased, and the advance of young players has been most encouraging.

David Sheppard will be this season's captain in what may be his last full season in first-class cricket—a most popular appointment—but that stalwart of so many years, James Langridge, is to retire from the game to become the coach following the match against Australia in June. It is appropriate that Langridge should have joined that distinguished band of cricketers who have scored over 30,000 runs and taken over 1,500 wickets before his retirement.

Jim Cornford is now coaching in Southern Rhodesia, but Sussex followers are hoping that young Ian Thomson, a right-arm fast-medium bowler, may prove a worthy successor, while Jim Parks, now out of the Services, will probably be given a chance to bowl his leg-breaks.

Tall Alan Oakman has already impressed as an all-rounder of more than average ability, and among the younger professionals Denis Foreman, a South African, who will be eligible for the county in 1954, will gain valuable experience with the second team.

Gordon Potter, a right-hand batsman and leg-break bowler, is another young player who should make progress this season, but pace bowler Donald Bates will not be out of the Forces until late autumn. When Robin Marlar and Hubert Doggart become available during the holidays the side will be appreciably strengthened.

A grass mound has been laid at the north end of the County Ground at Hove on which over a thousand members can watch play in the comfort of deck chairs.

A blend of experience with youth may make this season's Sussex side the county's strongest since the war.

Worcester Recruits

MID-WAY through a difficult transition period, **WORCESTERSHIRE'S** problems centre almost entirely on the attack.

The Midland county have greatly felt the loss of off-spinner Jackson and left arm spinner Howorth, and it was hardly surprising that last season they fell from fourth from the top in 1951 to fourth from the bottom.

A strong close-season bid has been made, however, to remedy this state of affairs and two Yorkshire bowlers have been taken on to the staff—left arm spinner John Ashman and pace bowler John Whitehead. With Jenkins and Perks, Worcester will thus have four bowlers, men of proved ability, but beyond that lies uncertainty.

The county have at call fast bowler Jack Flavell, who was out of action for much of last summer with a back injury; West Indian pace man Ken Lobban, who was among the wickets for a short spell until the Malvern schoolmaster G. H. Chesterton took his place, and Wilson, a young left arm pace bowler of promise.

Outstanding among Worcester's young players last summer was Peter Richardson, the opening bat, who in his first full season of county cricket, topped the 1,500 runs mark.

With four other men going over 1,500 runs—Kenyon again reached his 2,000—Worcester were contrastingly strong in batting. They should again lack nothing in run-getting powers for the five leading batsmen have much cricket in front of them.

R. E. Bird, who had his best season ever in 1952, will again be the captain. The club have appointed a new coach in G. V. Gunn.

The new terracing on the ground, begun last summer, has been continued. The river side section has been completed and new terracing has been laid on the New-road side, where formerly a wooden open stand structure existed. Future plans include the building of a new scoreboard.

A tubular stand will be put up for the Australian match and retained for public use throughout the season.

HAMPSHIRE'S BIG NEED

HAMPSHIRE'S greatest need last season was in spin bowling. The County Committee during the winter made an effort to secure the services of the Yorkshire bowler, Eddie Leadbeater, but he eventually decided to enter Lancashire League cricket. However, Hampshire will be better served in this department this season, for off-spin bowler C. J. Knott, whose business commitments last summer restricted his appearances, is likely to be available regularly.

A newcomer to the side will be Henry Horton, Worcestershire-born, and who is a noted member of the Southampton F.C. He was transferred to Southampton from Blackburn Rovers two seasons ago, and impressed the Hampshire committee by his all-round form last season in club and ground games.

A number of young players on the staff should show further advance. Jimmy Gray has proved himself as an adequate opening batsman—1,634 runs last summer—to partner Neville Rogers who was the first Hampshire batsman since the war to aggregate over 2,000 runs, last season. The youngest of these, Alan Rayment, topped the 1,000 and earned considerable praise for his stylish attack. Moreover, he is inspiring in the field at cover.

Reg. Dare, the slow left-arm slow bowler and useful batsman, and two young amateurs, D. E. Blake and A. C. D. Ingleby-Mackenzie—both left-handers and both able to keep wicket—are other players due to make considerable advance.

Hampshire's seam bowling, in the hands of Derek Shackleton and Vic. Cannings, can compare with that of most counties, but here as in the batting order, there are weaknesses. If these could be remedied, Hampshire could become a very competent all-round combination under Desmond Eagar's enthusiastic leadership.

Kent Have Talent

IT is surprising that, with so much young talent available, **KENT** have occupied relatively modest places in the County Championship in recent seasons. Their lowly position in the table belied their potential strength.

The nursery, under the guidance of Claude Lewis, produced some fine young cricketers who ought to have yielded adequate replacements and reserves for the County side. But for some reason they did not fulfil their promise. Yet the Second XI won the Minor Counties' Championship in 1951, and lost the challenge match in 1952. It is high time that some of these youngsters established themselves as seniors.

W. Murray Wood will captain the County again. He is a brilliant fielder and, with the additional experience, is confidently expected to become a consistent run-getter. If only he would be less modest about his bowling ability those leg breaks of his could be distinctly useful.

The captain should have plenty of batting at his disposal. Even at 38 Fagg retains his form in amazing fashion and in spite of absence through injury collected more runs last season than any other batsman. Evans, in his benefit year, Hearn, Mayes, Phebey and O'Linn are all expected to do well.

The reserve wicket-keeper, Upton, a left-hand bat, made such rapid strides that he may gain his place for his batting alone.

After the University match, that outstanding player, M. C. Cowdrey, will come into the side to its immense advantage. In the range and power of his strokes there is no more promising batsman in the country.

When it comes to bowling, the prospects are less promising. The brilliant but erratic Wright is again the potential match winner. He has shortened his run-up and should be able to bear the probable burden required of him, though at 38 he may well need longer rests between spells.

Dovey has not missed a match for two years. As a stock bowler he can be relied upon to wheel up his off-spinners for hours on end. After two winters in India on top of his bowling here, Ridgway seemed to lack his customary zip and had a poor bag of wickets. He is expected to do very much better this summer.

A. C. Shirreff, fast medium, hopes to be able to play for part of the season, as does J. W. Martin. Others who will be called upon are Page who can open at fast medium, and switch to off-spinners, Brian Edrich and G. Smith.

WILL WARWICK RECOVER ?

CHAMPIONS in 1951, **WARWICKSHIRE,** are hoping for a return to their best form this summer, following a disappointing season last year, when they never looked like retaining their title.

All last season's players will be available, and the side will again be led by professional skipper Tom Dollery. It is hoped, too, that the team will be strengthened by the return of Ray Hitchcock, the brilliant young New Zealander who was one of the 1951 stars.

Last season Hitchcock was unable to play regularly owing to spinal trouble, and did not appear at all after mid-July, but it is hoped that he will be fit again for the start.

Keith Dollery, the Australian fast bowler, who has spent the last two seasons qualifying for the Midland county, will be eligible this summer. Dollery has been playing in the Lancashire League during his qualifying period.

Another of Warwickshire's youngsters, Jimmy Stewart, has gone into the Forces and neither of the two young pace bowlers, Roland Thompson and Ray Carter, is expected to be available regularly, as they are not due for demobilisation until next winter.

Warwickshire's ambitious programme of ground development, by which they hope to bring the ground up to Test match standards, is still proceeding.

Essex Enterprise

THERE is much about the cricket played by **ESSEX** that deserves congratulation and merits even greater reward than has come their way. In the present urge for brighter cricket they have set themselves to be as attractive a batting side as possible, and last season won a trophy for the fastest scoring team in the County Championship.

With D. J. Insole, an astute and enterprising captain, to lead and encourage the side Essex have developed a fine team spirit, and Insole sets a magnificent example of attacking batmanship and swift and nimble action in the field.

It is to be hoped that other members of the team will smarten up their fielding to give their toiling bowlers better support. If they performed as well as P. A. Gibb does behind the wicket there would be little cause for complaint. He was a great success and not only did he snap up more victims—83—than any other wicket-keeper, but scored 1,500 runs.

The batting should again be strong with Dodds and Avery, of such contrasting methods, to lay the foundation of the innings. Dodds is not among those opening batsmen who wait until the shine is off the ball before dreaming of offensive strokes. Twice he set the Essex innings off to an invigorating start by hitting the first ball for six. He was estimated as the fastest scoring opener in first-class cricket, his 1,800 runs being obtained at a rate of over 40 per hour.

Essex has two of the best all rounders in T. E. Bailey and R. Smith. Bailey batted consistently last summer, and is a most reliable man to have coming in half way down the order. He did not quite capture his best bowling form. Ray Smith has now performed the "double" five times. He can switch from medium paced to off-spinners. He was far and away the best bowler on the side.

The attack, however, badly needs the addition of a class spinner, a left hander or off-spinner, to support Bailey, Preston and Smith. If Greensmith could spin the ball he might supply the need since he has a good command of length; Vigar, who takes his benefit in the Sussex match at Ilford, is another leg-spinner with possibilities.

The Cambridge Blue, C. J. M. Kenny, hopes to play when business permits, and will be a welcome strength to the attack with his medium paced "seamers." A comprehensive coaching scheme covers the whole county and membership is now 5,029, a record and a tribute to enterprising cricket.

BIG CHANCE FOR YOUNGSTERS

ANY doubts about **YORKSHIRE'S** outlook are chiefly centred on the bowling strength at the disposal of Norman Yardley, who will lead the side again. The fact that seven batsmen reached the thousand runs mark last year indicates that there should be little fear of the White Rose men being dismissed cheaply in many matches.

As Trueman will not finish his National Service until September, he will again not be frequently available to act as the attacking spearhead. It will be surprising, too, if Appleyard, after many months in hospital, is fit to return, although there are hopes that he will figure in some grade of cricket in 1953.

In these circumstances, the bowling mainstays will again be Close and Wardle. Most promising of the young bowlers whose turn will come, particularly, when Test match calls affect the team, are Burgin and Sutcliffe (Sheffield United), Holdsworth (Chester-le-Street) and Wood (Walsden). Along with other colts, these players have been given special pre-season coaching in the winter shed at Headingley.

Second-team captain will be J. R. Burnet (Baildon Green), while Cyril Turner, who played for the county between 1925 and 1946, succeeds Herbert Walker as first-team scorer.

Stand improvements costing £5,000 have been carried out at Park-avenue, Bradford, and a grant of £3,000 is to be made towards the cost of a new stand at Hull. Altogether, Yorkshire have earmarked £20,000 for ground improvements.

Brighter Red Rose?

RIGHTLY or wrongly, many people argued that **LANCASHIRE** lost their chances of winning the championship in the last two seasons through staleness of key men following arduous winter tours. In the circumstances, the county did well enough to finish third on each occasion, especially as they were weakened by representative calls, sickness and injuries.

Lancashire again will doubtless be called upon to supply men for the England teams against Australia, but the players can tackle their various commitments in the knowledge that they have had a restful winter and that last season's casualties Ikin, Wharton and Tattersall, are fit again.

Nigel Howard, also happily restored to health, has been re-appointed captain, and is looking forward to a welcome change in his personal fortunes.

Generally, therefore, the outlook is bright, and Lancashire again should be among the leading challengers. The batting is as varied and reliable as any in the country, and the chief problem appears to be to find an opening partner in attack for Statham. Twenty-three-year-old Ted Nutter, of Colne, may be the answer.

Young all-rounder, Peter Marner, who made a belated appearance on the first-class scene last summer will probably have further opportunities and the second team have a useful acquisition in Bramhall captain, Alastair Fraser-Thomson, who takes over the leadership from Barry Howard.

The Surrey match has been set apart as Johnny Ikin's benefit, and although under normal circumstances a big crowd could be expected to welcome the champions, thousands more will be eager to pay tribute to this popular all-rounder, who has rendered such outstanding service to county and country and who, it is hoped, will have the opportunity to do so again this summer.

Cambridge University will make one of their infrequent visits North in June, and if the weather is kind, Lancashire should have one of their best seasons financially. The county have spared no effort to provide for the extra comfort of visitors, and Old Trafford at last will have a "new look" about it.

LEICESTER'S INCENTIVE

THE **LEICESTERSHIRE** players have more than one reason to be stimulated into special effort this year. Their morale is high after last season's most successful campaign since 1935, and they are aiming to improve on sixth place in the championship.

Thanks to the efforts of the Supporters' Association formed in January, 1952, the club's financial position has never been comparable to that in which the new season is awaited. Important changes at the Grace-road ground include terraced seating for nearly 800 spectators, and the construction of a stand to accommodate a corresponding number.

Under the leadership of Charles Palmer, the team will differ very little from last season. One big gap which is not likely to be filled adequately is that left by the absence of pace bowler Terry Spencer on Army service, though he may be able to play occasionally.

Walsh, Jackson, Goodwin, Palmer and Munden will once more shoulder most of the attacking burden. Walsh's achievement of the double in 1952 indicates that he should be a batting force, in the more circumspect mood he went for runs last summer.

Munden, too, took his most important role with the bat last season, and there are high hopes for this left-hander, who also flights and spins the ball cleverly.

With six men who each made a thousand runs last year, the batting abounds in enterprise, but there may have to be more experimenting to find the best opening pair. The retirement of Berry posed a problem that certainly was not solved last season.

A testimonial fund is being raised for senior professional Gerald Lester this year.

New Speed Man

FOR once **NORTHAMPTONSHIRE** start the season without any new players, but by July, Frank Tyson, the Lancashire-born fast bowler, now at Durham University, will be available. Great hopes are pinned on Tyson, who displayed considerable pace against the Indian touring side last season. He should greatly strengthen a department of attack which needed reinforcing.

In addition, the former Werneth wick-keeper, Keith Andrew, who has impressed in Services cricket during the last two years, will start his year's residential qualification, which is an insurance against the possible retirement of Ken Fiddling at the end of the season.

It is the ambition of F. R. Brown, in his last year as captain, to lead Northants to their first championship or failing that, to one of the highest positions. All the players are available except the second-team pace bowler, Gordon Brice.

With such stalwarts as Dennis Brookes, Norman Oldfield, Jock Livingston, Fred Jakeman, Desmond Barrick, Doug Greasley, Eddie Davis and Vince Broderick to say nothing of the captain himself, the strength of the Northants batting is obvious. If the bowlers can supplement the efforts of the run-getters, the outlook should be bright.

It is hoped that the Australian spinner, George Tribe, will improve on his first season performances, especially as the batsman's wicket at Northampton is being treated to give bowlers a fairer chance. This should aid the efforts of Brown, Nutter, Clarke and Starkie who had varying success last year.

Oldfield and Nutter, who joined Northants from Lancashire in 1948, take a joint testimonial this season. Ground improvements at Northampton include a Mound Stand, providing seated accommodation for 1,800 spectators on the public side.

"AS YOU WERE" AT LORD'S

IN spite of one of the most comprehensive schemes for finding and encouraging young talent, **MIDDLESEX** will depend largely on the players who did duty last season, though the long career of that fine slow bowler, Jim Sims, must be nearing its close. He may not play very often.

After two seasons of joint captaincy, the county will have W. J. Edrich as sole leader. Last year this great all-rounder seemed to show an unwonted amount of caution in his batting, perhaps forced upon him by the knowledge that he could not rely on the later batsmen. Still he topped the batting averages.

Now that Denis Compton has been released from the anxieties of captaincy, it is hoped he will regain the form that made him an outstandingly successful and attractive batsman.

This would not only give the Middlesex batting the stiffening it so badly needed last season, but would allow Edrich to indulge more freely his inclination to attack the bowlers.

J. D. Robertson is still one of the soundest "openers" and made more runs than ever before in a season. The difficulty is to discover a reliable partner for him. S. M. Brown, who takes his benefit in the Whitsun Sussex match, and T. Thompson were not successful, though both possess batting ability of a high order.

The young amateur W. Knightley-Smith, a left-handed batsman, scored consistently, and gained a regular place. He goes up to Cambridge and should get his "blue." He will be available at the end of term.

The bowling should be adequate. At least it does not lack variety with J. A. Young, still one of the hardest of slow left-arm bowlers to score off, Edrich now off-spinning, Bennett, Moss, and J. J. Warr all brisk medium, and Sims leg-breaks.

R. W. V. Robins has been persuaded to captain the second eleven, and will not miss any signs of talent. The cricket school at Alexandra Palace is a tremendous success and is in full swing twelve hours a day, seven days a week.

Champions' Task

AS Champion County **SURREY** will have their work cut out to hold on to their supremacy, especially now that two of their most dependable performers, Fishlock and Parker, have retired. But the prospects of their doing so have been considerably enhanced since it became known that P. B. H. May, who has taken up an appointment in the city, will be available for the whole season.

With this very sound and often brilliant batsman regularly in the side, the Surrey batting will be a formidable proposition for opposing bowlers Last season the batting, for a variety of reasons was not as consistently good as it ought to have been with the talent available. The Championship was won chiefly by the excellence of the bowling, supported by superb fielding, and by the inspiring captaincy of W. S. Surridge. He will again lead the side.

In addition to May, there are batsmen of high quality in Fletcher, who recaptured his best form and settled down as a dependable opener with Eric Bedser; Whittaker, Clark, Brazier, Constable and McIntyre.

Neither Whittaker nor McIntyre did himself justice. It is hoped that Whittaker, who can hit as hard as anyone, will follow his natural bent and not allow himself to be tucked up by innocuous-looking bowling simply by not using his feet.

If McIntyre could curb his impetuosity at the start of an innings, he would make plenty of runs. He has the ability but threw his wicket away too often by rash strokes. But his wicket-keeping remained in the highest class.

The gallant and apparently tireless Alec Bedser will be supported by Surridge, Laker, Lock, Eric Bedser and Loader—a well-assorted attack. It only requires a good leg-spinner to be complete. Perhaps greater use will be made of Constable for this purpose. Young Loader showed great promise with his fast-medium bowling, and he has the great virtue of making the ball leave the bat.

Lock has been attending to his method of delivery during the winter, and there should be no question of its legality now.

Two youngsters R. C. E. Pratt and K. Barrington, did so well last season in the 2nd XI, they are bound to be in the running for a place in the county side. They both made over a thousand runs. M. J. Stuart, a right-hand bat, has joined the staff.

The Yorkshire match on July 4 has been allotted to Alec Bedser for his benefit. The Australians will be met on May 9 and July 29. Surrey have a full membership. There was a profit of nearly £1,000 on the 1952 season.

MANY SOMERSET CHANGES

THE prospects of **SOMERSET** depend very largely on what new material the club is able to recruit, for at the end of last season the Committee decided to make several changes, some of which have not entirely pleased the supporters.

Biggest surprise was the non-retention of their most successful slow bowler, Horace Hazell and Ellis Robinson, another off-spin bowler who came to Somerset from Yorkshire, will not be seen with the county this season. Jim Redman, the fast bowler, declined to sign professional forms again, and, if required, will play in future as an amateur. Leslie Angell, the opening batsman, too, has not been retained.

A former captain of Uppingham School, Tom Hall, comes from Derbyshire, under a special registration and will play as an amateur. He is a sound batsman and a useful right-handed fast medium bowler. S. S. Rogers has relinquished the captaincy, and will be succeeded by Berkshire farmer Ben Brocklehurst, a free scoring player who has appeared in a few games for this county since 1951.

Of the old stalwarts available, Harold Gimblett on whom the team depends so much; Bertie Buse (who takes his benefit this year), Maurice Tremlett, J. W. Lawrence, H. W. Stephenson and young Roy Smith, who is expected to fill Hazell's place, are likely to bear most of the burden.

Of the amateurs who may be available for part of the season at least, H. E. Watts, M. M. Walford and G. G. Tordoff are the most notable.

McConnon Back

THOUGH **GLAMORGAN** dropped to seventh position in the County Championship last season, Wilf Wooller, who will again captain the Welsh county, sees no reason why his men should not move up to the top four this year.

There were certainly extenuating circumstances for Glamorgan's slight drop in form, most important, of course, being the fact that for the greater part of the season they were without off-spin bowler Jim McConnon. The luck of the toss, too, was constantly against the side, for Wooller lost twenty out of thirty guesses.

The coming season should see a big improvement in attack. McConnon is fit again, and has been doing winter practice at the nets, and Alan Watkins has been developing a new bowling style which, supplemented with his normal fast-medium "cutters," should bring him more than the 84 wickets he secured last season. In addition, Don Shepherd, who claimed 115 wickets last season, is bowling better than ever.

With Norman Hever as a pace man and Wilf Wooller, Len Muncer and W. E. Jones, change bowlers, the attack should lack nothing in variety or ability.

Of the batsmen, Parkhouse, Clift and W. E. Jones, the latter of whom takes his benefit this summer, have put in a lot of early practice, while Emrys Davies, now in his 30th year of first-class cricket, is still there to provide steadiness at the start of an innings.

Don Ward, who has been with the Lord's school for the past couple of seasons, has now entered the Forces, but promising Swansea all-rounder Jim Pressdee has completed his term of National Service and will again be available, as will such other promising younger players as Bernard Hedges Bernard Shaw and Jim Pleass.

GLOUCESTER MAKE HISTORY

IN their 80th county season, **GLOUCESTERSHIRE** will be led for the first time by a professional—Jack Crapp, the England left-hander.

Crapp follows many illustrious names in the county's cricket, including W. G. Grace, G. L. Jessop and W R. Hammond, but the council, in making the decision, declared "their complete confidence in him, both as cricketer and man, on and off the field of play."

Two former captains, Sir Derrick Bailey and B. O. Allen, hope to play some games during the summer, but otherwise Gloucestershire will field the regulars of last season.

Tom Graveney has had a tonsils operation during the winter, and it is hoped he will return to cricket more vigorous than ever. Great faith, too, is pinned in the young all-rounder Arthur Milton, who, it is hoped, will fulfil all the optimistic forecasts made about him.

The county hopes to have the help at intervals of their two promising spin bowlers still in the Services, Brian Wells and John Mortimore.

Six of the younger professionals, Frank McHugh, Peter Rochford, Derek Hawkins, Tony Wignall, John Griffiths and Graham Wiltshire have spent some time at Gover's indoor school during the winter, while Andy Wilson, who has kept wicket for the county since 1936, is to have the Middlesex match at Bristol on June 20 as his benefit.

THIS YEAR'S TEST SELECTORS

Meeting at Lord's, the Board of Control appointed the following selection committee for the 1953 Test matches against Australia: F. R. Brown (chairman), R. E. S. Wyatt, N. W. D. Yardley and L. E. G. Ames. This is the same committee as in 1951 and 1952 except that Mr. Brown takes over the chairmanship from Mr. Yardley.

MILESTONES . . .

* Denotes not out.

1728 First recorded county match, Kent v. Sussex

1744 First laws published

1774 Ruling on maximum width of bat—4¼ inches

1775 Stumps to be 22 inches by 6 inches. Three stumps used for first time

1787 M.C.C. founded

1788 Stumps enlarged to 24 inches by 7 inches

1791 Hambledon Club broke up

1806 First Gentlemen v. Players match

1814 Lord's ground moved to present site from Regent's Park

1816 Stumps 26 inches by 7 inches

1816 Two bails first used

1817 Stumps 27 inches by 8 inches

1827 Round arm bowling legalised

1827 First Oxford v. Cambridge match

1835 Follow-on deficit fixed at 100 runs

1836 Pads first used

1844 United States first played Canada (first representative match out of England)

1846 W. Clarke founded All England XI

1850-51 Start of first-class cricket in Australia

1852 Foundation of United England XI

1859 First English team on tour—Parr's to North America

1859-60 Start of first-class cricket in New Zealand

1861-62 First English team (H. H Stephenson's) to Australia

1863-64 Start of first-class cricket in West Indies

1864 Overarm bowling legalised

1873 County Championship started

1876-77 England first played Australia

1878 First Australian team to England

1880 First Test in England

1882 "The Ashes" tradition established after Oval Test match

1882-86 Notts champions (joint in 1882)

1884-85 Five Tests played for first time

1887-92 Surrey champions (joint 1889)

1888-89 Start of first-class cricket in South Africa

1888-89 England first played South Africa

1889 Over increased to five balls

1892 Start of first-class cricket in India

1894 First South African team to England

1895 Second-class Counties' Competition started

1895 A. C. MacLaren makes record score in England, 424

1896 Record total by a county in England, 887 by Yorkshire

1898 Board of Control instituted

1900 Follow-on deficit fixed at 150 runs, and made optional

1900 Over increased to six balls

1900 First West Indies team to England

1902-03 Australia first played South Africa

1906 Hirst's unique double—2,385 runs and 208 wickets

1906 Hayward's record aggregate, 3,518 runs

1909 Imperial Cricket Conference instituted

1911 First Indian team to England

1912 Triangular Test Tournament, won by England

1912 First "timeless" Test in England (v. Australia at The Oval)

1913 Covering ends of wickets permitted

1914-18 First World War

1915 W. G. Grace died: career 1864-1908, 54,896 runs and 2,876 wickets

1920-21 Australia beat England in all five Tests

. . . OF CRICKET

1922 Over increased to 8 balls in Australia

1922–25 Yorkshire champions

1925 Covering whole pitch 24 hours before match allowed

1926–27 World's record score for a side—1,107 by Victoria

1927 Size of wickets increased to 28 inches by 9 inches

1927 Ball to be 8 13/16 ins. to 9 ins.

1927 First New Zealand team to England

1928 England first played West Indies

1928 Freeman's record aggregate 304 wickets

1929–30 England first played New Zealand

1929–30 D. G. Bradman's world record score—452 not out

1930 Rhodes retires (1898–1930)—record number of wickets, 4,188

1930 Record score by Australians in Tests—334 by D. G. Bradman

1932 England first played India

1932 Holmes and Sutcliffe make partnership of 555

1932–33 "Body-line" controversy in Australia during M.C.C. tour

1932–33 Record score in E.-N.Z. Tests (336*) by W. R. Hammond

1934 Hobbs retires (1905–1934)—record number of runs and centuries—61,237 and 197

1935 South Africa wins first Test rubber in England

1935 Lbw (N) rule

1935 M.C.C. rule against "body-line" bowling

1937 P. F. Warner knighted

1937 Parks (J. H.) performs unique double—3,003 runs and 101 wickets

1938 Record total in Test cricket —903 (7) by England v. Australia–and innings (364) by Hutton

1938–39 Fifth Test at Durban (England v. South Africa) lasted 10 days, and was drawn

1938–39 Don Bradman equalled C. B. Fry's feat of scoring six centuries in successive innings

1939 8-ball over used experimentally in first-class matches

1939–1945 Second World War

1940–41 A. Morris (N.S.W.) scored 148 and 111 in his first first-class match (world record)

1943–44 F. Worrell and J. Goddard scored 502 for Barbados v. Trinidad (4th wicket record)

1943–44 V. M. Merchant scored 359 not out at Bombay (Indian record)

1944 M.C.C. Select Committee's 6,000 word report on post-war needs, urged "dynamic attitude" by players

1945 W. R. Hammond scored two centuries in a match for the 7th time (world record)

1945 County Cup plan postponed

1947 Gul Mahomed and V. S. Hazare for Baroda v. Holkar made record partnership (577) for any wicket in first-class cricket

1947 Revision of the Laws of Cricket—first for 67 years.

1947 D. Compton scored 3,816 runs, including 18 hundreds

1948 W. G. Grace Centenary

1949 D. G. Bradman retired from first-class cricket and received Knighthood

1949 D. B. Close (Yorks.) played for England at age of 18 and completed "double" in first season

1950 W. Indies won first Test in England and also rubber.

1951 L. Hutton was given out "obstructing the field" in England's 2nd innings v. South Africa at the Oval—the first instance of this decision in a Test match.

1952 England appointed a professional (L. Hutton) as season's Test captain.

What's on at Lord's

(Three-day games, unless otherwise stated)

MAY

2 M.C.C. v. Yorkshire
6 M.C.C. v. Surrey
9 Middlesex v. Hampshire
13 Middlesex v. Derbyshire
16 M.C.C. v. Australians
21 M.C.C. v. R.M.A., Sandhurst (2 days)
23 Middlesex v. Sussex
27 M.C.C. v. Hampshire
30 Middlesex v. Northamptonshire

JUNE

3 Middlesex v. Somerset
6 Middlesex v. Yorkshire
10 Middlesex v. Leicestershire
13 Middlesex 2nd XI v. Surrey 2nd XI (2 days)
17 Middlesex v. Nottinghamshire
20 M.C.C. v. Gentlemen of Ireland (2 days)
25 ENGLAND v. AUSTRALIA (Second Test) (5 days)

JULY

1 Middlesex v. Essex
4 Oxford v. Cambridge
10 Eton v. Harrow (2 days)
13 Royal Artillery v. Royal Engineers (2 days)
15 Gentlemen v. Players
18 Middlesex v. Australians
22 Middlesex v. Kent
25 Beaumont v. Oratory (1 day)

JULY

27 Clifton v. Tonbridge (2 days)
29 Rugby v. Marlborough (2 days)
31 Cheltenham v. Haileybury & I.S.C. (2 days)

AUGUST

3 Southern Schools v. The Rest (2 days)
5 A Schools XI v. M.C.C. Young Professionals (1 day)
6 Combined Services v. Public Schools (2 days)
8 Middlesex v. Surrey
12 Royal Navy v. Royal Air Force (2 days)
14 M.C.C. v. de Flamingos (1 day)
15 Middlesex v. Worcestershire
19 Middlesex v. Gloucestershire
22 Army v. Royal Air Force (2 days)
25 M.C.C. Young Professionals v. English Schools C. A. (1 day)
26 Gentlemen of England v. Australians
29 Middlesex v. Lancashire

SEPTEMBER

2 M.C.C. Young Professionals v. London Federation of Boys' Clubs (1 day)
7 Cross Arrows C.C. match every week-day (Saturdays excluded) until Friday, Sept. 25

First-Class Fixtures

(all 3 days unless otherwise stated)

APRIL

29—Worcester, Worcestershire v. Australians
29—Cambridge, Cambridge University v. Sussex

MAY

2—Southampton, Hampshire v. Essex
2—Leicester, Leicestershire v. Australians
2—Lord's, M.C.C. v. Yorkshire
2—Peterborough, Northants v. Middlesex
2—Warwickshire v. Kent
2—Worcester, Worcestershire v. Somerset
2—Oxford, Oxford University v. Gloucestershire
2—Cambridge, Cambridge University v. Surrey
6—Bradford, Yorkshire v. Australians
6—Lord's, M.C.C. v. Surrey
6—Portsmouth, Hampshire v. Gloucestershire
6—Oxford, Oxford University v. Lancashire
6—Cambridge, Cambridge University v. Middlesex
9—The Oval, Surrey v. Australians
9—Bristol—Gloucestershire v. Leicestershire
9—Swansea, Glamorgan v. Worcestershire

MAY—Continued

9—Manchester, Lancashire v. Warwickshire
9—Lord's, Middlesex v. Hampshire
9—Nottingham, Notts v. Kent
9—Taunton, Somerset v. Sussex
9—Hull, Yorkshire v. Essex
9—Cambridge, Cambridge University v. Free Foresters
9—Northampton, Northants v. R.A.F.
13—**Cambridge, Cambridge University v. Australians**
13—Cardiff, Glamorgan v. Kent
13—Liverpool, Lancashire v. Sussex
13—Lord's, Middlesex v. Derbyshire
13—Northampton, Northants v. Somerset
13—Nottingham, Notts v. Warwickshire
13—Oxford, Oxford University v. Yorkshire
16—**Lord's, M.C.C. v. Australians**
16—Chesterfield, Derbyshire v. Glamorgan
16—Westcliff, Essex v. Middlesex
16—Gloucester, Gloucestershire v. Notts
16—Gravesend, Kent v. Lancashire
16—Loughborough, Leicestershire v. Hampshire
16—The Oval, Surrey v. Warwickshire
16—Hove, Sussex v. Northants
16—Leeds, Yorkshire v. Somerset
16—Cambridge, Cambridge University v. Worcestershire
20—**Oxford, Oxford University v. Australians**
20—Westcliff, Essex v. Glamorgan
20—Portsmouth, Hampshire v. Leicestershire
20—Gravesend, Kent v. Northants
20—Taunton, Somerset v. Derbyshire
20—The Oval, Surrey v. Gloucestershire
20—Huddersfield, Yorkshire v. Worcestershire
20—Birmingham, Warwickshire v. Combined Services
23—**Stoke, Minor Counties v. Australians**
23—Southampton, Hampshire v. Kent
23—Manchester, Lancashire v. Yorkshire
23 Lord's, Middlesex v. Sussex (**S. M. Brown's Benefit**)
23—Northampton, Northants v. Leicestershire
23—Nottingham, Notts v. Surrey
23—Taunton, Somerset v. Gloucestershire
23—Birmingham, Warwickshire v. Derbyshire
23—Worcester, Worcestershire v. Essex
27—**Birmingham, TEST TRIAL MATCH**
27—**Manchester, Lancashire v. Australians**
27—Derby, Derbyshire v. Sussex
27—Ilford, Essex v. Northants
27—Folkestone, Kent v. Glamorgan
27—Leicester, Leicestershire v. Gloucestershire
27—Taunton, Somerset v. Surrey
27—Lords, M.C.C. v. Hampshire
27—Oxford, Oxford University v. Middlesex
27—Cambridge, Cambridge University v. Warwickshire
27—Jesmond, Northumberland v. Yorkshire (2 days)
30—**Nottingham, Notts v. Australians**
30—Burton-on-Trent, Derbyshire v. Worcestershire
30—Ilford, Essex v. Sussex (**F. Vigar's Benefit**)
30—Bristol, Gloucestershire v. Hampshire
30—Manchester, Lancashire v. Surrey (**J. T. Ikin's Benefit**)
30—Lord's, Middlesex v. Northants
30—Coventry (Courtaulds), Warwickshire v. Somerset
30—Sheffield, Yorkshire v. Glamorgan
30—Oxford, Oxford University v. Leicestershire

JUNE

3—**Hove, Sussex v. Australians**
3—Llanelly, Glamorgan v. Essex

JUNE—Continued

3—Bristol, Gloucestershire v. Combined Services
3—Lord's, Middlesex v. Somerset
3—Nottingham, Notts v. Worcestershire
3—The Oval, Surrey v. Derbyshire
3—Birmingham, Warwickshire v. Lancashire
3—Harrogate, Yorkshire v. Leicestershire
3—Oxford, Oxford University v. Hampshire
3—Cambridge, Cambridge University v. Northants
6—Southampton, Hampshire v. Australians
6—Pontypridd, Glamorgan v. Derbyshire
6—Gillingham, Kent v. Gloucestershire
6—Leicester, Leicestershire v. Sussex
6—Lord's, Middlesex v. Yorkshire
6—Bath, Somerset v. Lancashire (**H. T. F. Buse's Benefit**)
6—The Oval, Surrey v. Northants
6—Kidderminster, Worcestershire v. Notts
6—Cambridge, Cambridge University v. M.C.C.
10—Brentwood, Essex v. Surrey
10—Lord's, Middlesex v. Leicestershire
10—Bath, Somerset v. Kent
10—Horsham, Sussex v. Warwickshire
10—Bradford, Yorkshire v. Notts
10—Oxford, Oxford University v. Derbyshire
10—Peterborough, Northants v. Scotland
11—Nottingham, ENGLAND v. AUSTRALIA (First Test—5 days)
13—Brentwood, Essex v. Hampshire
13—Manchester, Lancashire v. Derbyshire
13—Northampton, Northants v. Notts
13—Bath, Somerset v. Leicestershire
13—The Oval, Surrey v. Kent
13—Horsham, Sussex v. Glamorgan
13—Birmingham, Warwickshire v. Gloucestershire
13—Worcester, Worcestershire v. Middlesex
13—Hull, Yorkshire v. Cambridge University
13—Oxford, Oxford University v. Free Foresters
17—Chesterfield, Derbyshire v. Australians
17—Neath, Glamorgan v. Northants
17—Tunbridge Wells, Kent v. Leicestershire
17—Manchester, Lancashire v. Cambridge University
17—Lord's, Middlesex v. Notts
17—The Oval, Surrey v. Essex
17—Dudley, Worcestershire v. Sussex
17—Oxford, Oxford University v. Warwickshire
17—In Scotland, Scotland v. Yorkshire
20—Sheffield, Yorkshire v. Australians
20—Derby, Derbyshire v. Surrey
20—Swansea, Glamorgan v. Somerset
20—Bristol, Gloucestershire v. Middlesex (**A. E. Wilson's Benefit**)
20—Tunbridge Wells, Kent v. Sussex
20—Leicester, Leicestershire v. Lancashire
20—Kettering, Northants v. Essex
20—Nottingham, Notts v. Cambridge University
20—Birmingham, Warwickshire v. Hampshire
20—Worcester, Worcestershire v. Oxford University
20—Lord's, M.C.C. v. Gentlemen of Ireland (2 days)
24—Newport, Glamorgan v. Hampshire
24—Bristol, Gloucestershire v. Warwickshire
24—Folkestone, Kent v. Cambridge University
24—Hinckley, Leicestershire v. Worcestershire
24—Nottingham, Notts v. Middlesex
24—The Oval, Surrey v. Oxford University
24—Leeds, Yorkshire v. Northants
25—Lord's, ENGLAND v. AUSTRALIA (Second Test—5 days)
27—Ilkeston, Derbyshire v. Notts
27—Romford, Essex v. Kent

JUNE—Continued

27—Cardiff, Glamorgan v. Yorkshire
27—Bournemouth, Hampshire v. Northants
27—Manchester, Lancashire v. Middlesex
27—Hinckley, Leicestershire v. Warwickshire
27—Yeovil, Somerset v. Worcestershire
27—Guildford, Surrey v. Cambridge University
27—Hove, Sussex v. Oxford University

JULY

1—**Bristol, Gloucestershire v. Australians**
1—Chesterfield, Derbyshire v. Northants
1—Manchester, Lancashire v. Hampshire
1—Lord's, Middlesex v. Essex
1—Nottingham, Notts v. Glamorgan
1—Yeovil, Somerset v. Yorkshire
1—Guildford, Surrey v. Sussex
1—Worcester, Worcestershire v. Warwickshire
1—Sandhurst, The Army v. Oxford University (2 days)
1—Eastbourne, L. C. Stevens' XI v. Cambridge University (2 days)
4—**Northampton, Northants v. Australians**
4—Blackheath, Kent v. Essex
4—Liverpool, Lancashire v. Glamorgan
4—Nottingham, Notts v. Derbyshire (**E. A. Meads's Benefit**)
4—Taunton, Somerset v. Hampshire
4—The Oval, Surrey v. Yorkshire (**A. V. Bedser's Benefit**)
4—Hove, Sussex v. Leicestershire
4—Birmingham, Warwickshire v. Middlesex
4—Dudley, Worcestershire v. Gloucestershire
4—**Lord's, Oxford University v. Cambridge University**
8—Chesterfield, Derbyshire v. Kent
8—Leicester, Leicestershire v. Somerset
8—Nottingham, Notts v. Northants
8—Worthing, Sussex v. Hampshire
8—Birmingham, Warwickshire v. Surrey
8—Worcester, Worcestershire v. Lancashire
8—Sheffield, Yorkshire v. Gloucestershire
9—**Manchester, ENGLAND v. AUSTRALIA (Third Test—5 days)**
10—**Lord's, Eton v. Harrow (2 days)**
11—Colchester, Essex v. Lancashire
11—Gloucester, Gloucestershire v. Glamorgan
11—Portsmouth, Hampshire v. Somerset
11—Blackheath—Kent v. Surrey
11—Ashby-de-la-Zouch, Leicestershire v. Derbyshire
11—Northampton, Northants v. Warwickshire
11—Worthing, Sussex v. Worcestershire
11—Bradford, Yorkshire v. Middlesex
11—Nottingham, Notts v. R.A.F.
13—Lord's, Royal Artillery v. Royal Engineers (2 days)
15—**Lord's, Gentlemen v. Players**
15—Derby, Derbyshire v. Middlesex
15—Colchester, Essex v. Leicestershire
15—Cardiff, Glamorgan v. Notts
15—Gloucester, Gloucestershire v. Yorkshire
15—Maidstone, Kent v. Warwickshire
15—Northampton, Northants v. Lancashire
15—The Oval, Surrey v. Worcestershire
18—**Lord's, Middlesex v. Australians**
18—Chesterfield, Derbyshire v. Yorkshire
18—Swansea, Glamorgan v. Gloucestershire (**W. E. Jones's Benefit**)
18—Bournemouth, Hampshire v. Sussex
18—Maidstone, Kent v. Worcestershire
18—Manchester, Lancashire v. Essex
18—Taunton, Somerset v. Northants
18—The Oval, Surrey v. Leicestershire
18—Birmingham, Warwickshire v. Notts

JULY—Continued

22—Ebbw Vale, Glamorgan v. Warwickshire
22—Bristol, Gloucestershire v. Essex
22—Bournemouth, Hampshire v. Notts
22—Manchester, Lancashire v. Somerset
22—Lord's, Middlesex v. Kent
22—Hastings, Sussex v. Yorkshire
22—Dudley, Worcestershire v. Derbyshire
23—Leeds, ENGLAND v. AUSTRALIA (Fourth Test—5 days)
25—Chesterfield, Derbyshire v. Lancashire
25—Cardiff, Glamorgan v. Middlesex
25—Bristol, Gloucestershire v. Surrey
25—Northampton, Northants v. Hampshire
25—Nottingham, Notts v. Yorkshire
25—Hastings, Sussex v. Kent
25—Birmingham, Warwickshire v. Essex
25—Worcester, Worcestershire v. Leicestershire (**R. O. Jenkins's Benefit**)
25—Lord's, Beaumont v. Oratory (1 day)
27—Lord's, Clifton v. Tonbridge (2 days)
29—The Oval, Surrey v. Australians
29—Chelmsford, Essex v. Somerset
29—Southampton, Hampshire v. Middlesex
29—Blackpool, Lancashire v. Worcestershire
29—Northampton, Northants v. Sussex
29—Nottingham, Notts v. Gloucestershire
29—Coventry (Courtaulds), Warwickshire v. Leicestershire
29—Scarborough, Yorkshire v. Kent
29—Lord's, Rugby v. Marlborough (2 days)
31—Lord's, Cheltenham v. Haileybury (2 days)

AUGUST

1—Swansea, Glamorgan v. Australians
1—Derby, Derbyshire v. Warwickshire
1—Chelmsford, Essex v. Worcestershire
1—Bristol, Gloucestershire v. Somerset
1—Canterbury, Kent v. Hampshire (**T. G. Evans's Benefit**)
1—Canterbury, Kent v. Hampshire
1—Leicester, Leicestershire v. Northants
1—The Oval, Surrey v. Notts
1—Hove, Sussex v. Middlesex
1—Sheffield, Yorkshire v. Lancashire
3—Lord's, Southern Schools v. The Rest (2 days)
5—Birmingham, Warwickshire v. Australians
5—Canterbury, Kent v. Middlesex
5—Leicester, Leicestershire v. Yorkshire
5—Rushden, Northants v. Gloucestershire
5—Nottingham, Notts v. Lancashire
5—Weston-super-Mare, Somerset v. Glamorgan
5—The Oval, Surrey v. Hampshire
5—Hove, Sussex v. Derbyshire
6—Lord's, Combined Services v. Public Schools (2 days)
8—Manchester, Lancashire v. Austrailans
8—Cheltenham, Gloucestershire v. Sussex
8—Loughborough, Leicestershire v. Kent
8—Lord's, Middlesex v. Surrey
8—Wellingborough, Northants v. Derbyshire
8—Nottingham, Notts v. Hampshire
8—Weston-super-Mare, Somerset v. Essex
8—Worcester, Worcestershire v. Glamorgan
8—Bradford, Yorkshire v. Warwickshire
12—Southend, Essex v. Australians
12—Cheltenham, Gloucestershire v. Worcestershire
12—Portsmouth, Hampshire v. Glamorgan
12—Manchester, Lancashire v. Northants
12—Loughborough, Leicestershire v. Surrey
12—Weston-super-Mare, Somerset v. Notts

AUGUST—Continued

12—Birmingham, Warwickshire v. Sussex
12—Scarborough, Yorkshire v. Derbyshire
12—Lord's, Royal Navy v. R.A.F. (2 days)
15—The Oval, ENGLAND v. AUSTRALIA (Fifth Test—5 days)
15—Derby, Derbyshire v. Leicestershire
15—Southend, Essex v. Notts
15—Cardiff, Glamorgan v. Sussex
15—Cheltenham, Gloucestershire v. Lancashire
15—Portsmouth, Hampshire v. Warwickshire
15—Dover, Kent v. Somerset
15—Lord's, Middlesex v. Worcestershire
15—Leeds, Yorkshire v. Surrey
19—Chesterfield, Derbyshire v. Somerset
19—Swansea, Glamorgan v. Lancashire
19—Dover, Kent v. Yorkshire
19—Leicester, Leicestershire v. Essex
19—Lord's, Middlesex v. Gloucestershire
19—Northampton, Northants v. Surrey
19—Eastbourne, Sussex v. Notts
19—Birmingham, Warwickshire v. Worcestershire
22—**Taunton, Somerset v. Australians**
22—Buxton, Derbyshire v. Essex
22—Manchester, Lancashire v. Kent
22—Northampton, Northants v. Glamorgan
22—Nottingham, Notts v. Leicestershire
22—The Oval, Surrey v. Middlesex
22—Eastbourne, Sussex v. Gloucestershire
22—Birmingham, Warwickshire v. Yorkshire
22—Worcester, Worcestershire v. Hampshire
22—Lord's, The Army v. R.A.F. (2 days)
26—**Lord's, Gentlemen of England v. Australians**
26—Clacton, Essex v. Gloucestershire
26—Southampton, Hampshire v. Derbyshire
26—Manchester, Lancashire v. Notts
26—Northampton, Northants v. Kent
26—The Oval, Surrey v. Glamorgan
26—Worcester, Worcestershire v. Yorkshire
26—Hove, Sussex Amateurs v. Sussex Professionals
29—**Canterbury, Kent v. Australians**
29—Clacton, Essex v. Warwickshire
29—Bristol, Gloucestershire v. Derbyshire
29—Bournemouth, Hampshire v. Yorkshire
29—Leicester, Leicestershire v. Glamorgan
29—Lord's, Middlesex v. Lancashire
29—Nottingham, Notts v. Somerset
29—Hove, Sussex v. Surrey
29—Worcester, Worcester v. Northants

SEPTEMBER

2—**Hastings, An England XI v. Australians**
2—Bournemouth, Hampshire v. Surrey
2—Hove, Sussex v. Lancashire
2—Scarborough, Yorkshire v. M.C.C.
5—**Kingston, Combined Services v. Australians**
5—Hastings, The South v. Rest of England
5—Scarborough, Gentlemen v. Players
9—**Scarborough, T. N. Pearce's XI v. Australians**
9—Kingston, An England XI v. Commonwealth XI

CORONATION YEAR AND SPORT

THE DUKE AS CRICKETER

Praised by Don Bradman and Frank Chester

by IVAN SHARPE

IN this Coronation Year H.R.H. the Duke of Edinburgh is no mere figure-head in sport. All his life he has shown that he delights in it.

At the age of eleven, at his preparatory school at Cheam, he was in the cricket, football and Rugby teams, and won the under-12 hurdles and diving competitions.

He also got himself into all the usual schoolboy scrapes. "I had to cane him more than once," said the headmaster, the Rev. H. M. S. Taylor.

At Gordonstoun, in Scotland, where he studied under Dr. Hahn, he was captain of the school cricket and hockey teams and, later, as cadet at the Royal Naval College at Dartmouth, played in cricket matches against rival training-barracks.

Again, at the Naval Gunnery School at Whale Island, he was invited by the ship's company to appear in the Soccer eleven—a compliment few officers receive. It means that he was a footballer of more than average ability.

WHAT BRADMAN SAID

WHEN the Australian team of 1948, captained by Don Bradman, attended the Cricket Writers' Club dinner on the season's eve in London, the Duke was the guest of honour—again no figure-head compliment. The Club knew of his genuine attachment to the game and ability as a player.

Indeed, Don Bradman stated during the toast list that he had personal knowledge of the Duke's ability and offered sincere compliments on his spin bowling. "I suggest the England Test match selectors should have a look at it," he added with a smile.

FRIENDS OR MEDALS?

Inspiration for Younger End

By 1949-50, the Duke was President of the M.C.C. (of which he is now an honorary life-member) and had become an accomplished polo-player. He has also held the presidency of the British Amateur Athletics Board and the Central Council of Physical Recreation.

LOOKS THE PART AND PLAYS IT

IT is as President of the National Playing Fields Association and leader of its £500,000 drive for more grounds and pitches for the youngsters, however, that he has so plainly proved his love of sport. He is no passive leader.

He has played in various of the cricket matches for this good cause and when appeared for little Combe against Oxfordshire he said : "As a village cricketer myself, I think this is the backbone of our national game."

After playing at Taunton he declared : "There's no need to have a Rolls-Royce scheme. You want a reasonably flat piece of ground and some goal-posts. Then you're half-way home. Put on the fancy waistcoats later."

"SURPRISED ME"

AT Bournemouth in September, 1949, he captained a team of Test and County cricketers against Hampshire, scored 12 runs and took one wicket for 25 with 10,000 people there to spotlight and analyse his form . . . quite an ordeal, especially as stars like R. W. V. Robins, F. R. Brown, G. O. Allen and Leslie and Denis Compton were in his eleven.

Frank Chester, the famous umpire, was in action, too, and he said afterwards : "The Duke surprised me by his ability and keenness. With regular play he would make a good 'un."

He has been a spectator at several Tests, the New Zealand match at Manchester in 1949 among them, and after a visit to the Olympic Games at Helsinki in 1952 he uttered a reminder of current trends when he remarked :

"Perhaps I'm old-fashioned but I feel it is much more important to come away from the Games with a good reputation, and having made friends with everybody there, than to come back with a bagful of medals."

TIMELY INSPIRATION

IN the Duke of Edinburgh British sport has a firm and influential friend. Almost all branches of outdoor life appeal to him.

"I have always loved Scotland," he told a friend. "I have always loved fishing up there."

The First Gentleman of the Realm not only looks the part but, to the younger generation in British sport, is destined to be a timely inspiration.

designed for men

of good taste and discernment, Van Heusen Collar-attached Shirts also prove the most practical and economical in wear. Fine quality materials, generous cut, expert tailoring and finish—these are the qualities that have made Van Heusen so popular for so long.

Van Heusen

THE DUKE AS BOWLER

"The **DUKE OF EDINBURGH** surprised me by his ability," said Umpire Frank Chester after a match at Bournemouth

AUSTRALIA'S GREATEST ALL-ROUNDER

KEITH MILLER—fast bowler, dashing batsman and fieldsman—may be the key man of the 1953 Tests

ON THEIR TOES FOR TRUEMAN

This was Trueman's field to P. Roy (India) in the Old Trafford Test last summer. There are eight behind-the-wicket fieldsmen in the picture. A ninth is at deep third man and, apart from the bowler, only one fieldsman, at short mid-on (not on the picture) is in front of the wicket

CRICKET WITH A SMILE

LINDSAY HASSETT, genial cricketer, sound and steady batsman, succeeded Bradman as Australia's captain

CAN BE VERY AWKWARD CUSTOMER

BILL JOHNSTON, left-arm fast-medium bowler, and still one of Australia's best bets

RECORD BREAKER

With 30 wickets in a Test series, H. TAYFIELD (South Africa), achieved a new record for the Springboks against Australia in last winter's series. Batsman is COLIN McDONALD (Victoria), one of Australia's newcomers to England this summer

YOUNGEST EVER

At seventeen, and already a batsman of Test ranking, IAN CRAIG (New South Wales) is the youngest-ever player to be chosen by Australia for an English tour

HEADINGLEY HERO

NEIL HARVEY was the budding " boy " batsman of the party in 1948. Now, at 24, he's a brilliant, stable bat

AUSTRALIAN MENACE

All-out action by **RAY LINDWALL**, whose pace may again be a menace to England's batsmen in the Tests

ALL ROUNDER

GRAEME HOLE (South Australia) may make his mark with bat and ball on his first tour of England this season

STAR STUMPER

G. R. LANGLEY (South Australia) may be Australia's first choice behind the stumps in this summer's Tests

ENGLAND OPENER ?

D. S. SHEPPARD, Sussex and Cambridge, may be Len Hutton's partner at the start of England's batting this summer

AMONG ENGLAND'S HOPES

PETER MAY, brilliant England batsman, will come to full bloom, it is hoped, in 1953

STYLE & EFFECT

TOM GRAVENEY, of Gloucestershire, looks the part and often gets results as well. Another of England's hopes

HIS BIG YEAR

JOHN IKIN, of Lancashire, left-hand bat, useful change bowler, and finest close-to-the-wicket fieldsman in the country . . . Test candidate and beneficiary in 1953

HIS BENEFIT YEAR, TOO

ALEC BEDSER, twin cricketer of Surrey, and more than once named by Bradman as the best medium bowler in the world, has more help in the Tests this time

Always look for the name
MORLEY

CHIEF RECORDS . . .

First-Class Cricket

Highest Match Aggregate: 2,376, Bombay v. Maharashtra, Bombay, 1948-49.

Highest Innings Total: 1,107, Victoria v. New South Wales, Melbourne, 1926-27.

Highest Match Aggregate (England): 1,723 England v. Australia, Leeds, 1948.

Highest Innings Total (England): 903(7), England v. Australia, The Oval, 1938.

Lowest Match Aggregate: 105, M.C.C. v. Australia, Lord's, 1878.

Lowest Innings Total: 12, Northamptonshire v. Gloucestershire, Gloucester, 1907; 12, Oxford University v. M.C.C., Oxford, 1877.

Most Runs (Individual): J. B. Hobbs, 61,237 (1905-1934)

Most Runs in a Season (England): D. Compton, 3,816 (1947). **(Australia):** D. G. Bradman, 1,690 (1928-29).

1,000 Runs in a Season: 28 times, W. G. Grace and F. E. Woolley.

1,000 Runs in May: W. G. Grace and W. R. Hammond (each 22 days); C. Hallows (27 days)

Most Hundreds: J. B. Hobbs, 197; E. Hendren, 170.

Most Hundreds in a Season: 18—D. Compton, 1947

Most Hundreds in Consecutive Innings: 6—C. B. Fry and D. G. Bradman.

Most Hundreds in a Match: 9, Bombay v. Maharashtra, 1948-49.

Most Hundreds in an Inns.: 6 Holkar v. Mysore, 1945-46.

Highest Innings: 452 not out, D. G. Bradman, New South Wales v. Queensland, 1929-30.

Longest Innings: 364 in 800 minutes, L. Hutton, England v. Australia, 1938.

Most Innings Over 300: 6—D. G. Bradman.

Two Double Hundreds in a Match: 244, 202*, A. Fagg, Kent v. Essex, Colchester, 1938.

Two Hundreds in a Match: W. R. Hammond, 7 times.

Quickest Hundred: 35 minutes—P. G. H. Fender, Surrey v. Northamptonshire, Northampton, 1920.

Biggest Partnership: 577—Gul Mahomed and V. S. Hazare (4th wicket), Baroda v. Holkar, 1946-47

Most Century Stands: 74—P. Holmes and H. Sutcliffe.

... AT A GLANCE

Bowling

Most Wickets: 4,188—W. Rhodes (1898-1930).

Most Wickets in a Season: 304—A. P. Freeman (1928).

Most Wickets in a Match: 17—A. P. Freeman and W. Mead (each twice).

Most in a Day: 17—C. Blythe, T. W. Goddard, H. Verity.

Most Wickets in an Innings: 10—A. P. Freeman (3 times), V. E. Walker and H. Verity (each twice).

Most in Consecutive Balls: 4, by twenty-two bowlers.

100 Wickets in a Season: W. Rhodes (23 times).

Quickest 100 Wickets: June 12—J. T. Hearne and C. W. L. Parker.

Best Innings Analysis: 10 wickets for 10 runs—H. Verity, 1932.

Most Hat-tricks: 7—D. V. P. Wright.

All-Rounders

2,000 Runs and 200 Wkts. in a Season: G. H. Hirst, 1906.

3,000 Runs and 100 Wkts. in a Season: J. H. Parks, 1937.

2,000 Runs and 100 Wicket-keeping Dismissals: L. E. G. Ames, 1932.

Most "Doubles": W. Rhodes (16), G. H. Hirst (14), V. W. C. Jupp (10).

Most "Doubles" in Consecutive Seasons: 11—G. H. Hirst, 1903-1913.

Fielding

Most Catches: F. E. Woolley 913, W. G. Grace 871.

Most Catches in a Season: 78—W. R. Hammond, 1928.

Most Catches in a Match: 10—W. R. Hammond, 1928.

Wicket-keeping

Most Dismissals: 1,493—H. Strudwick, 1902-1927.

Most Dismissals in a Season: 127—L. E. G. Ames, 1929

Most in a Match: 12—E. Pooley and D. Tallon.

Most Dismissals in an Innings: 7—W. Farrimond, W. F. Price, R. Saggers, E. J. Smith, D. Tallon, H. Yarnold.

Most Stumpings: 413—L. E. G. Ames, 1926-1938.

Most Catches at the Wicket: 1,235—H. Strudwick.

YEAR'S BENEFITS

Test Players' Turn

IN 1953, fourteen cricketers will receive benefits or testimonials. The career-figures below are complete to October 1, 1952:

A. V. BEDSER (1939-1952), **Surrey.**

Having played only two matches against the Universities in 1939, Alec Bedser can be regarded as a post-war product. In 1946 he took 128 wickets for 20.13 runs each, made a record Test debut by taking 11 wickets in each of the first two England-India Tests, and ever since has been the mainstay of the Surrey and England bowling. In his last 4 Test series Bedser took 82 wickets (av. 17.16), and needs only 8 Australian Test wickets in 1953 to pass S. F. Barnes's record of 189. In 1952 he took his 1,000th wicket in first-class cricket, all having been taken since the war.

TEST CRICKET: Runs 640 (av. 13.06); wkts. 182 (av. 26.10).

ALL CRICKET: Runs 4,072 (av. 17.10); wkts. 1,034 (av. 21.49).

S. M. BROWN (1937-1952), **Middlesex.**

As No. 2 batsman, Brown has shared many notable first-wicket partnerships with J. D. Robertson, his highest innings being 232 not out v. Somerset at Lord's in 1951. Has scored 19 centuries. Good outfield.

Runs 12,391 (av. 30.00).

H. T. F. BUSE (1929-1952), **Somerset.**

Useful batsman who has strengthened the middle of Somerset's not too strong batting order, and a bowler who has frequently opened Somerset's bowling. Scored 1,000 runs in 5 seasons.

Runs 9,856 (av. 22.92); wkts. 608 (av. 28.63).

T. G. EVANS (1939-1952), **Kent.**

Evans has been England's No. 1 wicketkeeper since 1946, and still is one of the few Test "indispensables." In 1952 he dismissed his 100th Test batsman and, having already scored 1,000 Test runs, equalled W. A. Oldfield's "double" of 1,000 runs and 100 dismissals in Test matches.

A dashing batsman determined to play brighter cricket or get out, he scored 104 v. West Indies in 1950, and averaged 60.50 against India in 1952.

Runs 8,629 (av. 23.91); dismissals 586 (st. 151, ct. 435).

J. T. IKIN (1939-1952), **Lancashire.**

Sound left-hand batsman who opens the innings with Washbrook, and on occasion can bowl a useful leg-break. A brilliant fielder near the wicket, Ikin, with Watkins and Lock, in 1952 formed the most formidable Test leg-trap seen in England since 1946. Has scored 21 centuries.

Runs 12,818 (av. 40.30); wkts. 263 (av. 31.11).

R. O. JENKINS (1938-1952), **Worcestershire.**

Useful bat, good leg-break bowler and fine fielder at cover. Has played in 9 Tests against South Africa, West Indies and India, scoring 198 runs (av. 18.00) and taking 32 wickets. Completed "doubles" in 1949 and 1952.

Runs 7,840 (av. 24.96); wkts. 951 (av. 23.91).

W. E. JONES (1937-1952), **Glamorgan.**

Left-hand bat and bowler—one of the all-rounders who form the backbone of the Glamorgan side. In 1948 Jones scored 1,656 runs (av. 40.39), including 2 centuries over 200, and took 47 wickets (av. 25.53).

Runs 7,847 (av. 27.15); wkts. 146 (av. 28.62).

Men in the Money

Wicketkeeper's 400 Victims

E. A. MEADS (1939-1952), **Nottinghamshire.**

Wicketkeeper who got his County "cap" in his first season. Has dismissed over 400 opponents at the wicket, his best seasons being 1948 and 1952 in each of which he had 66 victims. Single-figure batsman.

Runs 1,426 (av. 9.90); dismissals 408 (st. 74, ct. 334).

F. H. VIGAR (1938-1952), **Essex.**

Useful all-rounder—sound bat, fast-medium change bowler, and good fielder. In 1947 Vigar shared a last wicket stand of 218 with P. Smith v. Derby at Chesterfield; and in 1946 took 8 Leicestershire wickets in an innings for 128 runs. Has scored 12 centuries.

Runs 7,441 (av. 27.16); wkts. 230 (av. 37.33).

A. E. WILSON (1932-1952), **Gloucestershire.**

First appeared for Middlesex, but in 1936 had qualified for Gloucestershire. A left-hand bat who has scored 5 centuries, and a sound wicket-keeper. Is now the Gloucestershire coach.

Runs 9,155 (av. 25.86); dismissals 494 (st. 156, ct. 338).

TESTIMONIALS

	Runs	100's	Aver.	Wkts.	Aver.
C. GLADWIN (1939-1952)... Derbyshire	4,246	1	19.34	901	19.01
G. LESTER (1937-1952)...... Leicestershire	7,341	5	21.52	256	31.45
†**A. NUTTER** (1935-1952)..... Lancs., Northants	4,604	1	19.67	551	25.44
†**N. OLDFIELD** (1935-1952).. Lancs., Northants.	16,296	33	37.43	—	—

† Joint testimonial

INDIA v. PAKISTAN

Test Matches of 1952

India won 2, Pakistan 1. Drawn 2.

First Test, at Delhi, October 16, 17, 18, 1952. India won by innings and 70 runs. **India** 372 (Adhikari not out 81). **Pakistan** 150 (Mankad 8-62) and 152 (Mankad 5-79).

Second Test, at Lucknow, October 23, 24, 25, 26, 1952. Pakistan won by innings and 43 runs. **India** 106 (Fazal Mahmoud 5-50) and 182 (Fazal Mahmoud 7-42). **Pakistan** 331 (Nazar Mohammed not out 124).

Third Test, at Bombay, November 13, 14, 15, 16, 1952. India won by 10 wickets. **Pakistan** 186 (Amarnath 4-40) and 242. **India** 387 for 4 dec. (Hazare not out 146, Umrigar 102 and 45 (0 wkt.).

Fourth Test, at Madras, November 28, 29, 30, December 1, 1952. Abandoned as a draw owing to rain. **Pakistan** 344. **India** 175 (6 wkts.).

Fifth Test, at Calcutta, December 12, 13, 14, 15, 1952. Match drawn. **Pakistan** 257 (Phadkar 5-72) and 236 (7 wkts. dec.). **India** 397 (Deepak Shoda 110) and 28 (0 wkt.).

Denis Compton's 100 Hundreds

DENIS COMPTON, then 18, scored his maiden hundred — 101 not out — for Middlesex v. Northants at Northampton on June 18, 1936. In 1952 at Lord's he scored his 100th century, also against Northants, and became the fourteenth batsman to complete a hundred centuries in first-class cricket. Details of this performance are given below.

TEST CRICKET (14)

IN ENGLAND (11)

5 v. South Africa, 3 v. Australia, 2 v. New Zealand, 1 v. West Indies.

ABROAD (3) : 2 v. Australia, 1 v. South Africa.

OTHER FIRST-CLASS CRICKET (86)

IN ENGLAND (65)

FOR MIDDLESEX : 6, Lancashire, Northants ; 5, Surrey, Sussex ; 4, Essex, Kent ; 3, Hampshire, Leicestershire, Somerset ; 2, Derbyshire, Gloucestershire, Warwickshire, Worcestershire ; 1, Notts, Yorkshire, Cambridge University, Oxford University, South Africans, New Zealanders.

FOR M.C.C. : 2, Surrey ; 1, Oxford University, Yorkshire, South Africans, West Indies.

Miscellaneous : 5.

ABROAD (21)

FOR M.C.C. : 4, Combined XI's ; 2, Natal, Victoria ; 1, Cape Province, Eastern Province, Griqualand West, N.E. Transvaal, Tasmania, Western Australia.

Miscellaneous (in India, 1944-45-46) : 7.

Compton's hundreds were scored on 20 English grounds and 15 overseas, four or more being made on the following : Lord's (38), Manchester (5), Nottingham (5), Oval (5), Bombay (4), Northampton (4).

In 1947 he scored 18 centuries during the season, including 4 in the Test matches against South Africa—both records for an English batsman in an English season.

Compton's 300 in 180 minutes v. N.E. Transvaal at Benoni in 1948-49 is the fastest treble hundred scored in first-class cricket.

PRINCIPAL RECORDS

To March 1, 1953.

CHIEF INDIVIDUAL SCORES

FIRST CLASS MATCHES :— [*Signifies not out.]

452*, D. G. Bradman, New South Wales v. Queensland, Sydney, 1929-30. (6hrs 55m. 49 4's)
443*, B. B. Nimbalkar, Maharashtra v. W. India States, Poona, 1948-49
437, W. H. Ponsford, Victoria v. Queensland, Melbourne, 1927-28. (10hrs 21m. 42 4's)
429, W. H. Ponsford, Victoria v. Tasmania, Melbourne, 1922-23. (7hrs 57m. 42 4's)
424, A. C. MacLaren, Lancs v. Somerset, Taunton, 1895. (7hrs 50m. A 6. 62 4's)
385, B. Sutcliffe, Otago v. Canterbury, Christchurch, 1952-53.
383, C. W. Gregory, New South Wales v. Queensland, Brisbane, 1906-07. (5¾hrs. 55 4's)
369, D. G. Bradman, South Australia v. Tasmania, Adelaide, 1935-36. (4 6's, 48 4's)
365*, C. Hill, South Australia v. New South Wales, Adelaide, 1900-01. (8hrs 35m. An 8, 35 4's)
364, Hutton (L.), England v. Australia, Oval, 1938. (13hrs 20m. 35 4's)
359*, V. M. Merchant, Bombay v. Maharashtra, Bombay, 1943-44.
357*, Abel (R.), Surrey v. Somerset, Oval, 1899. (8hrs 35m. A 6, 7 5's, 38 4's)
357, D. G. Bradman, South Australia v. Victoria, Melbourne, 1935-36. (7hrs. 40 4's)
355, B. Sutcliffe, Otago v. Auckland, Dunedin, 1949-50. (38 4's)
352, W. H. Ponsford, Victoria v. New South Wales, at Melbourne, 1926-27. (6hrs. 36 4's)
345, C. G. Macartney, Australians v. Notts, Trent Bridge, 1921. (4hrs. 4 6's, 47 4's)
344*, G. Headley, Jamaica v. Tennyson's XI, Kingston, 1931-32. (39 4's)
344, W. G. Grace, M.C.C. v. Kent, Canterbury, 1876. (6hrs 20m. 51 4's)
343*, P. A. Perrin, Essex v. Derby, Chesterfield, 1904. (5¾hrs. 68 4's)
341, Hirst (G. H.), Yorks v. Leicestershire, Leicester, 1905. (7hrs. A 6, 53 4's)
340*, D. G. Bradman, New South Wales v. Victoria, Sydney, 1928-29. (7hrs 55m. 38 4's)
338, W. W. Read, Surrey v. Oxford U., Oval, 1888. (6½hrs. A 5, 46 4's)
338*, R. C. Blunt, Otago v. Canterbury, Christchurch, N.Z., 1931-32. (5½hrs. 41 4's)
336*, Hammond (W. R.), England v. New Zealand, Auckland, N.Z., 1932-3. (5hrs 18m. 10 6's, 33 4's)
336, W. H. Ponsford, Victoria v. South Australia, at Melbourne, 1927-28.
334, D. G. Bradman, Australia v. England, Leeds, 1930. (6¼hrs. 46 4's)
333, K. S. Duleepsinhji, Sussex v. Northants, Hove, 1930. (Made in a day.) (5½hrs. A 6, 34 4's)
332, Ashdown (W. H.), Kent v. Essex, Brentwood, 1934. (6hrs 15m. A 6, 45 4's.) (Record for Kent)
331*, Robertson (J. D.), Middlesex v. Worcestershire, Worcester, 1949. (6½hrs. 2 6's, 39 4's)
325*, H .L. Hendry, Victoria v. New Zealand, Melbourne, 1925-26. (5hrs 23m. 26 4's)
325, C. L. Badcock, South Australia v. Victoria, Adelaide, 1935-36. (9hrs 45m. 34 4's)
325, Sandham (A.), England v. West Indies, Kingston (W.I.), 1929-30. (10hrs. A 7, a 5, 27 4's)
324*, J. B. Stollmeyer, Trinidad v. British Guiana, Port of Spain, 1946-47
322, Paynter (E.), Lancashire v. Sussex, Hove, 1937. (5hrs. 3 6's, 39 4's)
321, W. L. Murdoch, New South Wales v. Victoria, Sydney, 1881-82.
319, Gul Mahomed, Baroda v. Holkar, Baroda, 1946-47
318*, W. G. Grace, Gloucester v. Yorks, Cheltenham, 1876. (8hrs 5m. A 7, 2 6's, 2 5's, 28 4's)
317, Hammond (W. R.), Gloucester v. Notts, Gloucester, 1936. (6½hrs. 3 6's, 34 4's)
316*, Hobbs (J. B.), Surrey v. Middlesex, Lord's, 1926. (6hrs. 41 4's)
316, R. H. Moore, Hampshire v. Warwickshire, Bournemouth, 1937.

(Continued on next page)

HIGHEST INNINGS

(*Continued from previous page*)

316,* V. S. Hazare, Maharashtra v. Baroda, Poona, 1939-40
315*, Hayward (T.), Surrey v. Lancs., Oval, 1898. (6¾hrs. 2 5's, 37 4's)
315*, Holmes (P.), Yorks v. Middlesex, Lord's, 1925. (6¾hrs. 38 4's)
315*, A. F. Kippax, New South Wales v. Queensland, at Sydney, 1927-28. (6hrs 28m. 41 4's)
314*, C. L. Walcott, Barbados v. Trinidad, Port of Spain, 1945-46.
313, Sutcliffe (H.), Yorks v. Essex, Leyton, 1932. (7hrs 25m. A 6, 33 4's)
312*, Keeton (W. W.), Nottinghamshire v. Middlesex. Oval, 1939.
311, Brown (J. T.), Yorks v. Sussex, Sheffield, 1897. (6¼hrs. 45 4's)
310, Gimblett (H.), Somerset v. Sussex, Eastbourne, 1948. (7hrs 45m. 2 6's, 37 4's)
309, V. S. Hazare, Rest v. Hindus, Bombay, 1943-44 (out of a total of 387)
308*, F. M. Worrell, Barbados v. Trinidad, Bridgetown, 1943-44.
306*, Ducat (A.), Surrey v. Oxford U., Oval, 1919. (4hrs 40m. 3 5's, 47 4's)
306*, E. A. B. Rowan, Transvaal v. Natal, Johannesburg, 1939-40
305*, Woolley (F. E.), M.C.C. v. Tasmania, Hobart, 1911-12. (3½hrs. 2 6's, 48 4's)
305*, F. R. Foster, Warwickshire v. Worcestershire, Dudley, 1914. (4hrs 20m. A 5, 44 4's)
305*, Ashdown (W. H.) Kent v. Derbyshire, Dover, 1935. (6¾hrs. 47 4's)
304*, P. H. Tarilton, Barbados v. Trinidad, Barbados, 1919-20. (6hrs 50m.)
304*, A.D.Nourse,Natal v.Transvaal,Johannesburg,1919-20. (6hrs. 52 4's)
304*, E. Weekes, West Indies v. Cambridge University, Cambridge, 1950.
304, R. M. Poore, Hants v. Somerset, Taunton, 1899. (6hrs 50m. 45 4's)
304, D. G. Bradman, Australia v. England, Leeds, 1934. (6hrs 55m. 2 6's, 43 4's)
303*, W. W. Armstrong, Australians v. Somerset, Bath, 1905. (6¼hrs. A 6, 38 4's)
302*, Holmes (P.), Yorks v. Hants, Portsmouth, 1920. (7¼hrs. 29 4's)
302*, Hammond (W. R.), Gloucestershire v. Glamorgan, Bristol, 1934.
302, W. R. Hammond, Gloucestershire v. Glamorgan, Newport, 1939.
301*, Hendren (E.), M'sex v. Worcester, Dudley, 1933. (6hrs 50m. 29 4's)
301, W. G. Grace, Gloucester v. Sussex, Bristol, 1896. (8½hrs. 29 4's)
300*, V. T. Trumper, Australians v. Sussex, Hove, 1899. (6hrs 20m. 36 4's)
300*, Watson (F.), Lancs. v. Surrey, Manchester, 1928. (8½hrs. A 5, 37 4's)
300, Brown (J. T.), Yorks v. Derby, Chesterfield, 1898. (5hrs 5m. 48 4's)
300, Compton (D.), M.C.C. v. N.E. Transvaal, Benoni, 1948-49. (3hrs 3m. 5 6's, 42 4's)
300*, Imtiaz Ahmed, Prime Minister's Combined XI v. Commonwealth XI, Bombay, 1951.

Minor Matches

628*, A. E. Collins, Clarke's v. North Town (Junior House Match), Clifton College, 1899. (Born in 1885. 6hrs 50m. A 6, 4 5's, 31 4's)

HIGHEST TOTALS

1,107, Victoria v. New South Wales, at Melbourne, 1926-27. (10hrs 33m.)
1,059, Victoria v. Tasmania, Melbourne, 1922-23. (10hrs 41m.)
918, New South Wales v. South Australia, Sydney, 1900-01. (9hrs 20m.)
912 (8) dec., Holkar v. Mysore, at Indore, 1945-46.
903 (7) dec., England v. Australia, Oval, 1938. (15hrs 45m.)
887, Yorkshire v. Warwickshire, Edgbaston, 1896. (10hrs 50m.)
849, England v. West Indies, Kingston, W.I., 1929-30
843, Australians v. Ox. and Camb. U., Past and Present, Portsm'th, 1893
839, New South Wales v. Tasmania, Sydney, 1898-99
826 (4 wkts), Maharashtra v. Western India States, Poona, 1948-49
815, New South Wales v. Victoria, Sydney, 1908-09
811, Surrey v. Somerset, Oval, 1899
807, New South Wales v. South Australia, Adelaide, 1899-1900
805, New South Wales v. Victoria, Melbourne, 1905-06
803 (9 wkts), Non-Smokers v. Smokers, East Melbourne, 1886-87
803 (4 wkts), Kent v. Essex, Brentwood, 1934
802, New South Wales v. South Australia, Sydney, 1920-21
801, Lancashire v. Somerset, Taunton, 1895

Minor Matches

1,094, Melbourne Univ. v. Essendon, Melbourne, 1897-98

LOWEST TOTALS (Under 20)

12—Oxford University v. M.C.C., Oxford, 1877. (1 man absent)
12—Northants v. Gloucestershire, Gloucester, 1907
13—Auckland v. Canterbury, Auckland, N.Z., 1877-8
13—Notts v. Yorkshire, Trent Bridge, 1901
15—M.C.C. v. Surrey, Lord's, 1839
15—Victoria v. England, Melbourne, 1903-4. (1 man absent)
15—Northants v. Yorkshire, Northampton, 1908. (Totals 27 and 15; 1 man absent each innings)
15—Hants v. Warwickshire, Edgbaston, 1922. (Hants put home side in, scored 15 and 521, and won by 155 after following-on)
16—M.C.C. v. Surrey, Lord's, 1872
16—Derbyshire v. Notts, Trent Bridge, 1879
16—Surrey v. Notts, Oval, 1880
16—Warwickshire v. Kent, Tonbridge, 1913
16—Barbados v. Trinidad, Bridgetown, 1942
17—Derbyshire v. Lancashire, Manchester, 1888
17—Gloucestershire v. Australians, Cheltenham, 1896
18—The B's v. England, Lord's, 1831
18—Kent v. Sussex, Gravesend, 1867. (1 man absent)
18—Tasmania v. Victoria, Melbourne, 1868-9
18—Australians v. M.C.C., Lord's, 1896. (1 man absent)
19—Sussex v. Surrey, Godalming, 1830
19—Sussex v. Notts, Hove, 1873. (1 man absent)
19—M.C.C. v. Australians, Lord's, 1878

HIGHEST MATCH AGGREGATES

FIRST CLASS MATCHES :—
2,376 for 38 wkts, Bombay (651, 714 for 8 wkts dec) v. Maharashtra (407, 604) at Poona, 1948-49. Semi-final of the Ranji Trophy
2,078 for 40 wkts, Bombay (462, 764) v. Holkar (360, 492) at Bombay, 1944-45
1,981 for 35 wkts, England v. South Africa, Durban, 1938-39
1,929 for 39 wkts, New South Wales v. South Australia, Sydney, 1925-26
1,911 for 34 wkts, New South Wales v. Victoria, Sydney, 1908-09
1,905 for 40 wkts, Otago v. Wellington, Dunedin, 1923-24
1,815 for 34 wkts, England v. West Indies, Kingston (W.I.), 1929-30
1,753 for 40 wkts, England v. Australia, Adelaide, 1920-21
1,752 for 34 wkts, New South Wales v. Queensland, Sydney, 1926-27
1,744 for 40 wkts, New South Wales v. South Africa, Sydney, 1910-11

RECORDS IN ENGLAND :—
1,601 for 29 wkts, England v. Australia, Lord's, 1930
1,502 for 28 wkts, M.C.C. v. New Zealand, Lord's, 1927
1,496 for 24 wkts, England v. Australia, Nottingham, 1938
1,492 for 33 wkts, Worcestershire v. Oxford University, Worcester, 1904
1,477 for 32 wkts, Hants v. Oxford University, Southampton, 1913
1,477 for 33 wkts, England v. South Africa, The Oval, 1947

LOWEST MATCH AGGREGATES

105 for 31 wkts, M.C.C. v. Australians, Lord's, 1878
153 for 31 wkts, Otago v. Canterbury, Dunedin, 1896-97
165 for 30 wkts, Middlesex v. Somerset, Lord's, 1899
165 for 30 wkts, Yorkshire v. Notts, Sheffield, 1888

LONGEST MATCH

In 1938-39 the fifth Test match between South Africa and England at Durban was abandoned as a draw at tea-time on the tenth day of the match

FOURTH INNINGS TOTALS IN FIRST-CLASS CRICKET

654 (5 wkts), England v. South Africa, Durban, 1938-39
604, Maharashtra v. Bombay, Poona, 1948-49
576 (8 wkts), Trinidad v. Barbados, Port of Spain, 1945-46
572, New South Wales v. South Australia, Sydney, 1907-8
518, Victoria v. Queensland, at Brisbane, 1926-7
507 (7 wkts), Cambridge University v. M.C.C., Lord's, 1896
502 (6 wkts), Middlesex v. Notts, Trent Bridge, 1925
502 (8 wkts), Players v. Gentlemen, Lord's, 1900

COMPLETED IN A DAY

LIST FOR LAST 60 YEARS

The following are the most important instances since 1890 of matches completed in one day:

1891 M.C.C. v. Notts, Lord's
1892 Lancs. v. Somerset, M'chester
1894 M.C.C. v. Sussex, Lord's
1894 Lancs. v. Somerset, M'chester
1894 Yorks. v. Somerset, Hud'field
1897 Leicester v. Surrey, Leicester
1898 Hants v. Yorks, Southampton
1899 Middlesex v. Somerset, Lord's
1900 Yorks v. Worcester, Bradford
1903 M.C.C. v. London Co., Lord's
1908 Middx v. Philadelphians, Lord's
1909 Gloucester v. Midd'x, Bristol
1912-13 Eastern Province v. Orange Free State, Pt Elizabeth
1919 Kent v. Sussex, Tonbridge
1925 Lancs v. Somerset, M'chester
1937 Ireland v. New Zealanders, Dublin
1947 Derbyshire v. Somerset, Chesterfield
1950 Lancs v. Sussex, Manchester

Somerset lost two matches in two days in 1894.

TEST RECORD

At Leeds in 1952 A. Bedser and F. Trueman took the first 4 wickets in India's second innings before a run or extra had been scored.

TIE-MATCHES (Since 1890)

1890—Somerset v. Middlesex, Taunton. (Former side not then first-class)
1894—Surrey v. Lancashire, Oval
1901—Worcestershire v. South Africans, Worcester
1904—Middlesex v. South Africans, Lord's
1905—Surrey v. Kent, Oval
1905—Lancashire v. An England XI, Blackpool. (Lancashire had 3 wickets in hand)
1907—M.C.C. v. Leicestershire, Lord's
1910-11—Jamaica v. M.C.C., Kingston
1919—Somerset v. Sussex, Taunton. (The last Sussex batsman, H. J. Heygate, forfeited his innings under Law 45)
1925-6—Orange Free State v. Eastern Province, at Bloemfontein. (Eastern Province had two wickets to fall)
1926—Essex v. Somerset, Chelmsford. (Essex had one wicket to fall. The 9th man was out ½-minute before time. M.C.C. ruled game was a tie)
1930—Gloucestershire v. Australians, Bristol
1932-3—Victoria v. M.C.C. Team, Melbourne. (Victoria had seven wickets to fall when time expired)
1939—Worcestershire v. Somerset, Kidderminster
1945-6—Southern Punjab v. Baroda, Patiala
1947—Essex v. Northamptonshire, Ilford
1947—Hampshire v. Lancashire, Bournemouth
1948-9—D. G. Bradman's XI v. A. L. Hassett's XI, Melbourne (Bradman's XI had one wicket to fall)
1950—Hampshire v. Kent, Southampton
1952—Warwickshire v. Sussex, Hove
1952—Lancashire v. Essex, Brentwood

In the match Totteridge v. Fortress Club, in 1929, each of the four innings amounted to 94.

Lieberman & Gortz

Famous 20 x 40 (Diam. OG. Lens)
PRISMATIC BINOCULARS

Sent for **39/6**

Cash Price £19·19·0

Normal size and weight 7¼ x 5¾, 21 ozs. The most powerful Continental glasses made. Unrepeatable. Amazing clarity in definition. Centre focus and separate eye adjustment. A comfortable power to use. Day and night lenses. Worth double the price. Sent for 39/6 deposit and 39/6 monthly. Complete with case and slings.

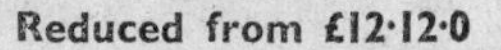

to **£4·9·6**

BRAND NEW

Yes, a third of the price of any comfortable dress suit to advertise our bumper catalogue. Excellent quality woollen mixture with dress faced lapels and braided side to trousers. Real tailored garments, smart and distinguished. Why hire or use a lounge suit ? Match a cocktail or evening gown whenever the occasion arises. Give chest, waist and inside leg. 42 to 50, 20/- extra. Post, 1/9. Money back guarantee.

Extends approx 10 ft. x 6 ft. x 6ft. Walls 3 ft. Finest value. Real waterproof canvas. Portable but very stout cloth. Complete, including valise, 22/6 Deposit, 25/- monthly. Carr. 5/-. Cash price, £9 12s. 6d. Also brand new RIDGE TENT sent for 6/- or cash price £2 15s. or with FLYSHEET sent for 15/- or cash price £4 2s. 6d. both carriage 1/-. Send for free illustrated list of 200 different Tents or inspect largest selection of Tents and Camping Equipment in England. 1,000 Binocular Bargains. Kapok filled sleeping bags, marquees, flysheets, etc. TERMS. State LISTS required.

HEADQUARTER & GENERAL SUPPLIES, LTD.

(Dept. SCCA), 196-200, Coldharbour Lane, Loughborough Junction, London, S.E.5. 1 p.m. WEDNESDAY. OPEN ALL SATURDAY.

100 OR MORE HUNDREDS

RECORDS OF LEADING PLAYERS

Player	No. of 100's	Where Scored Eng.	Where Scored Abr'd	First 100	100th 100	Last 100
J. B. Hobbs (1905-1934)	197	175	22	1905	1923	1934
E. Hendren (1907-1938)	170	151	19	1911	1928	1937
W. R. Hammond (1920-1947)	167	134	33	1923	1935	1947
C. P. Mead (1905-1936)	153	145	8	1906	1927	1936
H. Sutcliffe (1919-1945)	149	135	14	1919	1932	1939
F. E. Woolley (1906-1938)	145	135	10	1906	1929	1938
W. G. Grace (1865-1908)	126	125	1	1866	1895	1904
L. Hutton (1934-)	114	94	20	1934	1951	1952
A. Sandham (1911-1937)	107	87	20	1913	1935	1937
T. Hayward (1893-1914)	104	100	4	1893	1913	1914
E. Tyldesley (1909-1936)	102	94	8	1912	1935	1935
L. E. G. Ames (1926-)	102	89	13	1927	1950	1951
D. S. C. Compton (1936-)	101	77	24	1936	1952	1952

Hearne (J. W.) 96, C. B. Fry 94, Tyldesley (J. T.) 86, R. E. S. Wyatt 84, Hardstaff, jun. (J.) 80, Leyland (M.) 80, Hardinge (H. W. T.) 75, Abel (R.) 74, Langridge (John) 72, Quaife (W. G.) 72, K. S. Ranjitsinhji 72, O'Connor (J.) 71, Russell (A. C.) 71, W. J. Edrich 70, Denton (D.) 69, Holmes (P.) 67, Washbrook (C.) 66, P. A. Perrin 65, Gunn (G.) 62, Hirst (G. H.) 60, Sir P. F. Warner 60, Shrewsbury (A.) 59, Rhodes (W.) 58, Fishlock (L. B.) 56, Fagg (A.) 55, Hallows (C.), Keeton (W. W.) 54, W. Bardsley 53, Dipper (A. E.) 53, A. L. Hassett 53, G. L. Jessop 53, Seymour (Jas.) 53, Bowley (E.H.) 52, Ducat (A.) 52, Robertson (J. D.) 52, Whysall (W. W.) 51, Watson (F.) 51.

ONLY OVERSEAS PLAYER

Player	No. of 100's	Where Scored Eng.	Where Scored Aust.	First 100	100th 100	Last 100
D. G. Bradman (1927-1949)	117	41	76	1927	1947	1948

AGGREGATES OF 50,000 RUNS

Player * Not Out	Inns.	Not out	Runs	Highest inns.	Aver.
J. B. Hobbs (1905-1934)	1,315	106	61,221	316*	50.63
F. E. Woolley (1906-1938)	1,532	85	58,969	305*	40.75
E. Hendren (1907-1938)	1,300	166	57,610	301*	50.81
C. P. Mead (1905-1936)	1,335	185	55,060	280*	47.67
W. G. Grace (1865-1908)	1,493	105	54,896	344	39.55
W. R. Hammond (1920-1951)	1,002	104	50,415	336*	56.14
H. Sutcliffe (1919-1945)	1,087	123	50,135	313	52.00

CENTURIES IN ONE SEASON

18—By Compton (D.) in 1947.

16—By Hobbs (aged 42) in 1925.

15—By W. R. Hammond in 1938.

14—By Sutcliffe in 1932.

13—By C. B. Fry in 1901, Hayward in 1906, Hendren in 1923, 1927 and 1928, Mead in 1928, Sutcliffe in 1928 and 1931, and Hammond in 1933 and 1937, and D. G. Bradman in 1938.

12—By Abel (R.) in 1900, Hammond in 1927, Hobbs and Woolley (F. E.) in 1928, and K. S. Duleepsinhji in 1931, Hutton (L.) in 1939 and 1949, W. J. Edrich and Robertson (J. D.) in 1947, Langridge (John) in 1949.

11—By K. S. Ranjitsinhji in 1900, V. T. Trumper in 1902, Hayward in 1904, Hobbs in 1914 and 1920, Hallows (C.) in 1928, Woolley (F. E.) in 1929, Hendren in 1933, Parks (J. H.) in 1937, Hutton (L.) in 1947 and 1952, Washbrook (C.) in 1947, D. G. Bradman in 1948.

10—By W. G. Grace (1871), K. S. Ranjitsinhji (1896), C. B. Fry (1900, 1904, 1905), Hayward (1900), Mead (1921, 1926), Hobbs (1922, 1926, 1929 and 1931), Tyldesley (E.) (1926 and 1928), Hammond (1929), R. E. S. Wyatt (1929), D. G. Bradman (1930), Mead (1933), Woolley (F. E.) (1934), and Langridge (John) (1937), Compton (D.) (1946), Place (W.) (1947), Hutton (L.) (1948), P. B. H. May (1952), D. Sheppard (1952).

In 1928 as many as 139 men reached three figures, making 414 hundreds altogether—both records.

200 IN EACH INNINGS

Fagg (A.)—244 and 202*, Kent v. Essex, Colchester, 1938

200 AND 100 IN SAME MATCH

Innings	Player	For	Against	Ground	Season
125, 229	C. B. Fry	Sussex	Surrey	Bright'n	1900
157, 245	W. W. Armstrong	Victoria	S. Australia	Melb'rne	1920-21
207, 102	Hardinge (H. T. W.)	Kent	Surrey	B'heath	1921
113, 224	Mead (C. P.)	Hampshire	Sussex	Horsh'm	1921
115, 246	K. S. Duleepsinhji	Sussex	Kent	Hastings	1929
124, 225	D. G. Bradman	Woodfull's XI	Ryder's XI	Sydney	1929-30
243, 100*	B. Sutcliffe	N. Zealanders	Essex	Southend	1949

TWO 100's IN TEST

Innings	Player	For	Against	Ground	Season
136, 130	W. Bardsley	Australia	England	Oval	1909
140, 111	Russell (A. C.)	England	S. Africa	Durban	1922-23
176, 127*	Sutcliffe (H.)	England	Australia	Melb'rne	1924-25
119, 177	Hammond (W. R.)	England	Australia	Adelaide	1928-29
104, 109*	Sutcliffe (H.)	England	S. Africa	Oval	1929
114, 112	G. Headley	West Indies	England	Georget'n	1929-30
117, 100	Paynter (E.)	England	S. Africa	Jo'burg	1938-39
106, 107	G. Headley	West Indies	England	Lord's	1939
†147, 103*	Compton (D.)	England	Australia	Adelaide	1946-47
†122, 124*	A. Morris	Australia	England	Adelaide	1946-47
189, 104*	A. Melville	S. Africa	England	Nottingm	1947
120, 189*	B. Mitchell	S. Africa	England	Oval	1947
132, 127*	D. G. Bradman	Australia	India	Melb'rne	1947-48
116, 145	V. S. Hazare	India	Australia	Adelaide	1947-48
162, 101	E. Weekes	West Indies	India	Calcutta	1948-49
118, 101*	J. R. Moroney	Australia	S. Africa	Jo'burg	1949-50

* Not out † Same match

TWO 100's IN A MATCH

SEVEN TIMES.—W. R. Hammond. SIX TIMES.—Hobbs (J. B.). FIVE TIMES.—C. B. Fry. FOUR TIMES.—D. G. Bradman, Fishlock (L. B.), Hardinge (H. T. W.), Hendren (E.), G. L. Jessop, P. A. Perrin, B. Sutcliffe, Sutcliffe (H.).

R. E. Foster—102* and 136, Lord's, 1900—and King (J. H.)—104 and 109* on the same ground, 1904—made two separate hundreds on their first appearance in a Gentlemen v. Players match.

On November 1, 1952, two separate 100's in a match had been scored by 171 batsmen on 257 occasions.

TWO 100's NOT OUT IN A MATCH

When C. J. B. Wood made 107* and 117* for Leicester v. Yorks., Bradford, 1911, he carried his bat through both completed innings. Seven batsmen have scored not out hundreds in each innings of a match.—D. R. A. Gehrs at Fremantle, 1905-6; C. C. Dacre at Auckland, 1924; Hallows (C.) at Ashby, 1924; Parks (H.) at Leyton, 1933; Mitchell (A.) at Scarborough, 1933; Fishlock (L. B.) at The Oval, 1936; Gibbons (H. H.) at Worcester, 1939.

TWO 100's EACH FOR SAME SIDE

W. L. Foster, 140 and 172*, and R. E. Foster, 134 and 101*, for Worcestershire v. Hants, Worcester, 1899, Dacre (C. C.) 119 and 125, and Hammond (W. R.) 122 and 111*, for Gloucestershire v. Worcestershire, Worcester, 1933, C. L. Badcock, 120 and 102, and R. A. Hamence 130 and 103*, for South Australia v. Victoria, Melbourne, 1940-41, U. M. Merchant, 143 and 156, and D. G. Phadkar 131 and 160, for Bombay v. Maharashtra, at Poona, 1948-49, are the only instances of the same batsmen each scoring two separate hundreds in a first-class match for the same side.

CENTURY ON DEBUT

TWO SEPARATE HUNDREDS

148 and 111, A. Morris, N.S.W. v. Queensland, at Sydney, 1940-41

CHIEF INSTANCES IN BIG GAMES

IN FIRST TEST.—The following scored centuries in first Test innings:

C. Bannerman (A.), 165 v. England, Melbourne, 1877
R. E. Foster (E.), 287 v. Australia, Sydney, 1903
W. G. Grace (E.), 152 v. Australia, Oval, 1880
H. Graham (A.), 107 v. England, Lord's, 1893
G. Gunn (E.), 119 v. Australia, Sydney, 1907
A. Jackson (A.), 164 v. England, Adelaide, 1929
Nawab of Pataudi (E.), 102 v. Australia, Sydney, 1932
W. H. Ponsford (A.), 110 v. England, Sydney, 1924
S. C. Griffith (E.), 140 v. West Indies, Port of Spain, 1947-48
P. B. H. May (E.), 138 v. South Africa, Leeds, 1951
Deepak Shodan (Ind.), 110 v. Pakistan, Calcutta, 1952-53
B. Pairaudeau (W.I.), 115 v. India, Port of Spain, 1952-53

L. Amarnath (India); R. A. Duff, H. L. Collins and R. J. Hartigan (A.); P. A. Gibb, K. S. Ranjitsinhji, P. F. Warner, B. H. Valentine (E.); G. Headley (W.I.); J. W. E. Mills (N.Z.) scored centuries in their first Test matches.

FOR ENGLISH TEAMS IN AUSTRALIA :—

228, A. C. MacLaren, v. Victoria, Melbourne, 1894-95
115, Brown (J. T.), v. South Australia, Adelaide, 1894-95
189, K. S. Ranjitsinhji, v. South Australia, Adelaide, 1897-98
158, F. R. Foster, v. South Australia, Adelaide, 1911-12
117, Makepeace (H.), v. West Australia, Perth, 1920-21
103, Kilner (R.), v. West Australia, Perth, 1924-25
166, Nawab of Pataudi, v. West Australia, Perth, 1932-33

D. R. Jardine, in his first three innings, in 1928-9, made 109 v. West Australia, 104 v. Victoria, and 140 v. New South Wales.

IN FIRST MATCH FOR AUSTRALIANS IN ENGLAND :—

206, H. H. Massie, v. Oxford University, Oxford, 1882
175, A. G. Chipperfield v. Essex, Chelmsford, 1934
116*, M. A. Noble, v. London County, Crystal Palace, 1899

In his two first innings in first-class cricket in England—in 1926—W. M. Woodfull made 201 and 118; D. G. Bradman in his first two innings in England—in 1930—scored 236 and 185*

FOR IMPORTANT COUNTY :—

108, A. C. MacLaren, Lancashire v. Sussex, Hove, 1890
144, Marlow, Sussex v. M.C.C., Lord's, 1891
114, Bacon (F. H.), Hants v. Warwickshire, Edgbaston, 1894
150, K. S. Ranjitsinhji, Sussex v. M.C.C., Lord's, 1895
101*, S. H. Day, Kent v. Gloucestershire, Cheltenham, 1897
124, N. Miller, Surrey v. Sussex, Hove, 1899
124, H. C. Pretty, Surrey v. Notts, Oval, 1899
116,* B. L. Bisgood, Somerset v. Worcestershire, Worcester, 1907
137, J. G. C. Scott, Sussex v. Oxford University, Eastbourne, 1907
131*, Whitehead (R.), Lancashire v. Notts, Manchester, 1908
126, Lt. C. H. Abercrombie, Hants v. Oxford Univ., Southampton, 1913
103, W. G. M. Sarel, Sussex v. Oxford University, Hove, 1919
101, K. A. Higgs, Sussex v. Worcester, Hove, 1920
124, G. J. Bryan, Kent v. Notts, Trent Bridge, 1920
100*, Tyson (C.), Yorkshire v. Hampshire, Southampton, 1921
102, A. J. Evans, Kent v. Northants, Northampton, 1921
107*, H. O. Bloomfield, Surrey v. Northants, Northampton, 1921
103*, A. L. Hilder, Kent v. Essex, Gravesend, 1924
104, Nicol (M.), Worcestershire v. West Indies, Worcester, 1928
206, D. N. Moore, Gloucestershire v. Oxford Univ., Oxford, 1930
108, C. A. Fiddian-Green, Worcestershire v. Essex, Worcester, 1931
123, Gimblett (H.), Somerset v. Essex, Frome, 1935
157*, P. A. Gibb, Yorks. v. Notts, Sheffield, 1935
122, H. T. Bartlett, Sussex v. Oxford University, Worthing, 1937
11[illegible], Stocks (F. W.), Notts v. Kent, Nottingham, 1946
10[illegible], A. Fairbairn, Middlesex v. Somerset, Taunton, 1947

In his first innings in first-class cricket, G. H. G. Doggart (Camb. U.) scored 215* v. Lancashire, 1948.

FIRST WICKET RECORDS

FAMOUS OPENING PARTNERSHIPS

555, Sutcliffe (313) and Holmes (P.) (224*), Yorks v. Essex, Leyton, 1932. (7hrs. 25m.) *(See Best for Each Wicket records page 64).*
554, Brown (300) and Tunnicliffe (243), Yorks v. Derbyshire, Chesterfield, 1898. (5hrs. 5m.)
490, Bowley (E. H.) (283), and Langridge (John) (195), Sussex v. Middlesex, Hove, 1933.
456, W. H. Ponsford (248) and E. R. Mayne (209), Victoria v. Queensland, Melbourne, 1923-24.
428, Hobbs (261) and Sandham (183), Surrey v. Oxford Univ., Oval, 1926.
424, J. F. Nicolson (252*) and I. J. Siedle (174) Natal v. Orange Free State, at Bloemfontein, 1926-27.
391, A. O. Jones (250) and Shrewsbury (146), Notts v. Gloucs., Bristol, 1899
390, G. Gibbs and L. Wight, British Guiana v. Barbados, Bourda, 1951.
380, C. J. B. Wood (225) and Whitehead (174), Leics v. Worcs. W'rc'ter, 1906
379, Brockwell (225) and Abel (R.) (173), Surrey v. Hants, Oval, 1897.
378, Brown (311) and Tunnicliffe (147), Yorks v. Sussex, Sheffield, 1897.
375, W. H. Ponsford (352) and W. M. Woodfull (133), Victoria v. New South Wales, at Melbourne, 1926-27.
373, B. Sutcliffe (275) and L. A. Watt (96), Otago v. Auckland, Auckland, 1950-51.
368, A. C. MacLaren (204) and R. H. Spooner (168), Lancs v. Gloucester, Liverpool, 1903.
368, Bowley (E. H.) (280*) and Parks (J. H.) (110), Sussex v. Gloucester, Hove, 1929.
364, D. L. A. Jephson (213) and Abel (R.) (193), Surrey v. Derby, Oval, 1900
355, A. F. Rae (179) and J. B. Stollmeyer (198), W. Indies v. Sussex, Hove, 1950.
352, Hayward (204*) and Hobbs (159), Surrey v. Warwick, Oval, 1909.
350 *(unfinished)*, Washbrook (C.) (204*) and Place (W.) (134*), Lancashire v. Sussex, Manchester, 1947.
349, J. G. Dewes (212) and D. S. Sheppard (158), Cambridge University v. Sussex, Hove, 1950.
347, Holmes (302*) and Sutcliffe (131), Yorks v. Hants, Portsmouth, 1920.
346, H. T. Hewett (201) and L. C. H. Palairet (146), Somerset v. Yorks, Taunton, 1892.
343, J. G. Dewes (183) and D. S. Sheppard (227), Cambridge University v. West Indies, Cambridge, 1950.
340, J. H. Fingleton and W. A. Brown, N.S.W. v. Victoria, Sydney, 1933-34
338, T. Bowring (228) and H. Teesdale (108), Oxford University v. Gents. of England, Oxford, 1908.
337, C. McDonald (166) and A. Meuleman (150), Victoria v. South Australia, Adelaide, 1949-50.
333, J. F. Byrne (222) and Kinneir (158), Warwick v. Lancs, Edgbaston, 1905.
330, B. Mitchell (195) and E. Rowan (171), S. Africa v. Surrey, Oval, 1935.

RECORDS IN TESTS

359, Hutton (158) and Washbrook (195), England v. South Africa, Johannesburg, 1948-49.
323, Rhodes (179) and Hobbs (178), England v. Australia, Melb'rne, 1911-12.
283, Sutcliffe (176) and Hobbs (154), England v. Australia, Melbourne, 1924-25. (Batted the whole day when facing total of 600).
276, C. S. Dempster (136) and J. E. Mills (117), New Zealand v. England, Wellington, 1929-30.
268, Hobbs (211) and Sutcliffe (122), England v. S. Africa, Lord's, 1924.
260, B. Mitchell (123) and I. J. Siedle (141), South Africa v. England, Capetown, 1930-31.
221, Hobbs (187) and Rhodes (77), England v. S. Africa, Capetown, 1909-10.
203, V. M. Merchant (114) and Mushtaq Ali (112), India v. England, Manchester, 1936.

In three consecutive innings against Australia in 1924-5 Sutcliffe and Hobbs obtained 157 and 110 together at Sydney and 283 at Melbourne.

MINOR CRICKET

472, P. Coles (247*) and S. Colman (209), Devonshire Park v. G. W. Morrison's XI, Eastbourne, 1892.

BEST FOR EACH WICKET
IN ALL FIRST-CLASS CRICKET

1st—555, *See* earlier table (page 63).
2nd—455, B. B. Nimbalkar and K. V. Bhandarkar, Maharashtra v. Western India States, Poona, 1948-49.
3rd—445, W. N. Carson (290) and P. E. Whitelaw (195), Auckland v. Otago, Dunedin, 1936-37.
4th—†577, Gul Mahomed (319) and V. S. Hazare (254*), Baroda v. Holkar, 1946-47.
5th—405, D. G. Bradman and S. G. Barnes, Australia v. England, at Sydney, 1946-47.
6th—487, G. Headley (344*) and C. Passailigue (261*), All Jamaica v. Lord Tennyson's Team, Kingston (W.I.), 1931-32 (unfinished).
7th—344, K. S. Ranjitsinhji (230) and W. Newham (153), Sussex v. Essex, Leyton, 1902.
8th—433, V. T. Trumper (293) and A. Sims (184), an Australian XI v. Canterbury, Christchurch, 1913-14.
9th—283, J. Chapman (165) and Warren (A.) (123), Derbyshire v. Warwickshire, Blackwell, 1910.
10th—307, A. F. Kippax (260*) and H. Hooker (62), New South Wales v. Victoria, Melbourne, 1928-29.
† Highest partnership for any wicket in first-class cricket.

MINOR MATCHES :—

1st—472, *See* earlier table (page 63).
2nd—623* Capt. W. C. Oates (313*) and Pte. F. Fitzgerald (287*), 1st Royal Munster Fusiliers v. A.S.C., at the Curragh, 1895.
3rd—641, T. Patton (408) and N. Rippon (321), Buffalo v. Whorouly, Gapsted (Victoria), 1913-14.
4th—464, Lt. H. N. Dumbleton (325) and Capt. C. L. Young (204), Royal Engineers v. Royal Marines, Portsmouth, 1884.
5th—533, W. W. Armstrong (438) and E. Monfries (123), Melbourne v. University, Melbourne, 1901-02.
6th—370, G. H. Gatehouse (247) and O. Douglas (200*), Wellington v. Derwent, Hobart, 1900-01.
7th—429, C. J. Ealy (566) and W. Abbott (143), Break-o'-Day v. Wellington, Hobart, 1901-02.
8th—442, S. E. Gregory (235) and E. G. Noble (227), Sydney v. Warwick, Sydney, 1890-91.
9th—293, E. A. C. Druce (201*) and V. P. Johnstone (120), Trinity Wanderers v. Eastbourne, Eastbourne, 1900.
10th—289*, E. H. Kekewick (227*) and J. Matthews (141*), North Adelaide v. Sturt, Adelaide, 1901-02.

HUNDRED FOR FIRST WICKET

TIMES
69, Holmes and Sutcliffe for Yorks
66, Hobbs and Sandham for Surrey
46, Keeton and Harris for Notts

TIMES
40, Hayward and Hobbs for Surrey
40, Gunn (G.) & Whysall for Notts

Figures of other famous partnerships are :

33, C. B. Fry and Vine for Sussex
24, Iremonger and A. O. Jones, Notts
23, Hallows (C.) & Watson for Lancs
19, Brown and Tunnicliffe for Yorks

MOST IN CAREER—	Career		Stands
Hobbs	1905–1934	..	166
Sutcliffe	1919–1939	..	145
MOST IN SEASON—	**Stands**		**Season**
Ashdown-Hardinge	12	..	1928
Hallows-Watson	12	..	1928

For Notts v. Northants, at Northampton in 1950, Keeton and Harris shared a century partnership for the first wicket in each innings—122 and 151 unfinished—each batsman scoring 139 runs (Keeton 59, 80*; Harris 81, 58*).

CLUB SECRETARIES !

Have you received a copy of our booklet "YOUR TICKET TO PROSPERITY"?

Outlining The Popular Fund Raising Schemes For Clubs, Societies & Organisations, Etc.

This booklet is a **must** for secretaries of clubs who intend to augment club funds by the above methods, and is POST FREE on REQUEST from :—

G. F. HITCHEN (Successors) LTD.

PRINTERS

BACUP · LANCS.

BATSMEN'S BEST YEARS

HIGHEST TOTALS IN A SEASON

Year		Inns.	Not out	Most in inns.	Runs	Avge.
1947	Compton (D.)	50	8	246	3816	90.85
1947	W. J. Edrich	52	8	267*	3539	80.43
1906	Hayward (T.)	61	8	219	3518	66.37
1949	Hutton (L.)	56	6	269*	3429	68.58
1928	Woolley (F. E.)	59	4	198	3352	61.03
1932	Sutcliffe (H.)	52	7	313	3336	74.13
1933	Hammond (W. R.)	54	5	264	3323	67.81
1928	Hendren (E.)	54	7	209*	3311	70.44
1901	Abel (R.)	68	8	247	3309	55.15
1937	Hammond (W. R.)	55	5	217	3252	65.04
1933	Hendren (E.)	65	9	301*	3186	56.89
1921	Mead (C. P.)	52	6	280*	3179	69.10
1904	Hayward (T.)	63	5	205	3170	54.65
1899	K. S. Ranjitsinhji	58	8	197	3159	63.18
1901	C. B. Fry	43	3	244	3147	78.67
1900	K. S. Ranjitsinhji	40	5	275	3065	87.57
1933	Ames (L. E. G.)	57	5	295	3058	58.80
1901	Tyldesley (J. T.)	60	5	221	3041	55.29
1928	Mead (C. P.)	50	10	180	3027	75.67
1925	Hobbs (J. B.)	48	5	266*	3024	70.32
1928	Tyldesley (E.)	48	10	242	3024	79.57
1938	W. R. Hammond	42	2	271	3011	75.27
1923	Hendren (E.)	51	12	200*	3010	77.17
1931	Sutcliffe (H.)	42	11	230	3006	96.96
1937	Parks (J. H.)	63	4	168	3003	50.89
1928	Sutcliffe (H.)	44	5	228	3002	76.97

W. G. Grace's highest aggregate was 2,739 (average 78.25) in 1871.

FOR ENGLISH CRICKETERS (FIRST-CLASS MATCHES) ABROAD :—

Year		Inns.	Not out	Most in inns.	Runs	Avge.
1948-49	(S.A.) Compton (D.)	26	5	300	1781	84.80
1929-30	(W.I.) Hendren (E.)	18	5	254	1765	135.76
1928-29	(A.) Hammond (W. R.)	18	1	251	1553	91.35
1913-14	(S.A.) Hobbs (J. B.)	22	2	170	1489	67.68
1948-49	(S.A.) Hutton (L.)	21	1	174	1477	73.85

† FOR AUSTRALIANS IN ENGLAND :—

Year		Inns.	Not out	Most in inns.	Runs	Avge.
1930	D. G. Bradman	36	6	334	2960	98.66
1902	V. T. Trumper	53	0	128	2570	48.49
1938	D. G. Bradman	26	5	278	2429	115.66
1948	D. G. Bradman	31	4	187	2428	89.92
1921	C. G. Macartney	39	1	345	2305	60.65
1912	W. Bardsley	50	5	184	2291	50.91

† FOR SOUTH AFRICANS IN ENGLAND :—

Year		Inns.	Not out	Most in inns.	Runs	Avge.
1947	B. Mitchell	37	4	189*	2014	61.03

† FOR WEST INDIES IN ENGLAND :—

Year		Inns.	Not out	Most in inns.	Runs	Avge.
1950	E. Weekes	33	4	304*	2310	79.65

† FOR NEW ZEALANDERS IN ENGLAND :—

Year		Inns.	Not out	Most in inns.	Runs	Avge.
1949	B. Sutcliffe	49	5	243	2627	59.70
1949	M. P. Donnelly	45	8	206	2287	61.81

† FOR COMMONWEALTH TEAMS IN INDIA :—

Year		Inns.	Not out	Most in inns.	Runs	Avge.
1949-50	F. M. Worrell	26	4	223*	1640	74.54
1950-51	F. M. Worrell	33	3	285	1900	63.33

† First-class matches only

CONSECUTIVE HUNDREDS

SIX—

C. B. Fry, 1901.
D. G. Bradman, 1938-39

FOUR—

D. G. Bradman, 1931-32, 1948-49.
Compton (D.), 1946-47.
K. S. Duleepsinhji, 1931.
C. B. Fry, 1911.
W. R. Hammond, 1936-37, 1945-46.
Hardinge (H. T. W.), 1913.
Hayward (T.), 1906.
Hobbs (J. B.), 1920, 1925.
Langridge (John), 1949.
C. G. Macartney, 1921.
V. M. Merchant, 1941-42.
Mitchell (A.), 1933.
Nawab of Pataudi, 1931.
Sutcliffe (H.), 1931, 1939.
Tyldesley (E.), 1926.
Whysall (W. W.), 1930.
Woolley (F. E.), 1929.

THREE—

D. G. Bradman, 1929-30, 1934, 1935-36, 1937-38, 1946-47, 1947-48, 1943
W. G. Grace, 1871, 1872, 1873, 1874, 1876.
W. H. Ponsford, 1921-2-3, 1923-24, 1926-27, 1927-28, 1930-31.
W. R. Hammond, 1927, 1928-29, 1937, 1938.
Hobbs (J. B.), 1914, 1926, 1932, 1933.
Mead (C. P.), 1921, 1922, 1923, 1933.
A. L. Hassett, 1938, 1939-40, 1948.
Hendren (E.), 1929-30, 1931, 1933
Hutton (L.), 1937, 1947, 1952
C. G. Macartney, 1910-11, 1912, 1923-24.
K. S. Ranjitsinhji, 1896, 1900 (twice).
H. Sutcliffe, 1924-25, 1928, 1931.

In 1926 Tyldesley (E.) scored six hundreds in seven innings, seven in nine, and eight in twelve.

IN TEST CRICKET

5—E. WEEKES: 141 (Kingston) versus England in 1947-48; and 128 (New Delhi), 194 (Bombay), 162 and 101 (Calcutta) *versus* India in 1948-49.

4—J. H. FINGLETON: 112 (Capetown), 108 (Johannesburg), 118 (Durban) all *versus* South Africa in 1935-36, and 100 (Brisbane) *versus* England in 1936-37.

A. MELVILLE: 103 (Durban) in 1938-39, and 189 and 104* (Nottingham), 117 (Lord's) in 1947, all *versus* England.

OTHER RECORDS

DEBUT AT 14

C. C. Dacre (N.Z. and Glos.) made his debut in first-class cricket when he was 14½—for Auckland v. Wellington, at Auckland in 1914-15.

SHARED TWO 500 STANDS

F. M. Worrell (W.I.) is the only cricketer who has shared two partnerships of 500 runs—502 (with J. D. Goddard) at Bridgetown in 1943-44, and 574 (with C. L. Walcott) at Port of Spain in 1945-46. Both were for Barbados v. Trinidad.

THE OTHER SUTCLIFFE

In each of his first four seasons of first-class cricket, B. Sutcliffe scored two separate hundreds in a match.

791 RUNS BUT—

At one period of the match between Barbados and Trinidad, at Port of Spain in 1945-46, 791 consecutive runs were scored without the bowlers taking a wicket. The only two batsmen dismissed were run out.

FOURTH INNINGS FEAT

In the fourth innings of the match between Hindus and Rest at Bombay in 1943-44, V. S. Hazare (Rest) scored 309 of 368 runs scored from the bat. With his brother, V.J., he added 300 in 280 minutes for the fifth wicket, V. J. Hazare scoring 20.

1,000 RUNS IN MAY

	No. of inns.	Not out	Runs	Highest score	Avge.
1895 W. G. Grace	10	1	1,016	288	112.88
1927 Hammond (W. R.)	13	0	1,028	192	79.07
1928 Hallows (C.)	11	3	1,000	232	125.00
Commencing in April, the following scored 1,000 runs by the end of May:					
1900 Hayward, T.	13	2	1,074	193	97.63
1930 D. G. Bradman	11	4	1,001	252*	143.00
1938 D. G. Bradman	9	2	1,056	278	150.85
1938 Edrich (W. J.)	15	3	1,010	245	84.61

MOST RUNS IN A MONTH

	Runs	Month	Year
L. Hutton	1,294	June	1949
W. R. Hammond	1,281	August	1936
W. G. Grace	1,278	August	1876

(Hutton also scored 1,050 runs in August, 1949)

MOST RUNS IN A DAY

721 (10wkts), Australians (721) v. Essex, Southend, 1948.
666 (6wkts), Surrey (607 for 4) v. Northants (59 for 2), North'pt'n, 1920.
665 (20wkts), Rest of South Africa (339 for 10) v. Transvaal (326 for 10), Johannesburg, 1911-12.
651 (2wkts), West Indies v. Leicestershire, Leicester, 1950.

RAPID SCORING

Season	Player	Match	Inns.	Hits 6's	Hits 4's	Time (min)
1948-49	Compton (D.)	M.C.C. v. N.E. Trans.	300	5	42	183
1907	G. L. Jessop	Gents of S v. Players of S.	191	5	30	90
1911	†Alletson (E.)	Notts v. Sussex	189	8	23	90
1920	‡P. G. H. Fender	Surrey v. Northants	113	5	16	42
1897	G. L. Jessop	Glos v. Yorks	101	..	..	40

† Last 89 in 15 min. ‡ 100 in 35 min.

In 1949, for Notts v. Leicestershire, R. T. Simpson and Poole scored 251 in 97 minutes.

OTHER RECORDS

FATHER AND SON

For Notts v. Warwickshire, at Birmingham in 1931, G. Gunn scored 183 and G. V. Gunn 100 not out in the same innings. This is the only instance of a father and son scoring hundreds in the same innings in a first-class match.

709 NOT OUT

In 1947-48, K. C. Ibrahim (Bombay) scored 709 runs in first-class matches before he was dismissed—218, 36, 234, 77 (all not out) and 144.

HURRICANE HAMMOND

W. R. Hammond's first five innings in Test matches at Sydney were: 251, 112, 101, 75 not out, 231 not out--770 runs (average 256.66).

MAIDEN HUNDRED

S. C. Griffith scored his maiden hundred (140) in his first Test innings—for England v. West Indies, at Port of Spain in 1947-48.

When 17½ years of age, Haneef Mohammed scored 121 and 109 not out for Pakistan v. India at Amritsar (1952-53).

For the first time in Test cricket three bowlers in the same side had taken 100 Test wickets—R. Lindwall, K. Miller and W. Johnston at Melbourne in 1952.

ALL-ROUND ABILITY

THE CRICKETER'S "DOUBLE"

2,000 Runs and 200 Wickets in Season :—

1906, Hirst—2,385 runs (average 45.86) and 208 wickets (average 16.50).

3,000 Runs and 100 Wickets in Season :—

1937, Parks (J. H.)—3,003 runs (av. 50.89) and 101 wickets (av. 25.83)

2,000 Runs and 100 Wickets in Season :—

		Runs	Average.	Wickets.	Average
1873	W. G. Grace	2,139	71	106	12
1876	W. G. Grace	2,622	62	129	24
1899	C. L. Townsend	2,440	51	101	29
1900	G. L. Jessop	2,210	40	104	21
1904	Hirst	2,501	54	132	21
1905	Hirst	2,266	53	110	19
1909	Rhodes	2,094	40	141	15
1911	Rhodes	2,261	38	117	24
1911	Tarrant	2,030	46	111	19
1913	Hearne (J. W.)	2,036	44	124	22
1914	Hearne (J. W.)	2,116	60	123	22
1914	Woolley (F. E.)	2,272	45	125	19
1920	Hearne (J. W.)	2,148	55	142	17
1921	V. W. C. Jupp	2,169	38	121	22
1921	Woolley (F. E.)	2,101	42	167	16
1922	Woolley (F. E.)	2,022	45	163	18
1923	Woolley (F. E.)	2,091	41	101	19
1933	Townsend (L.)	2,268	44	100	18
1937	Davies (E.)	2,012	40	103	23
1937	Langridge (Jas.)	2,082	40	101	22

1,000 Runs and 200 Wickets in Season :—

		Runs	Average	Wickets	Average
1899	Trott (A. E.)	1,175	23	239	17
1900	Trott (A. E.)	1,337	23	211	23
1922	Kennedy	1,129	22	205	16
1923	Tate (M. W.)	1,168	22	219	13
1924	Tate (M. W.)	1,419	29	205	13
1925	Tate (M. W.)	1,290	23	228	14

ALL-ROUND RECORDS in TEST CRICKET

1.—G. Giffen (A.) v. England in 1894-95—475 runs (average 52.88) and 34 wickets (average 24.11).

2.—G. A. Faulkner (S.A.) v. England in 1909-10—545 runs (average 60.55) and 29 wickets (average 21.89).

FOUR TEST WICKETS IN OVER

In the second innings of South Africa, at Leeds in 1947, K. Cranston took the last four wickets in one over for no runs, and without doing the hat-trick.

BOWLED 552 BALLS IN A TEST INNINGS

A. L. Valentine (W.I.) set up a new bowling record in England's second innings at Nottingham in 1950: he bowled 92 overs (552 balls) in the innings.

In 1951-52 at Melbourne, Valentine took his 50th Test wicket in his 8th Test match.

V. Mankad (India) completed the quickest Test "double" at Bombay v. Pakistan in 1952. It was his 23rd Test match.

1,000 RUNS AND 100 WICKETS

16 Times—Rhodes 1903 to 1909, 1911, 1914, 1919 to 1924, 1926
14 „ —Hirst 1896, 1897, 1901, 1903 to 1913
10 „ —V. W. C. Jupp 1920, 1921, 1925, 1926, 1927, 1928, 1930, 1931, [1932, 1933
9 „ —Astill
8 „ —W. G. Grace, Nichols, Relf (A. E.), Tate, Tarrant and Woolley (F. E.)
6 „ —P. G. H. Fender and Langridge (Jas.)
5 „ —J. W. H. T. Douglas, Hearne (J. W.), Kennedy and Newman
4 „ —Arnold, Gunn (J.) and Kilner (R.)
3 „ —Braund, N. E. Haig, Howorth (R.), Townsend (L.), Llewellyn, Smith (R.), S. G. Smith and Wellard.

Twice—Andrews, T. E. Bailey, E. R. Brown, Close (D. B.), J. N. Crawford, Davies (E.), F. R. Foster, Hopwood, Jenkins (R.), G. L. Jessop, Lockwood, Martin (S. H.), Parks (J. H.), Pope (G. H.), Sinfield, C. T. Studd, Thompson, C. L. Townsend, Trott (A. E.) and J. C. White.

Once—Bailey (J.), Barratt, Booth, B. J. T. Bosanquet, Brockwell, Broderick (V.), F. S. G. Calthorpe, Cuffe, Cuttell, Davidson, Drake, Flowers, A. E. R. Gilligan, Haigh, Hallows (J.), Hayward, F. S. Jackson, Killick (E. H.), King (J. H.), J. R. Mason, Muncer (L.), Pearson, Peel, R. W. V. Robins, Root, H. L. Simms, Smailes, Smith (P.), Todd, Tribe (G.), Vine, Wainwright, Walsh (J.), Wensley.

In addition to the above the feat has been performed thirteen times during tours in England: By W. W. Armstrong (3 times); G. Giffen (3 times); H. L. Collins, J. M. Gregory, G. E. Palmer and H. Trumble (Australia); G. A. Faulkner (South Africa); V. Mankad (India); and L. N. Constantine (West Indies).

DEBUTANT'S DOUBLE AT 18

D. B. Close, in 1949, became the only cricketer to complete a "double" in his first season, and the youngest player (18) to do so. He also completed a "double" in his second full season (1952).

ODD EVENTS

BOWLING

When Cambridge University played Yorkshire at Cambridge in 1949, each of the four opening bowlers was making his first appearance in first-class cricket—J. J. Warr and O. J. Wait (Cambridge), Close and Trueman (Yorkshire).

In 1871, twenty-three bowlers took 343 wickets for M.C.C. in 20 first-class matches—and bowled only *one* no-ball.

ALL-ROUNDERS

For South Australia v. Victoria, in 1891-92, G. Giffen scored 271 in the South Australian innings (562), and took 16 wickets for 166 runs—9 for 96 and 7 for 70.

100 AND HAT-TRICK

Three Yorkshiremen completed "doubles" in 1904—Hirst, Rhodes and Haigh.

J. Briggs is the only cricketer who has scored a hundred and done the hat-trick in Test cricket.

Put it to
THE TEST!

Get the

IT SCORES
EVERY TIME

BOWLING RECORDS

MOST WICKETS

	Wickets		Runs		Avge.
Rhodes (W.)	4,188	..	69,986	..	16.71
Freeman (A. P.)	3,775	..	69,579	..	18.43
Parker (C. W. L.)	3,274	..	63,805	..	19.48
Hearne (J. T.)	3,055	..	54,278	..	17.76
Goddard (T. W.)	2,979	..	59,116	..	19.84
Kennedy (A. S.)	2,877	..	59,044	..	20.52
W. G. Grace	2,876	..	51,545	..	17.92
Tate (M. W.)	2,784	..	50,567	..	18.12

MOST WICKETS IN A SEASON

304, Freeman (A. P.) in 1928. Average 18.05
298, Freeman (A. P.) in 1933. Average 15.26
290, Richardson (T.) in 1895. Average 14.37
276, Freeman (A. P.) in 1931. Average 15.60
275, Freeman (A. P.) in 1930. Average 16.84
273, Richardson (T.) in 1897. Average 14.45
267, Freeman (A. P.) in 1929. Average 18.27
261 Rhodes (W.) in 1900. Average 13.81
257, Hearne (J. T.) in 1896. Average 14.28
253, Freeman (A. P.) in 1932. Average 16.39
251 Rhodes (W.) in 1901. Average 15.12

In his first full season R. Appleyard took 200 wickets (aver. 14.14), all for Yorkshire.

MOST WICKETS IN CONSECUTIVE SEASONS

8 Seasons—2,090, A. P. Freeman (1928-35).
4 Seasons—1,122, A. P. Freeman (1928-31).
1,027, A. P. Freeman (1927-30).
1,005, T. Richardson (1894-97).
3 Seasons— 846, A. P. Freeman (1928-30).
809, T. Richardson (1895-97).
725, W. Rhodes (1900-02).

Highest Career Average: 206 wickets per year, H. Verity (1930-1939).

In all matches F. R. Spofforth took 352 (1878), 391 (1880), and C. T. B. Turner 314 (1888) during English tours.

Only C. T. B. Turner has taken 100 wickets in an Australian season—106 (aver. 13.50) in 1887-88.

4 WICKETS IN 4 BALLS (Since 1890)

1890, Hide (J. B.), Sussex v. M.C.C., Lord's
1893, Shacklock, Notts v. Somerset, Trent Bridge
1893-4, A. Downes, Otago v. Auckland, Dunedin
1895, Martin, M.C.C. v. Derbyshire, Lord's
1895, Mold, Lancashire v. Notts, Trent Bridge
1905, W. Brearley, Lancashire v. Somerset, Manchester
1905-6, Haigh, England v. Army XI, Pretoria
1907 Trott, Middlesex v. Somerset, Lord's. (His benefit. He did hat-trick in same innings.)
1907, Tarrant, Middlesex v. Gloucestershire, Bristol
1914, Drake, Yorkshire v. Derbyshire, Chesterfield
1914, S. G. Smith, Northants v. Warwickshire, Edgbaston
1924, Peach, Surrey v. Sussex, Oval
1926-27, A. F. Borland, Natal v. Griqualand West, at Kimberley
1928-29, H. Hooker, New South Wales v. Victoria, Sydney
1929, Tyldesley (R.), Lancashire v. Derbyshire, at Derby
1931-32, R. J. Crisp, Western Province v. Griqualand West, Johannesburg
1933-34, R. J. Crisp, Western Province v. Natal, Durban
1935, Gover (A. R.), Surrey v. Worcestershire, Worcester
1937, Copson, Derbyshire v. Warwickshire, Derby
1937-38, W. A. Henderson, North-Eastern Transvaal v. Orange Free State, Bloemfontein
1951, Ridgway (F.), Kent v. Derbyshire, Folkestone

BEST BOWLING FIGURES

IN TEST AND COUNTY CRICKET (Since 1890)

10 for 10, Verity (H.), Yorkshire v. Notts, Leeds, 1932
9 ,, 11, Freeman (A. P.), Kent v. Sussex, Brighton, 1922
8 ,, 2, Laker (J. C.), England v. Rest, Bradford, 1950
8 ,, 7, Lohmann, England v. South Africa, Port Elizabeth, 1895-6
8 ,, 8, J. E. D. Sealey, Barbados v. Trinidad, 1942
8 ,, 8. M. Melle, Transvaal v. Griqualand West, 1950
*8 ,, 9, Dennett in first innings for Gloucestershire v. Northants, Gloucester, 1907
†7 ,, 12, Dennett, in second innings, above match
7 ,, 4, W. A. Henderson, N.E. Transvaal v. O.F.S. Bloemfontein, 1937-8
6 ,, 1, V. I. Smith, South Africans v. Derbyshire, Derby, 1947
6 ,, 2, Field, Warwickshire v. Worcestershire, Dudley, 1914
5 ,, 0, Pougher, M.C.C. v. Australians, Lord's, 1896
5 ,, 0, Cox (G. R.), Sussex v. Somerset, Weston-super-Mare, 1921
5 ,, 0, Tyldesley (R.), Lancashire v. Leicestershire, Manchester, 1924
5 ,, 0, Mills (P. T.), Gloucestershire v. Somerset, Bristol, 1928

In Test cricket, H. Ironmonger, Australia v. South Africa, Melbourne, 1931-2, took 5 wickets for 6 runs—in the match 11 for 24.

7 WICKETS AT ONE PERIOD OF AN INNINGS FOR NO RUNS :—

In 20 balls, Mold, Lancashire v. Somerset, Manchester, 1894
In 20 balls, King, Leicestershire v. Yorkshire, Leicester, 1911
In 25 balls, Hearne (J. W.), Middlesex v. Essex, Lord's, 1910

* Including the hat-trick. † All seven wickets that fell in second innings. Dennett took these 15 wickets in one day.

MOST WICKETS IN A DAY

17 for 48 runs, Blythe, Kent v. Northants, Northampton, 1907
17 for 91, Verity (H.), Yorkshire v. Essex, Leyton, 1933
17 for 106, Goddard, Gloucestershire v. Kent, Bristol, 1939

SEVENTEEN WICKETS IN A MATCH (Since 1890)

1893, Mead (W.), Essex v. Australians, Leyton. (205 runs) (Essex not then first-class)
1895, Mead (W.), Essex v. Hants, Southampton. (119 runs)
1902-03, W.P.Howell, Australians v. Western Province, Capetown. (54 runs)
1905, W. Brearley, Lancashire v. Somerset, Manchester, 1905. (137 runs)
1907, Blythe, Kent v. Northants, Northampton. (48 runs)
1913, Dean, Lancashire v. Yorkshire, Liverpool. (91 runs)
1913-14, Barnes (S. F.), England v. S. Africa, Johannesburg. (159 runs)
1922, Freeman (A. P.), Kent v. Sussex, Hove. (67 runs)
1923, Matthews (F. C. L.), Notts v. Northants, Trent Bridge. (89 runs)
1925, Parker, Gloucestershire v. Essex, Gloucester. (56 runs)
1926, Cox (G. R.), Sussex v. Warwickshire, Horsham. (106 runs)
1932, Freeman (A. P.), Kent v. Warwickshire, Folkestone. (92 runs)
1933, Verity (H.), Yorkshire v. Essex, Leyton. (91 runs)
1937, J. C. Clay, Glamorgan v. Worcestershire, Swansea. (212 runs)
1939, Goddard, Gloucestershire v. Kent, Bristol. (106 runs)

In 1911 Barnes (S. F.) took 17 Durham wickets for 83 runs at South Shields and scored an innings of 136 in the same match.

In 1937 Harding (N. W.) took 18 wickets for 100 runs for Kent 2nd XI v. Wiltshire at Swindon—nine for 39 and nine for 61.

ALL TEN WICKETS

MEMORABLE DEBUT AT OVAL

The most notable instances in important cricket of all ten wickets being taken by one bowler since 1890 :

S. M. J. Woods, Camb. Univ. v. C. I. Thornton's XI, Cambridge, 1890
Richardson, Surrey v. Essex, Oval, 1894
Pickett, Essex v. Leicestershire, Leyton, 1895
Tyler, Somerset v. Surrey, Taunton, 1895
W. P. Howell, Australians v. Surrey, Oval, 1899. (His first match in England)
Bland, Sussex v. Kent, Tonbridge, 1899
Briggs, Lancashire v. Worcestershire, Manchester, 1900
Trott, Middlesex v. Somerset, Taunton, 1900
Fielder, Players v. Gentlemen, Lord's, 1906
Dennett, Gloucestershire v. Essex, Bristol, 1906
A. E. E. Vogler, Eastern Province v. Griqualand West, Joh'sburg, 1906-7
Blythe, Kent v. Northants, Northampton 1907
Drake, Yorkshire v. Somerset, Weston-super-Mare, 1914
Bestwick, Derbyshire v. Glamorgan, Cardiff, 1921
A. A. Mailey, Australians v. Gloucestershire, Cheltenham, 1921
J. C. White, Somerset v. Worcestershire, Worcester, 1921
Rushby, Surrey v. Somerset, Taunton, 1921
Parker, Gloucestershire v. Somerset, Bristol, 1921
Collins, Kent v. Notts, Dover, 1922
Howell, Warwickshire v. Yorkshire, Edgbaston, 1923
Kennedy, Players v. Gentlemen, Oval, 1927
G. O. Allen, Middlesex v. Lancashire, Lord's, 1929
Freeman (A. P.), Kent v. Lancashire, Maidstone, 1929
Geary, Leicestershire v. Glamorgan, Pontypridd, 1929
C. V. Grimmett, Australians v. Yorkshire, Sheffield, 1930
Freeman (A. P.), Kent v. Essex, Southend-on-Sea, 1930
Verity, Yorkshire v. Warwickshire, Leeds, 1931
Freeman (A. P.), Kent v. Lancashire, Manchester, 1931
V. W. C. Jupp, Northants v. Kent, Tunbridge Wells, 1932
Verity, Yorks v. Notts, Leeds, 1932 (for 10 runs only)
T. W. Wall, South Australia v. New South Wales, Sydney, 1933
Mitchell (T. B.), Derbyshire v. Leicestershire, Leicester, 1935
Mercer, Glamorgan v. Worcestershire, Worcester, 1936
Goddard, Gloucestershire v. Worcestershire, Cheltenham, 1937
Smailes, Yorkshire v. Derbyshire, Sheffield, 1939
Watts, Surrey v. Warwickshire, Birmingham, 1939
Hollies (E.), (7 bowled, 3 l.b.w.) Warwickshire v. Notts, Birmingham, 1946
Sims (J.), East v. West, Kingston-on-Thames, 1948
T. E. Bailey, Essex v. Lancashire, Clacton, 1949
†Graveney (J. K.), Gloucestershire v. Derbyshire, Chesterfield, 1949
J. H. Cameron, of Taunton School, for The Rest v. Lord's Schools in 1932—the only success in a schools' match at Lord's
A. G. Eldridge *bowled down* all ten wickets in an innings for Wiltshire v. Monmouth, at Usk, in 1896

† In first season

FAMOUS HAT-TRICKS

WICKET HIT FIVE TIMES.—In his benefit match v. Yorkshire at Bristol, 1922, C. W. L. Parker (Gloucester) hit the wicket 5 times in 5 consecutive balls, the second being a no-ball.

TWO HAT-TRICKS IN A MATCH.—(1) At Manchester in 1912 T. J. Matthews (A.) did the hat-trick in each innings of South Africa.

(2) For Notts v. Gloucestershire in 1884 A. Shaw did the hat-trick in each innings, and also took 3 wickets in 4 balls.

(3) C. W. L. Parker did the hat-trick in each innings of Middlesex at Bristol in 1924.

(4) At Worcester in 1949 R. Jenkins did the hat-trick in each Surrey innings.

At Port Elizabeth in 1895-96 G. A. Lohmann did the first hat-trick in Tests between England and South Africa.

HAT-TRICK SEVEN TIMES.—Against Hampshire at Canterbury in 1949 D. V. P. Wright (Kent) did his 7th hat-trick (record).

R. Lindwall (Australia) took England's last 3 wickets in 4 balls in the first innings at Adelaide in 1946-47.

ALL THREE L.B.W.—When H. Fisher did the hat-trick for Yorks. v. Somerset at Sheffield in 1932 all three batsmen were l.b.w.

ALL THREE STUMPED.—In 1893 W. H. Brain (Gloucestershire) stumped three Somerset batsmen off successive balls from C. L. Townsend, who was 17 and still at school.

FIELDING

MOST CATCHES

	Career	Most in Season	Total
Woolley (F. E.)	1906–1938	45	913
W. G. Grace	1865–1908	60	871
W. R. Hammond	1920–1947	78	785
Hendren (E.)	1907–1938	42	722
Rhodes (W.)	1898–1930	43	708
Tunnicliffe (J.)	1891–1907	69	691

MOST CATCHES IN A SEASON: W. R. Hammond, 78 (1928)

MOST CATCHES IN A MATCH: 10 W. R. Hammond, Gloucestershire v. Surrey, Cheltenham, 1928

In his first full season, J. T. Ikin made 52 catches. K. Grieves (Lancashire) made 61 catches in 1950.

For Players v. Gentlemen at Lord's in 1952, L. Hutton made 5 catches in the Gentlemen's second innings. Players won by 2 runs.

DAVID SHEPPARD'S LAST YEAR IN TEST CRICKET

David Sheppard, England, Sussex and Cambridge University cricketer who is to enter the Church, says: "I shall play cricket whenever I can, but it is obvious that Test cricket is over for me after this year.

"I am to captain Sussex this summer, and shall play the whole season and be available for the Tests if required.

"I shall be at Ridley Hall for two years: after that I cannot say how much time I shall have for cricket."

Wicket-keeping Records

12 wickets (c 8, st 4) in match—Pooley, Surrey v. Sussex, Oval, 1868
12 wickets (c 9, st 3) in match—D. Tallon, Queensland v. New South Wales, Sydney, 1938-39
10 wickets (c 5, st 5) in match—Phillips, Sussex v. Surrey, Oval, 1872
10 wickets (c 2, st 8) in match—Pooley, Surrey v. Kent, Oval, 1878
10 wickets (c 9, st 1) in match—Oates, Notts v. Middx., Trent Bridge, 1906
10 wickets (c 1, st 9) in match—Huish, Kent v. Surrey, Oval, 1911
10 wickets (c 9, st 1) in match—Hubble, Kent v. Glouces, Cheltenh'm, 1923
10 wickets (c 8, st 2) in match—Elliott, Derbyshire v. Lancashire, Manchester, 1935
10 wickets (c 7, st 3) in match—Corrall, Leicestershire v. Sussex, Hove, 1936
10 wickets (c 9, st 1) in match—R. Saggers, New South Wales v. Victoria—Queensland, Brisbane, 1940-41
7 wickets (c 4, st 3) in innings—Smith (E. J.), Warwickshire v. Derby, Edgbaston, 1926
7 wickets (c 6, st 1) in innings—Farrimond, Lancashire v. Kent, Manchester, 1930
7 wickets (c 7) in innings—Price, Middlesex v. Yorkshire, Lord's, 1937
7 wickets (c 7) in innings—R. Saggers, New South Wales v. Victoria and Queensland, Brisbane, 1940-41
7 wickets (c 3, st 4) in innings—D. Tallon, Queensland v. Victoria, Brisbane, 1938-39
7 wickets (c 1, st 6) in innings—Yarnold, Worcestershire v. Scotland, Broughty Ferry, 1951
(Yarnold is the only wicketkeeper who has stumped 6 batsmen in an innings)
E. B. Lewis (Warwickshire) stumped one and caught 8 Oxford University batsmen in his debut match in 1949.
In 1952 four Yorkshire cricketers kept wicket regularly—Brennan (Yorks), Gibb (Essex), Fiddling (Northants), Firth (Leicester).

FAMOUS WICKET-KEEPERS' TOTALS

In 1st-class cricket Strudwick caught 1,235 and stumped 258—total 1,493
For Yorkshire, Hunter (D.) caught 920 and stumped 352—total 1,272
For Kent, Huish caught 906 and stumped 356—total 1,262
For Sussex, Butt caught 927 and stumped 274—total 1,201
For Notts, Oates caught 756 and stumped 233—total 988

MOST DISMISSALS IN A SEASON

Season	Player	Dismissals St.	Ct.	T.
1929	Ames	48	79	127
1928	Ames	52	69	121
1949	Yarnold	47	63	110
1928	Duckworth	30	77	107
1913	Huish	32	70	102
1932	Ames	64	36	100
1911	Huish	38	62	100
1930	Ames	48	49	97
1937	Price	29	68	97
1923	Street	26	71	97
1951	Yarnold	37	60	97
1929	Duckworth	37	58	95
1947	Evans	24	69	93
1934	Wood (A.)	17	76	93
1950	Yarnold	31	62	93
1903	Strudwick	20	71	91
1935	Elliott (H.)	21	69	90

WICKET-KEEPERS' HAULS

	Career	St.	Ct.	Total	Average per Year
Ames (L. E. G.)	1927–1939	413	550	963	80.25
Strudwick (H.)	1902–1927	258	1235	1493	67.86
Huish (F. H.)	1895–1914	376	952	1328	69.89
Hunter (D.)	1889–1909	372	955	1327	63.19
Butt (H.)	1890–1912	291	971	1262	54.86
Elliott (H.)	1920–1939	298	895	1193	59.70
Board (J. H.)	1891–1914	335	797	1132	47.14
Duckworth (G.)	1923–1938	328	720	1048	65.50
Oates (T.)	1897–1925	239	766	1005	43.69

Don't be stumped!

The test of a hand-made cigarette is that it's longer lasting, smoother and more satisfying. See your tobacconist today and ask for the

CHIEF RECORDS ...

This table covers ONLY PERFORMANCES
Tests and other representative

	Highest Total	Lowest Total	Highest Innings	Most 100's
Derbyshire...	645	16	274 G. Davidson	32 D. M. Smith
Essex.........	692	30	343* P. A. Perrin	70 J. O'Connor
Glamorgan...	587(8)	22	287* E. Davies	30 E. Davies
Gloucester....	653(6)	22	318* W. G. Grace	106 W. R. Hammond
Hampshire.....	672(7)	15	316 R. H. Moore	140 C. P. Mead
Kent..........	803(4)	18	332 W. H. Ashdown	122 F. E. Woolley
Lancashire....	801	25	424 A. C. MacLaren	90 E. Tyldesley
Leicestershire	701(4)	25	252* S. Coe	45 L. G. Berry
Middlesex....	642(3)	25	331* J. D. Robertson	123 E. Hendren
Northants.....	557(6)	12	258* F. Jakeman	47 D. Brookes
Notts.........	739(7)	13	312* W. W. Keeton	55 G. Gunn
Somerset.....	675	25	310 H. Gimblett	45 H. Gimblett
Surrey........	811	16	357 R. Abel	144 J. B. Hobbs
Sussex.......	705	19	333 K. S. Duleepsinhji	68 C. B. Fry
Warwickshire	657(6)	16	305* F. R. Foster	71 W. G. Quaife
Worcester.....	633	24	276 F. L. Bowley	44 H. H. Gibbons
Yorkshire.....	887	26	341 G. H. Hirst	112 H. Sutcliffe

* Not out

. . . of the COUNTIES

FOR COUNTY TEAMS in first-class games. matches are excluded.

‡ Most "Doubles" in a season	County Title Wins	Test Players	Test Players' Appearances	
2: L. F. Townsend, G. H. Pope	2	13	48 T. S. Worthington (9)	Derbyshire
14 M. S. Nichols (7)	—	14	108 J. W. H. T. Douglas (23)	Essex
3 E. Davies (2)	1	5	26 W. G. A. Parkhouse (5)	Glamorgan
3 R. A. Sinfield (2)	3†	19	186 W. R. Hammond (85)	Gloucester
9 J. Newman (5)	—	10	50 C. P. Mead (17)	Hampshire
7 F. E. Woolley (6)	4	32	315 F. E. Woolley (64)	Kent
2 J. L. Hopwood (2)	12†	41	383 A. C. MacLaren (35)	Lancashire
6 W. E. Astill (5)	—	6	33 G. Geary (14)	Leicestershire
12 F. A. Tarrant (6)	6†	40	376 E. Hendren (51)	Middlesex
7 V. W. C. Jupp (5)	—	6	41 F. R. Brown (14)	Northants
3 J. Gunn (2)	12†	25	261 W. Voce (27)	Notts
6: J. C. White (2), A. Wellard (2), W. Andrews (2)	—	12	57 L. C. Braund (23)	Somerset
7: W. Lockwood (2), J. Crawford (2), P. Fender (2)	12†	40	435 J. B. Hobbs (61)	Surrey
19: A. E. Relf (6), M. W. Tate (6)	—	27	177 C. B. Fry (26)	Sussex
2 F. R. Foster (2)	2	11	135 R. E. S. Wyatt (40)	Warwickshire
9 R. Howorth (3)	—	10	58 C. F. Walters (11)	Worcester
31 W. Rhodes (12)	23†	47	543 L. Hutton (60)	Yorkshire

† Includes joint Championships ‡ 1,000 runs and 100 wickets

AUSTRALIA v. SOUTH AFRICA

Tests, 1952-53

Played 5. Australia won 2, South Africa won 2, drawn 1

FIRST TEST (at Brisbane).—December 5, 6, 8, 9, 10, 1952.
Australia won by 96 runs.

1st inn.	AUSTRALIA		2nd inn.
A. R. Morris lbw b Watkins	29	c Melle b Tayfield	58
C. McDonald c and b Watkins	27	st Waite b Tayfield	17
R. N. Harvey c sub (Innes) b Melle	109	run out	52
A. L. Hassett c Waite b Watkins	55	c McGlew b Melle	17
K. Miller b Watkins	3	lbw b Tayfield	3
G. Hole c Tayfield b Melle	8	lbw b Melle	42
R. Lindwall lbw b Melle	5	not out	38
G. Langley c Tayfield b Melle	17	b Watkins	27
D. Ring c Mansell b Melle	13	b Melle	4
I. Johnson lbw b Melle	7	b Watkins	13
W. Johnston not out	1	c McGlew b Tayfield	0
Extras	6	Extras	6
Total	280	Total	277

1st inn.	SOUTH AFRICA		2nd inn.
D. J. McGlew c Ian Johnson b Miller	9	lbw b Lindwall	69
J. H. Waite lbw b Ring	39	st Langley b Ian Johnson	14
W. R. Endean c Langley b Ring	14	lbw b Lindwall	12
K. J. Funston b Ring	33	c Langley b W. Johnston	65
R. A. McLean c Miller b Ian Johnson	13	b Lindwall	38
J. E. Cheetham c Langley b Lindwall	26	b W. Johnston	18
J. C. Watkins c Miller b Ring	25	hit wkt b Ian Johnson	1
P. N. F. Mansell c Lindwall b Ring	31	b Lindwall	4
A. G. A. Murray lbw b W. Johnston	18	not out	11
H. A. Tayfield lbw b Ring	3	c Langley b Ian Johnson	1
M. G. Melle not out	7	b Lindwall	4
Extras	3	Extras	3
Total	221	Total	240

BOWLING ANALYSIS

AUSTRALIA	1st inn. O.	M.	R.	W.	2nd inn. O.	M.	R.	W.
Melle	20.5	0	71	6	26	2	95	3
Watkins	24	8	41	4	26	13	47	2
Murray	14	1	63	0	13	7	13	0
Tayfield	15	3	59	0	33.3	5	116	4
Mansell	8	0	40	0	...			

SOUTH AFRICA	O.	M.	R.	W.	O.	M.	R.	W.
Lindwall	12	0	48	1	30	8	60	5
Miller	10	0	46	1	...			
I. Johnson	12	3	31	3	30	7	52	3
Ring	21	2	72	6	17	2	58	0
W. Johnston	7.6	2	21	1	26	5	62	2
Hole	...				3	0	5	0
Harvey	...				1	1	0	0

SECOND TEST (at Melbourne).—December 24, 26, 27, 29, 30, 1952.
South Africa won by 82 runs.

1st inn.	SOUTH AFRICA		2nd inn.
D. J. McGlew b Lindwall	46	st Langley b Ring	13
J. H. B. Waite c Lindwall b Miller	0	c Hole b Miller	62
W. R. Endean c Benaud b Lindwall	2	not out	162
K. J. Funston c Ring b Miller	9	run out	26
R. A. McLean c Lindwall b Ring	27	lbw b Miller	42
J. E. Cheetham c Johnston b Miller	15	lbw b Johnston	6
J. C. Watkins c Langley b Benaud	19	b Johnston	3
P. N. F. Mansell b Lindwall	24	b Miller	18
A. G. A. Murray c Johnston b Benaud	51	st Langley b Ring	23
H. A. Tayfield c Langley b Miller	23	lbw b Lindwall	22
M. G. Melle not out	4	b Lindwall	0
Extras	7	Extras	11
Total	227	Total	388

1st inn.	AUSTRALIA		2nd inn.
C. McDonald c Fuller b Mansell	82	c Mansell b Murray	23
A. R. Morris c and b Tayfield	43	c Watkins b Melle	1
R. N. Harvey c Cheetham b Tayfield	11	c Watkins b Tayfield	60
A. L. Hassett c Melle b Mansell	18	lbw b Tayfield	21
K. Miller c Endean b Tayfield	52	b Tayfield	31
G. Hole c Waite b Mansell	13	b Tayfield	25
R. Benaud b Tayfield	5	c Melle b Tayfield	45
R. Lindwall run out	1	b Melle	19
D. Ring c McGlew b Tayfield	14	c Melle b Tayfield	53
G. Langley not out	2	b Tayfield	4
W. Johnston lbw b Tayfield	0	not out	0
Extras	2	Extras	8
Total	243	Total	290

BOWLING ANALYSIS	1st inn.				2nd inn.			
SOUTH AFRICA	O.	M.	R.	W.	O.	M.	R.	W.
Lindwall	14	2	29	3	31.5	4	87	2
Miller	21	3	62	4	22	5	51	3
Johnston	12	2	37	0	31	9	77	2
Ring	18	1	72	1	31	5	115	2
Benaud	6.6	1	20	2	6	0	23	0
Hole					7	0	24	0
AUSTRALIA	O.	M.	R.	W.	O.	M.	R.	W.
Melle	14	0	73	0	11	2	39	2
Watkins	6	1	15	0	10	2	34	0
Murray	3	1	11	0	23	7	59	1
Tayfield	29.4	9	84	6	37.1	13	81	7
Mansell	19	3	58	3	14	2	69	0

THIRD TEST (at Sydney).—January 9, 10, 12, 13, 1953.
Australia won by an innings and 38 runs.

1st inn.	SOUTH AFRICA		2nd inn.
D. J. McGlew run out	24	c Langley b Lindwall	9
J. H. B. Waite c Morris b Johnston	32	c Hole b Lindwall	0
W. R. Endean b Lindwall	18	lbw b Miller	71
K. J. Funston b Ring	56	c Hole b Miller	16
R. A. McLean b Lindwall	0	c Benaud b Lindwall	65
J. E. Cheetham c Johnston b Miller	5	c Morris b Lindwall	5
A. G. A. Murray c sub b Miller	4	c Hole b Benaud	17
J. C. Watkins c sub b Miller	17	c Miller b Johnston	48
P. N. F. Mansell b Lindwall	8	c Hole b Benaud	0
H. A. Tayfield not out	3	absent hurt	0
M. G. Melle c Langley b Lindwall	1	not out	0
Extras	5	Extra	1
Total	173	Total	232

THIRD TEST—Continued

1st inn. AUSTRALIA	
C. McDonald c Endean b Tayfield	67
A. R. Morris b Watkins	18
A. L. Hassett c Funston b Murray	2
R. N. Harvey c Watkins b Murray	190
K. G. Miller lbw b Tayfield	55
G. Hole run out	5
R. Benaud lbw b Melle	0
D. Ring b Tayfield	58
R. Lindwall b Murray	1
G. Langley c Mansell b Murray	20
W. Johnston not out	7
Extras	20
Total	443

BOWLING ANALYSIS SOUTH AFRICA	1st inn. O.	M.	R.	W.	2nd inn. O.	M.	R.	W.
Lindwall	14.2	1	40	4	20	3	72	4
Miller	17	1	48	3	18	6	33	2
Johnston	18	5	46	1	14.6	0	51	1
Ring	12	4	23	1	12	1	54	0
Hole	2	0	11	0				
Benaud					5	1	21	2

AUSTRALIA	O.	M.	R.	W.
Melle	23	3	98	1
Watkins	12	5	16	1
Murray	51.2	11	169	4
Tayfield	38	9	93	3
Mansell	7	0	46	0

FOURTH TEST (at Adelaide).—January 24, 26, 27, 28, 29, 1953. Drawn.

1st inn. AUSTRALIA		2nd inn.	
C. McDonald st Waite b Tayfield	154	b Mansell	15
A. R. Morris c Endean b Fuller	1	c Endean b Melle	77
A. L. Hassett c McGlew b Mansell	163		
R. N. Harvey c Tayfield b Fuller	84	c Endean b Watkins	116
K. R. Miller c Waite b Tayfield	9		
G. Hole c and b Mansell	59	not out	6
R. Benaud b Melle	6	not out	18
D. Ring c McLean b Tayfield	28		
R. Lindwall lbw b Tayfield	2		
G. Langley not out	5		
W. Johnston run out	11		
Extras	8	Extra	1
Total	530	Total (for 3 dec.)	233

1st inn. SOUTH AFRICA		2nd inn.	
D. J. McGlew c Hole b Johnston	26	c Langley b Johnston	54
W. R. Endean c Langley b Benaud	56	b Harvey	17
R. A. McLean c Hassett b Ring	11	c Hole b Benaud	17
J. H. B. Waite c Hole b Benaud	44	b Hole	20
K. J. Funston c and b Benaud	92	lbw b Johnston	17
J. C. Watkins b Benaud	76	b Morris	21
J. E. Cheetham b Johnston	6	not out	13
P. N. F. Mansell c Hole b Johnston	33	not out	2
H. A. Tayfield b Johnston	16		
E. Fuller c and b Johnston	0		
M. G. Melle not out	9		
Extras	18	Extras	16
Total	387	Total (for 6 wkts.)	177

FOURTH TEST—Continued

BOWLING ANALYSIS

AUSTRALIA	1st inn. O.	M.	R.	W.	2nd inn. O.	M.	R.	W.
Melle	26	1	105	1	10	1	50	1
Fuller	25	2	119	2	3	0	12	0
Tayfield	44	6	142	4	14	1	65	0
Mansell	32	1	113	2	7	0	40	1
McGlew	2	0	9	0	1	0	7	0
Watkins	6	1	34	0	12	1	58	1

SOUTH AFRICA	O.	M.	R.	W.	O.	M.	R.	W.
Lindwall	13	0	47	0				
Johnston	49.3	17	110	5	24	4	67	2
Miller	3	2	1	0				
Ring	30	8	88	1	11	3	25	0
Benaud	44	9	118	4	14	5	28	1
Hole	3	1	4	0	9	4	17	1
Harvey					7	2	9	1
Morris					5	0	11	1
Hassett					1	0	1	0
McDonald					1	0	3	0

FIFTH TEST (at Melbourne).—**February 6, 7, 9, 10, 11, 12, 1953.**
South Africa won by six wickets.

1st inn. AUSTRALIA		2nd inn.	
C. McDonald c McLean b Mansell	41	c Watkins b Fuller	11
A. R. Morris run out	99	lbw b Tayfield	44
R. N. Harvey c Cheetham b Fuller	205	b Fuller	7
A. L. Hassett run out	40	c Endean b Mansell	30
Ian Craig c Keith b Fuller	53	c Endean b Tayfield	47
R. Archer c Waite b Fuller	18	c Watkins b Tayfield	0
R. Benaud c and b Tayfield	20	c Watkins b Fuller	30
D. Ring b Tayfield	14	c Endean b Mansell	0
G. Langley b Murray	2	not out	26
W. Johnston c Endean b Tayfield	12	c Cheetham b Fuller	5
G. Noblet not out	13	b Fuller	1
Extras	3	Extras	8
Total	520	Total	209

1st inn. SOUTH AFRICA		2nd inn.	
W. R. Endean c Langley b W. Johnston	16	b Johnston	70
J. H. B. Waite run out	64	c Archer b Noblet	18
J. C. Watkins b Archer	92	b Ring	50
K. Funston lbw b Johnston	16	b Benaud	35
H. Keith b Johnston	10	not out	40
R. A. McLean lbw b Noblet	81	not out	76
J. E. Cheetham c McDonald b Johnston	66		
P. N. Mansell lbw b Johnston	52		
A. Murray c and b Johnston	17		
H. Tayfield c Benaud b Ring	17		
E. Fuller not out	0		
Extras	4	Extras	8
Total	435	Total (for 4)	297

BOWLING ANALYSIS

AUSTRALIA	1st inn. O.	M.	R.	W.	2nd inn. O.	M.	R.	W.
Fuller	19	4	74	3	30.2	4	66	5
Watkins	23	3	72	0	14	4	33	0
Tayfield	35.4	4	129	3	32	8	73	3
Murray	25	3	84	1				
Mansell	22	0	114	1	8	3	29	2
Keith	9	0	44	0				

FIFTH TEST—Continued

SOUTH AFRICA	O.	M.	R.	W.	O.	M.	R.	W.
Noblet	30	6	65	1	24	9	44	1
Archer	33	4	97	1	5	0	23	0
Johnston	46	8	152	6	28	7	114	1
Ring	19	1	62	1	13	2	55	1
Benaud	15	3	55	0	15	4	41	1
Hassett					5	0	12	0

TEST MATCH AVERAGES

AUSTRALIA

BATTING	No. of inns.	Total runs	Highest inns.	Not out	Avge.
R. N. Harvey	9	834	205	0	92.66
C. McDonald	9	437	154	0	48.55
A. L. Hassett	8	346	163	0	43.25
A. Morris	9	370	99	0	41.11
K. Miller	6	153	55	0	25.50
D. Ring	8	184	58	0	23.00
G. Hole	7	158	59	0	22.57
R. Benaud	7	124	45	1	20.66
G. Langley	8	103	27	3	20.60
R. Lindwall	6	66	*38	1	13.20
W. Johnston	8	36	12	3	7.20

Also batted: R. Archer, 18, 0; I. Craig, 53, 47; I. Johnson, 7, 13; G. Noblet, *13, 1.

BOWLING	Balls	Runs	Wickets	Avge.
K. Miller	728	241	13	18.53
R. Lindwall	1109	383	19	20.15
I. Johnson	330	83	4	20.75
R. Benaud	846	306	10	30.60
W. Johnston	2055	737	21	35.09
D. Ring	1473	624	13	48.00
G. Noblet	432	109	2	54.50

Also bowled:—N. Harvey, 1—9; A. Morris, 1—11; G. Hole, 1—17; R. Archer, 1—120; C. McDonald, 0—3; L. Hassett, 0—13.

SOUTH AFRICA

BATTING	No. of inns.	Total runs	Highest inns.	Not out	Avge.
W. Endean	10	438	162	1	48.77
R. McLean	10	370	81	1	41.11
K. Funston	10	365	92	0	36.50
J. Watkins	10	352	92	0	35.20
D. McGlew	8	250	69	0	31.25
J. Waite	10	293	64	0	29.30
A. Murray	7	141	51	1	23.50
P. Mansell	2	172	52	1	21.50
J. Cheetham	9	160	66	1	20.00
H. Tayfield	7	85	23	0	12.14
M. Melle	7	25	9*	4	8.33

Also batted:—E. Fuller, 0, *0; H. Keith, 10, *40.

BOWLING	Balls	Runs	Wickets	Avge.
E. Fuller	618	271	10	27.10
H. Tayfield	2208	843	30	28.10
M. Melle	1045	531	14	37.92
J. Watkins	1064	350	8	43.75
P. Mansell	936	509	9	56.55
A. Murray	1034	399	6	66.50

Also bowled:—D. McGlew, 0—16; H. Keith, 0—44.

* Not out

ENGLAND v. INDIA

Test Matches of 1952

Played 4 ; England won 3. Drawn 1.

FIRST TEST (at Leeds).—June 5, 6, 7, 9. England won by 7 wickets.

1st inn.	INDIA		2nd inn.
P. Roy st Evans b Jenkins	19	c Compton b Trueman	0
D. K. Gaekwad b Bedser	9	c Laker b Bedser	0
P. R. Umrigar c Evans b Trueman	8	c and b Jenkins	9
V. S. Hazare c Evans b Bedser	89	b Trueman	56
V. L. Manjrekar c Watkins b Trueman	133	b Trueman	0
D. G. Phadkar c Watkins b Laker	12	b Bedser	64
C. D. Gopinath b Trueman	0	lbw b Jenkins	8
M. K. Mantri not out	13	b Trueman	0
G. S. Ramchand c Watkins b Laker	0	st Evans b Jenkins	0
S. G. Shinde c May b Laker	2	not out	7
G. Ahmed b Laker	0	st Evans b Jenkins	14
Extras (b 1, lb 7)	8	Extras (lb 5, nb 1, w 1)	7
Total	293	Total	165

FALL OF WICKETS—1st innings

1	2	3	4	5	6	7	8	9
18	40	42	264	264	264	291	291	293

2nd innings

1	2	3	4	5	6	7	8	9
0	0	0	0	26	131	143	143	143

1st inn.	ENGLAND		2nd inn.
L. Hutton c Ramchand b Ahmed	10	b Phadkar	10
R. T. Simpson c Ramchand b Ahmed	23	c Mantri b G. Ahmed	51
P. B. H. May b Shinde	16	c Phadkar b G. Ahmed	4
D. C. S. Compton c Ramchand b Ahmed	14	not out	35
T. W. Graveney b Ghulam Ahmed	71	not out	20
A. J. Watkins lbw b Ghulam Ahmed	48		
T. G. Evans lbw b Hazare	66		
R. O. Jenkins c Mantri b Ramchand	38		
J. C. Laker b. Phadkar	15		
A. V. Bedser b Ramchand	7		
F. S. Trueman not out	0		
Extras (b 15, lb 11)	26	Extras (b 4, lb 3, nb 1)	8
Total	334	Total (for 3)	128

FALL OF WICKETS—1st innings

1	2	3	4	5	6	7	8	9
21	48	62	92	182	211	290	325	329

2nd innings

1	2	3
16	42	89

BOWLING ANALYSIS

	1st inn.				2nd inn.			
INDIA	O.	M.	R.	W.	O.	M.	R.	W.
Bedser	33	13	38	2	21	9	32	2
Trueman	26	6	89	3	9	1	27	4
Laker	22.3	9	39	4	13	4	17	0
Watkins	11	1	21	0	11	2	32	0
Jenkins	27	6	78	1	13	2	50	4
Compton	7	1	20	0				
ENGLAND	O.	M.	R.	W.	O.	M.	R.	W.
Phadkar	24	7	54	1	11	2	21	1
Ramchand	36.2	11	61	2	17	3	43	0
Ghulam Ahmed	63	24	100	5	22	8	37	2
Hazare	20	7	22	1	3	0	11	0
Shinde	22	5	71	1	2	0	8	0

SECOND TEST (at Lord's).—**June 19, 20, 21, 23, 24. England won by 8 wickets.**

1st inn.	INDIA		2nd inn.
V. Mankad c Watkins b Trueman	72	b Laker	184
P. Roy c and b Bedser	35	b Bedser	0
P. R. Umrigar b Trueman	5	b Trueman	14
V. S. Hazare not out	69	c Laker b Bedser	49
V. L. Manjrekar lbw b Bedser	5	b Laker	1
D. G. Phadkar b. Watkins	8	b Laker	16
H. R. Adhikari lbw b Watkins	0	b Trueman	16
G. S. Ramchand b Trueman	18	b Trueman	42
M. K. Mantri b Trueman	1	c Compton b Laker	5
S. G. Shinde st Evans b Watkins	5	c Hutton b Trueman	14
Ghulam Ahmed b Jenkins	0	not out	1
Extras	17	Extras	36
Total	235	Total	378

FALL OF WICKETS—1st innings

1	2	3	4	5	6	7	8	9
106	116	118	126	135	139	167	180	221

2nd innings

1	2	3	4	5	6	7	8	9
7	59	270	272	289	312	314	323	377

1st inn.	ENGLAND		2nd inn.
L. Hutton c Mantri b Hazare	150	not out	39
R. T. Simpson b Mankad	53	run out	2
P. B. H. May c Mantri b Mankad	74	c Roy b Ghulam Ahmed	26
D. C. S. Compton lbw b Hazare	6	not out	4
T. W. Graveney c Mantri b G. Ahmed	73		
A. J. Watkins b Mankad	0		
T. G. Evans c and b Ghulam Ahmed	104		
R. O. Jenkins st Mantri b Mankad	21		
J. C. Laker not out	23		
A. V. Bedser c Ramchand b Mankad	3		
F. S. Trueman b Ghulam Ahmed	17		
Extras	13	Extras	8
Total	537	Total (for 2)	79

FALL OF WICKETS—1st innings

1	2	3	4	5	6	7	8	9
106	264	272	292	292	451	468	506	514

2nd innings

1	2
8	71

BOWLING ANALYSIS

INDIA	1st inn. O.	M.	R.	W.	2nd inn. O.	M.	R.	W.
Bedser	33	8	62	2	36	13	60	2
Trueman	25	3	72	4	27	4	110	4
Jenkins	7.3	1	26	1	10	1	40	0
Laker	12	5	21	0	39	15	102	4
Watkins	17	7	37	3	8	0	20	0
Compton					2	0	10	0

ENGLAND	O.	M.	R.	W.	O.	M.	R.	W.
Phadkar	27	8	44	0				
Ramchand	29	8	67	0	1	0	5	0
Hazare	24	4	53	2	1	1	0	0
Mankad	73	24	196	5	24	12	35	0
Ghulam Ahmed	43.4	12	106	3	23.2	9	31	1
Shinde	6	0	43	0				
Umrigar	4	0	15	0				

THIRD TEST (at Manchester).—July 17, 18, 19. England won by an innings and 207 runs.

ENGLAND	1st inn.
L. Hutton c Sen b Divecha	104
D. S. Sheppard lbw b Ramchand	34
J. T. Ikin c Divecha b Ghulam Ahmed	29
P. B. H. May c Sen b Mankad	69
T. W. Graveney lbw b Divecha	14
A. J. Watkins c Phadkar b Mankad	4
T. G. Evans c and b Ghulam Ahmed	71
J. C. Laker c Sen b Divecha	0
A. V. Bedser c Phadkar b Ghulam Ahmed	17
G. A. R. Lock not out	1
Extras	4
Total (for 9 dec.)	347

F. S. Trueman did not bat.

FALL OF WICKETS

1	2	3	4	5	6	7	8	9
78	133	214	248	252	284	292	336	347

INDIA 1st inn.		2nd inn.	
V. Mankad c Lock b Bedser	4	lbw b Bedser	6
P. Roy c Hutton b Trueman	0	c Laker b Trueman	0
H. R. Adhikari c Graveney b Trueman	0	c May b Lock	27
V. S. Hazare b Bedser	16	c Ikin b Lock	16
P. R. Umrigar b Trueman	4	c Watkins b Bedser	3
D. G. Phadkar c Sheppard b Trueman	0	b Bedser	5
V. L. Manjrekar c Ikin b Trueman	22	c Evans b Bedser	0
R. V. Divecha b Trueman	4	b Bedser	2
G. S. Ramchand c Graveney b Trueman	2	c Watkins b Lock	1
P. Sen c Lock b Trueman	4	not out	13
Ghulam Ahmed not out	1	c Ikin b Lock	0
Extras	1	Extras	9
Total	58	Total	82

FALL OF WICKETS—1st innings

1	2	3	4	5	6	7	8	9
4	4	5	17	17	45	51	53	53

2nd innings

1	2	3	4	5	6	7	8	9
7	7	55	59	66	66	66	67	77

BOWLING ANALYSIS

ENGLAND	1st inn. O.	M.	R.	W.	2nd inn. O.	M.	R.	W.
Phadkar	22	10	30	0				
Divecha	45	12	102	3				
Ramchand	33	7	78	1				
Mankad	28	9	67	2				
Ghulam Ahmed	9	3	43	3				
Hazare	7	3	23	0				
INDIA	O.	M.	R.	W.	O.	M.	R.	W.
Bedser	11	4	19	2	15	6	27	5
Trueman	8.4	2	31	8	8	5	9	1
Laker	2	0	7	0				
Watkins					4	3	1	0
Lock					9.3	2	36	4

FOURTH TEST (at the Oval).—**August 14, 15, 16, 18, 19. Drawn.**

1st inn.	**ENGLAND**
L. Hutton c Phadkar b Ramchand	86
D. S. Sheppard lbw b Divecha	119
J. T. Ikin c Sen b Phadkar	53
P. B. H. May c Manjrekar b Mankad	17
T. W. Graveney c Divecha b Ghulam Ahmed	13
W. Watson not out	18
T. G. Evans c Phadkar b Mankad	1
J. C. Laker not out	6
Extras	13
Total (for 6 dec.)	326

A. V. Bedser, G. A. R. Lock, F. S. Trueman did not bat.

FALL OF WICKETS

1	2	3	4	5	6
143	261	273	293	304	307

1st inn.	**INDIA**
V. Mankad c Evans b Trueman	5
P. Roy c Lock b Trueman	0
H. R. Adhikari c Trueman v. Bedser	0
V. S. Hazare c May b Trueman	38
V. L. Manjrekar c Ikin b Bedser	0
P. R. Umrigar b Bedser	0
D. G. Phadkar b Trueman	17
R. V. Divecha b Bedser	16
G. S. Ramchand c Hutton b Bedser	5
P. Sen b Trueman	9
Ghulam Ahmed not out	2
Extras	5
Total	98

FALL OF WICKETS

1	2	3	4	5	6	7	8	9
0	5	5	6	6	64	71	78	94

BOWLING ANALYSIS 1st inn.

ENGLAND	O.	M.	R.	W.	O.	M.	R.	W.
Divecha	33	9	60	1				
Phadkar	32	8	61	1				
Ramchand	14	2	50	1				
Mankad	48	23	88	2				
Ghulam Ahmed	24	1	54	1				
Hazare	3	3	0	0				
INDIA	O.	M.	R.	W.				
Bedser	14.5	4	41	5				
Trueman	16	4	48	5				
Lock	6	5	1	0				
Laker	2	0	3	0				

TEST AVERAGES, 1952

ENGLAND

BATTING	Matches	No. of inns.	Total runs	Highest score	Not out	Avge.
L. Hutton	4	6	399	150	1	79.80
D. S. Sheppard	2	2	153	119	0	76.50
T. G. Evans	4	4	242	104	0	60.50
T. W. Graveney	4	5	191	73	1	47.75
J. T. Ikin	2	2	82	53	2	41.00
P. B. H. May	4	6	206	74	0	34.33
R. T. Simpson	2	4	129	53	0	32.25
D. C. S. Compton	2	4	59	35*	2	29.50
R. O. Jenkins	2	2	59	38	0	29.50
J. C. Laker	4	4	44	23*	2	22.00
A. J. Watkins	3	3	52	48	0	17.33
F. S. Trueman	4	2	17	17	1	17.00
A. V. Bedser	4	3	27	17	0	9.00
G. A. R. Lock	2	1	1	1*	1	—

Also batted :—W. Watson 18*.

BOWLING	Overs	Maidens	Runs	Wickets	Avge.
G. A. R. Lock	15.3	7	37	4	9.25
F. S. Trueman	119.4	25	386	29	13.31
A. V. Bedser	163.5	57	279	20	13.95
J. C. Laker	90.3	33	189	8	23.62
R. O. Jenkins	57.3	10	194	6	32.33
A. J. Watkins	51	13	111	3	37.00
D. C. S. Compton	9	1	30	0	—

INDIA

BATTING	Matches	No. of inns.	Total runs	Highest score	Not out	Avge.
V. S. Hazare	4	7	333	89	1	55.50
V. Mankad	3	5	271	184	0	54.20
V. L. Manjrekar	4	7	162	133	0	23.14
D. G. Phadkar	4	7	122	64	0	17.42
P. Sen	2	3	26	13*	1	13.00
G. S. Ramchand	4	7	68	42	0	9.71
S. G. Shinde	2	4	28	14	1	9.33
H. R. Adhikari	3	5	43	27	0	8.60
P. Roy	4	7	54	35	0	7.71
R. V. Divecha	2	3	22	16	0	7.33
M. K. Mantri	2	4	19	13*	1	6.33
P. R. Umrigar	4	7	43	14	0	6.14
Ghulam Ahmed	4	7	18	14	3	4.50

Also batted :—D. K. Gaekwad, 9 and 0 ; C. D. Gopinath, 0 and 8.

BOWLING	Overs	Maidens	Runs	Wickets	Avge.
Ghulam Ahmed	185	57	371	15	24.73
V. S. Hazare	58	18	109	3	36.33
R. V. Divecha	78	21	162	4	40.50
V. Mankad	173	68	386	9	42.88
D. G. Phadkar	116	35	210	3	70.00
G. S. Ramchand	130.2	31	304	4	76.00
S. G. Shinde	30	5	122	1	122.00

Also bowled :—P. R. Umrigar, 4—0—15—0.

The following three-figure innings were scored in the Test matches :—

For ENGLAND—L. Hutton (2) 150 at Lord's (second Test), 104 at Manchester (third Test) ; T. G. Evans (1) 104 at Lord's (second Test) ; D. S. Sheppard (1) 119 at the Oval (fourth Test).

For INDIA—V. L. Manjrekar (1) 133 at Leeds (first Test) ; V. Mankad (1) 184 at Lord's (second Test).

* Not out.

Indians' Visit, 1952

	P.	W.	L.	D.
Test Matches	4	0	3	1
All Matches	33	5	5	23

(Selected Results)

May 7, 8, 9, v. Surrey at The Oval. Surrey won by 141 runs. Surrey 219 (L. B. Fishlock 57, J. F. Parker 52, G. S. Ramchand 5 for 20) and 188 (B. Constable 57); India 158 (J. C. Laker 6 for 64) and 108.

May 10, 12, 13, v. Leicestershire at Leicester. Drawn. Leicester 161 (G. A. Smithson 55) and 156 (8 wickets, Ghulam Ahmed 5 for 52); India 202 (9 wickets dec., V. S. Hazare 57).

May 24, 26, 27, v. Essex at Ilford. Drawn. India 195 (H. R. Adhikari 61, Smith 6 for 36) and 368 (6 wickets dec., D. K. Gaekwad 75, P. R. Umrigar 74, V. L. Manjrekar 81, D. G. Phadkar 86); Essex 410 (D. J. Insole 116, T. C. Dodds 81, T. E. Bailey 67) and 144 (9 wickets, H. G. Gaekwad 5 for 44).

May 28, 29, 30, v. Somerset at Taunton. Drawn. Somerset 330 (J. Lawrence not out 103) and 188 (9 wickets dec., F. L. Angell 64, S. S. Rogers 53, P. Roy 5 for 53); India 238 (D. K. Gaekwad 83) and 118 (8 wickets).

May 31, June 2, 3, v. Glamorgan at Cardiff. Drawn. Glamorgan 164 (P. B. Clift 58, W. G. A. Parkhouse 57, G. S. Ramchand 8 for 33) and 170; India 217 (P. R. Umrigar 55, V. L. Manjrekar 55) and 85 (8 wickets).

June 29, 30, July 1, v. Lancashire at Manchester. India won by 10 wickets. Lancashire 363 (N. D. Howard 87, W. Place 85, A. Wharton 68) and 68 (Ramchand 7 for 27); India 427 (P. R. Umrigar 204, R. V. Divecha 61) and 5 (0 wicket).

July 5, 7, 8, v. Notts at Nottingham. Drawn. India 436 (4 wickets dec., P. Roy 163, V. S. Hazare 96, D. K. Gaekwad 70) and 16 (0 wicket); Notts 468 (C. J. Poole 222 not out, J. Hardstaff 54, Shinde 5 for 107).

July 9, 10, 11, v. Derbyshire at Chesterfield. Drawn. Derbyshire 162 (Chowdhury 5 for 30) and 296 (A. Hamer 76, D. Morgan 65, G. L. Willatt 63); India 86 (Jackson 6 for 39) and 115 (3 wickets).

July 12, 14, 15, v. Yorkshire at Sheffield. Drawn. Yorkshire 192 (D. B. Close not out 71, Divecha 5 for 81) and 296 (4 wickets, E. Lester 110 not out, H. Halliday 77, F. A. Lowson 69); India 377 (5 wickets dec., P. R. Umrigar not out 137, H. R. Adhikari 82, K. Mantri 80).

July 26, 28, 29, v. Surrey at The Oval. India won by 6 wickets. Surrey 71 (Divecha 6 for 29) and 319 (P. B. H. May 143); India 179 (P. J. Loader 5 for 63) and 214 (4 wickets, H. R. Adhikari 98 not out, D. G. Phadkar 50 not out).

July 30, 31, August 1, v. Northants at Northampton. Drawn. Northants 365 (7 wickets dec., D. Brookes 156) and 107 (1 wicket, D. Brookes 51 not out); India 309 (V. L. Manjrekar 83, H. R. Adhikari 73, P. R. Umrigar 59).

August 2, 4, 5, v. Glamorgan at Swansea. Drawn. No play third day. Glamorgan 204 (9 wickets dec., J. Pleass 75, Divecha 8 for 74) and 5 (0 wicket); India 306 (9 wickets dec., G. S. Ramchand 78, P. Sen 75 not out, V. L. Manjrekar 59).

August 6, 7, 8, v. Warwickshire at Birmingham. Drawn. India 172 (2 wickets dec., H. R. Adhikari 101 not out); Warwickshire 96 (2 wickets, N. F. Horner 57).

August 9, 11, 12, v. Gloucestershire at Cheltenham. India won by 6 wickets. Gloucester 198 (G. M. Emmett 63, T. W. Graveney 56 not out) and 47 (7 wickets dec.); India 138 (H. R. Adhikari 80) and 108 (4 wickets).

Continued on next page

INDIANS' VISIT

Continued from previous page

August 20, 21, 22, v. Sussex at Hove. Sussex won by 6 wickets. India 186 (D. K. Gaekwad 87, D. J. Wood 5 for 34) and 210 (V. S. Hazare 52, N. Thompson 5 for 54); Sussex 220 (Ramchand 6 for 67) and 177 (4 wickets, John Langridge 80).

August 23, 25, 26, v. Middlesex at Lord's. Drawn. India 289 (V. L. Manjrekar 104, D. K. Gaekwad 62) and 294 (5 wickets dec., P. Roy 131, P. R. Umrigar 86); Middlesex 255 (J. D. Robertson 85, Hazare 7 for 50) and 289 (5 wickets, W. J. Edrich 129, J. D. Robertson 81, D. Compton 70).

August 27, 28, 29, v. Kent at Canterbury. Drawn. Kent 217 (A. E. Fagg 76, A. H. Phebey 61) and 225 (M. C. Cowdrey 101); India 392 (P. R. Umrigar 204, C. T. Sarwate 57) and 45 (4 wickets).

August 30, September 1, 2, v. Hampshire at Bournemouth. Drawn. Hampshire 256 (A. C. D. Ingleby-MacKenzie 91, E. D. R. Eager 88) and 206 (8 wickets dec., A. W. H. Rayment 58, J. R. Gray 55); India 357 (7 wickets dec., P. R. Umrigar 165, D. K. Gaekwad 69) and 100 (8 wickets, D. Shackleton 6 for 41).

INDIANS' AVERAGES

First-Class Matches Only.

BATTING	No. of inns.	Total runs	Highest score	Not cut	Avge.
V. Mankad	5	271	184	0	54.20
P. R. Umrigar	41	1688	229*	6	48.22
V. L. Manjrekar	33	1059	133	6	39.22
H. R. Adhikari	29	879	101*	3	33.80
V. S. Hazare	40	1077	161*	5	30.77
D. K. Gaekwad	34	852	87	3	27.48
G. S. Ramchand	32	644	134	6	24.76
D. G. Phadkar	32	689	94	4	24.60
M. K. Mantri	27	550	80	3	22.91
P. Roy	38	788	163	2	21.88
R. V. Divecha	17	294	61	3	21.00
C. D. Gopinath	19	356	79	2	20.94
P. Sen	13	195	75*	3	19.50
S. G. Shinde	18	165	30*	8	16.50
H. G. Gaekwad	15	182	51*	2	14.00
C. T. Sarwate	15	146	57	1	10.42
Ghulam Ahmed	18	107	30	7	9.72
N. Chowdhury	10	21	9*	3	3.00

* Not out

BOWLING	Overs	Maidens	Runs	Wickets	Avge.
P. Roy	29.2	5	82	5	16.40
Ghulam Ahmed	767.5	233	1754	80	21.92
V. S. Hazare	486.5	156	1061	44	24.11
G. S. Ramchand	665.5	173	1655	64	25.85
R. V. Divecha	484.0	120	1294	50	25.88
D. G. Phadkar	639.0	191	1427	53	26.92
H. G. Gaekwad	187.1	50	464	17	27.29
N. Chowdhury	249.1	52	744	24	31.00
S. G. Shinde	443.3	91	1371	39	35.15
C. T. Sarwate	159.1	40	459	12	38.25
V. Mankad	173.0	68	386	9	42.88
P. R. Umrigar	90.0	24	214	4	53.50

Also bowled :-D. K. Gaekwad, 1—0—6—0 ; C. D. Gopinath, 1—0—1—0

English Cricket . . .

(In Matches at Home and Overseas)

ENGLAND v. AUSTRALIA

Abel, R., 1888, 1891-2, 1896, 1902
Absolom, C. A., 1878-9
Allen, G. O., 1930, 1932-3, 1934, 1936-7
Ames, L. E. G., 1932-3, 1934, 1936-7, 1938
Armitage, T., 1876-7
Arnold, E. G., 1903-4, 1905
Attewell, W., 1884-5, 1887-8, 1890, 1891-2

Bailey, T. E., 1950-51
Barlow, R. G., 1881-2, 1882, 1882-3, 1884, 1886, 1886-7
Barnes, S. F., 1901-2, 1902, 1907-8, 1909, 1911-12, 1912
Barnes, W., 1880, 1882, 1882-3, 1884, 1884-5, 1886, 1886-7, 1888, 1890
Barnett, C. J., 1936-7, 1938, 1948
Bates, W., 1881-2, 1882-3, 1884-5, 1886-7
Bean, G., 1891-2
Bedser, A. V., 1946-7, 1948, 1950-51
Bligh, Hon. Ivo, 1882-3
Blythe, C., 1901-2, 1905, 1907-8, 1909
Bosanquet, B. J. T., 1903-4, 1905
Bowes, W. E., 1932-3, 1934, 1938
Bradley, W. M., 1899
Braund, L. C., 1901-2, 1902, 1903-4, 1907-8
Brearley, W., 1905, 1909
Briggs, J., 1884-5, 1886, 1886-7, 1887-8, 1888, 1891-2, 1893, 1894-5, 1896, 1897-8, 1899
Brockwell, W., 1893, 1894-5, 1899
Brown, F. R., 1950-51
Brown, G., 1921
Brown, J. T., sen., 1894-5, 1896, 1899

Carr, A. W., 1926
Carr, D. W., 1909
Chapman, A. P. F., 1924-25, 1926, 1928-9, 1930
Charlwood, H. R. J., 1876-7
Christopherson, S., 1884
Clark, E. C., 1934
Close, D. B., 1950-51
Compton, D., 1938, 1946-7, 1948, 1950-51
Coxon, A., 1948
Cranston, J., 1890
Cranston, K., 1948
Crapp, J. F., 1948
Crawford, J. N., 1907-8

Dean, H., 1912
Denton, D., 1905
Dewes, J., 1948, 1950-51
Dipper, A. E., 1921
Dollery, H. E., 1948
Dolphin, A., 1920-21
Douglas, J. W. H. T., 1911-12, 1912, 1920-1, 1921, 1924-5
Druce, N. F., 1897-8
Ducat, A., 1921
Duckworth, G. 1928-9, 1930
Duleepsinhji, K. S., 1930
Durston, T. J., 1921

Edrich, W. J., 1938, 1946-7, 1948
Emmett, G. H., 1948
Emmett, T., 1876-7, 1878-9, 1881-2
Evans, A. J., 1921
Evans, T. G., 1946-7, 1948, 1950-51

Fagg, A., 1936-7
Fane, F. L., 1907-8
Farnes, K., 1934, 1936-7, 1938
Fender, P. G. H., 1920-21, 1921
Fielder, A., 1903-4, 1907-8
Fishlock, L. B., 1946-7
Flowers, W., 1884-5, 1886-7, 1893
Ford, F. G. J., 1894-5
Foster, F. R., 1911-12, 1912
Foster, R. E., 1903-4
Freeman, A. P., 1924-5
Fry, C.B., 1899, 1902, 1905, 1909, 1912

Gay, L. H., 1894-5
Geary, G., 1926, 1928-9, 1930, 1934
Gibb, P. A., 1946-7
Gilligan, A. E. R., 1924-5
Goddard, T. W., 1930
Grace, E. M., 1880
Grace, G. F., 1880
Grace, W. G., 1880, 1882, 1884, 1886, 1888, 1890, 1891-2, 1893, 1896, 1899
Greenwood, A., 1876-7
Gunn, G., 1907-8, 1909, 1911-12
Gunn, J., 1901-2, 1905
Gunn, W., 1886-7, 1888, 1890, 1893, 1896, 1899

Haig, N. E. 1921
Haigh, S., 1905, 1909, 1912
Hallows, C., 1921
Hammond, W. R., 1928-9, 1930, 1932-3, 1934, 1936-7, 1938, 1946-7
Hardinge, H. T. W., 1921
Hardstaff, J., 1907-8
Hardstaff, J., jnr., 1936-7, 1938, 1946-7, 1948
Harris, Lord, 1878-9, 1880, 1884
Hayes, E. G., 1909
Hayward, T., 1896, 1897-8, 1899, 1901-2, 1902, 1903-4, 1905, 1909
Hearne, J. T., 1896, 1897-8, 1899
Hearne, J. W., 1911-12, 1912, 1920-1, 1921, 1924-5, 1926
Hendren, E., 1920-1, 1921, 1924-5, 1926, 1928-9, 1930, 1934
Hill, A., 1876-7
Hirst, G. H., 1897-8, 1899, 1902, 1903-4, 1905, 1909
Hitch, J. W., 1911-2, 1912, 1920-1, 1921

. . . Internationals

Hobbs, J. B., 1907-8, 1909, 1911-12, 1912, 1920-1, 1921, 1924-5, 1926, 1928-9, 1930
Hollies, W. E., 1948
Holmes, P., 1921
Hone, L., 1878-9
Hopwood, J. L., 1934
Hornby, A. N., 1878-9, 1882, 1884
Howell, H., 1920-21, 1921
Humphries, J., 1907-8
Hunter, J., 1884-5
Hutchings, K. L., 1907-8, 1909
Hutton, L., 1938, 1946-7, 1948, 1950-51

Ikin, J. T., 1946-7

Jackson, F. S., 1893, 1896, 1899, 1902, 1905
Jardine, D. R., 1928-9, 1932-3
Jessop, G. L., 1899, 1901-2, 1902, 1905, 1909
Jones, A. O., 1899, 1901-2, 1905, 1907-8, 1909
Jupp, H., 1876-7
Jupp, V. W. C., 1921

Keeton, W. W., 1934
Kilner, R., 1924-5, 1926
King, J. H., 1909
Kinneir, S. P., 1911-12
Knight, A. E., 1903-4
Knight, D. J., 1921

Laker, J. C., 1948
Larwood, H., 1926, 1928-9, 1930, 1932-3
Leslie, C. F. H., 1882-3
Leyland, M., 1928-9, 1930, 1932-3, 1934, 1936-7, 1938
Lilley, A. A., 1896, 1899, 1901-2, 1902, 1903-4, 1905, 1909
Lillywhite, J., 1876-7
Lockwood, W. H., 1893, 1894-5, 1899, 1902
Lohmann, G. A., 1886, 1886-7, 1887-8, 1888, 1890, 1891-2, 1896
Lucas, A. P., 1878-9, 1880, 1882, 1884
Lyttelton, Hon. A., 1880, 1882, 1884

Macaulay, G. G., 1926
McGahey, C. P., 1901-2
MacGregor, G., 1890, 1891-2, 1893
Mackinnon, F. A., 1878-9
McIntyre, A. J., 1950-51
MacLaren, A. C., 1894-5, 1896, 1897-8, 1899, 1901-2, 1902, 1905, 1909
Makepeace, H., 1920-21
Martin, F., 1890
Mason, J. R., 1897-8
Mead, C. P., 1911-12, 1921, 1928-9
Mead, W., 1899
Midwinter, W. E., 1881-2
Mitchell, T. B., 1932-3, 1934
Mold, A., 1893
Morley, F., 1880, 1882-3

Newham, W., 1887-8
Nichols, M. S., 1930

O'Brien, T. C., 1884, 1888

Palairet, L. C. H., 1902
Parker, C. W. L., 1921
Parkhouse, W. G., 1950-51
Parkin, C. H., 1920-21, 1921
Pataudi, Nawab of, 1932-3, 1934
Paynter, E., 1932-3, 1938
Peate, E., 1881-2, 1882, 1884, 1886
Peebles, I. A. R., 1930
Peel, R., 1884-5, 1887-8, 1888, 1890, 1891-2, 1893, 1894-5
Penn, F., 1880
Philipson, H., 1891-2, 1894-5
Pilling, R., 1881-2, 1884, 1886, 1887-8, 1888
Pollard, R., 1948
Price, W. F., 1938

Quaife, W. G., 1899, 1901-2

Ranjitsinhji, K. S., 1896, 1897-8, 1899, 1902
Read, J. M., 1882, 1884-5, 1886-7, 1887-8, 1890, 1891-2, 1893
Read, W. W., 1882-3, 1884, 1886, 1887-8, 1888, 1890, 1893
Relf, A. E., 1903-4, 1909
Rhodes, W., 1899, 1902, 1903-4, 1905, 1907-8, 1909, 1911-12, 1912, 1920-1, 1921, 1926
Richardson, T., 1893, 1894-5, 1896, 1897-8
Richmond, T. L., 1921
Robins, R. W. V., 1930, 1936-7
Root, F., 1926
Royle, V. P. F. A., 1878-9
Russell, A. C., 1920-21, 1921

Sandham, A., 1921, 1924-5
Schultz, S. S., 1878-9
Scotton, W. H., 1881-2, 1884, 1884-5, 1886, 1886-7
Selby, J., 1876-7, 1881-2
Sharp, J., 1909
Sharpe, J. W., 1890, 1891-2
Shaw, A., 1876-7, 1880, 1881-2
Sheppard, D. S., 1950-51
Sherwin, M., 1886-7, 1888
Shrewsbury, A., 1881-2, 1884, 1884-5, 1886, 1886-7, 1887-8, 1890, 1893
Shuter, J., 1888
Simpson, R. T., 1950-51
Sims, J., 1936-7
Sinfield, R. A., 1938
Smith, E. J., 1911-12, 1912
Smith, T. P. B., 1946-7
Southerton, J., 1876-7
Spooner, R. H., 1905, 1909, 1912
Steel, A. G., 1880, 1882, 1882-3, 1884, 1886, 1888
Stevens, G. T. S., 1926
Stoddart, A. E., 1887-8, 1891-2, 1893, 1894-5, 1896, 1897-8

ENGLAND v. AUSTRALIA—Continued

Storer, W., 1897-8, 1899
Strudwick, H., 1911-12, 1920-1, 1921 1924-5, 1926
Studd, C. T., 1882, 1882-3
Studd, G. B., 1882-3
Sugg, F. H., 1888
Sutcliffe, H., 1924-5, 1926, 1928-9, 1930, 1932-3, 1934
Tate, F. W., 1902
Tate, M. W., 1924-5, 1926, 1928-9, 1930
Tattersall, R. R., 1950-51
Tennyson, Hon. L. H., 1921
Thompson, G. J., 1909
Townsend, C. L., 1899
Tyldesley, E., 1921, 1926, 1928-9
Tyldesley, J. T., 1899, 1901-2, 1902, 1903-4, 1905, 1909
Tyldesley, R., 1924-5, 1930
Tylecote, E. F. S., 1882-3, 1886
Ulyett, G., 1876-7, 1878-9, 1881-2, 1882, 1884, 1884-5, 1886, 1887-8, 1888, 1890
Verity, H., 1932-3, 1934, 1936-7, 1938
Vernon, G. F., 1882-3
Vine, J., 1911-12
Voce, W., 1932-3, 1936-7 1946-7
Waddington, A., 1920-1
Wainwright, E., 1893, 1897-8
Walters, C. F., 1934
Ward, A., 1893, 1894-5
Warner, P. F., 1903-4, 1909, 1912
Warr, J. J., 1950-51
Warren, A. R., 1905
Washbrook, C., 1946-7, 1948, 1950-51
Watkins, A., 1948
Webbe, A. J., 1878-9
Wellard, A. W., 1938
White, J. C., 1921, 1928-9, 1930
Whysall, W. W., 1924-5, 1930
Wilson, E. R., 1920-21
Wood, A., 1938
Wood, H., 1888
Wood, R., 1886-7
Woolley, F. E., 1909, 1911-12, 1912, 1920-1,1921,1924-5,1926,1930,1934
Worthington, T. S., 1936-7
Wright, D. V. P., 1938, 1946-7, 1948 1950-51
Wyatt, R. E. S., 1930, 1932-3, 1934, 1936-7
Wynyard, E. G., 1896
Yardley, N. W. D., 1946-7, 1948
Young, H., 1899
Young, J. A., 1948
Young, R. A., 1907-8

ENGLAND v. SOUTH AFRICA

Abel, R., 1888-9
Allom, M. J. C., 1930-31
Ames, L. E. G., 1929, 1935, 1938-39
Archer, A. G., 1888-9
Arnold, E. G., 1907
Astill, W. E., 1927-28
Bailey, T. E., 1951
Bakewell, A. H., 1935
Barber, W., 1935
Barnes, S. F., 1912, 1913-14
Barnett, C. J., 1947
Barratt, F., 1929
Barton, V. A., 1891-2
Bedser, A. V., 1947, 1948-49, 1951
Bird, M. C., 1909-10, 1913-14
Blythe, C., 1905-6, 1907, 1909-10
Board, J. H., 1898-9, 1905-6
Booth, M. W., 1913-14
Bowden, M. P., 1888-9
Bowes, W., 1935
Bowley, E. H., 1929
Braund, L. C., 1907
Brearley, W., 1912
Brennan, D. V., 1951
Briggs, J., 1888-9
Bromley-Davenport, H. R., 1895-6, 1898-9
Brown, F. R., 1951
Brown, G., 1922-3
Buckenham, C. P., 1909-10
Butler, H. J., 1947
Butt, H. R., 1895-6
Carr, A. W., 1922-3, 1929
Chapman, A. P. F., 1924, 1930-31
Chatterton, W., 1891-2
Clark, E. C., 1929
Clay, J. C., 1935
Compton, D., 1947, 1948-49, 1951
Cook, C., 1947
Copson, W., 1947
Coventry, Hon. C. J., 1888-9
Cranston, K., 1947
Crapp, J. F., 1948-49
Crawford, J. N., 1905-6, 1907
Cuttell, W. R., 1898-9
Dawson, E. W., 1927-8
Dean, H., 1912
Denton, D., 1905-6, 1909-10
Dollery, H., 1947
Douglas, J. W. H. T., 1913-14, 1924
Duckworth, G, 1924, 1929, 1930-31, 1935
Duleepsinhji, K. S., 1929
Edrich, W. J., 1938-39, 1947
Elliott, H., 1927-28
Evans, T. G., 1947, 1948-49, 1951
Fane, F. L., 1905-6, 1909-10
Farnes, K., 1938-39
Farrimond, W., 1930-31, 1935
Fender, P. G. H., 1922-3, 1924, 1929
Ferris, J. J., 1891-2
Foster, F. R., 1912
Foster, R. E., 1907
Fothergill, A. J., 1888-9
Freeman, A. P. 1927-28, 1929

ENGLAND v. SOUTH AFRICA—Continued

Fry, C. B., 1895-6, 1907, 1912

Geary, G., 1924, 1927-8, 1929
Gibb, P. A., 1938-39
Gilligan, A. E. R., 1922-3, 1924
Gladwin, C., 1947, 1948-49
Goddard, T. W., 1938-39
Graveney, T. W., 1951
Grieve, B. A. F., 1888-9
Griffith, S. C., 1948-49

Haigh, S., 1898-9, 1905-6
Hammond, W. R., 1927-28, 1929, 1930-31, 1935, 1938-39
Hartley, J. C., 1905-6
Hardstaff, J., jun., 1935
Hawke, Lord, 1895-6, 1898-9
Hayes, E. G., 1905-6, 1912
Hayward, T., 1895-6, 1907
Hearne, A., 1891-2
Hearne, F., 1888-9
Hearne, G. G., 1891-2
Hearne, J. T., 1891-2
Hearne, J. W., 1912, 1913-14, 1924
Hendren, E., 1924, 1929, 1930-31
Heseltine, C., 1895-6
Hill, A. J. L., 1895-6
Hilton, M. J., 1951
Hirst, G. H., 1907
Hitch, J. W., 1912
Hobbs, J. B., 1909-10, 1912, 1913-14, 1924, 1929
Hollies, W. E., 1947
Holmes, E. R. T., 1935
Holmes, P., 1927-28
Howell, H., 1924
Howorth, R., 1947
Hutton, L., 1938-39, 1947, 1948-49, 1951

Iddon, J., 1935
Ikin, J. T., 1951

Jenkins, R., 1948-49
Jessop, G. L., 1907, 1912
Jupp, V. W. C., 1922-3

Kennedy, A. S., 1922-3
Killick, E. T., 1929
Kilner, R., 1924
Knox, N. A., 1907

Laker, J. C., 1951
Langridge, James, 1935
Larwood, H., 1929
Lee, H. W., 1930-31
Lees, W. S., 1905-6
Legge, G. B., 1927-28
Leveson-Gower, H. D. G., 1909-10
Leyland, M., 1929, 1930-31, 1935
Lilley, A. A., 1907
Lohmann, G. A., 1895-6
Lowson, F. A., 1951

Macaulay, G. G., 1922-3, 1924
MacBryan, J. C. W., 1924
McMaster, E. J., 1888-9
Mann, F. G., 1948-49
Mann, F. T., 1922-3
Martin, F., 1891-2
Martin, J. W., 1947
May, P. B. H., 1951
Mead, C. P., 1913-14, 1922-3
Miller, A. M., 1895-6
Milligan, F. W., 1898-9
Mitchell, A., 1935
Mitchell, F., 1898-9
Mitchell-Innes, N. S., 1935
Mitchell, T. B., 1935
Moon, L. J., 1905-6
Murdoch, W. L., 1891-2

Nichols, M. S., 1935

O'Brien, T. C., 1895-6
O'Connor, J., 1929

Parkin, C. H., 1924
Paynter, E., 1938-39
Peebles, I. A. R., 1927-8, 1930-31
Perks, R. T. D., 1938-39
Pope, G., 1947
Pougher, A. D., 1891-2

Read, H. D., 1935
Read, J. M., 1888-9
Read, W. W., 1891-2
Relf, A. E., 1905-6, 1913-14
Rhodes, W., 1909-10, 1912, 1913-14
Robertson, J. D., 1947
Robins, R. W. V., 1929, 1935
Russell, A. C., 1922-3

Sandham, A., 1922-3, 1924
Shackleton, D., 1951
Simpson-Hayward, G. H., 1909-10
Simpson, R. T., 1948-49, 1951
Sims, J. M., 1935
Smith, C. A., 1888-9
Smith, D., 1935
Smith, E. J., 1912, 1913-14
Spooner, R. H., 1912
Stanyforth, R. T., 1927-28
Staples, S. J., 1927-28
Statham, B., 1951
Stevens, G. T. S., 1922-3, 1927-8
Street, G. B., 1922-3
Strudwick, H., 1909-10, 1913-14, 1924
Sutcliffe, H., 1924, 1927-8, 1929, 1935

Tate, M. W., 1924, 1929, 1930-31, 1935
Tattersall, R., 1951
Tennyson, Hon. L. H., 1913-14
Thompson, G. J., 1909-10
Trott, A. E., 1898-9
Tufnell, N. C., 1909-10
Turnbull, M. J., 1930-31
Tyldesley, E., 1924, 1927-8
Tyldesley, J. T., 1898-9, 1907
Tyldesley, R., 1924
Tyler, E. J., 1895-6

Ulyett, G., 1888-9

Valentine, B. H., 1938-39
Verity, H., 1935, 1938-39
Voce, W., 1930-31

Wardle, J. H., 1951
Warner, P. F., 1898-9, 1905-6, 1912
Washbrook, C., 1947, 1948-49

ENGLAND v. SOUTH AFRICA—Continued

Watkins, A., 1948-49
Watson, W., 1951
White, J. C., 1929, 1930-31
Wilkinson, L. L., 1938-39
Wilson, C. E. M., 1898-9
Wood, G. E. C., 1924
Wood, H., 1888-9, 1891-2
Woods, S. M. J., 1895-6
Woolley, F. E., 1909-10, 1912, 1913-14, 1922-3, 1924, 1929
Wright, C. W., 1895-6
Wright, D. V. P., 1938-39, 1947, 1948-49
Wyatt, R. E. S., 1927-8, 1929, 1930-31, 1935
Wynyard, E. G., 1905-6
Yardley, N. W. D., 1938-39, 1947
Young, J., 1947, 1948-49

ENGLAND v. INDIA

Allen, G. O., 1936
Ames, L. E. G., 1932

Bakewell, A. H., 1933-34
Barnett, C. J., 1933-34, 1936
Bedser, A. V., 1946, 1952
Bowes, W. E., 1932, 1946
Brown, F. R., 1932

Carr, D. B., 1951-2
Clark, E. C., 1933-34
Compton, D., 1946, 1952

Duckworth, G., 1936

Edrich, W. J., 1946
Elliott, H., 1933-34
Evans, T. G., 1946, 1952

Fagg, A., 1936
Fishlock, L. B., 1936, 1946

Gibb, P. A., 1946
Gimblett, H., 1936
Gover, A. R., 1936, 1946
Graveney, T. W., 1951-2, 1952

Hammond, W. R., 1932, 1936, 1946
Hardstaff, J., 1936, 1946
Hilton, M. J., 1951-2
Holmes, P., 1932
Howard, N. D., 1951-2
Hutton, L., 1946, 1952

Ikin, J. T., 1946, 1952

Jardine, D. R., 1932, 1933-34
Jenkins, R. O., 1952

Kenyon, D. J., 1951-2

Laker, J. C., 1952
Langridge, Jas., 1933-34, 1936, 1946
Leadbeater, E., 1951-2
Levett, W. H. V., 1933-34
Leyland, M., 1936
Lock, G. A. R., 1952
Lowson, F. A., 1951-2

May, P. B. H., 1952
Mitchell, A., 1933-34, 1936

Nichols, M. S., 1933-34

Paynter, E., 1932
Pollard, R., 1946
Poole, S. J., 1951-2

Ridgway, F., 1951-2
Robertson, J. D., 1951-2
Robins, R. W. V., 1932, 1936

Shackleton, D., 1951-2
Sheppard, D. S., 1952
Simpson, R. T., 1952
Sims, J., 1936
Smailes, T. F., 1946
Smith, T. P. B., 1946
Spooner, R. T., 1951-2
Statham, B., 1951-2
Sutcliffe, H., 1932

Tattersall, R., 1951-2
Townsend, L., 1933-34
Trueman, F. S., 1952
Turnbull, M. J., 1936

Valentine, B. H., 1933-34
Verity, H., 1933-34, 1936
Voce, W., 1932, 1936, 1946

Walters, C. F., 1933-34
Washbrook, C., 1946
Watkins, A. J., 1951-2, 1952
Watson, W., 1952
Woolley, F. E., 1932
Worthington, T. S., 1936
Wright, D. V. P., 1946
Wyatt, R. E. S., 1936

SEASON'S ARRANGEMENTS

Decisions reached at the Advisory County Cricket Board meeting at Lord's in November included:—Test Trial, 1953: To be staged at Edgbaston, Birmingham, starting May 27. Continued experimental rule permitting declarations at any time in county games. Recommended: Six points a-side in tied championship games. Unchanged: Lbw law.

SANDHAM, STRUDWICK & GOVER

AND

EAST HILL INDOOR CRICKET SCHOOL AND SPORTS CLUB

172, EAST HILL, WANDSWORTH, S.W.18

Phone : VANDYKE 1796

OPEN DAILY 10 a.m. to 11 p.m.
SUNDAYS 9 a.m. to 10 p.m.

Four full-size Nets with ample run-up for Bowlers and the latest form of Shadowless Lighting. Pitches made to conform to outdoor play. Air Conditioning—Showers—Dressing Rooms —Lockers.

FEES :

Club Practice Net, 14/- per hour (with Coaching)
Private Lessons, 10/- ; or 12 for £6-0-0

The School is under the direction of ANDREW SANDHAM (Surrey and England XI and Official Coach to Surrey County Cricket Club) and ALFRED GOVER (Surrey and England XI).

ALL COACHES FIRST CLASS PLAYERS

BILLIARDS—LOUNGE (Fully Licensed)— SNACKS—AFTERNOON TEAS
SPORTS OUTFITTERS and RETAILERS

County Championship 1952

FINAL POSITIONS

	P.	W.	D.	L.	Tie	No Dec.	1st innings lead in match D.	1st innings lead in match L.	Pts.
Points awarded	—	12	—	—	8/4	—	4	4	—
Surrey (6)	28	20	5	3	0	0	4	0	256
Yorkshire (2)	28	17	8	2	0	1	5	0	224
Lancashire (3)	28	12	11	3	†1	1	8	1	188
Derbyshire (11)	28	11	9	8	0	0	6	2	164
Middlesex (7)	28	11	4	12	0	1	1	0	136
Leicestershire (15)	28	9	9	9	0	1	5	1	132
Glamorgan (5)	28	8	13	7	0	0	6	2	130
Northamptonshire (13)	28	7	12	8	0	1	8	3	128
Gloucestershire (12)	28	7	11	10	0	0	6	4	124
Essex (8)	28	8	13	4	1	2	4	1	120
Warwickshire (1)	28	8	8	10	†1	1	4	0	120
Hampshire (9)	28	7	9	11	0	1	3	4	112
Sussex (10)	28	7	6	12	1	2	2	0	96
Worcestershire (4)	28	6	10	11	0	1	3	1	90
Kent (16)	28	5	8	15	0	0	4	2	84
Nottinghamshire (17)	28	3	13	11	0	1	7	2	72
Somerset (14)	28	2	13	12	0	1	4	1	44

† Includes eight points for first innings lead in match tied.
Sussex and Essex records include four points for tie without first innings lead.
Glamorgan and Worcestershire records include two points for tie on first innings in match drawn.
Figures in parentheses indicate positions in the 1951 table.

Full List of Winners

(Since 1873, when the qualification of players came into operation)

1873 Notts and Glos
1874 Derbyshire
1875 Notts
1876-7 Gloucester
1878 Middlesex
1879 Notts and Lancs
1880 Notts
1881 Lancashire
1882 Lancs and Notts
1883-4-5-6 Notts
1887-8 Surrey
1889 Surrey, Notts and Lancashire
1890-1-2 Surrey
1893 Yorkshire
1894-5 Surrey
1896 Yorkshire
1897 Lancashire
1898 Yorkshire
1899 Surrey
1900-1-2 Yorkshire
1903 Middlesex
1904 Lancashire
1905 Yorkshire
1906 Kent
1907 Notts
1908 Yorkshire
1909-10 Kent
1911 Warwickshire
1912 Yorkshire
1913 Kent
1914 Surrey
1915-18 No Contests
1919 Yorkshire
1920-1 Middlesex
1922-3-4-5 Yorkshire
1926-7-8 Lancashire
1929 Notts
1930 Lancashire
1931-2-3 Yorkshire
1934 Lancashire
1935 Yorkshire
1936 Derbyshire
1937-8-9 Yorkshire
1940-45 No Contests
1946 Yorkshire
1947 Middlesex
1948 Glamorgan
1949 Middlesex and Yorkshire
1950 Lancashire and Surrey
1951 Warwickshire
1952 Surrey

SURREY

BATTING	No. of inns.	Total runs	Highest score	Not out	Avge.
P. B. H. May	14	804	197	3	73.09
Fletcher	45	1674	142	2	38.93
Brazier	5	191	78	0	38.20
Constable	46	1482	205*	6	37.05
Bedser (E. A.)	48	1541	116	4	35.02
Parker	37	1109	113	4	33.60
Clark	45	1184	92	9	32.88
Fishlock	35	953	102*	3	29.78
Whittaker	26	553	68*	2	23.04
McIntyre	39	623	81	7	19.46
W. S. Surridge	31	489	59	3	17.46
Lock	21	139	24*	12	15.44
P. J. Loader	7	30	19*	5	15.00
Laker	22	190	23	3	10.00
Bedser (A. V.)	21	119	20	7	8.50
Cox	10	39	13	3	5.57
McMahon	5	3	3*	3	1.50

BOWLING	Overs	Maidens	Runs	Wickets	Avge.
Bedser (A. V.)	739.1	173	1583	102	15.51
Lock	942.1	351	1918	116	16.53
Laker	730.2	247	1451	86	16.87
Bedser (E. A.)	632.4	204	1335	56	23.83
P. J. Loader	156.3	37	409	16	25.56
W. S. Surridge	681.1	147	1762	68	25.91
Clark	112.4	32	273	9	30.33
Cox	177.0	34	461	13	35.46
McMahon	90.0	19	303	7	43.28
Constable	29.0	6	96	2	48.00

YORKSHIRE

BATTING	No. of inns.	Total runs	Highest score	Not out	Avge.
Hutton	26	1482	189	1	59.28
Watson	32	1305	114	8	54.37
Lester	33	1432	178	5	51.14
W. H. H. Sutcliffe	29	952	181	6	41.39
Lowson	37	1274	155	3	37.47
Wilson	32	1095	230	2	36.50
Close	35	978	87*	8	36.22
Booth	4	66	30	2	33.00
Halliday	35	1058	118	2	32.06
N. W. D. Yardley	28	564	77	4	23.50
Wardle	33	503	50	8	20.12
G. Cawthray	3	57	30	0	19.00
Illingworth	3	38	17*	1	19.00
Burgin	6	76	32	1	15.20
D. V. Brennan	24	191	27*	10	13.64
Leadbeater	8	44	18*	3	8.80
P. B. Brayshay	3	20	13	0	6.66
Holdsworth	9	22	7*	5	5.50
Wood	5	25	17	0	5.00
Foord	4	9	5	2	4.50

BOWLING	Overs	Maidens	Runs	Wickets	Avge.
Trueman	162.4	32	455	32	14.21
Wardle	1522.2	686	2707	158	17.13
Wood	176.1	76	384	18	21.33
Halliday	405.1	137	907	41	22.12
Burgin	241.0	65	540	24	22.50
Close	953.0	283	2356	98	24.04
Foord	213.0	50	534	21	25.42

YORKSHIRE—Continued

BOWLING.	Overs	Maidens	Runs	Wickets	Avge.
N. W. D. Yardley	357.1	105	795	31	25.64
Illingworth	57.0	14	121	4	30.25
Leadbeater	145.0	39	405	13	31.15
Holdsworth	201.0	50	487	15	32.46
P. B. Brayshay	32.0	4	104	3	34.66
Padgett	38.0	6	98	2	49.00
G. Cawthray	69.0	21	165	3	55.00

LANCASHIRE

BATTING	No. of inns.	Total runs	Highest score	Not out	Avge.
Ikin	35	1638	154	4	52.83
Grieves	36	1198	145*	7	41.31
Place	33	1208	133	3	40.26
Edrich	44	1627	162	2	38.73
Washbrook	37	1185	211*	4	35.90
Wharton	33	875	85	3	29.16
N. D. Howard	34	663	138*	5	22.86
Hilton (J.)	3	54	33	0	18.00
Tattersall	25	195	40	14	17.72
Lomax	33	572	78	0	17.33
P. Marner	3	47	30	0	16.33
Parr	15	182	42	3	15.16
Smith	6	85	40	0	14.16
Hilton (M. J.)	24	260	48*	5	13.68
Statham	30	255	54*	10	12.75
Berry	9	31	21*	6	10.33
Greenwood	7	61	15	1	10.16
Wilson	14	41	13*	6	5.12

BOWLING	Overs	Maidens	Runs	Wickets	Avge.
Tattersall	1019.4	361	2261	130	17.39
Statham	797.5	166	1799	100	17.99
Hilton (M. J.)	682.1	249	1450	65	22.30
Lomax	484.0	120	1068	43	24.83
Berry	452.3	187	893	34	26.26
Wharton	257.2	43	697	24	29.04
C. S. Smith	34.0	7	118	4	29.50
Ikin	358.3	101	820	27	30.37
Grieves	233.4	83	556	13	42.76
Greenwood	60.0	13	192	4	48.00
Hilton (J.)	24.0	6	58	0	—

DERBYSHIRE

BATTING	No. of inns.	Total runs	Highest score	Not out	Avge.
Elliott	46	1569	168	2	35.65
G. L. Willatt	42	1354	146	2	33.85
Revill	50	1431	101	4	31.10
Hamer	50	1377	165	0	27.54
Morgan	47	854	73	9	22.47
D. B. Carr	39	792	116	3	22.00
R. Sale	11	196	47	1	19.60
Kelly	31	557	93	1	18.56
Dawkes	48	551	55*	15	16.69
Rhodes	42	646	60	2	16.15
Gladwin	41	446	53*	10	14.38
Richardson	3	21	9	1	10.50
T. A. Hall	3	17	9	1	8.50
Jackson	33	168	32	5	6.00
Smith (E.)	13	23	11	8	4.60

DERBYSHIRE—Continued

BOWLING	Overs	Maidens	Runs	Wickets	Avge.
Jackson	828.4	205	1988	108	18.40
Gladwin	1220.2	398	2802	151	18.55
Morgan	583.2	119	1608	67	24.00
Rhodes	765.5	235	2025	81	25.00
Smith	285.0	85	747	26	28.73
T. A. Hall	19.0	4	66	2	33.00
D. B. Carr	95.1	26	321	8	40.12
Hamer	115.2	21	309	6	51.50

MIDDLESEX

BATTING	No. of inns.	Total runs	Highest score	Not out	Avge.
Compton (D.)	41	1439	130	2	36.89
W. J. Edrich	50	1689	175*	4	36.71
Robertson	52	1750	162	2	35.00
Thompson	39	1019	158	1	26.81
Brown	53	1190	123	3	23.80
Sharp	22	459	110*	1	21.85
Murray	13	127	59*	7	21.16
W. Knightley-Smith	41	814	64	2	20.87
M. P. Murray	4	52	23	1	17.33
Sims	29	376	52	6	16.34
Compton (L.)	34	550	91	0	16.17
Bennett	37	472	56	5	14.75
J. J. Warr	24	167	30*	9	11.13
Routledge	13	122	31	2	11.09
Titmus	6	47	28	1	9.40
Young	37	252	32	7	8.40
Moss	38	50	12	18	2.50

BOWLING	Overs	Maidens	Runs	Wickets	Avge.
Young	1298.0	474	2805	137	20.47
Titmus	33.2	9	88	4	22.00
Moss	792.1	153	2108	88	23.95
Bennett	315.5	70	844	33	25.57
Compton (D.)	590.1	85	1916	74	25.89
W. J. Edrich	406.0	79	1163	41	28.36
J. J. Warr	326.2	69	866	28	30.92
Sims	262.2	35	856	17	50.35
Routledge	22.0	5	51	1	51.00
Sharp	18.0	4	58	1	58.00
Robertson	61.0	14	182	3	60.66
Brown	5.0	0	19	0	—
W. Knightley-Smith	5.5	0	72	0	—

LEICESTERSHIRE

BATTING	No. of inns.	Total runs	Highest score	Not out	Avge.
C. H. Palmer	45	1819	123	4	44.36
Tompkin, M.	37	1577	156	1	43.80
Munden, V.	44	1220	103	6	32.10
Jackson, V. E.	42	1239	142	3	31.76
Smithson, G. A.	47	1264	111*	2	28.08
Walsh, J. E.	42	991	102	1	24.17
Lester, G.	48	905	88*	5	21.04
Firth, J.	40	499	51	14	19.19
Saunders, P. F.	10	82	30	4	13.66
Hallam, M.	21	255	33	0	12.14
Sargent, M. A. J.	18	178	29	3	11.86
Spence, L.	16	156	44	2	11.14
Sperry, J.	3	22	20*	1	11.00
Spencer, T.	35	243	34	8	9.00
Goodwin, J.	26	37	10*	13	2.84

LEICESTERSHIRE—Continued

BOWLING	Overs	Maidens	Runs	Wickets	Avge.
Jackson, V. E	784.3	317	1763	81	21.76
C. H. Palmer	444.5	199	768	32	24.00
Walsh, J. E	854.1	184	2737	112	24.43
Goodwin, J	624.0	128	1841	64	28.76
Munden, V	479.5	178	1076	37	29.08
Spencer, T	800.3	159	2365	76	31.11
Saunders, P. F	73.0	18	190	6	31.66
Sperry, J	76.0	22	164	5	32.80
Lester, G	87.1	17	290	3	96.66

GLAMORGAN

BATTING	No. of inns.	Total runs	Highest score	Not out	Avge.
Watkins, A. J	39	1081	107	9	36.03
Davies, E	50	1626	97	1	33.18
Parkhouse, W. G. A	50	1317	99*	5	29.26
Muncer, B. L	46	1058	135	4	25.19
Montgomery, S. W	5	15	59	0	23.00
Clift, P. B	48	1048	100	2	22.78
Jones, W. E	37	782	94	2	22.34
Hedges, B	26	429	54	2	17.87
Pleass, J	22	374	51	1	17.80
McConnon, J. F	6	83	63	1	16.60

BOWLING	Overs	Maidens	Runs	Wickets	Avge.
Montgomery, S. W	33.0	10	88	5	17.60
Muncer, B. L	816.2	249	1693	96	17.63
Watkins, A. J	649.1	157	1601	81	19.76
Shepherd, D. J	823.4	176	2209	101	21.87
Hever, N. G	584.2	153	1382	61	22.65
McConnon, J. E	124.3	28	323	13	24.84
W. Wooller	698.4	175	1862	65	28.64

NORTHAMPTONSHIRE

BATTING	No. of inns.	Total runs	Highest score	Not out	Avge.
Brookes	48	1991	204*	6	47.40
Livingston	23	834	127	2	39.71
Barrick	47	1540	211	6	37.56
Oldfield	34	1050	129*	3	33.87
Davis	9	243	108	1	30.37
F. R. Brown	37	1006	145	3	29.58
Jakeman	28	796	77	1	29.48
Tribe	45	969	78	12	29.36
Reynolds	3	56	23	1	28.00
Greasley	24	613	98	1	26.65
Broderick	41	1038	115	1	25.95
Clarke	30	368	50	10	18.40
Arnold	3	55	27	0	18.33
Davis	14	175	37	3	15.90
Fiddling	11	66	11*	6	13.20
Nutter	37	356	62	9	12.71
Starkie	24	167	34*	7	9.82

BOWLING	Overs	Maidens	Runs	Wickets	Avge.
F. R. Brown	911.3	224	2182	88	24.79
Tribe	1150.5	230	2954	116	25.46
Nutter	844.5	214	1896	62	30.58
Barrick	82.0	18	217	7	31.00
Broderick	139.3	36	352	11	32.00
Starkie	480.4	123	1123	35	32.08
Clarke	822.1	154	2354	61	38.59
Greasley	25.5	2	118	3	39.33
Brice	38.0	2	184	1	184.00

Also bowled :—Jakeman, 7—0—23—0.

GLOUCESTERSHIRE

BATTING	No. of inns.	Total runs	Highest score	Not out	Avge.
Milton	51	1881	146*	9	44.78
Graveney	33	1285	171	4	44.31
Crapp	52	1607	110	8	36.52
Young	53	1774	125	2	34.78
Emmett	48	1604	120	0	33.41
Wilson	43	939	90	12	30.29
Sir D. Bailey	37	809	82	4	24.51
Scott	37	473	71	10	17.51
Wells	8	53	23	4	13.25
Goddard	11	110	19	2	12.22
Lambert	33	358	42	2	11.54
C. Monks	4	30	10	0	7.50
Mortimore	5	27	10*	1	6.75
J. N. Mitchell	6	39	12	0	6.50
Hawkins	9	42	17*	1	5.25
Cook	28	89	26	10	4.94
McHugh	10	18	6	3	2.57
Griffiths	5	5	2	0	1.00

BOWLING	Overs	Maidens	Runs	Wickets	Avge.
Mortimore	68.0	21	132	7	18.85
Lambert	865.2	152	2399	105	22.84
Goddard	424.2	113	1063	45	23.62
Cook	1036.3	349	2191	89	24.61
Scott	1039.1	218	2460	98	25.10
Wells	246.1	72	632	24	26.33
Graveney	57.5	6	207	6	34.50
McHugh	239.3	26	869	25	34.76
Sir D. Bailey	96.0	20	254	6	42.33
Griffiths	28.0	4	97	2	48.50
Milton	281.0	68	743	13	57.15
Hawkins	15.0	4	50	0	—

ESSEX

BATTING	No. of inns.	Total runs	Highest score	Not out	Avge.
Avery	35	1396	224	4	54.03
D. J. Insole	42	1502	130	2	37.55
T. E. Bailey	38	1115	155*	7	35.96
Dodds	44	1565	150	0	35.56
Horsfall	45	1369	143	4	33.39
Gibb	47	1316	132	2	29.24
Smith (R.)	43	937	107*	6	25.32
Greensmith	34	488	79	14	24.40
C. Griffiths	23	459	105	3	22.95
Vigar	39	523	63*	15	21.79
Preston	30	283	56*	12	15.72
Stanley	8	99	23	1	14.14
C. J. M. Kenny	9	7	4*	5	1.75

Also batted :—A. B. Quick, 1 and 57 ; Rist, 18 and 10.

BOWLING	Overs	Maidens	Runs	Wickets	Avge.
Smith (R.)	1279.4	282	3510	124	28.30
Vigar	139.1	18	526	18	29.22
C. J. M. Kenny	332.0	66	980	32	30.62
T. E. Bailey	865.3	207	2202	71	31.01
Preston	808.4	150	2308	74	31.18
Greensmith	622.1	192	1595	49	32.55
D. J. Insole	163.0	32	586	10	58.60

Also bowled :—Avery, 4—0—17—0 ; Dodds, 3—1—11—1 ; C. Griffiths, 3—0—22—0 ; Horsfall, 2—0—4—0 ; A. B. Quick, 1.5—0—10—0; Rist, 4.1—2—8—1 ; Stanley, 0.3—0—8—0.

WARWICKSHIRE

BATTING	No. of inns.	Total runs	Highest score	Not out	Avge.
Dollery	50	2036	212	2	42.41
Gardner	52	1630	184*	6	35.43
Spooner	50	1320	117	5	29.33
Hitchcock	26	673	93	2	28.04
Townsend	45	894	65*	8	24.16
Bromley	20	368	121*	4	23.00
Ord	38	756	91	2	21.00
J. R. Thompson	10	193	69	0	19.30
Taylor	18	276	54*	2	17.25
Wolton	21	310	50*	2	16.31
Horner	28	338	54	1	15.65
Pritchard	30	391	76	0	13.03
Grove	42	392	38	4	10.31
M. Robinson	7	72	22	0	10.28
Weeks	29	164	25*	8	7.80
Bannister	12	54	16	2	5.40
I. King	3	16	10	0	5.33
Hollies	37	70	17	18	3.68
Thompson	3	7	4	1	3.50

Also batted :—E. B. Lewis, 9 and 2 ; Cartwright (T. W.), 82 and 22*.

BOWLING	Overs	Maidens	Runs	Wickets	Avge.
Thompson	54.1	12	152	11	13.81
Grove	910.3	224	1977	113	17.49
Townsend	450.2	90	1178	60	19.63
Hollies	1134.4	435	2393	118	20.27
Bannister	210.5	51	587	28	20.96
Bromley	87.0	22	286	11	26.00
Weeks	574.4	242	1159	37	31.32
Pritchard	535.3	105	1514	46	32.91
Wolton	41.0	12	101	1	101.00
I. King	21.0	10	46	0	—
Gardner	3.4	0	21	0	—

Also bowled :—Ord, 1—0—4—0.

HAMPSHIRE

BATTING	No. of inns.	Total runs	Highest score	Not out	Avge.
Rogers	51	2014	119	3	41.95
Gray	50	1574	139	2	32.79
J. R. Bridger	11	292	92	1	29.20
Harrison	45	1187	153	3	28.26
A. C. D. Ingleby-MacKenzie	10	260	57	0	26.00
Rayment	45	994	106	2	23.11
E. D. R. Eager	46	945	104	2	21.47
D. E. Blake	17	283	52	2	18.86
Walker	18	317	54*	1	18.64
Cannings	37	383	43*	15	17.40
Dare	46	592	109*	11	16.91
Hill	37	547	83	4	16.57
Shackleton	39	498	29	4	14.17
Carty	14	114	36	5	12.66
Prouton	39	335	51*	9	11.16
C. J. Knott	7	18	9*	4	6.00

Also batted :—Barnard 4 and 0 ; Jewel 0 and 1.

HAMPSHIRE—Continued

BOWLING	Overs	Maidens	Runs	Wickets	Avge.
Shackleton	1037.1	312	2243	119	18.84
Cannings	933.5	265	2224	106	20.98
C. J. Knott	180.3	52	464	17	27.28
Hill	341.1	61	953	33	28.87
Gray	542.1	113	1517	48	31.60
Dare	724.2	256	1833	54	33.94
Carty	207.4	43	657	19	34.57
E. D. R. Eagar	47.2	4	218	2	109.00
Walker	53.0	14	155	1	155.00

Also bowled :—Bailey (J.), 30—9—64—3 ; Barnard, 3—0—12—0 ; J. R. Bridger, 0.2—0—4—0 ; Harrison, 7—0—47—0 ; Jewel, 11-1-52-1 ; Rayment 11.3—1—54—0.

SUSSEX

BATTING	No. of inns.	Total runs	Highest score	Not out	Avge.
D. S. Sheppard	10	453	140	1	50.33
G. H. G. Doggart	13	519	135	1	43.25
Suttle	33	880	114*	9	36.66
Langridge (John)	52	1633	135	3	33.32
Cox	40	1292	128	0	32.30
Langridge (Jas.)	44	1049	109	8	29.13
Oakman	45	1188	99	3	28.28
Parks	28	719	138	2	27.65
Oakes	38	711	76*	1	19.21
Smith (D. V.)	27	413	49	0	15.29
James	37	318	47*	11	12.24
N. I. Thomson	24	253	43	2	11.50
Webb	35	304	36	6	10.48
R. G. Marlar	16	144	32	2	10.28
Wood	37	167	20	11	6.42
S. C. Griffith	7	34	19	0	4.85
Cornford	25	67	10	5	3.35
C. E. Winn	4	8	5	0	2.00

Also batted :—Lawrence, 0 and 0 ; P. A. Kelland, 11 and 5*.

BOWLING	Overs	Maidens	Runs	Wickets	Avge.
R. G. Marlar	333.5	98	845	55	15.36
Oakes	179.5	23	596	31	19.22
Wood	853.4	201	2308	93	24.81
Cornford	464.3	92	1173	46	25.50
Oakman	582.4	145	1650	62	26.61
N. I. Thomson	400.4	83	1061	35	30.31
James	814.5	244	2078	63	32.98
Langridge (Jas.)	9.0	1	33	1	33.00
Parks	8.5	0	34	1	34.00
Cox	81.2	20	235	6	39.16
Smith (D. V.)	25.0	6	70	1	70.00

Also bowled :—G. H. G. Doggart, 1—0—6—0 ; P. A. Kelland, 26—6—80—0 ; Langridge (John), 1—1—0—0.

WORCESTERSHIRE

BATTING	No. of inns.	Total runs	Highest score	Not out	Avge.
Kenyon	50	1978	171	2	41.20
P. J. Whitcombe	8	229	89*	2	38.16
R. E. Bird	42	1453	158*	3	37.25
Broadbent	44	1394	133	2	33.19
P. E. Richardson	49	1387	102	5	31.52
Dews	25	745	104	1	31.04
Outschoorn	45	1195	103	3	28.45
Jenkins	38	808	54*	3	23.08
Devereux	29	402	40*	4	16.08
Perks	39	465	41*	6	14.09
Yarnold	35	336	47*	7	12.00
Scholey	3	23	16	1	11.50

WORCESTERSHIRE—Continued

BATTING.	No. of inns.	Total runs	Highest score	Not out	Avge.
Whiting	12	113	32	2	11.30
Horton	25	216	37*	2	9.39
Flavell	5	15	9*	3	7.50
K. Lobban	7	18	7	4	6.00
G. H. Chesterton	7	22	9	3	5.50
G. Wilson	14	10	4*	6	1.25
Bradley	5	2	2*	5	—

BOWLING	Overs	Maidens	Runs	Wickets	Avge.
K. Lobban	148.4	23	545	23	23.69
Jenkins	844.5	136	2751	110	25.00
Perks	965.1	199	2752	104	26.46
G. H. Chesterton	214.5	55	636	20	31.80
Horton	361.0	96	1118	25	44.72
Devereux	300.5	55	994	22	45.18
Bradley	112.3	22	364	8	45.50
R. E. Bird	64.5	9	253	5	50.60
Flavell	109.3	7	261	5	52.20
G. Wilson	209.0	28	851	16	53.18
Outschoorn	44.0	9	148	2	74.00
Broadbent	46.0	6	185	2	92.50

Also bowled:—T. W. Larkin, 18—3—64—1; Whiting (N. W.), 15—4—49—0.

KENT

BATTING	No. of inns.	Total runs	Highest score	Not out	Avge.
A. C. Shireff	12	396	87*	2	39.60
Ufton	16	470	110*	2	33.57
Fagg	44	1442	143	1	33.53
Edrich (B. R.)	29	816	110	3	31.38
Hearn	27	751	85	3	31.29
Evans	39	1185	144	0	30.38
M. C. Cowdrey	17	455	95	1	28.43
O'Linn	39	913	111*	3	25.36
Phebey	40	964	83	1	24.71
Mayes	38	889	134	2	24.69
M. D. Fenner	3	73	41	0	24.33
Woollett	14	303	84	1	23.30
Wilson	6	104	52	1	20.80
J. W. Martin	10	100	24*	4	16.66
W. Murray-Wood	51	567	107	3	11.81
Dovey	50	463	40	6	10.52
Ridgway	25	184	28	4	8.76
Wright	44	297	39	10	8.73
G. Smith	7	47	10	1	7.83
Page	26	91	13*	14	7.58
Hellmuth	11	26	11	1	2.60

BOWLING	Overs	Maidens	Runs	Wickets	Avge.
J. W. Martin	186.1	42	484	21	23.04
Dovey	1020.0	285	2608	95	27.45
Wright	916.4	173	3075	111	27.70
A. C. Shireff	210.4	47	655	22	29.77
Ridgway	402.0	79	1123	37	30.35
Page	478.2	60	1725	56	30.80
G. Smith	148.0	32	466	14	33.28
W. Murray-Wood	103.3	10	349	10	34.90
Hellmuth	124.4	38	297	7	42.42
C. Cowdrey	46.0	4	173	4	43.25
Hearn	12.2	0	53	1	53.00
Edrich (B. R.)	81.5	8	311	5	62.20

Also bowled:—Evans, 6—1—19—0; Mayes, 3—0—20—0; O'Linn, 3—0—12—0.

NOTTINGHAMSHIRE

BATTING	No. of inns.	Total runs	Highest score	Not out	Avge.
R. T. Simpson	36	1674	216	1	47.82
Hardstaff	38	1543	144*	5	46.75
Poole	42	1410	219	3	36.15
Giles	35	1068	126	1	31.41
Stocks	44	1315	122	2	31.30
Martin	30	733	122	2	26.17
Clay	41	1063	192	0	25.92
Smales	21	273	37	6	18.20
Harvey	36	457	62	5	14.74
Jepson	35	376	85	2	11.39
Matthews	19	97	31	9	9.75
Butler	36	254	33	8	9.07
A. G. Baxter	4	31	22	0	7.75
Meads	36	177	21	13	7.69
Birtle	6	10	4*	2	2.50

Also batted :—Keeton, 5 and 0 ; Voce, 5.

BOWLING	Overs	Maidens	Runs	Wickets	Avge.
Butler	753.4	172	1819	74	24.58
Jepson	719.4	168	1900	52	36.53
Harvey	675.2	182	1728	45	38.40
Stocks	638.3	182	1671	41	40.75
R. T. Simpson	126.2	37	412	10	41.20
Matthews	299.0	64	867	19	45.63
Smales	460.3	128	1259	26	48.42
Hardstaff	65.4	25	177	3	59.00
Birtle	174.4	37	503	7	71.85

Also bowled :—A. G. Baxter, 1—0—8—0 ; Clay, 8.4—4—20—0 ; Giles, 1—0—5—0 ; Poole, 8—2—35—0 ; Voce, 27—11—53—1.

SOMERSET

BATTING	No. of inns.	Total runs	Highest score	Not out	Avge.
Gimblett	53	2068	169	1	39.76
G. G. Tordoff	20	636	101*	1	33.47
Tremlett	52	1481	100	4	30.85
Buse	47	945	102	8	24.23
Lawrence	46	774	111	12	22.76
H. E. Watts	13	295	93	0	22.69
Stephenson	47	951	114	0	20.23
Angell	29	541	90	0	18.65
S. S. Rogers	48	841	102*	2	18.28
Smith	28	413	58	4	17.20
Brocklehurst	10	160	40	0	16.00
M. M. Walford	14	194	61	1	14.92
Redman	26	270	29	6	13.50
Kitson	15	177	33	1	12.64
Robinson	39	237	29	8	7.64
Hazell	30	97	14	16	6.92
C. G. Mitchell	6	7	6*	4	3.50

Also batted :—J. Baker, 1* ; Harris, 18.

BOWLING	Overs	Maidens	Runs	Wickets	Avge.
Hazell	632.0	232	1341	63	21.28
Smith	127.0	32	320	14	22.85
Tremlett	184.0	28	578	19	30.42
Robinson	900.4	250	2139	70	30.55
Lawrence	808.2	150	2267	73	31.05
Buse	642.5	157	1685	54	31.20
Redman	358.1	62	1167	33	35.36
G. G. Tordoff	167.5	20	531	11	48.27
C. G. Mitchell	93.0	12	292	5	58.40

Also bowled :—Angell, 3—0—10—0 ; Baker, 17—4—40—0 ; Gimblett, 8—2—18—0 ; Harris, 21—3—60—0 ; S. S. Rogers, 9.5—0—54—0 ; M. M. Walford, 11—1—34—1 ; H. E. Watts, 3—0—8—0.

Leading First-Class Averages, 1952

BATTING

(Qualifications : 8 innings, average 25)

	No. of inns.	Total runs	Highest score	Not out	Avge.
D. S. Sheppard	39	2262	239*	4	64.62
P. B. H. May	47	2498	197	7	62.45
Hutton, L.	45	2567	189	3	61.11
Lester, E.	42	1786	178	6	49.61
Watson, W.	43	1651	114	9	48.55
Graveney, T. W	50	2066	171	7	48.04
Brookes, D.	54	2229	204*	7	47.42
Hardstaff, J	39	1597	144	5	46.97
Ikin, J. T.	46	1912	154	4	45.52
Milton, C. A.	55	1922	146*	11	43.68
Kenyon, D	60	2489	171	2	42.91
Place, W.	39	1483	133	4	42.37
Dollery, H. E.	51	2073	212	2	43.20
R. T. Simpson	54	2222	216	1	41.92
Tompkin, M.	46	1875	156	1	41.66
Edrich, G. A.	53	2067	162	3	41.34
R. Subba Row	19	661	94	3	41.31
Avery, A. V.	39	1441	224	4	41.17
Rogers, N. H.	58	2244	164	3	40.80
Washbrook, C.	43	1531	211*	5	40.28
C. H. Palmer	56	2071	127	4	39.82
Gimblett, H.	55	2134	169	1	39.51
W. H. H. Sutcliffe	31	987	181	6	39.48
Compton, D. C. S.	54	1880	132	6	39.16
W. J. Edrich	63	2281	239	4	38.66
Poole, C. J.	48	1700	222*	4	38.63
Fletcher, D. G. W.	55	1860	142	3	37.69
Robertson, J. D.	64	2337	162	2	37.69
Grieves, K.	42	1273	145*	8	37.44
Barrick, D.	48	1570	211	6	37.38
Gardner, F. C.	55	1826	184*	6	37.26
Langridge, John	60	2082	140	4	37.17
Cox, G.	46	1667	128	1	37.04
R. E. Bird	47	1591	158*	4	37.00
Livingston, L.	26	887	127	2	36.95
T. E. Bailey	56	1513	155*	15	36.90
Constable, B.	53	1726	205*	6	36.72
Crapp, J. F.	52	1607	110	8	36.52
Halliday, H.	44	1448	126*	4	36.20
Clark, T. H.	49	1410	137*	10	36.15
A. C. Shireff	15	469	87*	2	36.07
D. J. Insole	53	1816	130	2	35.60
Young, D. M.	57	1956	125	2	35.56
G. L. Willatt	48	1624	146	2	35.30
Bedser, E. A.	54	1723	116	5	35.16
Wilson, J. V.	45	1501	230	2	34.90
B. Boobbyer	23	802	120	0	34.86
Elliott, C. S.	48	1599	168	2	34.76
Lowson, F. A.	48	1562	155	3	34.71
Dodds, T. C.	52	1801	150	0	34.63
G. H. G. Doggart	17	549	135	1	34.31
Horsfall, R.	51	1560	143	5	33.91
Fagg, A. E.	46	1519	143	1	33.75

FIRST-CLASS AVERAGES—(*Continued*)

	No. of inns.	Total runs	Highest score	Not out	Avge.
Ufton, D. G.	16	470	119*	2	33.57
Suttle, K.	39	936	114*	11	33.42
Close, D. B.	45	1192	87*	9	33.11
M. C. Cowdrey	45	1391	101	3	33.11
Broadbent, R. G.	51	1556	133	4	33.10
J. E. Bush	13	395	67	1	32.91
Davies, E. (Glamorgan)	52	1678	97	1	32.90
Oldfield, N.	38	1149	129*	3	32.82
Gray, J. P.	52	1634	139	2	32.68
Parker, J. F.	41	1204	113	4	32.54
Watkins, A. J.	49	1267	107	10	32.48
F. C. M. Alexander	16	291	54	7	32.33
Emmett, G. M.	52	1680	120	0	32.30
Jakeman, F.	34	1000	119*	3	32.25
Outschoorn, L.	51	1504	120*	4	32.00
P. E. Richardson	52	1502	110	5	31.95
Stocks, F. W.	45	1362	122	2	31.67
G. G. Tordoff	39	1071	101*	5	31.50
Edrich, B. R.	29	816	110	3	31.38
Jackson, V. E.	44	1284	142	3	31.31
Parks, J. M.	35	930	138	5	31.00
Giles, R.	36	1083	126	1	30.94
Langridge, James	46	1128	109	9	30.48
Davis, E. (Northants)	9	243	108	1	30.37
Revill, A. C.	53	1471	101	4	30.02
Munden, V.	48	1259	103	6	29.97
Tremlett, M. F.	57	1586	100	4	29.92
Oakman, A. S.	51	1429	99	3	29.77
Tribe, G. E.	49	1039	78	14	29.68
Fishlock, L. B.	41	1126	102*	3	29.63
Ord, J. S.	42	1094	187*	5	29.56
A. C. D. Ingleby Mackenzie	12	353	91	0	29.41
Parkhouse, W. G. A.	56	1466	99*	6	29.32
Rev. J. R. Bridger	11	292	92	1	29.20
O'Linn, S.	41	1080	111*	4	29.18
Spooner, R. T.	57	1487	117	6	29.15
Wharton, A.	38	1017	85	3	29.05
Evans, T. G.	56	1613	144	0	28.80
F. R. Brown	42	1118	145	3	28.66
Wilson, A. E. (Gloucester)	45	940	90	12	28.48
Hamer, A.	52	1478	165	0	28.42
N. W. D. Yardley	37	852	93	7	28.40
Gibb, P. A.	56	1519	132	2	28.12
Hitchcock, R. E.	26	673	93	2	28.04
Dews, G. (Worcestershire)	31	838	104	1	27.93
W. G. E. Wiley	21	580	100	0	27.61
Smithson, G. A.	51	1351	111*	2	27.57
Harrison, L.	47	1191	153	3	27.06
Hearn, P.	31	753	85	3	26.89
Thompson, A.	44	1096	158	3	26.73
Greasley, D. G.	24	613	98	1	26.65
A. L. Dowding	19	506	69	0	26.63
P. J. Whitcombe	24	550	89*	3	26.19
Martin, E.	30	733	122	2	26.17
Whiting, N. H.	20	444	111	3	26.11
Broderick, V.	41	1038	115	1	25.95
Brown, S. M.	58	1408	123	3	25.60
Pheney, A. H.	42	1042	83	1	25.41
Clay, J. D.	42	1063	192	0	25.30
Lawrence, J.	48	885	111	13	25.29
R. H. Wollocombe	8	200	119	0	25.00

* Not out

BOWLING

(Qualification : 10 wickets)

	Overs	Maidens	Runs	Wickets	Avge.
Thompson, R. G.	82.5	14	229	18	12.72
Trueman, F. S.	282.2	57	841	61	13.78
W. Nichol	77.2	25	166	11	15.09
Shaw, G. B.	87.2	21	242	15	16.13
Bedser, A. V.	1185.4	296	2530	154	16.42
Lock, G. A. R.	1109.4	416	2237	131	17.07
Grove, C. W.	945.3	240	2022	118	17.13
Muncer, B. L.	862.2	259	1816	105	17.29
Townsend, A.	508.2	101	1310	74	17.70
Tattersall, R.	1165.5	409	2586	146	17.71
Laker, J. C.	1071.0	342	2219	125	17.75
Statham, J. B.	881.4	186	1989	110	18.08
Shackleton, D.	1147.1	351	2479	135	18.36
Jackson, L (Derbyshire)	917.5	233	2220	119	18.65
Wood, R. (Yorkshire)	234.0	96	511	27	18.92
Gladwin, C.	1258.2	402	2917	152	19.19
Wardle, J. H.	1857.2	810	3460	177	19.54
Young, J. A.	1440.1	514	3241	163	19.88
Hollies, W. E.	1146.4	438	2412	118	20.44
Bannister, J. D.	238.5	58	663	32	20.71
Oakes, C.	226.5	30	734	35	20.97
R. G. Marlar	880.2	256	2291	108	21.21
Hazell, H. L.	632.0	232	1341	63	21.28
Watkins, A. J.	772.1	195	1890	88	21.47
C. N. McCarthy	496.3	117	1097	51	21.50
Cannings, V. H. D.	989.0	275	2415	112	21.56
Bedser, E. A.	716.4	229	1530	70	21.85
Jackson, V. E. (Leicester)	797.3	319	1799	82	21.93
P. J. Loader	225.3	48	618	28	22.07
Goonesena, G.	91.1	18	288	13	22.15
Shepherd, D.	954.4	198	2675	120	22.29
Lambert, G. E.	952.0	174	2571	113	22.75
Hever, N. G.	606.2	159	1434	63	22.76
Smith, R. (Somerset)	127.0	32	320	14	22.85
Hilton, M. J.	790.1	286	1720	75	22.93
J. W. Martin	186.1	42	484	21	23.04
Morgan, D. C.	603.2	121	1662	71	23.40
Wells, B. D.	345.3	102	821	35	23.45
Moss, A. E.	850.2	170	2234	95	23.51
Cook, C.	1142.3	396	2378	101	23.54
Goddard, T. W.	424.2	113	1063	45	23.62
K. Lobban	148.4	23	545	23	23.69
C. H. Palmer	512.2	219	951	40	23.77
Close, D. B.	1107.4	330	2746	114	24.08
T. A. Hall	136.0	25	410	17	24.11
F. R. Brown	1006.0	239	2407	99	24.31
Wood, D. J (Sussex)	954.3	238	2530	103	24.56
Cox, D. F. (Surrey)	233.0	47	590	24	24.58
Scott, C. J.	1061.2	226	2499	101	24.74
Halliday, H.	468.1	145	1139	46	24.76
Graveney, T. W.	71.5	8	249	10	24.90
Rhodes, A. E. G.	779.5	239	2071	83	24.95
Burgin, E.	272.2	72	625	25	25.00
Butler, H. J.	780.4	183	1878	75	25.04
W. S. Surridge	770.1	165	1967	78	25.21
Tribe, G. E.	1230.3	234	3228	126	25.61
Jenkins, R. O.	1048.2	166	3489	136	25.65
Perks, R. T. D.	1020.1	208	2927	114	25.67
Bennett, D.	341.5	74	926	36	25.72
Walsh, J. E.	965.2	197	3157	122	25.87
C. S. Smith (Lancashire)	86.0	15	286	11	26.00
Foord, C. W.	251.0	62	599	23	26.04

Minor Counties' Championship

FINAL PLACINGS

	P.	W.	L.	1st Inns. W.	1st Inns. L.	No dec.	Pts.	Avge.
Buckinghamshire	10	6	0	3	1	0	70	7.00
Kent II	12	7	0	2	3	0	79	6.58
Surrey II	16	7	1	7	1	0	92	5.75
Berkshire	10	4	1	3	2	0	51	5.10
Lancashire II	14	6	0	1	6	1	71	5.07
Warwickshire II	10	3	*1	3	2	1	46	4.60
Middlesex II	12	3	†3	3	2	1	52	4.33
Staffordshire	10	3	2	3	1	1	42	4.20
Cambridgeshire	10	2	0	5	3	0	38	3.80
Durham	8	1	0	6	0	1	30	3.75
Hertfordshire	10	2	1	3	2	2	35	3.50
Yorkshire II	14	2	1	5	6	0	41	2.92
Northumberland	10	1	*3	4	2	0	27	2.70
Devon	10	1	1	4	4	0	26	2.60
Dorset	10	1	2	4	3	0	25	2.50
Suffolk	8	1	2	2	2	1	20	2.50
Oxfordshire	10	1	3	2	3	1	21	2.10
Norfolk	10	1	5	1	1	2	18	1.80
Bedfordshire	8	0	*2	2	3	1	14	1.75
Wiltshire	8	0	‡3	1	3	1	14	1.75
Lincolnshire	10	0	2	4	4	0	16	1.60
Essex II	12	1	5	1	4	1	19	1.58
Northants II	8	0	2	2	3	1	11	1.37
Hampshire II	8	0	3	2	2	1	10	1.25
Notts II	10	0	2	2	6	0	12	1.20
Cornwall	10	0	5	1	3	1	8	0.80
Cheshire	8	0	3	0	4	1	6	0.75

* 1st inns. pts. in one match ; † 1st inns. pts. in 3 matches ; ‡ 1st inns. pts. in 2 matches.

PREVIOUS WINNERS

Since 1895 the Minor Counties have arranged and played a Championship

1895 Norfolk
1896-7-8 Worcestershire
1899 Northamptonshire and Bucks
1900 Glamorganshire, Durham and N'hamptonshire
1901 Durham
1902 Wiltshire
1903-4 N'hamptonshire
1905 Norfolk
1906 Staffordshire
1907 Lancashire II
1908 Staffordshire
1909 Wiltshire
1910 Norfolk
1911 Staffordshire
1912 Norfolk
1913 Glamorganshire
1914 Staffordshire
1915-19 No Contests
1920 Staffordshire
1921 Staffordshire and Berkshire
1922-3 Buckingh'shire
1924 Berkshire
1925 Buckinghamshire
1926 Durham
1927 Staffordshire
1928 Berkshire
1929 Oxfordshire
1930 Durham
1931 Leicestershire II
1932 Buckinghamshire
1933 In abeyance
1934 Lancashire II
1935 Middlesex II
1936 Hertfordshire
1937 Lancashire II
1938 Buckinghamshire
1939 Surrey II
1940-45 No Contests
1946 Suffolk
1947 Yorkshire II
1948-49 Lancashire II
1950 Surrey II
1951 Kent II
1952 Buckinghamshire

In the challenge match, at High Wycombe, Buckinghamshire beat Kent II by 109 runs.

Minor Counties leaders in the last season pre-war (1939) were : 1, Surrey II; 2. Lancs II ; 3, Suffolk. There was no challenge match.

Minor County Secretaries

BEDFORDSHIRE: Frank Crompton, Shire Hall, Bedford.

BERKSHIRE: H. L. Lewis, c/o Huntley & Palmers, Ltd., Reading.

BUCKINGHAMSHIRE: H. Tyson-Chambers, J.P., "Caerleon," 28, London Road, Slough.

CAMBRIDGESHIRE: F. W. Wilkinson, M.A., M.M., "Charnwood," Cambridge Road, Ely.

CHESHIRE: Lewis Wilson, 50, Oxford Road, Bootle, Liverpool 20.

CORNWALL: Arthur Lugg, 28, Treliske Close, Truro.

DEVON: H. G. Cath, Kenilworth, Southfield Avenue, Paignton.

DORSET: C. J. P. C. Jowett, Dungiven, Sherborne.

DURHAM: J. Iley, "Kennington," 26, Long Acres, Durham City.

HERTFORDSHIRE: Major H. G. Lay, High Croft, Springfields, Broxbourne.

LINCOLNSHIRE: R. J. Charlton, Newton Hall, near Sleaford.

NORFOLK: Frank Inch, O.B.E., 37, St. Peter's Street, Norwich.

NORTHUMBERLAND: George H. Mallen, 223, Osborne Road, Newcastle-on-Tyne 2.

OXFORDSHIRE: L. B. Frewer, M.A., "Tal-y-Fan," Highfield Avenue, Oxford.

STAFFORDSHIRE: L. W. Hancock, 4, Kingsland Avenue, Oakhill, Stoke-on-Trent.

SUFFOLK: G. T. Barnard, 85, Constable Road, Ipswich.

WILTSHIRE: Reginald A. C. Forrester, B.A., 59, High Street, Malmesbury.

MINOR COUNTIES' CRICKET ASSOCIATION: Frank Crompton, High Knoll, Richmond Road, Bedford.

No More County Games For Saffrons Unless—

Eastbourne may lose county cricket at the Saffrons Ground after this summer unless the district provides more members for the Sussex county club.

Lt.-Col. G. S. Grimston the Sussex secretary, says: "We want 400 Eastbourne members by August, or we shall not continue fixtures there in 1954.

"At present we have about half that number from the district, and unless the support improves we may play more matches at our Hove headquarters, where there is plenty of enthusiasm for games during the holiday season."

Eastbourne cricket week this year is in August, when Nottinghamshire and Gloucestershire are the visitors.

Members of the Eastbourne Cricket and Football Club, whose ground is used, can go in without paying. They number about 1,600.

MINOR COUNTIES MATCHES

(Two days, unless otherwise stated)

MAY

6—The Oval, Surrey II v. Middlesex II.

13—Cricklewood, Middlesex II v. Northants II; Birmingham, Warwickshire II v. Lancashire II; Beckenham, Kent II v. Surrey II.

18—Manchester, Lancashire II v. Cheshire; Birmingham, Warwickshire II v. Northants II.

20—Newark, Notts II v. Northants II.

23—The Oval, Surrey II v. Kent II.

25—Scarborough—Yorkshire II v. Lancashire II; Newcastle, Northumberland v. Durham.

27—Wallasey, Cheshire v. Staffordshire; Ollerton, Notts II v. Lincolnshire.

JUNE

1—Rothwell, Northants II v. Warwickshire II.

3—Witham, Essex II v. Surrey II.

8—Bingley, Yorkshire II v. Cheshire; Wolverhampton, Staffordshire v. Durham.

10—Manchester, Lancashire II v. Warwickshire II; Wisbech, Cambridgeshire v. Northants II; Scunthorpe, Lincolnshire v. Yorkshire II; Gravesend, Kent II v. Essex II; Newcastle, Northumberland v. Cheshire.

13—Lord's, Middlesex II v. Surrey II.

17—Boston, Lincolnshire v. Notts II; Ely, Cambridgeshire v. Essex II.

22—Manchester, Lancashire II v. Lincolnshire; Newcastle, Northumberland v. Staffordshire; Woodford Wells, Essex II v. Kent II.

23—March—Cambridgeshire v. Bedfordshire.

24—Northampton, Northants II v. Notts II; Stockport, Cheshire v. Lancashire II; Newcastle, Northumberland v. Yorkshire II; Blackhill, Durham v. Staffordshire.

29—Doncaster, Yorkshire II v. Lincolnshire; The Oval, Surrey II v. Warwickshire II.

JULY

1—Newcastle, Northumberland v. Lancashire II; Harrogate, Yorkshire II v. Durham.

3—Penzance, Cornwall v. Devon.

8—Hertford, Hertfordshire v. Bedfordshire; Bury, Lancashire II v. Notts II; Dartford, Kent II v. Middlesex II; Bishop Auckland, Durham v. Yorkshire II; Sawston, Cambridgeshire v. Lincolnshire; Mistley, Essex II v. Norfolk.

13—Oxton, Cheshire v. Northumberland; Birmingham, Warwickshire II v. Surrey II.

15—Urmston, Lancashire II v. Northumberland; Teddington, Middlesex II v. Kent II; York, Yorkshire II v. Staffordshire.

20—Sleaford, Lincolnshire v. Lancashire II; Nottingham (Police Ground), Notts II v. Yorkshire II; Beddington, Surrey II v. Wiltshire.

22—Northampton, Northants II v. Cambridgeshire; Walthamstow, Essex II v. Middlesex II; Worksop, Notts II v. Lancashire II; Nantwich, Cheshire v. Yorkshire II; Birmingham, Warwickshire II v. Staffordshire; Broadstairs, Kent II v. Norfolk.

24—Plymouth, Devon v. Cornwall.

25—The Oval, Surrey II v. Essex II.

JULY—Continued

29—Luton, Bedfordshire v. Cambridgeshire; Sunderland, Durham v. Lancashire II; Knypersley, Staffordshire v. Warwickshire II; Camborne, Cornwall v. Berkshire; Norwich, Norfolk v. Buckinghamshire.

31—Trowbridge, Wiltshire v. Northants II; Liskeard, Cornwall v. Dorset; Exeter, Devon v. Berkshire.

AUGUST

3—Bedford School, Bedfordshire v. Lincolnshire; Manchester, Lancashire II v. Yorkshire II; Felixstowe, Suffolk v. Essex II; Chester-le-Street, Durham v. Northumberland; Seaton, Devon v. Dorset; Norwich, Norfolk v. Hertfordshire; Reading, Berkshire v. Buckinghamshire; Swindon, Wiltshire v. Surrey II.

5—Bedford School, Bedfordshire v. Buckinghamshire; Wakefield, Yorkshire II v. Notts II; Lakenham, Norwich, Norfolk v. Suffolk; Porthill, Staffordshire v. Cheshire; Mitcham, Surrey II v. Cornwall; Reading, Berkshire v. Oxfordshire; Histon, Cambridgeshire v. Hertfordshire.

7—Bedford School, Bedfordshire v. Hertfordshire; Felixstowe, Suffolk v. Middlesex II; Witney, Oxfordshire v. Cornwall; Lakenham (Norwich), Norfolk v. Essex II; High Wycombe, Buckinghamshire v. Berkshire; Sherborne, Dorset v. Wiltshire.

10—Felixstowe, Suffolk v. Hertfordshire; Reading, Berkshire v. Cornwall; Slough, Buckinghamshire v. Oxfordshire; Weymouth, Dorset v. Devon; Saffron Walden, Essex II v. Cambridgeshire.

12—Scunthorpe, Lincolnshire v. Bedfordshire; Rushden, Northants II v. Middlesex II; Uttoxeter, Staffordshire v. Yorkshire II; Aylesford, Kent II v. Wiltshire; Weymouth, Dorset v. Cornwall; Christ Church, Oxford, Oxfordshire v. Devon; Retford, Notts II v. Warwickshire II; St. Albans, Hertfordshire v. Buckinghamshire.

14—Lowestoft, Suffolk v. Norfolk; Christ Church, Oxford, Oxfordshire v. Dorset; Newbury, Berkshire v. Devon; Chesham, Buckinghamshire v. Hertfordshire.

17—Manchester, Lancashire II v. Durham; Banbury, Northants II v. Wiltshire; Stone, Staffordshire v. Northumberland; Lakenham, Norwich, Norfolk v. Kent II; Christ Church, Oxford, Oxfordshire v. Buckinghamshire; Guildford, Surrey II v. Devon; Birmingham, Warwickshire II v. Notts II; Reading, Berkshire v. Dorset.

19—Slough, Buckinghamshire v. Bedfordshire; Enfield, Middlesex II v. Suffolk; Middlesbrough, Yorkshire II v. Northumberland; Grimsby, Lincolnshire v. Cambridge; Blandford, Dorset v. Oxfordshire.

21—Letchworth, Hertfordshire v. Suffolk; Marlborough College, Wiltshire v. Kent II; Exmouth, Devon v. Oxfordshire.

24—Harlow, Essex II v. Suffolk; Penzance, Cornwall v. Oxfordshire; Watford, Hertfordshire v. Cambridgeshire; Dorchester, Dorset v. Berkshire.

25—Torquay, Devon v. Surrey II.

26—Winchmore Hill, Middlesex II v. Essex II; Ascott Park, Wing, Buckinghamshire v. Norfolk; Swindon, Wiltshire v. Dorset.

27—Banbury, Oxfordshire v. Berkshire.

28—Camborne, Cornwall v. Surrey II; Bishops Stortford, Hertfordshire v. Norfolk.

DROP IN TEST MATCH PROFITS

Profit on last summer's England v. India Tests was £39,429—down £19,000 on the England v. South Africa Tests of 1951. Each county's share of the profits was £1,314, a reduction of £900 on the 1951 figure. Counties on whose grounds the Tests were staged each received £3,943.

Inter-Club Fixtures

ADDISCOMBE

APRIL 25—Old Emanuel (a). **MAY** 2—Elmers End (h); 9—Purley (a); 16—Norwood (h); 23—Alleyn O.B. (a); 25—Weybridge (a); 30—West Wickham (h). **JUNE** 2—Honor Oak (h); 6—Thornton Heath (a); 13—Old Grammarians (a); 20—Orpington (h); 27—Streatham (a). **JULY** 4—Wallington (h); 5—H. E. Pierce's XI (h); 6—Surrey Club & Ground (h); 7—F. C. Woodham's XI (h); 8—Croydon Mayor's XI; 9—Oxted (h); 10—W. T. Cook's XI (h); 11—Alleyn O.B. (h); 18—Roehampton (a); 25—Orpington (a). **AUGUST** 1—Weybridge (h); 8—Norwood (a); 15—Barnes (h); 22—Oxted (a); 29—Elmers End (a). **SEPTEMBER** 5—Nat. Prov. Bank (a); 12—Lensbury (h); 19—Wallington (a); 26—Oxted (h).

ALTON

MAY 2—Romsey (h); 9—Fleet (a); 16—West Hill (h); 23—Petersfield (a); 30—Aldershot (h). **JUNE** 6—Basingstoke (h); 13—R.A.E. (h); 20—Thornycrofts (h); 27—Charterhouse (a). **JULY** 4—Fleet (h); 11—Basingstoke (a); 18—Guildford City (a); 25—Courage & Co. (h); **AUGUST** 1—Petersfield (h); 8—Courage & Co. (h); 15—Hartley Wintney (h); 22—Thornycroft (a); 29—West Hill (a). **SEPTEMBER** 5—Portsmouth Civil Service (a).

AMERSHAM

APRIL 25—Amersham Hill (a). **MAY** 2—High Wycombe (a); 9—Gerrards Cross (h); 16—Aylesbury (a); 23—Harrow Town (h); 25—Tring Park (h); 30—Uxbridge (a). **JUNE** 6—Chesham (h); 13—Beaconsfield (a); 20—Amersham Hill (h); 27—Harrow Town (a). **JULY** 4—Beaconsfield (h); 11—O.M.T. (h); 18—Chorley Wood (a); 25—Uxbridge (h). **AUGUST** 1—Tring Park (a); 3—Gerrards Cross (a); 8—Leighton Buzzard (a); 15—Aylesbury (h); 22—Chesham (a); 29—Slough (h). **SEPTEMBER** 5—O.M.T. (a); 12—High Wycombe (h); 19—Chorley Wood (h); 26—Slough (a).

ASHTEAD

APRIL 25—Epsom (a). **MAY** 2—Norwood (h); 9—Thames Ditton (h); 16—Cobham (h); 23—Cranleigh (h); 25—Leatherhead (h); 30—Cheam (a). **JUNE** 6—Sutton (a); 13—Oatland Park (h); 20—Wimbledon (h); 27—Banstead (h). **JULY** 4—Cobham (a); 11—Esher (a); 18—Wimbledon (a); 25—Sutton (h). **AUGUST** 1—Epsom (h); 3—Grasshoppers (h); 8—Oatland Park (a); 15—Cheam (h); 22—Barclays Bank (a); 29—Banstead (a). **SEPTEMBER** 5—Thames Ditton (a); 12—Esher (h); 19—Cranleigh (a); 26—Leatherhead (a).

BECONTREE

MAY 2—Stanford-le-Hope (a); 9—Eton Mission (h); 16—Crown and Manor (a); 23—Plaistow Red Triangle (a); 30—Hoffman's Athletic (a). **JUNE** 20—Stanford-le-Hope (h); 27—Shell (a). **JULY** 4—Eton Mission (a); 11—Old Bealonians (h); 18—Plaistow Red Triangle (h); 25—Hornchurch Athletic (h). **AUGUST** 1—Shell (h); 8—Old Clarkonians (h); 15—Hoffman's Athletic (h); 22—Crown and Manor (h); 29—Green and Siley Weir (a). **SEPTEMBER** 5—Old Bealonians (a); 12—Old Clarkonians (a); 19—Ilford Catholics (a); 26—Valentines (h).

BEDFORD TOWN

APRIL 25—Hitchin Town (h). **MAY** 2—Vauxhall Motors (h); 9—Chesham (a); 16—Three Counties Hospital (a); 23—March Town (a); 30—Letchworth (h). **JUNE** 6—Luton Town (h); 13—Brentham (h); 20—Queen's Works (h); 27—Peterborough Town (h). **JULY** 4—Mill Hill (a); 11—Wisbech Town (h); 18—Luton Town (a); 25—Harpur Sports (h). **AUGUST** 1—Peterborough Town (a); 8—March Town (h); 15—Hitchin Town (a); 22—Slough (a); 29—Leighton Buzzard (h). **SEPTEMBER** 5—Wisbech Town (a); 12—Welwyn Garden City (a); 19—Northampton Saints (a).

BEXLEY HEATH

MAY 2—Metrogas (a); 9—Old Grammarians (h); 16—Gore Court (h); 23—Norwood (a); 25—East Sussex (h); 30—Orpington (a). **JUNE** 2—Brittanic House (a); 6—Union Castle (h); 20—Elmers End (a); 27—Metrogas (h). **JULY** 4—Gore Court (a); 11—Siemens (a); 18—West Wickham (a); 25—Britannic House (h). **AUGUST** 1—Woolwich Polytechnic (h); 3—The Stage (h); 8—Blackheath Wanderers (a); 15—Lessa (a); 22—Woolwich Garrison (h); 29—Blackheath Wanderers (h). **SEPTEMBER** 5—Forest Hill (h); 12—East Sussex (a); 19—Erith Technical College (h); 26—Lessa (h).

BICKLEY PARK

APRIL 25—Sidcup (h). **MAY 2**—Sevenoaks Vine (a); **9**—Richmond (h); **16**—West Kent (a); **23**—The Mote (h); **25**—Beckenham (h); **30**—Bromley (h). **JUNE 6**—Hampstead (h); **13**—Bexley (a); **20**—Blackheath (a). **JULY 4**—Bromley (a); **11**—Wimbledon (a); **18**—H.A.C. (h); **25**—Dulwich (h). **AUGUST 1**—Reigate Priory (a); **3**—Beckenham (a); **8**—West Kent (h); **15**—Metropolitan Police (a); **22**—Bexley (h); **29**—The Mote (a). **SEPTEMBER 5**—Old Alleynians (h); **12**—Gravesend (a).

BLETCHLEY TOWN

MAY 2—Biggleswade (h); **9**—Vauxhall Motors (h); **23**—Pressed Steel (a); **25**—Kings Langley (a); **30**—Dunstable (a). **JUNE 6**—Vauxhall Motors (a); **13**—Hazels (h); **20**—Buckingham (a); **27**—Biggleswade (a). **JULY 4**—Outlaws (h); **11**—Three Counties Hospitals (a); **25**—Dunstable (h). **AUGUST 1**—Buckingham (a); **3**—Aylesbury (a); **8**—Boreham Wood (a); **15**—Hazels (a); **22**—Pressed Steel (h). **SEPTEMBER 12**—Swanbourne (a).

BOGNOR

MAY 2—Havant (h); **9**—Pagham (a); **16**—Littlehampton (h); **23**—Decca Record S.C. (h); **30**—Guys Hospital (a). **JUNE 6**—Littlehampton (a); **13**—South Bersted (h); **20**—Priory Park (h); **27**—Henfield (a). **JULY 4**—Pagham (h); **11**—H.M.S. Excellent (h); **18**—Carshalton (a); **25**—Chameleons (h). **AUGUST 1**—Hook & Newnham (h); **15**—Sussex Club & Ground (h); **29**—Priory Park (h).

BRIGGS SOCIAL AND ATHLETIC CLUB

MAY 2—Brentwood Mental Hospital (a); **9**—Royal Naval Barracks (a); **16**—Murex (a); **23**—Southampton Plant (h); **30**—Courtaulds (a). **JUNE 27**—Thurrock Interknit (a). **JULY 4**—Southampton Plant (a); **18**—Caribonum (a). **AUGUST 15**—Lyle Sports (a). **SEPTEMBER 12**—Hornchurch Athletic (a).

BROADWATER

MAY 2—Hove Nondescripts (h); **9**—Portslade (a); **16**—Hailsham (a); **23**—Brighton Banks (a); **30**—Burgess Hill St. Andrews (a). **JUNE 6**—Newhaven (h); **20**—Lewes Priory (a); **27**—Hailsham (h). **JULY 4**—Portslade (h); **11**—Shoreham (a); **18**—Brighton Telephones (a); **25**—Sussex Club and Ground (h). **AUGUST 1**—Burgess Hill St Andrews (h); **8**—Brighton Banks (h); **15**—Brighton & Hove (h); **22**—Lewes Priory (h); **29**—Shoreham (h). **SEPTEMBER 5**—Ifield (a); **12**—Brighton Telephones (h); **19**—Newhaven (a).

BUCKINGHAM TOWN

MAY 2—Northampton Saints (h); **9**—Banbury Twenty Club (h); **16**—Hazell's (Aylesbury) S.C. (a); **23**—Brackley Town (h); **30**—Swanbourne (h). **JUNE 6**—Queen's Works (Bedford) (h); **13**—Banbury Town (h); **20**—Bletchley Town (h); **27**—Dunstable Town (a). **JULY 4**—Queen's Works (Bedford) (a); **11**—Stowe School (a); **18**—Kineton (a); **25**—Hazell's (Aylesbury) S.C. (h). **AUGUST 1**—Bletchley Town (h); **8**—Brackley Town (a); **15**—Bicester Town (h); **22**—North Oxford (h); **29**—Cowley St. John (h); **SEPTEMBER 5**—Banbury N.A.C. (h); **12**—Banbury Twenty Club (h); **26**—Swanbourne (a).

CATFORD

APRIL 25—Private Banks (a). **MAY 2**—Gore Court (h); **9**—Catford Wanderers (h); **16**—National Prov. Bank (a); **23**—Mitcham (a); **30**—Dulwich (h). **JUNE 6**—Lensbury & Britannic House (h); **13**—Dartford (a); **20**—Horsham (a); **27**—Beddington (h). **JULY 4**—Horsham (h); **11**—Mitcham (h); **18**—Beddington (a); **25**—Honor Oak (a). **AUGUST 1**—Gravesend (a); **8**—Honor Oak (h); **15**—Catford Wanderers (a); **22**—Gravesend (h); **29**—Barclays Bank (a). **SEPTEMBER 5**—Beckenham (h); **12**—Dulwich (a); **19**—Gore Court (a); **26**—Dartford (h).

CATFORD WANDERERS

APRIL 25—Beddington (h). **MAY 2**—Crofton Park (h); **9**—Catford (a); **16**—Merton (a); **23**—Thornton Heath (h); **25**—West Wickham (h); **30**—Guildford (a). **JUNE 6**—Beckenham (h); **13**—Blackheath (h); **20**—Shepherds Bush (h); **27**—Merton (h). **JULY 11**—Honor Oak (h); **18**—Midland Bank (h); **25**—National Prov. Bank (a). **AUGUST 1**—Bexley (a); **3**—Britannic House (a); **8**—Crofton Park (a); **15**—Catford (h); **22**—Thornton Heath (a); **29**—Bexley (h). **SEPTEMBER 5**—Mitcham (a); **12**—Beckenham (a); **19**—Honor Oak (a); **26**—Mitcham (h).

CHELMSFORD

MAY 2—Chingford (a); **9**—Bishops Stortford (h); **16**—South Essex Waterworks (h); **23**—Old Chelmsfordians (a); **25**—Clacton (h); **30**—Southend (h). **JUNE 6**—Brentwood (a); **13**—Romford (a); **17**—Essex Club & Ground (h); **20**—Westcliff-on-Sea (a); **27**—Wanstead (h). **JULY 4**—Upminster (a); **11**—Old Parkonians (h); **18**—Southend (a); **25**—Chingford (h). **AUGUST 1**—South Essex Waterworks (a); **3**—Clacton (a); **8**—Brentwood (h); **15**—Witham (a); **22**—Old Chelmsfordians (h); **29**—Bishops Stortford (a). **SEPTEMBER 5**—Westcliff-on-Sea (h); **12**—Leigh and Chalkwell (a); **19**—Loughton (h); **26**—Old Parkonians (a).

CHINGFORD

APRIL 25—Woodford Wells (h). **MAY 2**—Chelmsford (h); **9**—Winchmore Hill (a); **16**—Brentwood (a); **23**—Edmonton (a); **25**—South Woodford (a); **30**—Ilford (h). **JUNE 6**—Wanstead (h); **13**—Loughton (h); **20**—Edmonton (h); **27**—Buckhurst Hill (a). **JULY 4**—Alexandra Park (h); **11**—Wanstead (a); **18**—Loughton (a); **25**—Chelmsford (a). **AUGUST 1**—North Middlesex (h); **3**—South Woodford (h); **8**—Winchmore Hill (h); **15**—Highgate (a); **22**—North Middlesex (a); **29**—Buckhurst Hill (h). **SEPTEMBER 5**—Alexandra Park (a); **12**—Ilford (a); **19**—Highgate (h); **26**—Woodford Wells (a).

CHIPSTEAD

APRIL 25—Bowring Sports (h). **MAY 2**—Wandgas Athletic (h); **9**—Walton Heath (a); **16** Brockham (h); **23**—Nutfield (a); **25**—Croydon Gas Co. (a); **30**—Sanderstead (a). **JUNE 6**—Carshalton (h); **13**—Merstham (a); **20**—Caterham Spartans (h); **27**—Kingswood (a). **JULY 4**—South Nutfield (h); **11**—Bowring Sports (a); **18**—Old Grammarians (h); **25**—Caterham Spartans (a). **AUGUST 1**—Merstham (h); **3**—Beckenham Wizards (h); **8**—Carshalton (a); **15**—Wandgas Athletic (a); **22**—Walton Heath (h); **29**—Nutfield (h). **SEPTEMBER 5**—South Nutfield (a); **12**—Kingswood (h); **19**—Brockham (a); **26**—Sanderstead (h).

COCKFOSTERS

MAY 2—Totteridge (h); **9**—Enfield (a); **16**—Keble (a); **23**—Potters Bar (h); **25**—Southgate County O.B. (h); **30**—Northampton Polytechnic (h). **JUNE 2**—Alexandra Park (a); **6**—Southgate Adelaide (h); **13**—Kenton (h); **20**—Mill Hill Village (a); **27**—Old Albanian (h). **JULY 4**—Southgate County O.B. (a); **11**—Clayhall (h); **18**—Welwyn Garden City (a); **25**—Old Elizabethans (a). **AUGUST 1**—Northampton Polytechnic (a); **3**—Southgate Adelaide (a); **8**—Old Albanian (a); **10**—President's XI (a); **11**—Arsenal F.C. (h); **12**—Tottenham Hotspur F.C. (h); **13**—Saracens R.F.C. (h); **14**—R. Lister's XI (h); **15**—Keble (h); **22**—Potters Bar (a); **29**—Old Elizabethans (h). **SEPTEMBER 5**—Totteridge (a); **12**—Mill Hill Village (h); **19**—Clayhall (a); **26**—Old Minchendenians (h).

DAGENHAM

MAY 2—Mann Crossman & Paulin (a); **9**—Britannic House (h); **16**—Shell (h); **23**—Tunnell Sports (h); **30**—Walthamstow NALGO (h). **JUNE 6**—Petts Wood (a); **2**—Prittlewell (a); **27**—Crown & Manor O.B. (h). **JULY 4**—Tunnell Sports (a); **11**—Goodmayes (h); **18**—Theydon Bois (a); **25**—Shell (a). **AUGUST 1**—Crown & Manor O.B. (a); **8**—Theydon Bois (h); **22**—Harvey Sports (h); **29**—Walthamstow NALGO (a).

DITCHLING

APRIL 28—Preston Nomads (h). **MAY 2**—St. Andrews (a); **9**—St. Andrews (h); **16**—Glenfield (a); **23**—Steyning (h); **30**—Cuckfield (h). **JUNE 6**—Brighton Banks (a); **13**—Storrington (a); **20**—Hassocks (a); **27**—Steyning (a). **JULY 4**—Storrington (h); **11**—Glenfield (a); **18**—Cuckfield (a); **25**—Hassocks (h). **AUGUST 1**—Morley (a); **8**—Furness Mill (a); **15**—Tiverton (h); **22**—Brighton Banks (h); **29**—Brighton and Hove (h). **SEPTEMBER 12**—Morley (h); **19**—Preston Nomads (a).

DOVER

MAY 9—Bretts (h); **13**—Hythe (h); **16**—R.M. (Deal) (a); **23**—Vauxhall Motors (h); **27**—N & S Nomads (h); **30**—St. Lawrence (a). **JUNE 3**—Kent Fire Brigade (a); **6**—Gore Court (h); **10**—Coutts Bank (h); **13**—Chinghoppers (h); **17**—Heathfield (h); **20**—Northampton Polytechnic (h); **24**—West Essex (h); **27**—Broadstairs (a). **JULY 4**—Dartford (h); **8**—Hendon (h); **11**—Caterham Strollers (h); **15**—R.M. (Deal) (h); **22**—Mediators (h); **25**—Ramsgate St. George's (h); **29**—Queen's Philippics (h). **AUGUST 1**—Folkestone (a); **3**—Folkestone (h); **5**—Selsted (h); **8**—Kent Club and Ground (h); **15-21**—County Cricket Week; **22**—Broadstairs (h); **26**—Kent Fire Brigade (h); **29**—Gore Court (a). **SEPTEMBER 5**—St. Lawrence (h); **9**—Selsted (a); **12**—Hythe (a).

DUNSTABLE TOWN

APRIL 25—Hemel Hempstead (a). **MAY 2**—Berkhamsted (h); **9**—Old Albanian (a); **16**—Abbotts Langley (h); **23**—Dickinsons (Apsley) (a); **25**—J. & E. Hall Ltd. (h); **30**—Bletchley (h). **JUNE 6**—Leighton Buzzard (h); **13**—Kings Langley (a) **20**—Letchworth (h); **27**—Buckingham (h). **JULY 4**—Letchworth (a); **11**—Dunstable School (a); **18**—Kings Langley (h); **25**—Bletchley (a). **AUGUST 1**—Berkhamsted (a); **3**—Northern Polytechnic (h); **8**—The Outlaws (h); **15**—Tring Park (h); **22**—Tring Park (a); **29**—Harpur Sports (h). **SEPTEMBER 5**—Three Counties Hospital (a); **12**—Hitchin (a); **19**—Vauxhall Motors (h).

EALING

APRIL 25—West Drayton (h). **MAY 2**—Southgate (a); **9**—South Hampstead (h); **16**—Hounslow (h); **23**—Old Citizens (h); **30**—Thornton Heath (a). **JUNE 6**—Malden Wanderers (h); **13**—Kenton (a); **20**—Finchley (h); **27**—Beaconsfield (a). **JULY 4**—Brentham (h); **11**—Hounslow (a); **18**—Ibis (h); **25**—Richmond (h). **AUGUST 1**—South Hampstead (a); **8**—Beaconsfield (h); **15**—Bank of England (h); **22**—Harrow Town (a); **29**—Southgate (h). **SEPTEMBER 5**—Malden Wanderers (a); **12**—Hampton Wick (h); **19**—Brondesbury (h); **26**—Finchley (a).

EALING DEAN

APRIL 25—Mill Hill (a). **MAY 2**—Guy's Hospital (a); **9**—Brondesbury (a); **16**—Brentham (h); **23**—Metropolitan Police (a); **25**—West Indies (h); **30**—Wembley (a). **JUNE 6**—Northampton Polytechnic (h); **13**—Sunbury (h); **20**—Alexandra Park (h); **27**—University College (h). **JULY 4**—Middlesex Club and Ground (h); **11**—Brentham (a); **18**—Mill Hill Park (a); **25**—Ilford (h). **AUGUST 1**—Winchmore Hill (h); **3**—West Essex (h); **8**—Gidea Park (h); **15**—Thornton Heath (h); **22**—Ilford (a); **29**—Laleham (a). **SEPTEMBER 5**—B.B.C. (h); **12**—Mill Hill Park (h); **19**—Metropolitan Police (h); **26**—Brondesbury (h).

EAST MOLESEY

MAY 2—Teddington (a); **9**—Hampton Wick (a); **16**—Richmond Town (a); **23**—Thames Ditton (a); **30**—Distillers (h). **JUNE 6**—Richmond Town (h); **13**—Roehampton (a); **20**—Ashford (a); **27**—Alleyn Old Boys (h). **JULY 4**—Old Emanuel (a); **11**—Oatlands Park (a); **18**—Weybridge (a); **25**—Banstead (h). **AUGUST 1**—Wallington (h); **8**—Olinda (a); **15**—Twickenham (h); **22**—Surrey Colts (h); **29**—Olinda (h). **SEPTEMBER 5**—Old Emanuel (h); **12**—Bessborough (a); **19**—Ashford (h); **26**—Banstead (a).

EDMONTON

APRIL 25—Winchmore Hill. **MAY 2**—Alexandra Park; **9**—Kenton; **16**—Leavesden Hospital; **23**—Chingford; **25**—Highgate; **30**—North London. **JUNE 6**—Cuaco; **13**—Cheshunt; **20**—Chingford; **27**—Enfield. **JULY 4**—Northampton Polytechnic; **11**—Old Colfeians; **18**—Cuaco; **25**—North Middlesex. **AUGUST 1**—Cheshunt; **3**—Highgate; **8**—Alexandra Park; **15**—Enfield; **22**—Winchmore Hill; **29**—Wembley. **SEPTEMBER 5**—Northampton Polytechnic; **12**—North London; **19**—North Middlesex.

ELMERS END

APRIL 25—Old Grammarians (h). **MAY 2**—Addiscombe (a); **9**—Boro Polytechnic (h); **16**—Roehampton (a); **23**—Wallington (h); **30**—Old Grammarians (a). **JUNE 6**—West Wickham (a); **13**—Alleyn Old Boys (h); **20**—Bexley Heath (h); **27**—Britannic House (a). **JULY 4**—Southern Railway (a); **11**—Boro Polytechnic (a); **18**—Southern Railway (a); **25**—Winchmore Hill (a). **AUGUST 1**—Purley (a); **8**—City of London College (a); **15**—Blackheath Wanderers (h); **22**—Wallington (a); **29**—Addiscombe (h). **SEPTEMBER 5**—Roehampton (h); **12**—Polytechnic (h); **19**—Crofton Park (h); **26**—Guildford (h).

ELSTREE

MAY 2—Shenley Hospital (a); **9**—North Mymms (a); **16**—Cheshunt (h); **23**—Southgate Adelaide (a); **25**—Midland Bank (h); **30**—Cheshunt (a). **JUNE 6**—Waterlows (Dunstable) (a); **13**—Highams Park (h); **20**—Hoddesdon Town (a); **27**—L.M.A.C. (a). **JULY 4**—Southgate Adelaide (h); **11**—Highams Park (a); **18**—Bushey (a); **25**—Waterlows (Dunstable) (h). **AUGUST 1**—Northampton Poly. (h); **3**—Bognor (a); **8**—Bushey (h); **15**—North-West Poly. (a); **22**—Headstone (h); **29**—North Mymms (h). **SEPTEMBER 5**—North-West Poly. (h); **12**—Totteridge (h); **19**—Hoddesdon Town (h); **26**—Laings (a).

ENFIELD

APRIL 25—Southgate (a). **MAY 2**—North Middlesex (h); **9**—Hornsey (a); **16**—Luton (h); **23**—Buckhurst Hill (h); **25**—Cheshunt (h); **30**—Barnet (a). **JUNE 2**—Southgate (h); **6**—Loughton (a); **13**—Brondesbury (a); **20**—Royston (h); **23**—Rye (a); **24**—Hythe (a); **26**—Selsted (a); **27**—Ashford (a); **28**—Folkestone (a). **JULY 4**—Harrow Town (a); **11**—Highgate (a); **18**—Barnet (h); **25**—Hertford (a). **AUGUST 1**—Buckhurst Hill (a); **3**—Cheshunt (a); **4**—Chichester Priory Park (a); **8**—Highgate (h); **15**—Edmonton (a); **22**—Loughton (h); **29**—Luton (a). **SEPTEMBER 5**—Hertford (h); **12**—Winchmore Hill (h); **19**—Wanstead (a); **26**—North Middlesex (a).

EPPING

APRIL 25—Hornchurch (h). **MAY 2**—Ongar (h); **9**—Loughton (a); **16**—Harlow (a); **23**—Highams Park (h); **25**—Barking Modern O.B. (11-30) (h); **30**—Hale End (a). **JUNE 6**—Goodmayes (a); **13**—Old Esthameians (h); **20**—Sawbridgeworth (h); **27**—Walthamstow (a). **JULY 4**—Clayhall (a); **11**—Ilford (h); **18**—Old Heronians (h); **25**—No. 3 Metropolitan Police (a). **AUGUST 1**—Romford (a); **3**—Goodmayes (11-30) (h); **8**—Harlow (h); **15**—Old Esthameians (a); **22**—Hoffman (a); **29**—Hoffman (h). **SEPTEMBER 2**—Essex County XI (F. Vigar's Benefit) (h); **5**—Romford (h); **12**—Hale End (h); **19**—Sawbridgeworth (a); **26**—South Woodford (h).

ETON MANOR

MAY 2—Old Esthameians (h); 9—Highams Park (h); 16—City of London Police (h); 23—Mill Hill Village (a); 30—Unilever (h). **JUNE 6**—Leigh & Chalkwell Park (a); 13—Old Hamptonians (h); 20—Goodmayes (h); 27—Highgate (h). **JULY 4**—Northern Polytechnic (a); 11—Unilever (a); 18—Old Esthameians (a); 25—Tour Oxford. **AUGUST 1**—Leavesden (a); 8—"The Times" (a); 15—Highams Park (a); 22—L.M.S. (London) Athletic (a); 29—Open. **SEPTEMBER 5**—Open; 12—Eton Mission (h); 19—Goodmayes (a).

FARNCOMBE

APRIL 25—Jeffites (h). **MAY 2**—Shepperton (a); 9—Farnham (h); 16—Haslemere (a); 23—Surrey Colts (h). **JUNE 6**—Godalming (a); 13—Shepperton (h); 20—Horsley (h); 27—Ripley (a). **JULY 4**—Farnham (a); 11—Godalming (h); 18—Horsell (a); 25—Charterhouse XI (h). **AUGUST 1**—Horsley (a); 8—Haslemere (h); 15—Cranleigh (a); 29—I.R.A.Q. P.C. (h). **SEPTEMBER 5**—Cranleigh (h); 19—Jeffites (h).

FOLKESTONE

MAY 2—Margate (h); 9—Broadstairs (a); 16—Ashford (a); 23—Aylesford P.M. (a); 30—Norfolk & Suffolk (h). **JUNE 6**—British Railways (a); 13—Gore Court (h); 20—Willesborough (a); 27—Hastings St. Leonards (h). **JULY 4**—Ashford (h); 11—Freebooters (h); 18—P E Murray Willis' XI (h); 25—Aylesford P.M. (h). **AUGUST 1**—Dover (h); 8—British Railways (a); 15—Broadstairs (h); 22—Willesborough (h); 29—Ramsgate St. George (h). **SEPTEMBER 5**—Gore Court (a); 12—St. Lawrence (h); 19—Hastings & St. Leonards (a); 26—Haversham (a).

FRINTON-ON-SEA

MAY 2—Witham (h); 9—Bromley (h); 16—Stowmarket (h); 23—Dovercourt (h); 25—Westcliff-on-Sea (h); 30—Mistley (a). **JUNE 6**—South Woodford (h); 13—Halstead (h); 17—Lloyds (h); 20—Romford (h); 27—Colchester & E. Essex (a). **JULY 4**—Royston (h); 8—K. Duke's XI (h); 11—Felixstowe (a); 16—Incidentals (h); 18—Mistley (h); 22—Territorial Army (h); 25—Clacton (h). **AUGUST 1**—Witham (a); 3—Colchester & E. Essex (h); 5—Shoeburyness Garrison (h); 6—President's XI (h); 8—Gentlemen of Essex (h); 13—Essex Club & Ground (h); 15—Clacton (a); 29—Ipswich & E. Suffolk (a). **SEPTEMBER 5**—Reserve Fleet, Harwich (h); 12—Felixstowe (h); 19—Ipswich & E. Suffolk (h); 26—Mr. M. R. Butcher's XI (h).

GODALMING

MAY 2—Witley (a); 9—Charterhouse (a); 16—Normandy (h); 23—Dunsfold (h); 25—Portsmouth Corin (h); 30—Busbridge (a). **JUNE 6**—Farncombe (h); 13—Old Guildfordians (a); 20—Vickers-Armstrong (a); 27—Brook (h). **JULY 4**—Haslemere (a); 11—Farncombe (a); 18—Busbridge (h); 25—Haslemere (h). **AUGUST 1**—Old Guildfordians (h); 3—Merton Wanderers (h); 8—Normandy (a); 22—Dunsfold (a); 29—Vickers-Armstrong (h). **SEPTEMBER 5**—Witley (h); 12—Guildford (h).

HARROW

MAY 2—Old Latymerians (h); 9—Northwood (h); 16—Woodside Park (a); 23—Ibis (a); 25—Aylesbury Town (a); 30—Foreign Office (a); **JUNE 2**—Harrow Town (a); 6—Ickenham (a); 13—Teddington Town (a); 20—Kenton (h); 27—Old Grammarians (h). **JULY 4**—Kenton (a); 11—Old Gaytonians (a); 18—West Drayton (h); 25—Teddington Town (h). **AUGUST 1**—Kings Langley (a); 3—Datchet (a); 8—Chesham (a); 15—Harefield (h); 22—Old Latymerians (a); 29—Kodak (a). **SEPTEMBER 5**—Old Gaytonians (h); 12—Uxbridge (h); 19—Bessborough (h); 26—Lyons Club (a).

HARROW TOWN

APRIL 25—Polytechnic (a). **MAY 2**—Ashford (a); 9—U.C.S. Old Boys (h); 16—Harrow School (a); 23—Amersham (a); 25—North London (a); 30—Richmond Town (h). **JUNE 2**—Harrow (h); 6—Pinner (a); 13—St Albans (h); 20—Twickenham (a); 27—Amersham (h). **JULY 4**—Enfield (h); 11—Rickmansworth (h); 18—Finchley (a); 25—Turnham Green (a). **AUGUST 1**—Richmond Town (a); 3—Sunbury-on-Thames (h); 8—Polytechnic (h); 15—North London (h); 22—Ealing (h); 29—Bessborough (h). **SEPTEMBER 5**—Mill Hill (a); 12—Highgate (a); 19—Roehampton (a); 26—Beaconsfield (a). **OCTOBER 3**—F. J. Payne's XI (h).

HASLEMERE

MAY 2—Priory Park (a); 9—Dorking (h); 16—Farncombe (h); 23—Portsmouth Civil Service (a); 25—Deanery (Southampton) (h); 30—Surrey Colts (h). **JUNE 6**—Havant (h); 13—Cranleigh (a); 20—Fleet (a); 27—Petersfield (a); 29—Bolton (h). **JULY 4**—Godalming (h); 11—St. Thomas's Hospital (a); 18—Farnham (h); 25—Godalming (a). **AUGUST 1**—Priory Park (h); 3—Portsmouth & Southsea (h); 8—Farncombe (a); 12—Dorking (Cricket Week) (a); 15—Portsmouth & Southsea (a); 22—Petersfield (h); 29—Cranleigh (h). **SEPTEMBER 5**—Oaklands Park (a); 12—Fareham (h); 19—Farnham (a).

HATCH END

MAY 2—Harpenden (h); **9**—North Enfield (a); **16**—Maurice (a); **23**—Old Gaytonians (h); **30**—Mill Hill Village (a). **JUNE 6**—Alexandra Park "B" (a); **13**—Northwood (a); **20**—Metropolitan Railway (h); **27**—Watford Town (h). **JULY 4**—Field End (h); **11**—Dickinsons Sports (a); **18**—Field End (a). **AUGUST 1**—Dickinsons Sports (h); **8**—Old Gaytonians (a); **15**—Metropolitan Railway (a); **22**—Shenley Hospital (a); **29**—British Oxygen Co. (a). **SEPTEMBER 5**—Ickenham (h); **12**—Alexandra Park "B" (h); **19**—Sudbury Court (h); **26**—British Oxygen Co. (h).

HAVANT

MAY 2—Bognor (a); **9**—Priory Park (a); **16**—Reading (a); **23**—Horsham (h); **25**—Brighton & Hove (h); **30**—Basingstoke & N.H. (a). **JUNE 6**—Haslemere (a); **13**—United Services (a); **20**—Royal Marines (a); **27**—Fareham (a). **JULY 4**—Basingstoke & N.H. (h); **11**—Brighton & Hove (a); **18**—Fareham (h); **25**—Horsell (a). **AUGUST 1**—Bournemouth Sports Club (a); **3**—Hampshire Hogs (h); **4**—Oddites (h); **5**—Seaford College (h); **6**—Hants Club & Ground (h); **7**—Susex Martlets (h); **8**—Hinckley St. Peter's (h); **11**—Littlehampton (a); **15**—Poole Park (a); **22**—Bournemouth Sports Club (h); **29**—Horsham (a). **SEPTEMBER 5**—Poole Park (h); **12**—Worthing (a); **19**—Lyndhurst (a).

HAYES

MAY 2—Bexley (h); **9**—Warlingham (a); **15**—Kenley (a); **23**—Blackheath (h); **25**—Elmers (h). **JUNE 2**—Wallington (a); **6**—Phoenix (a); **13**—Southern Railway (h); **27**—Phoenix (h). **JULY 4**—Crofton Park (h); **11**—Old Mid-Whitgiftians (a); **18**—Old Dunstonians (h); **25**—Bromley Town (a). **AUGUST 1**—Warlingham (h); **3**—Elmers End (a); **8**—Blackheath (a); **15**—Bexley (a); **22**—Crofton Park (a); **29**—Old Mid-Whitgiftians (h). **SEPTEMBER 5**—West Wickham (h); **12**—Bromley Town (h); **19**—Cuaco (a); **26**—Thornton Heath (h).

HIGHAMS PARK

MAY 2—Wickford (h); **9**—Eton Manor (a); **16**—Leigh & Chalkwell Park (h); **23**—Epping (a); **25**—Honor Oak (a); **30**—Harlow (h). **JUNE 2**—West Essex (a); **6**—North Middlesex (h); **13**—Elstree (a); **20**—Clayhall (a); **27**—No. 3 District (Metropolitan Police) (h). **JULY 4**—Unilever (Woodford) (a); **11**—Elstree (h); **18**—Old Southendians (h); **25**—Unilever (Woodford) (h). **AUGUST 1**—Clayhall (h); **3**—Hurlingham Oddfellows (h); **8**—Brentwood Mental Hospital (a); **15**—Eton Manor (h); **22**—Walthamstow (a). **SEPTEMBER 5**—Harlow (a); **12**—Gidea Park (a); **19**—Wickford (a).

HIGHGATE

APRIL 25—Barnet (a). **MAY 2**—Southgate (h); **9**—Finchley (h); **16**—Northampton Polytechnic (a); **23**—Alexandra Park (a); **30**—Totteridge (h). **JUNE 6**—North London (h); **13**—North Middlesex (a); **20**—North London (a); **27**—Eton Manor (a). **JULY 4**—North Middlesex (h); **11**—Enfield (h); **18**—Turnham Green (h); **25**—West Herts (a). **AUGUST 1**—Inter Club Match (h); **8**—Enfield (a); **15**—Chingford (h); **22**—Barnet (h); **29**—Alexandra Park (h). **SEPTEMBER 5**—Kenton (h); **12**—Harrow Town (h); **19**—Chingford (a); **26**—Cornhill (h).

HIGH WYCOMBE

MAY 2—Amersham (h); **9**—Shepherds Bush (a); **16**—South Hampstead (a); **23**—Gerrards Cross (h); **25**—Cambridge University Crusaders (h); **30**—Beaconsfield (a). **JUNE 6**—Shepherds Bush (h); **13**—Slough (a); **20**—Brondesbury (h); **27**—South Hampstead (h); **4**—Brondesbury (a); **11**—Oxford City (a); **18**—Chesham (a); **25**—Oxford City (h). **AUGUST 1**—Gerrards Cross (a); **15**—Slough (h); **22**—Leighton Buzzard (a); **29**—Beaconsfield (h). **SEPTEMBER 5**—Reading (a); **12**—Amersham (a); **19**—Chesham (h).

HODDESDON TOWN

MAY 2—Harlow (a); **9**—Gothic (h); **16**—Northmet House (a); **23**—Hatfield Estate (h); **25**—Old Owens (a); **30**—Walthamstow (h). **JUNE 6**—Sawbridgeworth (a); **13**—Mill Hill Village (a); **20**—Elstree (h); **27**—Harlow (h). **JULY 4**—Broxbourne (a); **11**—Potters Bar (a); **25**—Annual Sports and Fete (h). **AUGUST 1**—Sawbridgeworth (h); **3**—Southgate County Old Boys (h); **7**—Edmundian Casuals (a); **15**—Broxbourne (h); **22**—Hatfield Estate (a); **29**—Northmet House (h). **SEPTEMBER 5**—Gothic (a); **12**—Potters Bar (h); **19**—Elstree (a).

HONOR OAK

APRIL 25—Bexley (a). **MAY 2**—Cheam (a); **9**—Guy's Hospital (d); **16**—Shepherds Bush (h); **23**—Barclay's Bank (h); **25**—Highams Park (h); **30**—Shepherds Bush (a). **JUNE 2**—Addiscombe (a); **6**—Midland Bank (a); **13**—Hounslow (h); **20**—Bexley (h); **27**—Winchmore Hill (h). **JULY 4**—Merton (a); **11**—Catford Wanderers (a); **18**—Metropolitan Police (a); **25**—Catford (h); **29**—Surrey Club & Ground (h). **AUGUST 1**—Forest Hill (h); **3**—Old Olavians (h); **8**—Catford (a); **15**—Guildford (a); **22**—Spencer (a); **29**—Richmond Town (h). **SEPTEMBER 5**—Streatham (h); **12**—Hounslow (a); **19**—Catford Wanderers (h); **26**—Cheam (h).

HORLEY

MAY 2—Merstham (a); **9**—Burgess Hill (h); **16**—Burgess Hill (a); **23**—Ifield (h); **25**—Rustington (a); **30**—Fete (h). **JUNE 6**—Caterham Spartans (h); **13**—St. Andrews (a); **20**—Old Emanuel (a); **27**—Croydon Gas Sports (a). **JULY 4**—Merstham (h); **11**—Purley (h); **18**—St. Andrews (h); **25**—Frenches (a). **AUGUST 1**—Ditchling (h); **3**—Crowborough (h); **8**—Old Tiffinians (a); **15**—Croydon Gas Sports (h); **22**—Ifield (a); **29**—Surrey Constabulary (h). **SEPTEMBER 5**—Haywards Heath (a); **12**—Ditchling (a); **19**—South Nutfield (h); **26**—Frenches (h).

ICKENHAM

MAY 2—Pinner (h); **9**—Nth'n Polytechnic (a); **16**—Bessborough (h); **23**—Chalfont St. Peter (a); **25**—Eastcote (a); **30**—Richings Park (a). **JUNE 6**—Harrow (h); **13**—Harefield Hospital (h); **20**—Harefield (a); **27**—Gerrard's Cross (a). **JULY 4**—N.W. Polytechnic (h); **11**—Harlington (h); **18**—C.C.C. (a); **25**—Chalfont St. Peter (h). **AUGUST 1**—Rickmansworth (h); **3**—Eastcote (h); **8**—Ashford (a); **15**—South Hampstead (a); **22**—Bessborough (a); **29**—Gerrard's Cross (h). **SEPTEMBER 5**—Hatch End (a); **12**—N.W. Polytechnic (a); **19**—R.N.V.R. (h); **26**—Stanmore (a).

KENLEY

MAY 2—Wallington (a); **9**—Oxted (h); **16**—Hayes (Kent) (h); **23**—Westminster Bank (a); **30**—Marlborough (1870) (h). **JUNE 6**—Cyphers (h); **13**—Epsom (h); **20**—Purley (h); **27**—Guy's Hospital (a). **JULY 4**—Dorking (a); **11**—Streatham (h); **18**—Old Whitgiftians (h); **25**—Warlingham (a). **AUGUST 1**—Barclays Bank (a); **8**—Oxted (a); **15**—Old Grammarians (h); **22**—Epsom (a); **29**—Purley (a). **SEPTEMBER 5**—Dorking (h); **12**—Streatham (a); **19**—Warlingham (h); **26**—Wallington (h).

KINGS LANGLEY

MAY 2—Watford Town (h); **9**—Chorley Wood (h); **16**—Chipperfield (a); **23**—Amersham Hill (a); **25**—Leighton Buzzard (a); **30**—Hemel Hempstead (a). **JUNE 6**—Abbots Langley (h); **13**—Dunstable (h); **20**—Fencibles (h); **27**—Bushey (a). **JULY 4**—Abbots Langley (a); **11**—Hemel Hempstead (h); **18**—Dunstable (a); **25**—Berkhamsted (h). **AUGUST 1**—Harrow C.C. (h); **3**—Leighton Buzzard (h); **8**—Berkhamsted (a); **15**—Bushey (h); **22**—Chorley Wood (a); **29**—Amersham Hill (h). **SEPTEMBER 5**—Watford Town (a); **12**—Fencibles (a); **19**—Chipperfield (h).

LEIGH AND CHALKWELL PARK

MAY 2—Hutton (h); **9**—Old Parkonians (a); **16**—Highams Park (a); **23**—Upminster (a); **25**—Southend (h); **30**—Westcliff (a). **JUNE 13**—Winchmore Hill (a); **27**—Shoebury Garrison (a). **JULY 4**—Romford (h); **11**—Upminster (h); **18**—Lyons Club (a); **25**—Romford (a). **AUGUST 1**—Lyons Club (h); **3**—Southend (a); **8**—Lensbury & Brit House (h); **10**—Southend C.A. (h); **11**—J. Rowe's XI (h); **12**—Essex Club & Ground (h); **13**—Upminster (h); **14**—Hadleigh and Thundersley (h); **15**—Westcliff (h); **22**—London Hospital (a); **29**—Gravesend (h). **SEPTEMBER 5**—West Essex (a); **12**—Chelmsford (h); **19**—West Essex (h); **26**—Hutton (a).

LEIGHTON BUZZARD TOWN

APRIL 25—Leavesden Hospital (a). **MAY 9**—Hemel Hempstead (a); **23**—Abbots Langley (a); **30**—Aylesbury (a). **JUNE 6**—Dunstable Town (a); **13**—Tring Park (h); **20**—Berkhampsted (h); **27**—Vauxhall Motors (h). **JULY 4**—Tring Park (a); **11**—Berkhampsted (a); **18**—Abbots Langley (h). **AUGUST 1**—Aylesbury (h); **8**—Amersham (h); **15**—Vauxhall Motors (a); **22**—High Wycombe (h); **29**—Bedford Town (a). **SEPTEMBER 5**—Wolverton Town (h); **12**—Chipperfield (a).

LITTLEHAMPTON

APRIL 25—Graylingwell (a). **MAY 2**—Goring-by-Sea (a); **9**—Steyning (h); **16**—Bognor Regis (a); **23**—Shoreham (h); **25**—Brighton Banks (h); **30**—Worthing (a). **JUNE 2**—B.B.C. (h); **6**—Bognor Regis (h); **13**—Ferring (h); **20**—Goring-by-Sea (h); **24**—Bristol Wayfarers (h); **27**—Ferring (a). **JULY 4**—Priory Park (h); **11**—Steyning (a); **15**—Old Southendians (h); **18**—Pagham (h); **22**—Assassins C.C. (h); **25**—Burgess Hill St. A. (a); **29**—Fencibles (h). **AUGUST 1**—Pagham (a); **3**—South Beddington (h); **5**—St. Bart's Hospital (h); **8**—Shoreham (a). CRICKET WEEK: **10**—Streatham (h); **11**—Havant (h); **12**—Old Emanuel (h); **13**—Kenya Kongonis (h); **14**—Vandals (h); **15**—Burgess Hill St. A. (h). **19**—Old Roans (h); **22**—Priory Park (a); **26**—Sussex C. & G. (h); **29**—Worthing (h). **SEPTEMBER 5**—E. Preston (a); **12**—W. Chiltington (a); **19**—Graylingswell (a).

LOUGHTON

MAY 2—Ilford (a); **9**—Epping (h); **16**—Wanstead (a); **23**—Shenfield (h); **25**—Buckhurst Hill (a); **30**—Woodford Wells (h). **JUNE 2**—Club Match (h); **6**—Enfield (h); **13**—Chingford (a); **20**—Ilford (h); **27**—S. Woodford (a). **JULY 4**—S. Woodford (h); **11**—Woodford Wells (a); **18**—Chingford (h); **25**—Wanstead (h). **AUGUST 1**—Bishops Stortford (a); **3**—Buckhurst Hill (h); **4**—Gidea Park (h); **5**—Freebooters (h); **6**—A. B. Lavers XI (h); **7**—A. W. J. Osborne XI (h); **8**—Southgate (h); **15**—Harlow (h); **17**—Gidea Park (a); **22**—Enfield (a); **29**—Cheshunt (h). **SEPTEMBER 5**—Met. Police (a); **12**—Bishops Stortford (h); **19**—Chelmsford (a); **26**—Harlow (h).

LUTON TOWN

APRIL 25—Tring Park (a). **MAY 2**—Hitchin Town (h); **9**—Aylesbury (h); **16**—Enfield (a); **23**—Hertford (h); **24**—Middlesex County XI (S. M. Brown's benefit) (h); **25**—Pakistan Eaglets (11-30) (h); **26**—F. Appleyard's XI (11-30) (h); **30**—Mill Hill (h). **JUNE 6**—Bedford (a); **13**—Chesham (h); **20**—Wembley (a); **27**—West Herts (h). **JULY 4**—Cheshunt (h); **11**—St Albans (a); **18**—Bedford (h); **25**—Chesham (a). **AUGUST 1**—St. Albans (h); **8**—Vauxhall Motors (11-30) (h); **8**—Brentham (a); **15**—West Herts (a); **22**—Cheshunt (a); **29**—Enfield (h). **SEPTEMBER 5**—Oxford City (a); **12**—Tring Park (h); **19**—Barnet (2-0) (a).

MAIDENHEAD AND BRAY

MAY 2—Berkshire Gents (h); **5**—London Hospital (h); **9**—Reading (a); **16**—West Drayton (h); **30**—West Surrey (h). **JUNE 6**—Datchet (a); **13**—Ealing (a); **20**—Early Birds (h); **27**—Wellington College (a). **JULY 4**—Datchet (a); **11**—Boyne Hill (a); **18**—Ealing (h); **25**—Club Fete (h). **AUGUST 1**—Ashford (h); **3**—Becontree (h); **4**—Mr. C. E. Mott-Radclyffe's XI (h); **5**—Mr. Andrew Dawson's XI (h); **8**—West Drayton (a); **15**—Richmond (11-30) (h); **22**—Richmond (a). **SEPTEMBER 5**—Olinda (a); **12**—Ashford (a); **19**—Boyne Hill (h).

MALDEN WANDERERS

APRIL 25—Guildford (h). **MAY 2**—Beddington (h); **9**—Mitcham (h); **16**—Teddington (h); **23**—Orpington (h); **30**—Hounslow (a). **JUNE 6**—Ealing (a); **13**—Wimbledon (a); **20**—Merton (a); **27**—Wimbledon (h). **JULY 4**—Barclays Bank (h); **11**—Bank of England (h); **18**—Teddington (a); **25**—Horsham (a). **AUGUST 1**—Mitcham (a); **8**—Merton (h); **15**—Hounslow (h); **22**—Streatham (a); **29**—Cheam (a). **SEPTEMBER 5**—Ealing (h); **12**—Westminster Bank (h); **19**—Barclays Bank (a); **26**—Horsham (h).

MERTON

MAY 2—Horsham (a); **9**—Old Colfeians (a); **16**—Catford Wanderers (h); **23**—Barnes (a); **25**—Spencer (a); **30**—Old Rutlishians (a). **JUNE 2**—Wimbledon (a); **6**—Guildford (a); **13**—Teddington (h); **20**—Malden Wanderers (h); **27**—Catford Wanderers (a). **JULY 4**—Honor Oak (h); **11**—Wallington (a); **18**—Lloyds Register (a); **25**—Mitcham (h). **AUGUST 1**—Wembley (h); **3**—Spencer (h); **8**—Malden Wanderers (a); **12**—Surrey Club & Ground (h); **15**—Mitcham (a); **22**—Wanstead (h). **SEPTEMBER 5**—Norwood (h); **12**—L. B. Fishlock's XI (h); **19**—Alexandra Park (a); **26**—Epsom (h).

METROPOLITAN POLICE

MAY 2—Wembley (a); **9**—Marlborough (1870) (h); **16**—Ilford (h); **23**—Ealing Dean; **25**—Cheltenham (a); **26**—Stratford-on-Avon (a); **27**—North Warwickshire (a). **JUNE 13**—Royal Navy (h); **20**—Woodford Wells (a); **27**—Aldershot Services (h). **JULY 4**—West Indies (h); **11**—The Deanery (h); **18**—Honor Oak (h); **25**—Blackheath (a); **30**—Kent County Police (a) **AUGUST 3**—Mitcham (a); **5**—Banstead (a); **8**—Southgate (h); **15**—Wembley (h); **22**—Nomads (h); **29**—Finchley (h). **SEPTEMBER 4**—Mitcham (a); **5**—Southgate (a); **12**—Bexley (h); **19**—Ealing Dean (a); **26**—Richmond (h).

MITCHAM

MAY 2—Forest Hill (a); **9**—Malden Wanderers (a); **16**—Banstead (a); **23**—Catford (h); **30**—Beddington (a). **JUNE 6**—Spencer (a); **13**—Barnes (h); **20**—Dartford (h); **27**—Spencer (h). **JULY 4**—Barnes (a); **11**—Catford (a); **18**—Banstead (h); **25**—Merton (a). **AUGUST 1**—Malden Wanderers (h); **8**—Shepherds Bush (h); **15**—Merton (h); **22**—Dartford (a); **29**—Beddington (h). **SEPTEMBER 5**—Catford Wanderers (h); **12**—Forest Hill (h); **19**—Shepherds Bush (a); **26**—Catford Wanderers (a).

NORTH LONDON

APRIL 25—Woodside Park (h). **MAY 2**—Finchley (a); **9**—Barnet (a); **16**—Alexandra Park (h); **23**—B.B.C. (a); **25**—Harrow Town (h); **30**—Edmonton (a). **JUNE 2**—Highgate (a); **6**—Highgate (a); **13**—Finchley (h); **20**—Highgate (h); **27**—Stanmore (a). **JULY 11**—Barnet (h); **18**—Alexandra Park (a); **25**—Northampton Polytechnic (a). **AUGUST 1**—Kenton (h); **3**—Welwyn Garden City (a); **8**—Northampton Polytechnic (h); **15**—Harrow Town (a); **22**—Kenton (a); **29**—Leavesden Mental Hospital (a). **SEPTEMBER 5**—Turnham Green (a); **12**—Edmonton (h); **19**—Turnham Green (h); **26**—Winchmore Hill (h).

NORWOOD

MAY 2—Ashstead (a); **9**—Exiles (a); **16**—Addiscombe (a); **23**—Bexley Heath (h); **30**—Old Elthamians (a). **JUNE 6**—Exiles (h); **13**—Thornton Heath (a); **20**—Crofton Park (h); **27**—Old Rutlishians (a). **JULY 4**—Britannic House (a); **11**—Roehampton (a); **18**—Phoenix (a); **25**—West Wickham (h). **AUGUST 1**—Phoenix (h); **8**—Addiscombe (h); **9**—Surrey County XI (A. V. Bedser's Benefit) (h); **15**—Alleyn Old Boys (a); **22**—Old Emanuel (h); **29**—Twickenham (h). **SEPTEMBER 5**—Merton (a); **12**—Crofton Park (a); **19**—West Wickham (a); **26**—Old Rutlishians (h).

OLD MILLHILLIANS

MAY 2—Wimbledon (h); 9—Old Lyonians (h); 16—Northwood (a); 23—Old Albanians (a); 30—Old Cholmeleians (h). **JUNE** 6—Chorley Wood (h); 13—Mill Hill School (a); 20—Hertford (a); 27—Totteridge (h). **JULY** 4—Hampstead (a); 11—Old Dunstonians (a); 18—U.C.S. Old Boys (h); 25—Stanmore (a). **AUGUST** 1—Old Alleynians (h); 8—Mill Hill Village (h); 15—Hornsey (h); 22—Old Paulines (h); 29—Bushey (a). **SEPTEMBER** 5—Old Citizens (h); 19—Hornsey (a).

OXFORD CITY

MAY 2—Hertford College (a); 9—Stroud (h); 16—St. Peter's Hall (a); 23—Brasenose College (a); 30—St. John's College (a). **JUNE** 6—Banbury (a); 13—Magdalen College (a); 27—Swindon (h). **JULY** 4—Stroud (a); 11—High Wycombe (h); 18—Aylesbury (h); 25—High Wycombe (a). **AUGUST** 1—Reading (h); 8—North Oxford (a); 22—Swindon (a); 29—Cheltenham (h). **SEPTEMBER** 5—Luton (h); 12—Aylesbury (a).

PUTNEY

MAY 2—Imperial (NAAFI) (a); 9—Ministry of Works (h); 16—Wimbledon Village (a); 23—City of London Police (h); 30—Rootes (a). **JUNE** 6—Castle (h); 13—Rootes (h); 27—Argonauts (h). **JULY** 4—Streatham Wanderers (h); 11—Ministry of Works (a); 18—War Office (h); 25—Streatham Wanderers (a). **AUGUST** 1—Northolt Park (h); 8—Ministry of Health (a); 15—Wimbledon Village (h); 22—Burgh Heath (a); 29—South Belgravia (h). **SEPTEMBER** 12—War Office (a); 26—Ministry of Health (h).

REDHILL

MAY 2—Caterham Spartans (a); 9—Chaldon (h); 16—Tadworth (a); 23—Selsdon (a); 25—Australia House (h); 30—Edenbeck (h). **JUNE** 6—Tadworth (h); 13—Y.M.C.A. (Reigate) (h); 20—Sherwood Park (a); 27—Tolworthy Artisans (h). **JULY** 4—Woodmansterne (a); 11—Selsdon (h); 18—Y.M.C.A. (a). **AUGUST** 1—Edenbeck (a); 3—Y.M.C.A. (a); 15—Purley (a); 22—Sherwood Park (h); 29—East Coulsdon (a). **SEPTEMBER** 5—Wigmore (h); 12—Caterham Spartans (h).

RICHMOND

APRIL 25—Dulwich (a). **MAY** 2—Finchley (h); 9—Bickley Park (a); 16—Hornsey (a); 23—South Hampstead (h); 30—Beckenham (h). **JUNE** 6—Dulwich (h); 13—Hornsey (h); 29—Old Paulines (a); 27—Horsell (a). **JULY** 4—Beckenham (a); 11—Sutton (h); 18—Guildford (h); 25—Ealing (a). **AUGUST** 1—Hampstead (a); 8—Old Grammarians (a); 15—Maidenhead (a); 22—Wimbledon (a); 29—Leatherhead (a). **SEPTEMBER** 5—South Hampstead (a); 12—Sutton (a); 19—Richmond Town (h); 26—Metropolitan Police (a).

RICKMANSWORTH

MAY 2—Amersham Hill; 9—Great Western Railway; 16—Pinner; 23—Amersham; 25—U.C.S. Old Boys; 30—Abbots Langley. **JUNE** 6—Chalfont St. Peter; 13—Watford Grammar School; 20—Chorley Wood; 27—Tring Park. **JULY** 4—Chipperfield; 11—Harrow Town; 15—Herts County; 18—Totteridge; 25—Chorley Wood; 29—Hereford Ramblers. **AUGUST** 1—Ickenham; 3—Amersham Hill; 8—U.C.S. Old Boys; 15—Abbots Langley; 22—Amersham; 29—Old Lyonians. **SEPTEMBER** 5—Richings Park; 12—Northwood; 19—Chalfont St. Peter; 26—Fencibles.

RIPLEY

MAY 2—Shalford (h); 9—Pyrford (a); 16—Whiteley Village (h); 23—Ripley Court (a). **JUNE** 6—The Crickets (h); 13—Pyrford (h); 20—Shalford (a); 27—Farncombe (h). **JULY** 4—Bookham (a); 11—Old Guildfordians (h); 18—The Research G.E.C. Social & Athletic Club (h). **AUGUST** 1—Merton Wanderers (h); 15—United Services (Balham) (h); 22—Old Guildfordians (a); 29—Bookham (h).

ROEHAMPTON

APRIL 25—Barnes (a). **MAY** 2—Vickers Armstrong (a); 9—Old Rutlishians (a); 16—Elmers End (h); 23—Twickenham (h); 25—Cranleigh (a); 30—Teddington (h) **JUNE** 6—Cranleigh (h); 13—East Molesey (h); 20—Ibis (h); 27—Sunbury (h). **JULY** 4—Mill Hill Park (a); 11—Norwood (h); 18—Addiscombe (h); 25—Sunbury (a). **AUGUST** 3—Teddington (a); 8—Twickenham (a); 15—Hampton Wick Royal (h); 22—Wembley (h); 29—Barnes (h). **SEPTEMBER** 5—Elmers End (h); 12—Springfield Hospital (a); 19—Harrow Town (h); 26—Uxbridge (h).

ST. ALBANS

MAY 2—Radlett (a); **9**—Mill Hill (h); **16**—Harpenden (h); **23**—County Hall (h); **30**—Kenton (a). **JUNE 6**—Wembley (h); **13**—Harrow Town (a); **2**;—West Herts (11-30) (a); **27**—Hemel Hempstead (a). **JULY 4**—Hertford (a); **11**—Luton (h); **18**—Hemel Hempstead (h); **25**—Pinner (h). **AUGUST 1**—Luton (a); **8**—West Herts (h); **15**—Mill Hill (a); **22**—Harpenden (a); **29**—Northampton Polytechnic (h). **SEPTEMBER 5**—Radlett (h); **12**—Wembley (a); **19**—Pinner (a).

SEVENOAKS VINE

APRIL 18—Streatham (a); **25**—2nd XI (h). **MAY 2**—Bickley Park (h); **9**—Mote (h); **16**—Gravesend (h); **23**—Blackheath (a); **25**—Mote (a); **30**—Westminster Bank (h). **JUNE 1**—Yorkshire Owls (h); **2**—Nomads (h); **6**—Reigate Priory (h); **9**—Kent II v. Surrey United Hospitals (h); **13**—Gravesend (a); **17**—Sevenoaks School (h); **20**—Gore Court (h); **27**—Linden Park (a). **JULY 2**—King's School, Canterbury (a); **4**—Tunbridge Wells (h); **8**—Kent v. Surrey Women (h); **11**—Linden Park (h); **18**—Bromley (a); **21**—Old Bedfordians (a); **25**—B.B.C. (a). **AUGUST 1**—Buccaneers (h); **3**—M.C.C. (h); **4**—Stoics (h); **5**—Sir Ralph Smith Marriott's XI (h); **6**—The Wanderers (h); **7**—To be arranged (h); **8**—Dulwich (h); **14**—Dragons (h); **15**—Gore Court (a); **22**—Lloyds Bank (h); **24**—Evesham (h); **29**—Reigate Priory (a). **SEPTEMBER 2**—Sevenoaks Wednesday (h); **5**—Bromley (h); **12**—Tunbridge Wells (a); **19**—Blackheath (h); **26**—Streatham (h).

SLOUGH

MAY 2—Reading; **9**—Beaconsfield; **16**—Chesham; **23**—Brentham; **30**—Camberley. **JUNE 6**—Gerrards Cross; **13**—High Wycombe; **20**—South Hampstead; **27**—Brondesbury. **JULY 4**—Shepherds Bush; **11**—Chesham; **18**—Camberley; **25**—Lensbury. **AUGUST 1**—Shepherds Bush; **8**—Hounslow; **15**—High Wycombe; **22**—Bedford Town; **29**—Amersham. **SEPTEMBER 5**—Beaconsfield; **12**—South Hampstead; **19**—Old Merchant Taylors; **26**—Amersham.

SOUTHALL

APRIL 25—Club Match (h). **MAY 2**—Harlesden (a); **9**—Chertsey (a); **16**—Feltham (a); **23**—Midland Bank (a); **30**—Ashford (a). **JUNE 6**—Burnham (a); **13**—London Welsh (a); **20**—Turnham Green (h); **27**—Feltham (h). **JULY 4**—Pinner (h); **11**—Burnham (h). **AUGUST 8**—Old Latymerians (h); **15**—Devon Tour; **22**—Sunbury (a); **29**—Chertsey (h); **SEPTEMBER 5**—Hayes (h).

SOUTHEND-ON-SEA

MAY 2—Orsett (h); **9**—Walthamstow (a); **16**—Upminster (h); **23**—Romford (h); **25**—Leigh & Chalkwell (a); **30**—Chelmsford (a). **JUNE 6**—Wickford (a); **13**—Ilford (a); **20**—Hornchurch (a); **27**—Westcliff (h). **JULY 4**—Shoeburyness Garrison (a); **11**—Romford (a); **18**—Chelmsford (h); **25**—Gidea Park (h). **AUGUST 1**—Walthamstow (h); **3**—Leigh & Chalkwell (h); **8**—Westcliff (a); **15**—Shoeburyness Garrison (a); **22**—Upminster (a); **29**—Gidea Park (a). **SEPTEMBER 1**—Essex Club and Ground (h); **5**—Ilford (h); **12**—Wickford (h); **19**—Hornchurch (h); **26**—Hale End and South Essex (h).

SOUTHGATE

MAY 2—Ealing (h); **16**—United Services (Portsmouth) (a); **23**—Hornsey (a); **25**—Hertford (h); **30**—Finchley (h). **JUNE 2**—Enfield (a); **6**—Cambridge University Crusaders (h); **20**—Hampstead (h). **JULY 5**—Frogs (h); **13**—Sheffield University (h); **14**—Wanderers (h); **18**—Hornsey (h); **23**—M.C.C. (h); **25**—Finchley (a); **AUGUST 3**—Hertford (a); **15**—Hampstead (a); **29**—Ealing (a); **SEPTEMBER 5**—Metropolitan Police (h).

SYDENHAM

MAY 2—Cornhill (a); **9**—Siemens (h); **16**—Northern Assurance (a); **23**—Old Brockleians (a); **30**—West Essex (h). **JUNE 6**—Chislehurst (h); **13**—Siemens (a); **20**—Forest Hill (a); **27**—Old Dunstonians (a). **JULY 4**—Forest Hill (h); **11**—Hay's Wharf (a); **18**—Imperial (a). **AUGUST 1**—The Times (h); **8**—Harvey Sports Club (a); **15**—Borough Polytechnic (h); **22**—Croydon M.O. (a); **29**—Hay's Wharf (h). **SEPTEMBER 5**—Hongkong & Shanghai Bank (a); **12**—Northern Assurance (h); **19**—Chislehurst (a); **26**—Irving (h).

TAUNTON

APRIL 25—Chard (h). **MAY 2**—Exeter (a); **9**—Dorchester (a); **16**—Morlands (h); **23**—Yeovil (a); **25**—Torquay (a); **30**—Exeter St. James (a). **JUNE 6**—Bridgwater (h); **11**—Somerset Dragons (a); **13**—Optimists (Bristol) (h); **20**—Weston (a); **27**—Bridgwater (a). **JULY 4**—Bristol Bohemians (a); **11**—Bath (h); **18**—Bristol Bohemians (a); **25**—Flax Bourton (a); **30**—Pelicans (a). **AUGUST 1**—Exeter (h); **8**—Weston (h); **15**—Yeovil (h); **22**—Morlands (a); **29**—Bath (a). **SEPTEMBER 5**—Torquay (h); **12**—Optimists (Bristol) (a); **19**—South Petherton (a).

THAMES DITTON

APRIL 25—Hinchley Wood (a). **MAY** 2—Cobham (h); 9—Ashtead (a); 16—Hook (h); 23—East Molesey (h); 25—Esher (a); 30—Old Paulines (h). **JUNE** 6—Old Whitgiftians (h); 13—Vagabonds (h); 20—Cranleigh (h); 27—Horsham (a). **JULY** 4—Lensbury (h); 11—Old Citizens (a); 18—Oatlands Park (a); 25—Old Hamptonians (h). **AUGUST** 1—Cranleigh (a); 3—Esher (h); 4—C. H. Dixon's XI (h); 5—Incognite (h); 6—Barnes (h); 7—M.C.C. (h); 8—Guildford (h); 15—Cobham (a); 22—Old Whitgiftians (a); 29—Hampton Wick (h). **SEPTEMBER** 5—Ashtead (h); 12—Epsom (a); 19—Oatlands Park (h); 26—Hinchley Wood (h).

TORQUAY

MAY 2—Bovey Tracey (a); 9—Plymouth Bohemians (h); 16—United Services (a); 23—Heathcoat (h); 25—Taunton (h); 30—Paignton (a). **JUNE** 2—Ashford (Middlesex) (h); 6—R.N.E. College (h); 8—Leicester N. (h); 10-11—Devon v. Lancashire (h); 13—South Devon (a); 16—Turners' Sports (h); 17—Mitre (Notts) (h); 18—Kings Heath (h); 20—Paignton (h); 22—D. Ashpool's XI (h); 24—Caius College, Cambridge (h); 27-29—Torquay XI v. Gloucestershire (h); 30—Catford Wanderers (h). **JULY** 1—Hampstead (h); 3—Linden Park (h); 4—Exeter (a); 6—Imperial College (h); 7—Old Morlians (h); 8—Purley (h); 11—Plymouth (a); 13—Bath (h); 14—Holywood (N.I.) (h); 18—Paignton (h); 20—Harrow Town (h); 23—Reading (h); 25—South Devon (a); 27—Coventry & N. Warks (h); 28—Roehampton (h); 29—Polytechnic (h). **AUGUST** 1—Bovey Tracey (h); 3—Bournville (h); 4—Swansea (h); 6—U.C.S. Old Boys (h); 8—Exeter (h); 10—Sun of Canada (h); 11—Optimists (h); 12—Romford (h); 13—Malden Wanderers (h); 15—Plymouth (h); 18—Old Olavians (h); 19—Northants Amateurs (h); 20—Lydney (h); 22—South Devon (h); 25-26—Devon v. Surrey 2nd (h); 27—Hants & Sussex Bords. (h); 29—Heathcoat (a); 31—Devon Dumplings (h). **SEPTEMBER** 5—Taunton (a).

TUNBRIDGE WELLS

APRIL 25—Hastings Ramblers (h). **MAY** 2—Brighton & Hove (a); 9—Tonbridge (h); 16—Linden Park (h); 23—Frindsbury (a); 25—Thornton Heath (a); 30—Gore Court (a). **JUNE** 4—Yorkshire Owls (h); 6—Hastings Ramblers (a); 20—Kent County Cricket Week (h); 27—Barclays Bank (a). **JULY** 4—Sevenoaks Vine (a); 11—Bromley (a); 18—Lensbury (a); 25—Linden Park (a). **AUGUST** 1—Horsham (a); 8—Crowborough (a); 10—Blue Mantles (h); 15—East Grinstead (h); 22—Gore Court (h); 29—Eastbourne (a). **SEPTEMBER** 5—Brighton & Hove (h); 12—Sevenoaks Vine (h); 19—Gravesend (a); 26—Crowborough (h).

TURNHAM GREEN

APRIL 25—Old Medonians (a). **MAY** 2—Kenton (h); 9—Calthorpe (a); 16—Springfield Hospital (a); 30—Streatham (a). **JUNE** 6—Economicals (a); 13—Lyons (a); 20—Southall (a); 27—Twickenham (h). **JULY** 11—Northern Polytechnic (h); 18—Highgate (a); 25—Harrow Town (h). **AUGUST** 1—Standard Telephones (a); 8—Hornsey (h); 22—M.C.C. (h); 29—Northern Polytechnic (a). **SEPTEMBER** 5—North London (h); 19—North London (a); 26—Kenton (a).

UXBRIDGE

APRIL 25—Fencibles (a). **MAY** 2—Chalfont St. Peter (h); 9—Eastcote (a); 16—West Herts (a); 23—Pinner (h); 25—Old Lyonians (h); 30—Amersham (h). **JUNE** 6—West Drayton (a); 13—Boyne Hill (h); 20—Eastcote (h); 27—Pinner (a). **JULY** 4—Chalfont St. Peter (a); 11—Gerrards Cross (h); 18—West Herts (h); 25—Amersham (a). **AUGUST** 1—West Drayton (h); 3—Old Lyonians (a); 8—Kenton (a); 15—Ashford (h); 22—Gerrards Cross (a); 29—Boyne Hill (a). **SEPTEMBER** 5—Laleham (a); 12—Harrow (a); 19—Fencibles (h); 26—Roehampton (a).

VENTNOR

MAY 2—Shanklin (h); 9—Saunders Roe (a); 16—St. Helens (a); 23—Kayes Social Club (Enfield) (h); 25—Lathol (h); 30—Newport (I.O.W.) (h). **JUNE** 6—St Helens (h); 13—West Wight (a); 20—East Cowes (h); 27—Fairlee (a). **JULY** 4—Fairlee (h); 11—Ryde Borough (a); 12—Hampshire County XI (h); 18—East Cowes (a); 25—Newport (a). **AUGUST** 1—Northwood (h); 3—Bucks Mosquitoes (h); 8—Northwood (a); 15—Ryde Borough (h); 22—South Hants (h); 29—Shanklin (a). **SEPTEMBER** 5—St. Helens (h); 12—Saunders Roe (h); 19—Rookwood (h).

WALTHAM CROSS

MAY 2—Bengeo (h); 9—North Enfield (h); 16—Stanstead Abbotts (h); 23—Rochfords (a); 30—Hertingfordbury (h). **JUNE** 6—Beaumont Manor (a); 13—East Barnet Valley (h); 20—Much Hadham (a); 27—Loughton (h). **JULY** 4—Botany Bay (h); 11—Bengeo (a); 18—Knebworth Park (h); 25—Bayford and Hertford Nondescripts (h). **AUGUST** 1—Cockfosters (a); 8—R.A.F.A. Southgate (h); 15—Bleak Lodge (a); 22—Cockfosters (h); 29—Chaseville (h). **SEPTEMBER** 12—R.A.F.A. Southgate (a); 19—Stanstead Abbotts (a).

WALTHAMSTOW

MAY 2—Upminster (h); **9**—Southend (h); **16**—Buckhurst Hill (a); **25**—Kenton (h); **30**—London Hospital (a). **JUNE 6**—Romford (h); **13**—West Essex (a); **27**—Epping (h). **JULY 4**—Hornchurch (a); **11**—South Woodford (a); **25**—West Essex (h). **AUGUST 1**—Southend (a); **3**—Kenton (a); **8**—Upminster (a); **22**—Highams Park (h); **29**—No. 3 District Met. Police (a). **SEPTEMBER 5**—Hornchurch (h); **12**—Richmond Town (a); **19**—Harlesden (h); **26**—Buckhurst Hill (h).

WATERLOWS (DUNSTABLE)

MAY 2—Hazells (a); **9**—Biggleswade Town (a); **16**—Bedford Queens (a); **25**—A.C. Sphinx (h); **30**—Hartley Country Club (a). **JUNE 6**—Elstree (h); **13**—Heston (h); **20**—Watford Nomads (h); **27**—Tabulator Sports (h). **JULY 4**—West Willesden (h); **11**—Biggleswade Town (h); **18**—Hazells (h); **25**—Elstree (a). **AUGUST 3**—Luton Corinthians (h); **8**—Saints (Northampton) (h); **22**—Outlaws (h); **29**—Bedford Queens (h). **SEPTEMBER 5**—Tabulator Sports (a); **12**—Saints (Northampton) (a).

WELWYN GARDEN CITY

MAY 2—Chipperfield (h); **9**—King's Walden (h); **16**—Hornsey (h); **23**—Letchworth (a); **25**—R. W. Dale's XI (h); **30**—Harpenden (a). **JUNE 6**—Broxbourne (a); **13**—Three Counties (a); **20**—Hitchin (h); **27**—Hertford (a). **JULY 4**—King's Walden (a); **11**—Letchworth (h); **14**—Herts County Club (h); **16**—S. F. Brown's XI (h); **18**—Cockfosters (h); **25**—Chipperfield (a). **AUGUST 1**—Stevenage (h); **3**—North London (h); **8**—Hitchin (a); **15**—Harpenden (h); **22**—Hertford (a); **29**—Hornsey (a). **SEPTEMBER 5**—Broxbourne (h); **12**—Bedford (h); **19**—Stevenage (a).

WEMBLEY

APRIL 25—Ashford (a). **MAY 2**—Metropolitan Police (h); **9**—Stanmore (h); **16**—Ashford (h); **21**—Wanderers (h); **23**—Mill Hill (a); **25**—Hampton Wick Royal (h); **30**—Ealing Dean (h) **JUNE 2**—Mill Hill (h); **6**—St. Albans (a); **13**—Leavesden Hospital (h); **20**—Luton Town (h); **27**—Northampton Polytechnic (a). **JULY 4**—Thornton Heath (h); **9**—Wasps R.F.C. (h); **11**—Cheshunt (a); **18**—Thornton Heath (a); **25**—Mill Hill (h). **AUGUST 1**—Merton (a); **3**—Hounslow (a); **8**—Finchley (h); **15**—Metropolitan Police (a); **22**—Roehampton (a); **29**—Edmonton (a). **SEPTEMBER 5**—Barnet (h); **12**—St. Albans (h); **19**—Northampton Polytechnic (h); **26**—West Herts (h). **OCTOBER 3**—Brondesbury (h).

WINCHMORE HILL

APRIL 25—Edmonton (a). **MAY 2**—Woodford Wells (a); **9**—Chingford (h); **16**—South Woodford (h); **23**—Wanstead (a); **30**—North Middlesex (h). **JUNE 6**—Finchley (a); **13**—Brighton & Hove (a); **20**—London University (h); **27**—Honor Oak (a). **JULY 4**—M.C.C. (h); **11**—Westcliff (h); **18**—Wanstead (h); **25**—Westcliff (a). **AUGUST 1**—Ealing Dean (a); **8**—Chingford (a); **15**—Upper Clapton (h); **22**—Edmonton (h); **29**—Woodford Wells (h). **SEPTEMBER 5**—North Middlesex (a); **12**—Enfield (a); **19**—Finchley (h); **26**—Hertford (a).

WINDSOR AND ETON

APRIL 25—Burnham (h). **MAY 2**—Datchet (a); **16**—Watford Town (h); **23**—Victoria C.C. (h); **25**—Wargrave (a); **30**—Laleham (a). **JUNE 2**—Victoria C.C. (h); **6**—The Outlaws (h); **13**—Harrow St. Marys (h); **20**—Leavesden Hospital (a); **27**—Royal Household C.C. (a); **28**—Berkshire Gentlemen (h). **JULY 4**—Richings Park (h); **5**—Cookham Dene (a); **11**—Chiswick (h); **12**—Chiswick (a); **18**—Major Mott Radclyffe's XI (h); **19**—Cippenham (a); **25**—Burnham (a); **26**—Cookham Dene (h). **AUGUST 1**—White Waltham (h); **3**—Broadwater, Worthing (a); **8**—Royal Household C.C. (h); **15**—Victoria C.C. (a); **22**—Englefield Green (a); **29**—Ritchings Park (a). **SEPTEMBER 5**—Boyne Hill, Maidenhead (a); **12**—Laleham (h); **19**—Cippenham (h); **26**—Harrow St. Marys (a).

WITLEY

MAY 2—Godalming (h); **9**—Shalford (a); **16**—Guildford City Social Club (a); **23**—Hambledon (a); **25**—Severn C.C. (h); **30**—Ewhurst (h). **JUNE 6**—Dennis Athletic (h); **13**—Valley End (h); **20**—Worplesdon (a); **27**—Dennis Athletic (a). **JULY 4**—Carshalton (h); **11**—Ewhurst (a); **18**—Milford (a); **25**—Worplesdon (h). **AUGUST 1**—Valley End (a); **3**—Tolworth Artisans (h); **8**—Shalford (h); **15**—Milford (h); **29**—Hambledon (h). **SEPTEMBER 5**—Godalming (a).

Cricket League Secretaries

BASSETLAW LEAGUE: W. H. Tomlins, 33, Park Street, Worksop, Notts.

BIRMINGHAM LEAGUE: K. Spooner, 53, Strensham Rd., Birmingham, 12.

BRADFORD LEAGUE: W. Snowden, 228, Westfield Lane, Shipley, Yorks.

BOLTON ASSOCIATION: H. Roberts, 28, Warwick Street, Bolton.

BOLTON LEAGUE: K. H. Mercer, 2, Westcliffe Road, Bolton.

BURY AMATEUR LEAGUE: W. Yates, 38, Higher Ainsworth Rd., Radcliffe.

CENTRAL LANCASHIRE LEAGUE: J. Kay, 15, Townscroft Avenue, Middleton, Lancs.

CHORLEY AND DISTRICT AMATEUR LEAGUE: H. Taylor, 1a, Lodge Bank, Brinscall, near Chorley, Lancs.

DURHAM SENIOR LEAGUE: M. A. Coombs, "Fairhurst," 3, Stannington Grove, Sunderland.

EAST YORKSHIRE CUP: W. R. Batty, 68, Jamieson Terrace, York.

GLOSSOP AND DISTRICT LEAGUE: C. Elliott, High View, 3, Ashes Lane, Dinting Road, Glossop.

HUDDERSFIELD AND DISTRICT LEAGUE: J. Wilson Senior, 79, Birch Road, Berry Brow, Huddersfield.

LANCASHIRE LEAGUE: J. Isherwood, 118, Manor Street, Accrington.

LANCASHIRE AND CHESHIRE LEAGUE: S. M. Screeton, 65, Scholes Lane, Prestwich, Manchester.

LEEDS LEAGUE: W. Sheard, Croft House, New Farnley, Leeds.

NORTHERN LEAGUE: W. Horner, 4, Carlton Avenue, Barrow-in-Furness.

NORTH LANCASHIRE LEAGUE: T. Lindow, 3a, Romney Park, Dalton-in-Furness.

NORTH STAFFORDSHIRE LEAGUE: A. Hodson, 3, Douglas Avenue, Oakhill, Stoke-on-Trent.

NORTH-WESTERN LEAGUE: A. H. Thomas, 32, Brookthorpe Avenue, Burnage, Manchester 19.

NORTH YORKSHIRE AND SOUTH DURHAM LEAGUE: H. Trenholm, "Etherley," 36, Grosvenor Road, Stockton-on-Tees.

RIBBLESDALE LEAGUE: F. Dugdale, 36, Park Avenue, Clitheroe.

SADDLEWORTH LEAGUE: H. Clayton, 660, Huddersfield Road, Hey Heads, Stalybridge.

SOUTH LANCASHIRE LEAGUE: R. Berry, 78, Gardner Road, Prestwich, Manchester.

WEST BRADFORD LEAGUE: R. Newiss, 6, Arnside Avenue, Riddlesden, Keighley.

YORKSHIRE COUNCIL: N. Stead, "Chez Nous," 337, Barwick Road Scholes, near Leeds, Yorks.

League Fixtures

BASSETLAW LEAGUE

SECTION "A"

APRIL

25 Blidworth C v. Dinnington C I
25 Bolsover Col v. Worksop
25 British Ropes v. Ransome & M
25 Harthill M W v. Rose Bros
25 Kiveton Col v. Ruston's

MAY

2 Bolsover Col v. Ransome & M
2 Dinnington C I v. Steetley W
2 Rose Bros v. British Ropes
2 Ruston's v. Harthill M W
2 Worksop v. Blidworth Col
9 Blidworth Col v. Rose Bros
9 British Ropes v. Worksop
9 Harthill M W v. Bolsover Col
9 Ransome & M v. Dinnington C I
9 Steetley Works v. Kiveton Col
16 Bolsover Col v. British Ropes
16 Dinnington C I v. Harthill M W
16 Kiveton Col v. Ransome & M
16 Rose Bros v. Blidworth Col
16 Ruston's v. Steetley Works
23 Bolsover Col v. Rose Bros
23 Dinnington C I v. Ruston's
23 Harthill M W v. Kiveton Col
23 Ransome & M v. Worksop
23 Steetley Works v. Blidworth C
25 Blidworth Col v. Ransome & M
25 Dinnington C I v. Bolsover Col
25 Kiveton Col v. Steetley Works
25 Ruston's v. Rose Bros
25 Worksop v. British Ropes
26 Steetley W v. Dinnington C I
26 Worksop v. Harthill M W
30 British Ropes v. Harthill M W
30 Dinnington C I v. Blidworth Col
30 Ransome & M v. Bolsover Col
30 Ruston's v. Kiveton Col
30 Worksop v. Rose Bros

JUNE

6 Blidworth Col v. Worksop
6 Harthill M W v. Ruston's
6 Kiveton Col v. Dinnington C I
6 Rose Bros v. Ransome & M
6 Steetley Works v. British Ropes
13 Bolsover Col v. Steetley Works
13 British Ropes v. Rose Bros
13 Ransome & M v. Harthill M W
13 Ruston's v. Blidworth Col
13 Worksop v. Kiveton Col
20 Blidworth Col v. Ruston's
20 Dinnington C I v. Ransome & M
20 Harthill M W v. British Ropes
20 Kiveton Col v. Bolsover Col
20 Steetley Works v. Worksop
27 Blidworth Col v. Steetley Works
27 British Ropes v. Dinnington C I
27 Ransome & M v. Kiveton Col

JUNE

27 Rose Bros v. Bolsover Col
27 Worksop v. Ruston's

JULY

4 Dinnington C I v. Worksop
4 Harthill M W v. Ransome & M
4 Kiveton Col v. British Ropes
4 Ruston's v. Bolsover Col
4 Steetley Works v. Rose Bros
11 Bolsover Col v. Kiveton Col
11 British Ropes v. Steetley Works
11 Ransome & M v. Ruston's
11 Rose Bros v. Dinnington C I
18 Blidworth Col v. Kiveton Col
18 Rose Bros v. Harthill M W
18 Ruston's v. British Ropes
18 Steetley Works v. Bolsover Col
25 Bolsover Col v. Ruston's
25 British Ropes v. Blidworth Col
25 Rose Bros v. Steetley Works
25 Worksop v. Dinnington C I

AUGUST

1 Blidworth Col v. Bolsover Col
1 Dinnington C I v. British Ropes
1 Kiveton Col v. Worksop
1 Steetley Works v. Harthill M W
3 British Ropes v. Kiveton Col
3 Harthill M W v. Dinnington C I
3 Ransome & M v. Blidworth Col
3 Rose Bros v. Ruston's
3 Worksop v. Steetley Works
4 Kiveton Col v. Harthill M W
8 Blidworth Col v. British Ropes
8 Bolsover Col v. Harthill M W
8 Dinnington C I v. Rose Bros
8 Ruston's v. Worksop
8 Steetley Works v. Ransome & M
15 Harthill M W v. Blidworth Col
15 Ransome & M v. British Ropes
15 Rose Bros v. Kiveton Col
15 Ruston's v. Dinnington C I
15 Worksop v. Bolsover Col
22 British Ropes v. Ruston's
22 Bolsover Col v. Blidworth Col
22 Dinnington C I v. Kiveton Col
22 Harthill M W v. Worksop
22 Ransome & M v. Rose Bros
29 Blidworth Col v. Harthill M W
29 British Ropes v. Bolsover Col
29 Kiveton Col v. Rose Bros
29 Steetley Works v. Ruston's
29 Worksop v. Ransome & M

SEPTEMBER

5 Bolsover Col v. Dinnington C I
5 Harthill M W v. Steetley Works
5 Kiveton Col v. Blidworth Col
5 Rose Bros v. Worksop
5 Ruston's v. Ransome & M
12 Ransome & M v. Steetley W

BASSETLAW LEAGUE—Continued

SECTION "B"

April

25 Langwith Col v. Wales Church
25 Teversal & S C v. Gainsbro' B
25 Thurcroft M v. Clipstone Col

May

2 Clipstone C v. Langwith Col
2 Creswell Col v. Teversal & S C
2 Retford v. Shirebrook Col
2 Wales Church v. Gainsbro' B
2 Warsop M v. Thurcroft M
9 Langwith Col v. Killamarsh J
9 Retford v. Warsop M
9 Shirebrook Col v. Clipstone Col
9 Thurcroft M v. Gainsbro' B
9 Wales Church v. Creswell Col
16 Clipstone Col v. Creswell Col
16 Killamarsh Col v. Gainsbro' B
16 Langwith Col v. Retford
16 Shirebrook Col v. Thurcroft M
16 Teversal & S C v. Wales Church
23 Creswell Col v. Clipstone Col
23 Gainsbro' B v. Wales Church
23 Thurcroft M v. Langwith Col
23 Warsop M v. Teversal & S C
25 Clipstone Col v. Wales Church
25 Gainsbro' B v. Retford
25 Killamarsh J v. Thurcroft M
25 Langwith Col v. Warsop M
25 Shirebrook Col v. Creswell Col
26 Creswell Col v. Langwith Col
26 Teversal & SC v. Clipstone Col
26 Wales Church v. Killamarsh J
26 Warsop M v. Shirebrook Col
30 Killamarsh J v. Clipstone Col
30 Langwith Col v. Gainsbro' B
30 Retford v. Wales Church
30 Thurcroft M v. Warsop M

June

6 Clipstone Col v. Gainsbro' B
6 Killamarsh J v. Warsop M
6 Teversal & S C v. Retford
6 Wales Church v. Thurcroft M
13 Gainsbro' B v. Teversal & S C
13 Shirebrook Col v. Wales Church
13 Thurcroft M v. Creswell Col
13 Retford v. Langwith Col
13 Warsop M v. Killamarsh J
20 Clipstone Col v. Retford
20 Creswell Col v. Warsop M
20 Langwith Col v. Thurcroft M
20 Teversal & SC v. Killamarsh J
20 Wales Church v. Shirebrook Col
27 Clipstone Col v. Shirebrook Col
27 Gainsbro' B v. Thurcroft M
27 Killamarsh J v. Langwith Col
27 Retford v. Creswell Col
27 Teversal & S C v. Warsop M

July

4 Creswell Col v. Killamarsh J
4 Shirebrook Col v. Gainsbro' B
4 Thurcroft M v. Teversal & S C
4 Wales Church v. Retford
4 Warsop M v. Clipstone Col
11 Gainsbro' B v. Creswell Col
11 Killamarsh J v. Teversal & S C
11 Thurcroft M v. Wales Church
11 Warsop M v. Retford
18 Creswell Col v. Thurcroft M
18 Gainsbro' B v. Langwith Col
18 Retford v. Killamarsh J
18 Teversal & SC v. Shirebrook Col
18 Wales Church v. Warsop M
25 Clipstone Col v. Warsop M
25 Creswell Col v. Wales Church
25 Gainsbro' B v. Killamarsh J
25 Langwith Col v. Teversal & S C
25 Shirebrook Col v. Retford

August

1 Gainsbro' B v. Clipstone Col
1 Killamarsh J v. Creswell Col
1 Langwith Col v. Shirebrook Col
1 Retford v. Teversal & S C
1 Warsop M v. Wales Church
3 Creswell Col v. Shirebrook Col
3 Retford v. Gainsbro' B
3 Teversal & SC v. Langwith Col
3 Thurcroft M v. Killamarsh J
3 Wales Church v. Clipstone Col
4 Clipstone Col v. Teversal & S C
4 Killamarsh J v. Wales Church
4 Langwith Col v. Creswell Col
4 Shirebrook Col v. Warsop M
8 Clipstone Col v. Killamarsh J
8 Gainsbro' B v. Shirebrook Col
8 Wales Church v. Teversal & S C
8 Warsop M v. Creswell Col
8 Thurcroft M v. Retford
15 Creswell Col v. Gainsbro' B
15 Killamarsh J v. Shirebrook Col
15 Retford v. Clipstone Col
15 Teversal & S C v. Thurcroft M
15 Warsop M v. Langwith Col
22 Clipstone Col v. Thurcroft M
22 Creswell Col v. Retford
22 Gainsbro' B v. Warsop M
22 Shirebrook Col v. Killamarsh J
22 Wales Church v. Langwith Col
29 Killamarsh J v. Retford
29 Langwith Col v. Clipstone Col
29 Teversal & S C v. Creswell Col
29 Thurcroft M v. Shirebrook Col
29 Warsop M v. Gainsbro' B

September

5 Retford v. Thurcroft M
5 Shirebrook Col v. Langwith Col

To be arranged 30th May or Mid-week.

Shirebrook Col v. Teversal & SC

SECTION "C"

April

25 CWS Glasswks v. K.P.S.W.W.
25 Mansfield Col v. Welbeck Col
25 Manton Col v. Whitwell Col
25 Ollerton Col v. Marshalls

BASSETLAW LEAGUE—Continued

MAY

2 K.P.S.W.W. v. Mansfield Col
2 Manton Col v. Bilsthorpe Col
2 Marshalls v. Welbeck Col
2 Shireoaks MW v. CWS Glasswks
2 Whitwell Col v. Ollerton Col
9 CWS Glasswks v. Manton Col
9 K.P.S.W.W. v. Whitwell Col
9 Mansfield Col v. Bilsthorpe Col
9 Marshalls v. Shireoaks M W
9 Welbeck Col v. Ollerton Col
16 Bilsthorpe Col v. Marshalls
16 Manton Col v. K.P.S.W.W.
16 Ollerton Col v. CWS Glasswks
16 Shireoaks M W v. Welbeck Col
16 Whitwell Col v. New Hucknall C
23 CWS Glasswks v. Shireoaks MW
23 K.P.S.W.W. v. Bilsthorpe Col
23 Marshalls v. Ollerton Col
23 New Hucknall C v. Mansfield C
23 Welbeck Col v. Whitwell Col
25 Bilsthorpe Col v. New Hucknall
25 Mansfield Col v. Marshalls
25 Ollerton Col v. Manton Col
25 Shireoaks M W v. K.P.S.W.W.
25 Whitwell Col v. CWS Glasswks
26 Bilsthorpe Col v. Ollerton Col
26 Welbeck Col v. New Hucknall C
26 Whitwell Col v. Shireoaks M W
30 CWS Glasswks v. Marshalls
30 K.P.S.W.W. v. Ollerton Col
30 Mansfield Col v. Whitwell Col
30 New Hucknall Col v. Manton C
30 Welbeck Col v. Shireoaks M W

JUNE

6 Manton Col v. Mansfield Col
6 Marshalls v. CWS Glasswks
6 Ollerton Col v. Welbeck Col
6 Shireoaks MW v. New Hucknall
6 Whitwell Col v. Bilsthorpe Col
13 Bilsthorpe Col v. Manton Col
13 K.P.S.W.W. v. CWS Glasswks
13 Mansfield Col v. Shireoaks MW
13 New Hucknall C v. Ollerton C
13 Welbeck Col v. Marshalls
20 CWS Glasswks v. Mansfield Col
20 Manton Col v. New Hucknall Col
20 Marshalls v. Whitwell Col
20 Ollerton Col v. K.P.S.W.W.
20 Shireoaks MW v. Bilsthorpe Co
27 Bilsthorpe Col v. CWS Glasswks
27 K.P.S.W.W. v. Welbeck Col
27 Mansfield Col v. Ollerton Col
27 Manton Col v. Shireoaks M W
27 New Hucknall Col v. Marshalls

JULY

4 CWS Glasswks v. New Hucknall
4 Marshalls v. K.P.S.W.W.
4 Ollerton Col v. Bilsthorpe Col
4 Shireoaks MW v. Mansfield Col
4 Welbeck Col v. Manton Col
11 Bilsthorpe Col v. Welbeck Col
11 Mansfield Col v. K.P.S.W.W.
11 Manton Col v. CWS Glasswks
11 New Hucknall v. Shireoaks MW
11 Whitwell Col v. Marshalls
18 CWS Glasswks v. Bilsthorpe Col
18 K.P.S.W.W. v. Manton Col
18 Marshalls v. New Hucknall Col
18 Shireoaks MW v. Whitwell Col
18 Welbeck Col v. Mansfield Col
25 Bilsthorpe Col v. K.P.S.W.W.
25 Manton Col v. Marshalls
25 New Hucknall v. CWS Glasswks
25 Ollerton Col v. Mansfield Col
25 Whitwell Col v. Welbeck Col

AUGUST

1 CWS Glasswks v. Whitwell Col
1 K.P.S.W.W. v. New Hucknall C
1 Mansfield Col v. Manton Col
1 Shireoaks M W v. Ollerton Col
1 Welbeck Col v. Bilsthorpe Col
3 Bilsthorpe Col v. Shireoaks MW
3 Manton Col v. Welbeck Col
3 Marshalls v. Mansfield Col
3 New Hucknall C v. K.P.S.W.W.
3 Ollerton Col v. Whitwell Col
4 New Hucknall C v. Bilsthorpe C
4 Shireoaks M W v. Manton Col
4 Whitwell Col v. Mansfield Col
8 Bilsthorpe Col v. Whitwell Col
8 K.P.S.W.W. v. Marshalls
8 Mansfield Col v. New Hucknall
8 Manton Col v. Ollerton Col
8 Welbeck Col v. CWS Glasswks
15 Bilsthorpe Col v. Mansfield Col
15 CWS Glasswks v. Ollerton Col
15 K.P.S.W.W. v. Shireoaks M W
15 Marshalls v. Manton Col
15 New Hucknall C v. Whitwell C
22 Mansfield C v. CWS Glasswks
22 Ollerton C v. New Hucknall Col
22 Shireoaks M W v. Marshalls
22 Welbeck Col v. K.P.S.W.W.
22 Whitwell Col v. Manton Col
29 CWS Glasswks v. Welbeck Col
29 Marshalls v. Bilsthorpe Col
29 Ollerton Col v. Shireoaks M W
29 Whitwell Col v. K.P.S.W.W.

To arrange Mid-week.
New Hucknall C v. Welbeck C

BIRMINGHAM AND DISTRICT LEAGUE

MAY

9 Stourbridge v. Dudley
9 Kidderminster v. Smethwick
9 Aston Unity v. Moseley
9 Mitchells & Butlers v. Walsall
9 W B Dartmouth v. Old Hill
16 Dudley v. W B Dartmouth
16 Walsall v. Stourbridge
16 Aston Unity v. Mitchells & B

BIRMINGHAM & DISTRICT LEAGUE—Continued

MAY
16 Smethwick v. Moseley
16 Old Hill v. Kidderm'nster
23 Stourbridge v. Aston Unity
23 Dudley v. Walsall
23 Moseley v. Old Hill
23 Mitchells & B v. Smethwick
23 WBDartmouthv.Kidderminster
25 Walsall v. W B Dartmouth
25 Aston Unity v. Dudley
25 Smethwick v. Stourbridge
25 Old Hill v. Mitchells & Butlers
25 Kidderminster v. Moseley
26 Dudley v. Stourbridge
30 Stourbridge v. Old Hill
30 Dudley v. Smethwick
30 Walsall v. Aston Unity
30 Mitchells & B v. Kidderminster
30 W B Dartmouth v. Moseley

JUNE
6 Aston U v. W B Dartmouth
6 Smethwick v. Walsall
6 Old Hill v. Dudley
6 Kidderminster v. Stourbridge
6 Moseley v. Mitchells & Butlers
13 Stourbridge v. Moseley
13 Dudley v. Kidderminster
13 Walsall v. Old Hill
13 Aston Unity v. Smethwick
13 W B Dartmouth v. Mitchells & B
20 Old Hill v. Aston Unity
20 Kidderminster v. Walsall
20 Moseley v. Dudley
20 Mitchells & B v. Stourbridge
20 W B Dartmouth v. Smethwick
27 Stourbridge v. W B Dartmouth
27 Dudley v. Mitchells & Butlers
27 Walsall v. Moseley
27 Aston Unity v. Kidderminster
27 Smethwick v. Old Hill

JULY
4 Walsall v. Mitchells & Butlers
4 Moseley v. Aston Unity
4 Smethwick v. Kidderminster
4 Old Hill v. W B Dartmouth
11 Stourbridge v. Walsall
11 Kidderminster v. Old Hill
11 Moseley v. Smethwick
11 Mitchells & B v. Aston Unity
11 W B Dartmouth v. Dudley
18 Aston Unity v. Walsall
18 Smethwick v. Dudley
18 Old Hill v. Stourbridge
18 Kidderminster v. Mitchells & B
18 Moseley v. W B Dartmouth
25 Stourbridge v. Kidderminster
25 Dudley v. Old Hill
25 Walsall v. Smethwick
25 Mitchells & Butlers v. Moseley
25 W B Dartmouth v. Aston Unity

AUGUST
1 Walsall v. Dudley
1 Aston Unity v. Stourbridge
1 Smethwick v. Mitchells & B
1 Old Hill v. Moseley
1 Kidderminster v. W B Dartm'th
3 Stourbridge v. Smethwick
3 Dudley v. Aston Unity
3 Moseley v. Kidderminster
3 Mitchells & Butlers v. Old Hill
3 W B Dartmouth v. Walsall
4 Moseley v. Walsall
8 Smethwick v. Aston Unity
8 Old Hill v. Walsall
8 Kidderminster v. Dudley
8 Moseley v. Stourbridge
8 Mitchells & B v. W B Dartmouth
15 Stourbridge v. Mitchells & B
15 Dudley v. Moseley
15 Walsall v. Kidderminster
15 Aston Unity v. Old Hill
15 Smethwick v. W B Dartmouth
22 Old Hill v. Smethwick
22 Kidderminster v. Aston Unity
22 Mitchells & Butlers v. Dudley
22 W B Dartmouth v. Stourbridge
29 Champions v. The Rest

BOLTON AND DISTRICT ASSOCIATION

APRIL
25 Atherton C v. Barton Hall
25 Clifton v. Farnworth S C
25 Edgworth R v. Adlington
25 Little Hulton v. Walker Inst
25 Taylor Bros v. Astley & T C
25 Tootals S C v. Walkden M M

MAY
2 Adlington v. Taylor Bros
2 Astley & T C v. Tootals S C
2 Barton Hall v. Clifton
2 Farnworth S C v. Little Hulton
2 Walkden M M v. Edgworth R
2 Walker Institute v. Atherton C
9 Atherton C v. Adlington
9 Clifton v. Walkden M M
9 Edgworth R v. Walker Inst
9 Little Hulton v. Astley & T C
9 Taylor Bros v. Farnworth S C
9 Tootals S C v. Barton Hall
11-12 *Cross Cup (1st Round)*
11-12 Adlington v. Atherton C
11-12 Astley & T C v. Walkden MM
11-12 Farnworth SC v. Walker In
11-12 Little Hulton v. Clifton
11-12 Taylor Bros v. Edgworth R
11-12 Tootals S C v. Barton Hall
16 Adlington v. Little Hulton
16 Astley & T C v. Clifton
16 Barton Hall v. Edgworth R
16 Farnworth S C v. Tootals S C
16 Walkden M M v. Atherton C
16 Walker Institute v. Taylor Bros

BOLTON & DISTRICT ASSOCIATION—Continued

MAY

19-20 Adlington v. Farnworth S C
19-20 Atherton C v. Astley & T C
19-20 Barton Hall v. Taylor Bros
19-20 Edgworth R v. Clifton
19-20 Walkden M M v. Little Hulton
19-20 Tootals S C v. Walker Inst
23 Edgworth R v. Astley & T C
23 Farnworth S C v. Atherton C
23 Little Hulton v. Barton Hall
23 Taylor Bros v. Walkden M M
23 Tootals S C v. Adlington
23 Walker Institute v. Clifton
30 Adlington v. Walker Institute
30 Astley & T C v. Farnworth S C
30 Barton Hall v. Walkden M M
30 Clifton v. Atherton C
30 Little Hulton v. Edgworth R
30 Tootals S C v. Taylor Bros

JUNE

6 Adlington v. Clifton
6 Atherton C v. Tootals S C
6 Barton Hall v. Walker Institute
6 Edgworth R v. Farnworth S C
6 Taylor Bros v. Little Hulton
6 Walkden M M v. Astley & T C
13 Astley & T C v. Adlington
13 Clifton v. Taylor Bros
13 Edgworth R v. Atherton C
13 Farnworth S C v. Barton Hall
13 Little Hulton v. Tootals S C
13 Walker Inst v. Walkden M M
16-17 Astley & T C v. Atherton C
16-17 Clifton v. Edgworth R
16-17 Farnworth S C v. Adlington
16-17 Little Hulton v. Walkden M M
16-17 Taylor Bros v. Barton Hall
16-17 Walker Inst v. Tootals S C
20 Atherton C v. Little Hulton
20 Barton Hall v. Astley & T C
20 Farnworth S C v. Walker Inst
20 Taylor Bros v. Edgworth R
20 Tootals S C v. Clifton
20 Walkden M M v. Adlington
27 Adlington v. Barton Hall
27 Edgworth R v. Tootals S C
27 Little Hulton v. Clifton
27 Taylor Bros v. Atherton C
27 Walkden M M v. Farnworth S C
27 Walker Inst v. Astley & T C

JULY

4 Adlington v. Edgworth R
4 Astley & T C v. Taylor Bros
4 Barton Hall v. Atherton C
4 Farnworth S C v. Clifton
4 Walkden M M v. Tootals S C
4 Walker Inst v. Little Hulton
11 Atherton C v. Walker Institute
11 Clifton v. Barton Hall
11 Edgworth R v. Walkden M M
11 Little Hulton v. Farnworth S C
11 Taylor Bros v. Adlington
11 Tootals S C v. Astley & T C
18 Adlington v. Atherton C
18 Astley & T C v. Little Hulton
18 Barton Hall v. Tootals S C
18 Farnworth S C v. Taylor Bros
18 Walkden M M v. Clifton
18 Walker Inst v. Edgworth R
25 Atherton C v. Walkden M M
25 Clifton v. Astley & T C
25 Edgworth R v. Barton Hall
25 Little Hulton v. Adlington
25 Taylor Bros v. Walker Inst
25 Tootals S C v. Farnworth S C

AUGUST

1 Adlington v. Tootals S C
1 Astley & T C v. Edgworth R
1 Atherton C v. Farnworth S C
1 Barton Hall v. Little Hulton
1 Clifton v. Walker Institute
1 Walkden M M v. Taylor Bros
8 Atherton C v. Clifton
8 Edgworth R v. Little Hulton
8 Farnworth S C v. Astley & T C
8 Taylor Bros v. Tootals S C
8 Walkden M M v. Barton Hall
8 Walker Institute v. Adlington
15 Astley & T C v. Walkden M M
15 Clifton v. Adlington
15 Farnworth S C v. Edgworth R
15 Little Hulton v. Taylor Bros
15 Tootals S C v. Atherton C
15 Walker Inst v. Barton Hall
22 Adlington v. Astley & T C
22 Atherton C v. Edgworth R
22 Barton Hall v. Farnworth S C
22 Taylor Bros v. Clifton
22 Tootals S C v. Little Hulton
22 Walkden M M v. Walker Inst
29 Adlington v. Walkden M M
29 Astley & T C v. Barton Hall
29 Clifton v. Tootals S C
29 Edgworth R v. Taylor Bros
29 Little Hulton v. Atherton C
29 Walker Inst v. Farnworth S C

SEPTEMBER

5 Astley & T C v. Walker Inst
5 Atherton C v. Taylor Bros
5 Barton Hall v. Adlington
5 Clifton v. Little Hutton
5 Farnworth S C v. Walkden M M
5 Tootals S C v. Edgworth R

BOLTON LEAGUE

APRIL

18 Astley Bridge v. Kearsley
18 Egerton v. Farnworth
18 Little Lever v. Eagley
18 Tonge v. Horwich R M I

BOLTON LEAGUE—Continued

APRIL
18 Walkden v. Bradshaw
18 Westhoughton v. Heaton
25 Bradshaw v. Astley Bridge
25 Eagley v. Tonge
25 Farnworth v. Westhoughton
25 Heaton v. Egerton
25 Horwich R M I v. Walkden
25 Kearsley v. Little Lever

MAY
2 Astley Bridge v. Heaton
2 Egerton v. Horwich R M I
2 Little Lever v. Bradshaw
2 Tonge v. Farnworth
2 Walkden v. Kearsley
2 Westhoughton v. Eagley
5–6 Astley Bridge v. Horwich RMI
5–6 Egerton v. Eagley
5–6 Farnworth v. Bradshaw
5–6 Little Lever v. Heaton
5–6 Tonge v. Kearsley
5–6 Walkden v. Westhoughton
9 Bradshaw v. Westhoughton
9 Eagley v. Walkden
9 Farnworth v. Astley Bridge
9 Heaton v. Tonge
9 Horwich R M I v. Little Lever
9 Kearsley v. Egerton
16 Tonge v. Bradshaw
16 Eagley v. Astley Bridge
16 Heaton v. Walkden
16 Horwich R M I v. Kearsley
16 Little Lever v. Farnworth
16 Egerton v. Westhoughton
23 Astley Bridge v. Little Lever
23 Bradshaw v. Egerton
23 Farnworth v. Eagley
23 Westhoughton v. Horwich R M I
23 Kearsley v. Heaton
23 Walkden v. Tonge
30 Eagley v. Bradshaw
30 Egerton v. Astley Bridge
30 Heaton v. Horwich R M I
30 Kearsley v. Farnworth
30 Little Lever v. Walkden
30 Tonge v. Westhoughton

JUNE
6 Bradshaw v. Kearsley
6 Farnworth v. Heaton
6 Horwich R M I v. Eagley
6 Tonge v. Little Lever
6 Walkden v. Egerton
6 Westhoughton v. Astley Bridge
9 *Hamer Cup (1st Semi-Final)*
13 Astley Bridge v. Walkden
13 Egerton v. Tonge
13 Farnworth v. Horwich R M I
13 Heaton v. Bradshaw
13 Kearsley v. Eagley
13 Little Lever v. Westhoughton
16 *Hamer Cup (2nd Semi-Final)*
20 Eagley v. Heaton
20 Egerton v. Little Lever

JUNE
20 Horwich R M I v. Bradshaw
20 Tonge v. Astley Bridge
20 Walkden v. Farnworth
20 Westhoughton v. Kearsley
27 Bradshaw v. Walkden
27 Eagley v. Little Lever
27 Farnworth v. Egerton
27 Heaton v. Westhoughton
27 Horwich R M I v. Tonge
27 Kearsley v. Astley Bridge

JULY
4 Astley Bridge v. Bradshaw
4 Egerton v. Heaton
4 Little Lever v. Kearsley
4 Tonge v. Eagley
4 Walkden v. Horwich R M I
4 Westhoughton v. Farnworth
11 Bradshaw v. Little Lever
11 Eagley v. Westhoughton
11 Farnworth v. Tonge
11 Heaton v. Astley Bridge
11 Horwich R M I v. Egerton
11 Kearsley v. Walkden
18 Astley Bridge v. Farnworth
18 Egerton v. Kearsley
18 Little Lever v. Horwich R M I
18 Tonge v. Heaton
18 Walkden v. Eagley
18 Westhoughton v. Bradshaw
21–22 Bradshaw v. Farnworth
21–22 Eagley v. Egerton
21–22 Heaton v. Little Lever
21–22 Horwich RMI v. Astley B
21–22 Kearsley v. Tonge
21–22 Westhoughton v. Walkden
25 Astley Bridge v. Eagley
25 Westhoughton v. Egerton
25 Farnworth v. Little Lever
25 Kearsley v. Horwich R M I
25 Bradshaw v. Tonge
25 Walkden v. Heaton

AUGUST
1 Eagley v. Farnworth
1 Egerton v. Bradshaw
1 Heaton v. Kearsley
1 Little Lever v. Astley Bridge
1 Tonge v. Walkden
1 Horwich RMI v. Westhoughton
8 Astley Bridge v. Egerton
8 Bradshaw v. Eagley
8 Farnworth v. Kearsley
8 Horwich R M I v. Heaton
8 Walkden v. Little Lever
8 Westhoughton v. Tonge
15 Astley Bridge v. Westhoughton
15 Eagley v. Horwich R M I
15 Egerton v. Walkden
15 Heaton v. Farnworth
15 Kearsley v. Bradshaw
15 Little Lever v. Tonge
22 Bradshaw v. Heaton
22 Eagley v. Kearsley
22 Horwich R M I v. Farnworth

BOLTON LEAGUE—Continued

AUGUST
22 Tonge v. Egerton
22 Walkden v. Astley Bridge
22 Westhoughton v. Little Lever
29 Astley Bridge v. Tonge
29 Bradshaw v. Horwich R M I
29 Farnworth v. Walkden
29 Heaton v. Eagley
29 Kearsley v. Westhoughton
29 Little Lever v. Egerton
Hamer Cup (Final)

HAMER CUP COMPETITION

First Round (commencing May 12)—Egerton v. Westhoughton; Heaton v. Tonge; Horwich RMI v. Little Lever; Walkden v. Kearsley. *Byes*—Astley Bridge, Bradshaw, Eagley, Farnworth.

Second Round (commencing May 26)—Astley Bridge v. Horwich RMI *or* Little Lever; Eagley v. Walkden *or* Kearsley; Egerton *or* Westhoughton v. Heaton *or* Tonge; Farnworth v. Bradshaw.

BRADFORD LEAGUE

APRIL
DIVISION I
25 Baildon v. Lightcliffe
25 Bingley v. Great Horton
25 Lidget Green v. Farsley
25 Queensbury v. Salts
25 Yeadon v. Idle
INTER-DIVISIONAL
25 Pudsey St L v. Spen Victoria
DIVISION II
25 Bankfoot v. East Bierley
25 Brighouse v. Windhill
25 Keighley v. Bowling Old Lane
25 Saltaire v. Eccleshill
25 Undercliffe v. Bradford

MAY
DIVISION I
2 Farsley v. Baildon
2 Great Horton v. Pudsey St L
2 Idle v. Queensbury
2 Lightcliffe v. Lidget Green
2 Salts v. Bingley
INTER-DIVISIONAL
2 Eccleshill v. Yeadon
DIVISION II
2 Bowling O L v. Undercliffe
2 Bradford v. Saltaire
2 East Bierley v. Brighouse
2 Spen Victoria v. Keighley
2 Windhill v. Bankfoot
DIVISION I
9 Baildon v. Great Horton
9 Bingley v. Farsley
9 Idle v. Lightcliffe
9 Pudsey St Lawrence v. Salts
9 Queensbury v. Yeadon
INTER-DIVISIONAL
9 Lidget Green v. Bowling O L
DIVISION II
9 Bradford v. Spen Victoria
9 Brighouse v. Eccleshill
9 East Bierley v. Windhill
9 Saltaire v. Keighley
9 Undercliffe v. Bankfoot
16 *Priestley Cup Competition (First Round)*
16 Bankfoot v. Yeadon
16 Bingley v. Lightcliffe
16 Bradford v. Bowling Old Lane
16 Brighouse v. Idle
16 Eccleshill v. Lidget Green
16 Great Horton v. Queensbury
16 Keighley v. Salts
16 Pudsey St L v. Spen Victoria
16 Saltaire v. Farsley
16 Undercliffe v. Baildon
16 Windhill v. East Bierley
DIVISION I
23 Baildon v. Lidget Green
23 Great Horton v. Idle
23 Lightcliffe v. Farsley
23 Pudsey St L v. Queensbury
23 Yeadon v. Bingley
INTER-DIVISIONAL
23 Windhill v. Salts
DIVISION II
23 Bankfoot v Bradford
23 Bowling O L v. East Bierley
23 Keighley v. Brighouse
23 Saltaire v. Spen Victoria
23 Undercliffe v. Eccleshill
DIVISION I
25 Bingley v. Baildon
25 Farsley v. Yeadon
25 Lidget Green v. Pudsey St L
25 Queensbury v. Lightcliffe
25 Salts v. Great Horton
INTER-DIVISIONAL
25 Idle v. Undercliffe
DIVISION II
25 Bradford v. East Bierley
25 Brighouse v. Bowling Old Lane
25 Eccleshill v. Keighley
25 Spen Victoria v. Bankfoot
25 Windhill v. Saltaire
DIVISION I
26 Baildon v. Salts
26 Great Horton v. Farsley
26 Lightcliffe v. Bingley
26 Pudsey St Lawrence v. Idle
26 Yeadon v. Lidget Green
INTER-DIVISIONAL
26 Bankfoot v. Queensbury

BRADFORD LEAGUE—Continued

MAY

DIVISION II

26 Bowling Old Lane v. Eccleshill
26 East Bierley v. Spen Victoria
26 Keighley v. Bradford
26 Saltaire v. Brighouse
26 Undercliffe v. Windhill

DIVISION I

30 Farsley v. Salts
30 Idle v. Baildon
30 Lidget Green v. Great Horton
30 Queensbury v. Bingley
30 Yeadon v. Pudsey St Lawrence

INTER-DIVISIONAL

30 Brighouse v. Lightcliffe

DIVISION II

30 Bradford v. Windhill
30 Eccleshill v. Bankfoot
30 Keighley v. East Bierley
30 Saltaire v. Undercliffe
30 Spen Victoria v. Bowling O L

JUNE

DIVISION I

2 Farsley v. Pudsey St Lawrence
2 Idle v. Bingley
2 Lidget Green v. Queensbury
2 Lightcliffe v. Great Horton
2 Yeadon v. Salts

INTER-DIVISIONAL

2 Saltaire v. Baildon

DIVISION II

2 Bankfoot v. Brighouse
2 Bowling Old Lane v. Bradford
2 Eccleshill v. East Bierley
2 Keighley v. Windhill
2 Spen Victoria v. Undercliffe

DIVISION I

6 Bingley v. Lidget Green
6 Lightcliffe v. Yeadon
6 Pudsey St L v. Baildon
6 Queensbury v. Farsley
6 Salts v. Idle

INTER-DIVISIONAL

6 Great Horton v. Bradford

DIVISION II

6 Bankfoot v. Keighley
6 Bowling Old Lane v. Saltaire
6 Spen Victoria v. Brighouse
6 Undercliffe v. East Bierley
6 Windhill v. Eccleshill
8 *Priestley Cup Competition (Second Round)*

DIVISION I

13 Baildon v. Yeadon
13 Great Horton v. Queensbury
13 Idle v. Farsley
13 Pudsey St L v. Lightcliffe
13 Salts v. Lidget Green

INTER-DIVISIONAL

13 Keighley v. Bingley

DIVISION II

13 Bankfoot v. Bowling Old Lane
13 Brighouse v. Undercliffe
13 East Bierley v. Saltaire
13 Eccleshill v. Bradford

JUNE

13 Windhill v. Spen Victoria

DIVISION I

20 Bingley v. Pudsey St Lawrence
20 Lidget Green v. Idle
20 Lightcliffe v. Salts
20 Queensbury v. Baildon
20 Yeadon v. Great Horton

INTER-DIVISIONAL

20 Farsley v. East Bierley

DIVISION II

20 Bowling Old Lane v. Windhill
20 Bradford v. Brighouse
20 Saltaire v. Bankfoot
20 Spen Victoria v. Eccleshill
20 Undercliffe v. Keighley
22 *Priestley Cup Competition (Third Round)*

DIVISION I

27 Farsley v. Lidget Green
27 Great Horton v. Bingley
27 Idle v. Yeadon
27 Lightcliffe v. Baildon
27 Salts v. Queensbury

INTER-DIVISIONAL

27 Spen Victoria v. Pudsey St L

DIVISION II

27 Bowling Old Lane v. Keighley
27 Bradford v. Undercliffe
27 East Bierley v. Bankfoot
27 Eccleshill v. Saltaire
27 Windhill v. Brighouse

JULY

DIVISION I

4 Baildon v. Farsley
4 Bingley v. Salts
4 Lidget Green v. Lightcliffe
4 Pudsey St L v. Great Horton
4 Queensbury v. Idle

INTER-DIVISIONAL

4 Yeadon v. Eccleshill

DIVISION II

4 Bankfoot v. Windhill
4 Brighouse v. East Bierley
4 Keighley v. Spen Victoria
4 Saltaire v. Bradford
4 Undercliffe v. Bowling O L

DIVISION I

6 Bingley v. Idle
6 Great Horton v. Lightcliffe
6 Pudsey St Lawrence v. Farsley
6 Queensbury v. Lidget Green
6 Salts v. Yeadon

INTER-DIVISIONAL

6 Baildon v. Saltaire

DIVISION II

6 Bradford v. Bowling Old Lane
6 Brighouse v. Bankfoot
6 East Bierley v. Eccleshill
6 Undercliffe v. Spen Victoria
6 Windhill v. Keighley

DIVISION I

11 Farsley v. Bingley
11 Great Horton v. Baildon
11 Lightcliffe v. Idle

BRADFORD LEAGUE—Continued

JULY

11 Salts v. Pudsey St Lawrence
11 Yeadon v. Queensbury

INTER-DIVISIONAL

11 Bowling O L v. Lidget Green

DIVISION II

11 Bankfoot v. Undercliffe
11 Eccleshill v. Brighouse
11 Keighley v. Saltaire
11 Spen Victoria v. Bradford
11 Windhill v. East Bierley
13 *Priestley Cup Competition (Semi-Finals)*

DIVISION I

18 Bingley v. Yeadon
18 Farsley v. Lightcliffe
18 Idle v. Great Horton
18 Lidget Green v. Baildon
18 Queensbury v. Pudsey St L

INTER-DIVISIONAL

18 Salts v. Windhill

DIVISION II

18 Bradford v. Bankfoot
18 Brighouse v. Keighley
18 East Bierley v. Bowling O L
18 Eccleshill v. Undercliffe
18 Spen Victoria v. Saltaire

DIVISION I

25 Baildon v. Bingley
25 Great Horton v. Salts
25 Lightcliffe v. Queensbury
25 Pudsey St L v. Lidget Green
25 Yeadon v. Farsley

INTER-DIVISIONAL

25 Undercliffe v. Idle

DIVISION II

25 Bankfoot v. Spen Victoria
25 Bowling O L v. Brighouse
25 East Bierley v. Bradford
25 Keighley v. Eccleshill
25 Saltaire v. Windhill

AUGUST

DIVISION I

1 Bingley v. Lightcliffe
1 Farsley v. Great Horton
1 Idle v. Pudsey St Lawrence
1 Lidget Green v. Yeadon
1 Salts v. Baildon

INTER-DIVISIONAL

1 Queensbury v. Bankfoot

DIVISION II

1 Bradford v. Keighley
1 Brighouse v. Saltaire
1 Eccleshill v. Bowling Old Lane
1 Spen Victoria v. East Bierley
1 Windhill v. Undercliffe
3 *Priestley Cup Final, Park Ave.*

AUGUST

DIVISION I

8 Baildon v. Idle
8 Bingley v. Queensbury
8 Great Horton v. Lidget Green
8 Pudsey St Lawrence v. Yeadon
8 Salts v. Farsley

INTER-DIVISIONAL

8 Lightcliffe v. Brighouse

DIVISION II

8 Bankfoot v. Eccleshill
8 Bowling O L v. Spen Victoria
8 East Bierley v. Keighley
8 Undercliffe v. Saltaire
8 Windhill v. Bradford

DIVISION I

15 Baildon v. Pudsey St Lawrence
15 Farsley v. Queensbury
15 Idle v. Salts
15 Lidget Green v. Bingley
15 Yeadon v. Lightcliffe

INTER-DIVISIONAL

15 Bradford v. Great Horton

DIVISION II

15 Brighouse v. Spen Victoria
15 East Bierley v. Undercliffe
15 Eccleshill v. Windhill
15 Keighley v. Bankfoot
15 Saltaire v. Bowling Old Lane

DIVISION I

22 Farsley v. Idle
22 Lidget Green v. Salts
22 Lightcliffe v. Pudsey St L
22 Queensbury v. Great Horton
22 Yeadon v. Baildon

INTER-DIVISIONAL

22 Bingley v. Keighley

DIVISION II

22 Bowling Old Lane v. Bankfoot
22 Bradford v. Eccleshill
22 Saltaire v. East Bierley
22 Spen Victoria v. Windhill
22 Undercliffe v. Brighouse

DIVISION I

29 Baildon v. Queensbury
29 Great Horton v. Yeadon
29 Idle v. Lidget Green
29 Pudsey St Lawrence v. Bingley
29 Salts v. Lightcliffe

INTER-DIVISIONAL

29 East Bierley v. Farsley

DIVISION II

29 Bankfoot v. Saltaire
29 Brighouse v. Bradford
29 Eccleshill v. Spen Victoria
29 Keighley v. Undercliffe
29 Windhill v. Bowling Old Lane

CENTRAL LANCASHIRE LEAGUE

APRIL

25 Ashton v. Radcliffe
25 Oldham v. Castleton Moor
25 Rochdale v. Werneth

APRIL

25 Littleborough v. Royton
25 Crompton v. Middleton
25 Stockport v. Walsden

CENTRAL LANCASHIRE LEAGUE—Continued

APRIL
25 Heywood v. Milnrow
MAY
2 Walsden v. Ashton
2 Radcliffe v. Oldham
2 Werneth v. Littleborough
2 Royton v. Heywood
2 Milnrow v. Crompton
2 Castleton Moor v. Stockport
2 Middleton v. Rochdale
9 Ashton v. Castleton Moor
9 Oldham v. Walsden
9 Heywood v. Werneth
9 Rochdale v. Royton
9 Crompton v. Radcliffe
9 Stockport v. Milnrow
9 Littleborough v. Middleton
12 Ashton v. Milnrow
12 Royton v. Oldham
12 Werneth v. Crompton
12 Middleton v. Stockport
12 Heywood v. Castleton Moor
12 Walsden v. Rochdale
12 Littleborough v. Radcliffe
16 Werneth v. Ashton
16 Middleton v. Oldham
16 Royton v. Stockport
16 Castleton Moor v. Crompton
16 Radcliffe v. Rochdale
16 Milnrow v. Littleborough
16 Walsden v. Heywood
19 *Wood Cup (First Round)*
19 Rochdale v. Werneth
19 Ashton v. Milnrow
19 Oldham v. Royton
19 Littleborough v. Crompton
19 Castleton Moor v. Heywood
19 Stockport v. Walsden
23 Heywood v. Ashton
23 Oldham v. Werneth
23 Crompton v. Royton
23 Stockport v. Littleborough
23 Radcliffe v. Middleton
23 Castleton Moor v. Walsden
23 Rochdale v. Milnrow
29 Ashton v. Rochdale
29 Crompton v. Oldham
29 Radcliffe v. Werneth
29 Walsden v. Royton
29 Stockport v. Heywood
29 Middleton v. Milnrow
29 Castleton Moor v. Littleborough
30 Middleton v. Ashton
30 Oldham v. Stockport
30 Werneth v. Walsden
30 Royton v. Radcliffe
30 Littleborough v. Crompton
30 Milnrow v. Castleton Moor
30 Heywood v. Rochdale
JUNE
1 Royton v. Ashton
1 Littleborough v. Oldham
1 Milnrow v. Werneth
1 Crompton v. Walsden
1 Radcliffe v. Stockport
1 Heywood v. Middleton
1 Castleton Moor v. Rochdale
6 Ashton v. Littleborough
6 Oldham v. Milnrow
6 Werneth v. Royton
6 Heywood v. Crompton
6 Stockport v. Rochdale
6 Walsden v. Middleton
6 Castleton Moor v. Radcliffe
9 *Wood Cup (Second Round)*
9 Ashton or Milnrow v. Rochdale *or* Werneth
9 Castleton Moor *or* Heywood v. Littleborough *or* Crompton
9 Oldham *or* Royton v. Radcliffe
9 Middleton v. Stockport *or* Walsden
13 Ashton v. Oldham
13 Castleton Moor v. Werneth
13 Royton v. Middleton
13 Crompton v. Stockport
13 Littleborough v. Rochdale
13 Milnrow v. Walsden
13 Radcliffe v. Heywood
16 Stockport v. Ashton
16 Oldham v. Heywood
16 Middleton v. Werneth
16 Royton v. Castleton Moor
16 Rochdale v. Crompton
16 Radcliffe v. Milnrow
16 Littleborough v. Walsden
20 Crompton v. Ashton
20 Rochdale v. Oldham
20 Werneth v. Stockport
20 Milnrow v. Royton
20 Middleton v. Castleton Moor
20 Walsden v. Radcliffe
20 Heywood v. Littleborough
27 Ashton v. Crompton
27 Oldham v. Rochdale
27 Stockport v. Werneth
27 Royton v. Milnrow
27 Castleton Moor v. Middleton
27 Radcliffe v. Walsden
27 Littleborough v. Heywood
30 Ashton v. Stockport
30 Heywood v. Oldham
30 Werneth v. Middleton
30 Castleton Moor v. Royton
30 Crompton v. Rochdale
30 Milnrow v. Radcliffe
30 Walsden v. Littleborough
JULY
4 Oldham v. Ashton
4 Werneth v. Castleton Moor
4 Middleton v. Royton
4 Stockport v. Crompton
4 Rochdale v. Littleborough
4 Walsden v. Milnrow
4 Heywood v. Radcliffe
7 *Wood Cup (Semi-finals)*
11 Littleborough v. Ashton
11 Milnrow v. Oldham
11 Royton v. Werneth

CENTRAL LANCASHIRE LEAGUE—Continued

JULY
11 Crompton v. Heywood
11 Rochdale v. Stockport
11 Middleton v. Walsden
11 Radcliffe v. Castleton Moor
15 Ashton v. Royton
15 Oldham v. Littleborough
15 Werneth v. Milnrow
15 Walsden v. Crompton
15 Stockport v. Radcliffe
15 Middleton v. Heywood
15 Castleton Moor v. Rochdale
18 Ashton v. Middleton
18 Stockport v. Oldham
18 Walsden v. Werneth
18 Radcliffe v. Royton
18 Crompton v. Littleborough
18 Castleton Moor v. Milnrow
18 Rochdale v. Heywood
25 Rochdale v. Ashton
25 Oldham v. Crompton
25 Werneth v. Radcliffe
25 Royton v. Walsden
25 Heywood v. Stockport
25 Milnrow v. Middleton
25 Littleborough v. Castleton Moor
28 Milnrow v. Ashton
28 Oldham v. Royton
28 Crompton v. Werneth
28 Stockport v. Middleton
28 Castleton Moor v. Heywood
28 Rochdale v Walsden
28 Radcliffe v. Littleborough

AUGUST
1 Ashton v. Heywood
1 Werneth v. Oldham
1 Royton v. Crompton
1 Littleborough v. Stockport
1 Middleton v. Radcliffe
1 Walsden v. Castleton Moor
1 Milnrow v. Rochdale
8 Ashton v. Werneth
8 Oldham v. Middleton
8 Stockport v. Royton
8 Crompton v. Castleton Moor
8 Rochdale v. Radcliffe
8 Milnrow v. Littleborough
8 Heywood v. Walsden
15 Castleton Moor v. Ashton
15 Walsden v. Oldham
15 Werneth v. Heywood
15 Royton v. Rochdale
15 Radcliffe v. Crompton
15 Milrow v. Stockport
15 Middleton v. Littleborough
22 Ashton v. Walsden
22 Oldham v. Radcliffe
22 Littleborough v. Werneth
22 Heywood v. Royton
22 Crompton v. Milnrow
22 Stockport v. Castleton Moor
22 Rochdale v. Middleton
29 Radcliffe v. Ashton
29 Castleton Moor v. Oldham
29 Werneth v. Rochdale
29 Royton v. Littleborough
29 Middleton v. Crompton
29 Walsden v. Stockport
29 Milnrow v. Heywood

Second eleven Fixtures *vice versa* except for evening matches and June 1 fixtures, which are First Eleven only. Evening matches may be arranged by mutual consent, and the Wood Cup Final is provisionally arranged to commence on July 21. Wickets pitched 2-30 p.m. Saturday and holiday fixtures, and 6-30 p.m. each night for evening games.

DERBYSHIRE AND CHESHIRE LEAGUE

APRIL
25 Chapel-en-le-Frith v. Compstall
25 Hayfield v. Bredbury
25 New Mills v. Hazel Grove
25 Romiley v. Dove Holes
25 Poynton v. Birch Vale
25 Stockport S.S. v. Whaley B

MAY
2 Dove Holes v. Hayfield
2 Whaley Bridge v. Romiley
2 Birch Vale v. Stockport S.S.
2 Bredbury v. Poynton
2 Compstall v. New Mills
2 Hazel Grove v. Chapel-en-le-F
9 Chapel-en-le-F v. Birch Vale
9 Hayfield v. Compstall
9 New Mills v. Dove Holes
9 Romiley v. Hazel Grove
9 Poynton v. Whaley Bridge
9 Stockport S.S. v. Bredbury
16 Dove Holes v. Poynton
16 Whaley Bridge v. Hayfield
16 Birch Vale v. Romiley
16 Bredbury v. Chapel-en-le-Frith
16 Compstall v. Hazel Grove
16 Stockport S.S. v. New Mills
23 Chapel-en-le-F v. Stockport S.S.
23 Hayfield v. Birch Vale
23 New Mills v. Whaley Bridge
23 Romiley v. Bredbury
23 Hazel Grove v. Dove Holes
23 Poynton v. Compstall
25 Dove Holes v. Chapel-en-le-F
29 Whaley Bridge v. Birch Vale
29 Hayfield v. Hazel Grove
29 New Mills v. Poynton
29 Bredbury v. Compstall

DERBYSHIRE & CHESHIRE LEAGUE—Continued

MAY

29 Romiley v. Stockport S.S.
30 Chapel-en-le-Frith v. Hayfield
30 Birch Vale v. New Mills
30 Bredbury v. Dove Holes
30 Compstall v. Romiley
30 Hazel Grove v. Whaley Bridge
30 Stockport S.S. v. Poynton

JUNE

6 Dove Holes v. Birch Vale
6 Whaley Bridge v. Compstall
6 New Mills v. Bredbury
6 Romiley v. Hayfield
6 Hazel Grove v. Stockport S.S.
6 Poynton v. Chapel-en-le-Frith
13 Chapel-en-le-Frith v. New Mills
13 Hayfield v. Stockport S.S.
13 Birch Vale v. Hazel Grove
13 Bredbury v. Whaley Bridge
13 Compstall v. Dove Holes
13 Poynton v. Romiley
20 Whaley Br. v. Chapel-en-le-F
20 Hayfield v. Poynton
20 Birch Vale v. Compstall
20 Romiley v. New Mills
20 Hazel Grove v. Bredbury
20 Stockport S.S. v. Dove Holes
27 Chapel-en-le-Frith v. Romiley
27 Dove Holes v. Whaley Bridge
27 New Mills v. Hayfield
27 Bredbury v. Birch Vale
27 Compstall v. Stockport S.S.
27 Poynton v. Hazel Grove

JULY

4 Dove Holes v. New Mills
4 Whaley Bridge v. Bredbury
4 Birch Vale v. Hayfield
4 Romiley v. Poynton
4 Hazel Grove v. Compstall
4 Stockport S.S. v. Chapel-en-le-F
11 Hayfield v. Chapel-en-le-Frith
11 New Mills v. Birch Vale
11 Bredbury v. Romiley
11 Compstall v. Whaley Bridge
11 Poynton v. Dove Holes
11 Stockport S.S. v. Hazel Grove
18 Chapel-en-le-F v. Dove Holes
18 Whaley Bridge v. New Mills
18 Birch Vale v. Bredbury
18 Romiley v. Compstall
18 Hazel Grove v. Hayfield
18 Poynton v. Stockport S.S.
25 Dove Holes v. Bredbury
25 Hayfield v. Whaley Bridge
25 New Mills v. Chapel-en-le-F
25 Compstall v. Birch Vale
25 Hazel Grove v. Poynton
25 Stockport S.S. v. Romiley

AUGUST

1 Chapel-en-le-Frith v. Poynton
1 Dove Holes v. Stockport S.S.
1 New Mills v. Romiley
1 Birch Vale v. Whaley Bridge
1 Bredbury v. Hazel Grove
1 Compstall v. Hayfield
8 Whaley Bridge v. Dove Holes
8 Hayfield v. New Mills
8 Romiley v. Chapel-en-le-Frith
8 Hazel Grove v. Birch Vale
8 Poynton v. Bredbury
8 Stockport S.S. v. Compstall
15 Chapel-en-le-F v. Whaley B
15 Dove Holes v. Compstall
15 New Mills v. Stockport S.S.
15 Birch Vale v. Poynton
15 Bredbury v. Hayfield
15 Hazel Grove v. Romiley
22 Dove Holes v. Romiley
22 Whaley Bridge v. Hazel Grove
22 Birch Vale v. Chapel-en-le-F
22 Bredbury v. New Mills
22 Compstall v. Poynton
22 Stockport S.S. v. Hayfield
29 Chapel-en-le-F v. Hazel Grove
29 Whaley Bridge v. Stockport S.S.
29 Hayfield v. Dove Holes
29 Romiley v. Birch Vale
29 Compstall v. Bredbury
29 Poynton v. New Mills

SEPTEMBER

5 Chapel-en-le-Frith v. Bredbury
5 Dove Holes v. Hazel Grove
5 New Mills v. Compstall
5 Romiley v. Whaley Bridge
5 Poynton v. Hayfield
5 Stockport S.S. v. Birch Vale
12 Whaley Bridge v. Poynton
12 Hayfield v. Romiley
12 Birch Vale v. Dove Holes
12 Bredbury v. Stockport S.S.
12 Compstall v. Chapel-en-le-F
12 Hazel Grove v. New Mills

EAST YORKSHIRE CUP

APRIL

25 Scarborough 'A' v. Malton

MAY

5 Driffield v. Bridlington
5 Scarborough 'A' v. Hull No. 2
5 York 'A' v. Beverley
9 Bridlington v. Driffield
9 Hull Zingari v. Malton
9 Pickering v. Hull No. 2
16 Beverley v. Hull No. 2
16 Malton v. Pickering
16 Scarborough 'A' v. Bridlington
16 York 'A' v. Hull Zingari
23 Driffield v. Hull Zingari
23 Hull No. 2 v. York 'A'
23 Scarborough 'A' v. Pickering
25 Beverley v. Scarborough 'A'

EAST YORKSHIRE CUP—Continued

MAY
25 Hull No. 2 v. Malton
25 York 'A' v. Pickering
30 Driffield v. Hull No. 2
30 Hull Zingari v. Bridlington
30 Malton v. Beverley
30 Scarborough 'A' v. York 'A'

JUNE
6 Beverley v. Hull Zingari
6 Hull No. 2 v. Scarborough 'A'
6 Pickering v. Driffield
6 York 'A' v. Malton
13 Malton v. Driffield
13 Pickering v. Beverley
13 Scarborough 'A' v. Hull Zingari
13 York 'A' v. Bridlington
20 Bridlington v. Hull No. 2
20 Driffield v. Beverley
20 Hull Zingari v. Pickering
20 Malton v. York 'A'
27 Beverley v. York 'A'
27 Driffield v. Pickering
27 Hull No. 2 v. Bridlington
27 Hull Zingari v. Scarborough 'A'

JULY
4 Bridlington v. Malton
4 Hull No. 2 v. Hull Zingari
4 Pickering v. York 'A'
4 Scarborough 'A' v. Driffield
11 Hull No. 2 v. Driffield
11 Hull Zingari v. Beverley

JULY
11 Pickering v. Bridlington
11 York 'A' v. Scarborough 'A'
18 Bridlington v. Hull Zingari
18 Driffield v. Malton
18 Hull No. 2 v. Beverley
18 Pickering v. Scarborough 'A'
25 Beverley v. Bridlington
25 Hull Zingari v. Driffield
25 Malton v. Scarborough 'A'

AUGUST
1 Beverley v. Malton
1 Bridlington v. Pickering
1 Driffield v. Scarborough 'A'
1 York 'A' v. Hull No. 2
3 Driffield v. York 'A'
8 Bridlington v. Beverley
8 Malton v. Hull No. 2
8 Pickering v. Hull Zingari
15 Beverley v. Driffield
15 Bridlington v. Scarborough 'A'
15 Hull Zingari v. York 'A'
15 Pickering v. Malton
22 Beverley v. Pickering
22 Hull Zingari v. Hull No. 2
22 Malton v. Bridlington
22 York 'A' v. Driffield
29 Bridlington v. York 'A'
29 Hull No. 2 v. Pickering
29 Malton v. Hull Zingari
29 Scarborough 'A' v. Beverley

GLOSSOP AND DISTRICT LEAGUE

APRIL
25 Broadbottom S v. Ashton T
25 Hadfield St A v. Hollingworth
25 Old Glossop v. Charlesworth
25 Tintwistle v. Mottram
25 Bardsley v. Newton
25 Dinting v. I C I

MAY
2 Hollingworth v. Tintwistle
2 Mottram v. Broadbottom S
2 Newton v. Old Glossop
2 Ashton T v. Hadfield St A
2 Charlesworth v. Dinting
2 I C I v. Bardsley
9 Old Glossop v. Ashton T
9 Dinting v. Newton
9 Charlesworth v. Hollingworth
9 Broadbottom S v. Tintwistle
9 Bardsley v. Mottram
9 Hadfield St A v. I C I
16 Ashton T v. Charlesworth
16 Hollingworth v. Bardsley
16 Newton v. Hadfield St A
16 Dinting v. Broadbottom S
16 Tintwistle v. Old Glossop
16 I C I v. Mottram
23 Hadfield St A v. Dinting
23 Mottram v. Charlesworth

MAY
23 Newton v. Hollingworth
23 Broadbottom S v. Bardsley
23 Old Glossop v. I C I
23 Ashton T v. Tintwistle
29 Hadfield St A v. Tintwistle
29 Hollingworth v. Mottram
29 Dinting v. Old Glossop
29 I C I v. Newton
29 Ashton T v. Bardsley
29 Broadbottom S v. Charlesworth
30 Tintwistle v. Hadfield St A
30 Motttram v. Hollingworth
30 Old Glossop v. Dinting
30 Newton v. I C I
30 Bardsley v. Ashton T
30 Charlesworth v. Broadbottom S

JUNE
6 Old Glossop v. Broadbottom S
6 Mottram v. Hadfield St A
6 Tintwistle v. Newton
6 Bardsley v. Charlesworth
6 Hollingworth v. I C I
6 Ashton T v. Dinting
13 Old Glossop v. Mottram
13 Hollingworth v. Dinting
13 Charlesworth v. Hadfield St A
13 Broadbottom S v. Newton

GLOSSOP & DISTRICT LEAGUE—Continued

JUNE
13 Tintwistle v. Bardsley
13 I C I v. Ashton T
20 Hadfield St A v. Bardsley
20 Hollingworth v. Old Glossop
20 Motttram v. Dinting
20 Charlesworth v. Tintwistle
20 I C I v. Broadbottom S
20 Ashton T v. Newton
27 Old Glossop v. Hadfield St A
27 Newton v. Charlesworth
27 Dinting v. Bardsley
27 Broadbottom S v. Hollingworth
27 Tintwistle v. I C I
27 Ashton T v. Mottram

JULY
4 Hadfield St A v. Broadbottom S
4 Hollingworth v. Ashton T
4 Mottram v. Newton
4 Tintwistle v. Dinting
4 Bardsley v. Old Glossop
4 I C I v. Charlesworth
11 Hollingworth v. Hadfield St A
11 Broadbottom S v. Ashton T
11 Charlesworth v. Old Glossop
11 Mottram v. Tintwistle
11 Newton v. Bardsley
11 IC I v. Dinting
18 Hadfield St A v. Ashton T
18 Tintwistle v. Hollingworth
18 Broadbottom S v. Mottram
18 Old Glossop v. Newton
18 Dinting v. Charlesworth
18 Bardsley v. I C I
25 Ashton T v. Old Glossop
25 Newton v. Dinting
25 Hollingworth v. Charlesworth
25 Tintwistle v. Broadbottom S
25 Mottram v. Bardsley
25 I C I v. Hadfield St A

AUGUST
1 Charlesworth v. Ashton T
1 Bardsley v. Hollingworth
1 Hadfield St A v. Newton
1 Broadbottom S v. Dinting
1 Old Glossop v. Tintwistle
1 Mottram v. I C I
8 Dinting v. Hadfield St A
8 Tintwistle v. Ashton T
8 Charlesworth v. Motttram
8 Hollingworth v. Newton
8 Bardsley v. Broadbottom S
8 I C I v. Old Glossop
15 Dinting v. Ashton T
15 Broadbottom S v. Old Glossop
15 Hadfield St A v. Mottram
15 Newton v. Tintwistle
15 Charlesworth v. Bardsley
15 I C I v. Hollingworth
22 Motttram v. Old Glossop
22 Dinting v. Hollingworth
22 Hadfield St A v. Charlesworth
22 Newton v. Broadbottom S
22 Bardsley v. Tintwistle
22 Ashton T v. I C I
29 Bardsley v. Hadfield St A
29 Newton v. Ashton T
29 Old Glossop v. Hollingworth
29 Dinting v. Mottram
29 Tintwistle v. Charlesworth
29 Broadbottom S v. I C I

SEPTEMBER
5 Mottram v. Ashton T
5 Hadfield St A v. Old Glossop
5 Charlesworth v. Newton
5 Bardsley v. Dinting
5 Hollingworth v. Braodbottom S
5 I C I v. Tintwistle
12 Broadbottom S v. Hadfield St A
12 Newton v. Mottram
12 Dinting v. Tintwistle
12 Old Glossop v. Bardsley
12 Charlesworth v. I C I
12 Ashton T v. Hollingworth

HIGH PEAK LEAGUE

APRIL
25 Buxworth v. British Railways
25 High Lane v. Cheadle Heath
25 Offerton v. Newton Mill
25 Trinity Methodist v. Marple
25 Norbury v. Hyde
25 Hawk Green v. Hope Congos

MAY
2 Marple v. Norbury
2 Hyde v. Offerton
2 Newton Mill v. Trinity Meth
2 Cheadle Heath v. Buxworth
2 British Railways v. Hawk Green
2 Hope Congos v. High Lane
9 Hawk Green v. Cheadle Heath
9 High Lane v. British Railways
9 Offerton v. Marple
9 Trinity Methodist v. Hyde
9 Norbury v. Newton Mill
9 Buxworth v. Hope Congos
16 Marple v. Trinity Methodist
16 Hyde v. Norbury
16 Newton Mill v. Offerton
16 Cheadle Heath v. High Lane
16 British Railways v. Buxworth
16 Hope Congos v. Hawk Green
23 Hawk Green v. Trinity Meth
23 Buxworth v. Marple
23 High Lane v. Offerton
23 Cheadle Heath v. Newton Mill
23 British Railways v. Norbury
23 Hope Congos v. Hyde
29 Marple v. Cheadle Heath

HIGH PEAK LEAGUE—Continued

MAY
29 Hyde v. High Lane
29 Newton Mill v. Buxworth
29 Offerton v. Hawk Green
29 Trinity Meth v. British Rail
29 Norbury v. Hope Congos
30 Hawk Green v. Hyde
30 Buxworth v. Offerton
30 High Lane v. Marple
30 Cheadle Heath v. Norbury
30 British Railways v. Newton Mill
30 Trinity Meth v. Hope Congos

JUNE
6 Marple v. Hawk Green
6 Hyde v. Newton Mill
6 High Lane v. Buxworth
6 Offerton v. Cheadle Heath
6 Norbury v. Trinity Methodist
6 Hope Congos v. British Rail
13 Hyde v. British Railways
13 Hawk Green v. High Lane
13 Newton Mill v. Marple
13 Trinity Methodist v. Offerton
13 Norbury v. Buxworth
13 Cheadle Heath v. Hope Congos
20 Marple v. Hyde
20 Buxworth v. Hawk Green
20 High Lane v. Trinity Methodist
20 British Rail v. Cheadle Heath
20 Offerton v. Norbury
20 Hope Congos v. Newton Mill
27 Hyde v. Cheadle Heath
27 Newton Mill v. Hawk Green
27 Offerton v. British Railways
27 Trinity Methodist v. Buxworth
27 Norbury v. High Lane
27 Marple v. Hope Congos

JULY
4 Hawk Green v. Norbury
4 Buxworth v. Hyde
4 High Lane v. Newton Mill
4 Cheadle Heath v. Trinity Meth
4 British Railways v. Marple
4 Hope Congos v. Offerton
11 Marple v. Buxworth
11 Newton Mill v. Cheadle Heath
11 Offerton v. High Lane
11 Trinity Meth v. Hawk Green
11 Norbury v. British Railways
11 Hyde v. Hope Congos
18 Hawk Green v. Offerton
18 Buxworth v. Newton Mill
18 High Lane v. Hyde
18 Cheadle Heath v. Marple

JULY
18 British Rail v. Trinity Meth
18 Hope Congos v. Norbury
25 Marple v. High Lane
25 Hyde v. Hawk Green
25 Newton Mill v. British Railways
25 Offerton v. Buxworth
25 Norbury v. Cheadle Heath
25 Hope Congos v. Trinity Meth

AUGUST
1 Newton Mill v. Hyde
1 Hawk Green v. Marple
1 Buxworth v. High Lane
1 Cheadle Heath v. Offerton
1 Trinity Methodist v. Norbury
1 British Rail v. Hope Congos
8 British Railways v. Hyde
8 Marple v. Newton Mill
8 Buxworth v. Norbury
8 High Lane v. Hawk Green
8 Offerton v. Trinity Methodist
8 Hope Congos v. Cheadle Heath
15 Hyde v. Marple
15 Hawk Green v. Buxworth
15 Cheadle Heath v. British Rail
15 Trinity Methodist v. High Lane
15 Norbury v. Offerton
15 Newton Mill v. Hope Congos
22 Hawk Green v. Newton Mill
22 Buxworth v. Trinity Methodist
22 Cheadle Heath v. Hyde
22 High Lane v. Norbury
22 British Railways v. Offerton
22 Hope Congos v. Marple
29 Marple v. British Railways
29 Hyde v. Buxworth
29 Newton Mill v. High Lane
29 Trinity Meth v. Cheadle Heath
29 Norbury v. Hawk Green
29 Offerton v. Hope Congos

SEPTEMBER
5 Hawk Green v. British Railways
5 Buxworth v. Cheadle Heath
5 Offerton v. Hyde
5 Trinity Methodist v. Newton M
5 Norbury v. Marple
5 High Lane v. Hope Congos
12 Marple v. Offerton
12 Hyde v. Trinity Methodist
12 Newton Mill v. Norbury
12 Cheadle Heath v. Hawk Green
12 British Railways v. High Lane
12 Hope Congos v. Buxworth

LANCASHIRE LEAGUE

APRIL
18 Rawtenstall v. Nelson
18 Haslingden v. East Lancashire
18 Accrington v. Bacup
18 Church v. Burnley

APRIL
18 Lowerhouse v. Enfield
18 Colne v. Rishton
18 Todmorden v. Ramsbottom
25 Bacup v. Church

LANCASHIRE LEAGUE—Continued

APRIL

25 Ramsbottom v. Todmorden
25 Enfield v. Lowerhouse
25 Rishton v. Haslingden
25 East Lancashire v. Colne
25 Burnley v. Accrington
25 Nelson v. Rawtenstall

MAY

2 Rawtenstall v. Rishton
2 Ramsbottom v. Lowerhouse
2 Accrington v. Nelson
2 Church v. Bacup
2 Burnley v. East Lancashire
2 Colne v. Haslingden
2 Todmorden v. Enfield
9 Bacup v. Colne
9 Haslingden v. Todmorden
9 Enfield v. Rawtenstall
9 Rishton v. Burnley
9 East Lancashire v. Accrington
9 Lowerhouse v. Church
9 Nelson v. Ramsbottom
16 Rawtenstall v. Enfield
16 Ramsbottom v. Haslingden
16 Accrington v. Church
16 Rishton v. East Lancashire
16 Burnley v. Nelson
16 Colne v. Lowerhouse
16 Todmorden v. Bacup
19 Nelson v. Accrington
23 Bacup v. Ramsbottom
23 Haslingden v. Rawtenstall
23 Enfield v. Rishton
23 Church v. Accrington
23 East Lancashire v. Todmorden
23 Lowerhouse v. Burnley
23 Nelson v. Colne
25 Enfield v. Accrington
25 Rishton v. Church
25 Colne v. Rawtenstall
25 Lowerhouse v. East Lancashire
26 Accrington v. Haslingden
26 Church v. Ramsbottom
26 Burnley v. Bacup
29 Bacup v. Burnley
29 Haslingden v. Rishton
29 Ramsbottom v. Nelson
29 Todmorden v. Colne
30 Bacup v. East Lancashire
30 Haslingden v. Nelson
30 Accrington v. Enfield
30 Rishton v. Lowerhouse
30 Burnley v. Rawtenstall
30 Colne v. Ramsbottom
30 Todmorden v. Church

JUNE

1 Bacup v. Haslingden
1 Rawtenstall v. Lowerhouse
1 Ramsbottom v. Rishton
6 Rawtenstall v. Haslingden
6 Ramsbottom v. Bacup
6 Enfield v. Colne
6 Church v. East Lancashire
6 Lowerhouse v. Rishton
6 Nelson v. Burnley
6 Todmorden v. Accrington
13 Bacup v. Todmorden
13 Haslingden v. Ramsbottom
13 Accrington v. Rawtenstall
13 Rishton v. Enfield
13 East Lancashire v. Church
13 Burnley v. Lowerhouse
13 Colne v. Nelson
16 Lowerhouse v. Rawtenstall
16 Nelson v. Enfield
17 Rishton v. Colne
20 Rawtenstall v. Bacup
20 Ramsbottom v. Accrington
20 Enfield v. Burnley
20 Church v. Todmorden
20 East Lancashire v. Rishton
20 Lowerhouse v. Colne
20 Nelson v. Haslingden
23 Colne v. Church
27 Bacup v. Rishton
27 Ramsbottom v. Rawtenstall
27 Accrington v. East Lancashire
27 Church v. Colne
27 Burnley v. Enfield
27 Nelson v. Lowerhouse
27 Todmorden v. Haslingden

JULY

1 Enfield v. East Lancashire
4 Rawtenstall v. Burnley
4 Haslingden v. Accrington
4 Enfield v. Church
4 Rishton v. Nelson
4 East Lancashire v. Ramsbottom
4 Lowerhouse v. Bacup
4 Colne v. Todmorden
8 Accrington v. Todmorden
8 Haslingden v. Bacup
9 East Lancashire v. Enfield
11 Bacup v. Rawtenstall
11 Ramsbottom v. East Lancashire
11 Accrington v. Rishton
11 Church v. Nelson
11 Burnley v. Haslingden
11 Colne v. Enfield
11 Todmorden v. Lowerhouse
18 Rawtenstall v. Colne
18 Ramsbottom v. Burnley
18 Enfield v. Todmorden
18 Rishton v. Accrington
18 East Lancashire v. Bacup
18 Lowerhouse v. Haslingden
18 Nelson v. Church
23 Todmorden v. Burnley
25 Rawtenstall v. East Lancashire
25 Haslingden v. Enfield
25 Accrington v. Lowerhouse
25 Church v. Rishton
25 Burnley v. Ramsbottom
25 Colne v. Bacup
25 Todmorden v. Nelson

AUGUST

1 Bacup v. Accrington

LANCASHIRE LEAGUE—Continued

AUGUST

1 Haslingden v. Church
1 Enfield v. Ramsbottom
1 Rishton v. Rawtenstall
1 East Lancashire v. Lowerhouse
1 Nelson v. Todmorden
1 Colne v. Burnley
3 Rawtenstall v. Ramsbottom
3 Church v. Lowerhouse
3 East Lancashire v. Nelson
3 Burnley v. Todmorden
8 Rawtenstall v. Accrington
8 Ramsbottom v. Enfield
8 Church v. Haslingden
8 Rishton v. Bacup
8 Burnley v. Colne
8 Lowerhouse v. Nelson
8 Todmorden v. East Lancashire
15 Bacup v. Enfield
15 Haslingden v. Burnley
15 Accrington v. Colne
15 Church v. Rawtenstall
15 Lowerhouse v. Ramsbottom
15 Nelson v. East Lancashire
15 Todmorden v. Rishton
22 Bacup v. Lowerhouse
22 Rawtenstall v. Todmorden
22 Enfield v. Nelson
22 Rishton v. Ramsbottom
22 East Lancashire v Haslingden
22 Burnley v. Church
22 Colne v. Accrington
29 Haslingden v. Colne
29 Ramsbottom v. Church
29 Accrington v. Burnley
29 Enfield v. Bacup
29 East Lancashire v. Rawtenstall
29 Lowerhouse v. Todmorden
29 Nelson v. Rishton

SEPTEMBER

5 Bacup v. Nelson
5 Haslingden v. Lowerhouse
5 Accrington v. Ramsbottom
5 Church v. Enfield
5 Burnley v. Rishton
5 Colne v. East Lancashire
5 Todmorden v. Rawtenstall
12 Rawtenstall v. Church
12 Ramsbottom v. Colne
12 Enfield v. Haslingden
12 Rishton v. Todmorden
12 East Lancashire v. Burnley
12 Lowerhouse v. Accrington
12 Nelson v. Bacup

LANCASHIRE AND CHESHIRE LEAGUE

APRIL

18 Bollington v. East Levenshulme
18 Cheetham v. Stalybridge
18 Denton St Lawrence v. Stand
18 Dukinfield v. Swinton
18 Levenshulme v. Glossop
18 Prestwich v. Longsight
18 Unsworth v. Macclesfield
25 East Levenshulme v. Unsworth
25 Glossop v. Prestwich
25 Longsight v. Cheetham
25 Macclesfield v. Dukinfield
25 Stalybridge v. Bollington
25 Stand v. Levenshulme
25 Swinton v. Denton St Lawrence

MAY

2 Bollington v. Longsight
2 Cheetham v. Glossop
2 Denton St L v. Macclesfield
2 Dukinfield v. Stand
2 Levenshulme v. Swinton
2 Prestwich v. East Levenshulme
2 Unsworth v. Stalybridge
9 East Levenshulme v. Bollington
9 Glossop v. Levenshulme
9 Longsight v. Unsworth
9 Macclesfield v. Cheetham
9 Stalybridge v. Prestwich
9 Stand v. Denton St Lawrence
9 Swinton v. Dukinfield
16 Bollington v. Cheetham
16 Denton St Lawrence v. Swinton
16 Dukinfield v. Unsworth
16 Glossop v. Longsight
16 Levenshulme v. Stalybridge
16 Prestwich v. Macclesfield
16 Stand v. East Levenshulme
23 Bollington v. Glossop
23 Cheetham v. Levenshulme
23 East Levenshulme v. Dukinfield
23 Longsight v. Stand
23 Stalybridge v. Macclesfield
23 Swinton v. Prestwich
23 Unsworth v. Denton St Lawrence
25 Cheetham v. Prestwich
25 Levenshulme v. Longsight
25 Macclesfield v. E Levenshulme
29 Cheetham v. Bollington
29 Denton St Lawrence v. Glossop
29 Dukinfield v. Longsight
29 E Levenshulme v. Levenshulme
29 Prestwich v. Stalybridge
29 Stand v. Unsworth
30 Bollington v. Macclesfield
30 Denton St L v. Dukinfield
30 Glossop v. Stand
30 Longsight v. East Levenshulme
30 Stalybridge v. Levenshulme
30 Swinton v. Cheetham
30 Unsworth v. Prestwich

JUNE

6 Cheetham v. Dukinfield
6 East Levenshulme v. Stand

LANCASHIRE & CHESHIRE LEAGUE—Continued

JUNE
6 Levenshulme v. Bollington
6 Macclesfield v. Longsight
6 Prestwich v. Glossop
6 Stalybridge v. Denton St L
6 Unsworth v. Swinton
13 Bollington v. Unsworth
13 Denton St L v. E Levenshulme
13 Dukinfield v. Stalybridge
13 Glossop v. Macclesfield
13 Longsight v. Prestwich
13 Stand v. Cheetham
13 Swinton v. Levenshulme
16-17 Denton St L v. Bollington
16-17 Glossop v. Dukinfield
16-17 Stalybridge v. Longsight
16-17 Stand v. Macclesfield
16-17 Swinton v. Unsworth
20 Cheetham v. Swinton
20 East Levenshulme v. Glossop
20 Levenshulme v. Dukinfield
20 Macclesfield v. Denton St L
20 Prestwich v. Bollington
20 Stalybridge v. Stand
20 Unsworth v. Longsight
27 Bollington v. Stalybridge
27 Denton St L v. Levenshulme
27 Dukinfield v. Cheetham
27 Glossop v. Unsworth
27 Longsight v. Macclesfield
27 Stand v. Prestwich
27 Swinton v. East Levenshulme

JUNE AND JULY
30-1 E Levenshulme v. Denton S L
30-1 Stalybridge v. Glossop
30-1 Swinton v. Stand
30-1 Unsworth v. Dukinfield

JULY
4 Cheetham v. Stand
4 E Levenshulme v. Macclesfield
4 Glossop v. Bollington
4 Longsight v. Denton St L
4 Prestwich v. Swinton
4 Stalybridge v. Dukinfield
4 Unsworth v. Levenshulme
11 Cheetham v. Unsworth
11 Denton St L v. Stalybridge
11 Dukinfield v. Prestwich
11 Levenshulme v. E Levenshulme
11 Macclesfield v. Bollington
11 Stand v. Glossop
11 Swinton v. Longsight
14-15 Bollington v. Swinton
14-15 Dukinfield v. Levenshulme
14-15 Glossop v. Denton St L
14-15 Macclesfield v. Stalybridge
14-15 Prestwich v. Stand
14-15 Unsworth v. Cheetham
18 Cheetham v. Macclesfield
18 Glossop v. East Levenshulme
18 Levenshulme v. Denton St L
18 Longsight v. Dukinfield
18 Prestwich v. Unsworth
18 Stalybridge v. Swinton

JULY
18 Stand v. Bollington
25 Bollington v. Prestwich
25 Denton St L v. Longsight
25 Dukinfield v. Glossop
25 East Levenshulme v. Cheetham
25 Levenshulme v. Macclesfield
25 Swinton v. Stalybridge
25 Unsworth v. Stand

AUGUST
1 Cheetham v. E Levenshulme
1 Dukinfield v. Denton St L
1 Glossop v. Swinton
1 Longsight v. Levenshulme
1 Macclesfield v. Prestwich
1 Stand v. Stalybridge
1 Unsworth v. Bollington
3 East Levenshulme v. Longsight
3 Macclesfield v. Levenshulme
3 Prestwich v. Cheetham
3 Swinton v. Bollington
8 Bollington v. Dukinfield
8 Denton St L v. Prestwich
8 Levenshulme v. Cheetham
8 Longsight v. Glossop
8 Macclesfield v. Unsworth
8 Stalybridge v. E Levenshulme
8 Stand v. Swinton
15 Bollington v. Stand
15 Cheetham v. Longsight
15 Dukinfield v. Macclesfield
15 East Levenshulme v. Swinton
15 Glossop v. Stalybridge
15 Levenshulme v. Unsworth
15 Prestwich v. Denton St L
22 DentonStLawrencev.Cheetham
22 Dukinfield v. Bollington
22 Longsight v. Stalybridge
22 Macclesfield v. Stand
22 Prestwich v. Levenshulme
22 Swinton v. Glossop
22 Unsworth v. E Levenshulme
29 Bollington v. Denton St L
29 Dukinfield v. E Levenshulme
29 Glossop v. Cheetham
29 Levenshulme v. Prestwich
29 Stalybridge v. Unsworth
29 Stand v. Longsight
29 Swinton v. Macclesfield

SEPTEMBER
5 Cheetham v. Denton St L
5 E Levenshulme v. Stalybridge
5 Levenshulme v. Stand
5 Longsight v. Bollington
5 Macclesfield v. Swinton
5 Prestwich v. Dukinfield
5 Unsworth v. Glossop
12 Bollington v. Levenshulme
12 DentonStLawrencev.Unsworth
12 E Levenshulme v. Prestwich
12 Longsight v. Swinton
12 Macclesfield v. Glossop
12 Stalybridge v. Cheetham
12 Stand v. Dukinfield

LIVERPOOL COMPETITION

APRIL

25 Birkenhead v. Formby
25 Bootle v. Boughton Hall
25 Hightown v. Southport
25 Huyton v. Northern
25 Liverpool v. Wallasey
25 New Brighton v. Neston
25 Ormskirk v. Sefton
25 St. Helens Recs v. Oxton

MAY

2 Boughton Hall v. St. Helens R
2 Formby v. Liverpool
2 Neston v. Bootle
2 Northern v. Birkenhead Park
2 Oxton v. Huyton
2 Sefton v. Hightown
2 Southport v. New Brighton
2 Wallasey v. Ormskirk
9 Bootle v. Southport
9 Boughton Hall v. Oxton
9 Birkenhead Park v. Huyton
9 Hightown v. Wallasey
9 Liverpool v. Northern
9 New Brighton v. Sefton
9 Ormskirk v. Formby
9 St. Helens Recs v. Neston
16 Birkenhead Park v. Liverpool
16 Formby v. New Brighton
16 Huyton v. Ormskirk
16 Neston v. Oxton
16 Northern v. Hightown
16 Sefton v. St. Helens Recs
16 Southport v. Boughton Hall
16 Wallasey v. Bootle
23 Bootle v. Formby
23 Boughton Hall v. Sefton
23 Hightown v. Huyton
23 Neston v. Southport
23 New Brighton v. Northern
23 Ormskirk v. Birkenhead Park
23 Oxton v. Liverpool
23 St. Helens Recs v. Wallasey
25 Birkenhead Park v. Oxton
25 Boughton Hall v. Neston
25 Formby v. Hightown
25 Liverpool v. Huyton
25 New Brighton v. Wallasey
25 Northern v. Ormskirk
25 Sefton v. Bootle
25 Southport v. St. Helens Recs.
30 Birkenhead Park v. Hightown
30 Formby v. St. Helens Recs
30 Huyton v. New Brighton
30 Liverpool v. Ormskirk
30 Northern v. Bootle
30 Sefton v. Neston
30 Southport v. Oxton
30 Wallasey v. Boughton Hall

JUNE

6 Bootle v. Huyton
6 Boughton Hall v. Formby
6 Hightown v. Liverpool
6 Neston v. Wallasey
6 New Brighton v. Birkenhead P
6 Oxton v. Ormskirk
6 St. Helens Recs v. Northern
6 Southport v. Sefton
13 Birkenhead Park v. Bootle
13 Formby v. Neston
13 Huyton v. St. Helens Recs
13 Liverpool v. New Brighton
13 Northern v. Boughton Hall
13 Ormskirk v. Hightown
13 Sefton v. Oxton
13 Wallasey v. Southport
20 Bootle v. Liverpool
20 Boughton Hall v. Huyton
20 Neston v. Northern
20 New Brighton v. Ormskirk
20 Oxton v. Hightown
20 St. Helens R v. Birkenhead P
20 Sefton v. Wallasey
20 Southport v. Formby
27 Birkenhead Park v. Boughton H
27 Formby v. Sefton
27 Hightown v. New Brighton
27 Huyton v. Neston
27 Liverpool v. St. Helens Recs
27 Northern v. Southport
27 Ormskirk v. Bootle
27 Wallasey v. Oxton

JULY

4 Bootle v. Hightown
4 Boughton Hall v. Liverpool
4 Neston v. Birkenhead Park
4 Oxton v. New Brighton
4 St. Helens Recs v. Ormskirk
4 Sefton v. Northern
4 Southport v. Huyton
4 Wallasey v. Formby
11 Birkenhead Park v. Southpor
11 Formby v. Oxton
11 Hightown v. St. Helens Recs
11 Huyton v. Sefton
11 Liverpool v. Neston
11 New Brighton v. Bootle
11 Northern v. Wallasey
11 Ormskirk v. Boughton Hall
18 Boughton Hall v. Hightown
18 Formby v. Northern
18 Neston v. Ormskirk
18 Oxton v. Bootle
18 St. Helens R v. New Brighton
18 Sefton v. Birkenhead Park
18 Southport v. Liverpool
18 Wallasey v. Huyton
25 Birkenhead Park v. Wallasey
25 Bootle v. St. Helens Recs
25 Hightown v. Neston
25 Huyton v. Formby
25 Liverpool v. Sefton
25 New Brighton v. Boughton Hall
25 Northern v. Oxton
25 Ormskirk v. Southport

AUGUST

1 Boughton Hall v. Bootle
1 Formby v. Birkenhead Park

LIVERPOOL COMPETITION—Continued

AUGUST
1 Neston v. New Brighton
1 Northern v. Huyton
1 Oxton v. St. Helens Recs
1 Sefton v. Ormskirk
1 Southport v. Hightown
1 Wallasey v. Liverpool
3 Bootle v. Sefton
3 Hightown v. Formby
3 Huyton v. Liverpool
3 Neston v. Boughton Hall
3 Ormskirk v. Northern
3 Oxton v. Birkenhead Park
3 St Helens Recs v. Southport
3 Wallasey v. New Brighton
8 Birkenhead Park v. Northern
8 Bootle v. Neston
8 Hightown v. Sefton
8 Huyton v. Oxton
8 Liverpool v. Formby
8 New Brighton v. Southport
8 Ormskirk v. Wallasey
8 St. Helens Recs v. Boughton H
15 Formby v. Ormskirk
15 Huyton v. Birkenhead Park
15 Neston v. St. Helens Recs
15 Northern v. Liverpool
15 Oxton v. Boughton Hall
15 Sefton v. New Brighton
15 Southport v. Bootle
15 Wallasey v. Hightown
22 Bootle v. Wallasey
22 Boughton Hall v. Southport
22 Hightown v. Northern
22 Liverpool v. Birkenhead Park
22 New Brighton v. Formby
22 Ormskirk v. Huyton

AUGUST
22 Oxton v. Neston
22 St Helens Recs v. Sefton
29 Birkenhead Park v. Ormskirk
29 Formby v. Bootle
29 Huyton v. Hightown
29 Liverpool v. Oxton
29 Northern v. New Brighton
29 Sefton v. Boughton Hall
29 Southport v. Neston
29 Wallasey v. St Helens Recs

SEPTEMBER
5 Bootle v. Northern
5 Boughton Hall v. Wallasey
5 Hightown v. Birkenhead Park
5 Neston v. Sefton
5 New Brighton v. Huyton
5 Ormskirk v. Liverpool
5 Oxton v. Southport
5 St Helens Recs v. Formby
12 Birkenhead P v. New Brighton
12 Formby v. Boughton Hall
12 Huyton v. Bootle
12 Liverpool v. Hightown
12 Northern v. St Helens Recs
12 Ormskirk v. Oxton
12 Sefton v. Southport
12 Wallasey v. Neston
19 Bootle v. Birkenhead Park
19 Boughton Hall v. Northern
19 Hightown v. Ormskirk
19 Neston v. Formby
19 New Brighton v. Liverpool
19 Oxton v. Sefton
19 St Helens Recs v. Huyton
19 Southport v. Wallasey

MANCHESTER ASSOCIATION

* Denotes matches not in the Association

APRIL
18 Ashton-on-Mersey v. Weaste
18 Bramhall v. Didsbury
18 Urmston v. Brooklands
18 S W Manchester v. Bury
18 Heaton Mersey v. Castleton
18 Cheadle v. Chorlton
18 Broughton v. Cheetham Hill
18 Newton Heath v. Earlestown
18 Leigh v. Bolton
18 CheadleH v. Newton-le-Willows
18 Sale v. Whalley Range
18 Flixton v. Timperley
25 Ashton-on-Mersey v. Leigh
25 Newton-le-W v. Bramhall
25 Brooklands v. Bury
25 Castleton v. Chorlton
25 Prescot v. Cheadle
25 Whalley Range v. Cheetham H
25 Crosfield's Recs v. Bolton
25 Didsbury v. Sale
25*Earlestown v. Winton
25 Heaton M v. S W Manchester

APRIL
25*Lytham v. Weaste
25 Monton v. Cheadle Hulme
25 St Helens v. Newton Heath
25 Timperley v. Northwich
25 Warrington v. Urmston
25 Broughton v. Wigan
25 Worsley v. Flixton
25*Bowdon v. Winnington Park

MAY
2 Whalley Range v. Ashton-on-M
2 Bramhall v. Heaton Mersey
2 Cheadle v. Brooklands
2 Bury v. Weaste
2 Castleton v. Worsley
2 Cheetham Hill v. Winnington P
2 Chorlton v. Cheadle Hulme
2 Crosfield's R v. Earlestown
2 Urmston v. Didsbury
2 Leigh v. Lytham
2 Bolton v. Broughton
2*Middlewich v. Holmes Chapel
2 Flixton v. Monton

MANCHESTER ASSOCIATION—Continued

MAY

2*Winton v. Newton Heath
2 St Helens v. Newton-le-Willows
2 Northwich v. Prescot
2 Timperley v. Sale
2 Wigan v. Warrington
4*Manchester v. Leigh
5*Manchester v. Lytham
6*Urmston v. Manchester
9 Flixton v. Ashton-on-Mersey
9*Alderley Edge v. Bramhall
9 Brooklands v. Timperley
9 Cheadle Hulme v. Bury
9 Weaste v. Castleton
9 Cheadle v. Prescot
9 Cheetham Hill v. Urmston
9 Wigan v. Chorlton
9 S W Manchester v. Crosfield's R
9 Didsbury v. Whalley Range
9*Rainhill H v. Earlestown
9*Bowdon v. Heaton Mersey
9 Leigh v. Broughton
9 Warrington v. Middlewich
9 Monton v. Winnington Park
9 Newton Heath v. St Helens
9 Newton-le-willows v. Northwich
9*Sale v. Manchester
9 Worsley v. Bolton
9*Grappenhall v. Winton
11*Bolton v. Manchester
16 Newton-le-W v. Ashton-on-M
16 Bramhall v. Cheadle Hulme
16*Manchester v. Brooklands
16 Heaton Mersey v. Bury
16 Castleton v. Cheetham Hill
16 Broughton v. Cheadle
16*Chorlton v. Bowdon
16 Northwich v. Crosfield's Recs
16 Worsley v. Didsbury
16 Earlestown v. St Helens
16 Lytham v. Wigan
16 Prescot v. Middlewich
16 Monton v. Bolton
16 Winnington P v. Newton Heath
16 Sale v. S W Manchester
16 Whalley Range v. Timperley
16 Urmston v. Warrington
16 Weaste v. Flixton
16*Oughtrington P v. Winton
19–20 Castleton v. Bolton
19–20*St Helens v. Sutton
21*Manchester v. Ashton-on-M
23 Ashton-on-Mersey v. Heaton M
23 Castleton v. Bramhall
23 Brooklands v. Cheadle Hulme
23 Cheetham Hill v. Bury
23 Lytham v. Cheadle
23 Chorlton v. Whalley Range
23 Warrington v. Didsbury
23 Newton-le-W v. Earlestown
23 St Helens v. Leigh
23*Middlewich v. Alderley Edge
23 Weaste v. Monton
23 Broughton v. Northwich
23 Prescot v. Crosfield's Recs

MAY

23 Wigan v. Sale
23*S W Manchester v. Manchester
23 Timperley v. Winnington Park
23 Flixton v. Urmston
23 Bolton v. Worsley
23*Lancs S C v. Winton
25*Bramhall v. Bowdon
25 Worsley v. Brooklands
25*Latchford v. Castleton
25 Heaton Mersey v. Cheadle
25 Chorlton v. Cheetham Hill
25 Warrington v. Crosfield's Recs
25 Timperley v. Didsbury
25*Flixton v. Manchester U
25 Leigh v. Newton-le-Willows
25 Monton v. Middlewich
25*Newton Heath v. Droylsden
25 Northwich v. St Helens
25 Prescot v. Lytham
25 Urmston v. Sale
25 S W Manchester v. Broughton
25 Whalley Range v. Cheadle H
25 Wigan v. Bolton
27 Cheetham Hill v. Chorlton
27*Prescot v. Sefton
27*Longsight v. Manchester
28 Bramhall v. Weaste
28 Cheetham Hill v. Heaton M
28 Flixton v. Cheadle Hulme
29*Bowdon v. Bramhall
29 Brooklands v. Urmston
29 Cheadle v. Cheadle Hulme
29*Cheetham Hill v. Manchester
29 S W Manchester v. Chorlton
29 Didsbury v. Broughton
29 Flixton v. Whalley Range
29 Sale v. Heaton Mersey
29*Flixton v. Newton Heath
29*Worsley v. Bolton League XI
30*Ashton-on-M v. Manchester
30 Broughton v. Bramhall
30*Brooklands v. Alderley Edge
30 Bury v. Monton
30 Cheetham Hill v. Castleton
30 Cheadle Hulme v. Bolton
30 Cheadle v. Didsbury
30 Middlewich v. Chorlton
30 Earlestown v. Northwich
30 Heaton Mersey v. Sale
30 Leigh v. Winnington Park
30 Newton Heath v. Newton-le-W
30 Prescot v. Weaste
30 St Helens v. Wigan
30 Timperley v. S W Manchester
30 Urmston v. Whalley Range
30 Warrington v. Flixton
30*Worsley v. Bowdon
30*Widnes v. Winton

JUNE

2*Liverpool v. Manchester
2 Brooklands v. Sale
2 Monton v. Worsley
2*St Helens v. St Helens Recs
2*Roe Green v. Winton

MANCHESTER ASSOCIATION—Continued

JUNE

3*Prescot v. Liverpool University
4*Manchester v. St Helens Recs
6 Ashton-on-Mersey Club Fete
6*Bramhall v. Styal
6*Oughtrington P v. Winton
6 Brooklands v. Worsley
6 Wigan v. Bury
6 Castleton v. Earlestown
6 Cheadle v Broughton
6 Didsbury v. Cheetham Hill
6 Lytham v. Chorlton
6*Crosfield's R v. London C W G
6 Whalley Range v. Heaton M
6 Leigh v. St Helens
6*Alderley Edge v. Middlewich
6 Monton v. Weaste
6 Newton-le-W v. Warrington
6 Prescot v. Northwich
6 Winnington Park v. Sale
6 Cheadle H v. S W Manchester
6*Bowdon v. Timperley
6*Manchester v. Urmston
6 Bolton v. Flixton
10*Liverpool University v. Prescot
10*Manchester v. Didsbury
13*Ashton-on-M v. Knutsford
13*Buxton v. Bramhall
13*Bowdon v. Brooklands
13 Bury v. Cheetham Hill
13 Castleton Fete Day
13 Urmston v. Cheadle
13 Winnington Park v. Chorlton
13 Newton-le-W v. Crosfield's R
13 Didsbury v. S W Manchester
13*Earlestown v. Rainhill
13 Heaton Mersey v. Monton
13 Leigh v. Worsley
13 Broughton v. Lytham
13*Sandbach v. Middlewich
13 Newton Heath v. Prescot
13 Northwich v. Weaste
13*St Helens v. Manchester
13 Sale v. Wigan
13*Lostock G v. Winton
13 Timperley v. Flixton
13 Bolton v. Cheadle Hulme
13*Warrington v. Colwyn Bay
15–16*Cheetham Hill v. Cheetham
16–17 Bolton v. Castleton
16*Chorlton v. Manchester
18–19*Lancashire Co. Police v. Manchester (Newton-le-W.)
20 S W Manchester v. Ashton-on-M
20 Bramhall v. Timperley
20 Middlewich v. Brooklands
20 Bury v. Wigan
20 Flixton v. Castleton
20 Cheadle v. Warrington
20 Cheetham Hill v. Whalley R
20 Chorlton v. Urmston
20*Price's v. Crosfield's Recs
20 Monton v. Didsbury
20*Winton v. Earlestown
20 Cheadle Hulme v. Heaton M

JUNE

20 Worsley v. Leigh
20 St Helens v. Lytham
20 Prescot v. Newton-le-Willows
20 Northwich v. Winnington Park
20 Sale v. Bolton
27 Brooklands v. Ashton-on-M
27*Bramhall v. Holmes Chapel
27 Bury v. S W Manchester
27 Whalley Range v. Castleton
27 Cheadle v. Sale
27 Chorlton v. Worsley
27 Crosfield's R v. Newton Heath
27 Didsbury v. Cheadle Hulme
27 Earlestown v. Newton-le-W
27*Heaton Mersey v. Buxton
27*Leigh v. Oughtrington Park
27 Wigan v. Lytham
27 Northwich v. Middlewich
27 Bolton v. Monton
27 St Helens v. Prescot
27*Timperley v. Bowdon
27 Weaste v. Urmston
27*Warrington v. Manchester
27 Winnington P v. Cheetham Hill
27 Broughton v. Flixton
27*Winton v. Maxonians

JULY

1–2*St Helens Recs v. St Helens
3*Mr Tipping's XI v. Crosfield's R
4 Ashton-on-M v. S W Manchester
4 Bramhall v. Broughton
4 Brooklands v. Cheadle
4 Whalley Range v. Bury
4 Castleton v. Flixton
4 Sale v Cheetham Hill
4 Urmston v. Chorlton
4 Crosfield's Recs v. Northwich
4 Heaton Mersey v. Didsbury
4*Earlestown v. Rainhill H
4*Oughtrington Park v. Leigh
4 Lytham v. Prescot
4 Middlewich v. Monton
4 Newton-le-W v. Cheadle Hulme
4 Warrington v. St Helens
4 Timperley v. Wigan
4*Bowdon v. Worsley
4 Weaste v. Winnington Park
4*Bowdon V v. Winton
6*Hereford v. Cheetham Hill
6*Manchester v. Newton Heath
7*Leominster v. Cheetham Hill
7*Manchester v. Bolton
7–8*St Helens Recs v. Prescot
8*Cheltenham v. Cheetham Hill
9*Gloucester v. Cheetham Hill
10*Dumbleton v. Cheetham Hill
11 Ashton-on-Mersey v. Cheadle
11*Styal v. Bramhall
11 Heaton Mersey v. Brooklands
11 Bolton v. Bury
11 Castleton v. Lytham
11*Knutsford v. Cheetham Hill
11 Chorlton v. Broughton
11 Crosfield's R v. Newton-le-W

MANCHESTER ASSOCIATION—Continued

JULY

11 Sale v. Didsbury
11*Earlestown v. Withington
11 Wigan v. Leigh
11*Middlewich v. Sandbach
11 Monton v. Urmston
11*Newton Heath v. Manchester
11 St Helens v. Northwich
11*Winton v. W Park
11 Prescot v. Warrington
11 S W Manchester v. Timperley
11 Cheadle Hulme v. Whalley R
11 Flixton v. Worsley
11*Winnington Park v. Bowdon
14*Leigh v. Manchester
18 Ashton-on-M v. Newton-le-W
18 Bramhall v. Monton
18 Cheadle Hulme v. Brooklands
18 Worsley v. Bury
18 Chorlton v. Castleton
18 Cheadle v. Middlewich
18*Cheetham Hill v. Bowdon
18 Crosfield's Recs v. Leigh
18 Didsbury v. Heaton Mersey
18 Prescot v. Earlestown
18 Lytham v. St Helens
18 Newton Heath v. Winnington P
18 Weaste v. Northwich
18 S W Manchester v. Sale
18 Timperley v. Whalley Range
18 Urmston v. Flixton
18 Warrington v. Wigan
18 Broughton v. Bolton
18*Winton v. Wythenshawe
25 Leigh v. Ashton-on-Mersey
25 Bramhall v. Castleton
25*Alderley Edge v. Brooklands
25 Broughton v. Bury
25 Cheadle Hulme v. Cheadle
25 Urmston v. Cheetham Hill
25 Bolton v. Chorlton
25 Middlewich v. Crosfield's Recs
25 S W Manchester v. Didsbury
25 Northwich v. Earlestown
25*Heaton Mersey v. Bowdon
25 Newton-le-Willows v. Lytham
25 Worsley v. Monton
25 Prescot v. St Helens
25 Warrington v. Sale
25 Wigan v. Timperley
25 Whalley Range v. Flixton
25 Winnington Park v. Weaste
25*Winton v. Ashley
27*Manchester v. Chorlton
28*Cheadle v. Southampton Univ
30*Bolton v. Southampton Univ

AUGUST

1 Urmston v. Ashton-on-Mersey
1*Bramhall v. Buxton
1 Sale v. Brooklands
1 Bury v. Bolton
1 Castleton v. Weaste
1 Timperley v. Cheadle
1 Cheetham Hill v. Lytham
1 Whalley Range v. Chorlton

AUGUST

1 St Helens v. Crosfield's Recs
1 Didsbury v. Worsley
1 Earlestown v. Newton Heath
1 Monton v. Heaton Mersey
1 Prescot v. Leigh
1*Middlewich v. Bowdon
1 Warrington v. Newton-le-W
1 Northwich v. Broughton
1 Flixton v. S W Manchester
1 Cheadle Hulme v. Wigan
1*Winton v. Lostock G
1*Winnington Park v. Southampton University
3 Ashton-on-M v. Brooklands
3*Bramhall v. Alderley Edge
3 Cheadle v. Urmston
3 Cheetham Hill v. Sale
3 Worsley v. Chorlton
3 Crosfield's R v. Warrington
3 Didsbury v. Monton
3 St Helens v. Earlestown
3*Buxton v. Heaton Mersey
3 Newton-le-Willows v. Leigh
3 Weaste v. Lytham
3 Middlewich v. Northwich
3 Prescot v. Newton Heath
3 S W Manchester v. Flixton
3 Winnington P v. Timperley
3*Bowdon v. Whalley Range
3 Bolton v. Wigan
4*Middlewich v. Western Comm
5*Manchester v. Cheetham Hill
5 Middlewich v. Chorlton
6 Middlewich v. Whalley Range
6*Prescot v. A M Wolstenholme's XI
6*Manchester v. Lancs. C. Police
7*Manchester v. Cheadle Hulme
8 Northwich v. Ashton-on-M
8 Middlewich v. Bramhall
8*Brooklands v. Bowdon
8 Bury v. Castleton
8 Sale v. Cheadle
8*Worsley v. Cheetham Hill
8 Cheadle Hulme v. Chorlton
8*Crosfield's Recs v. Watson's
8 Broughton v. Didsbury
8*L S Corpn (Irlam) v. Earlestown
8 Heaton Mersey v. Whalley R
8 Leigh v. Wigan
8 Lytham v. Newton-le-Willows
8 Winnington Park v. Monton
8*Newton Heath v. Winton
8 S W Manchester v. Prescot
8 St Helens v. Warrington
8*Timperley v. Manchester
8 Urmston v. Weaste
8 Flixton v. Bolton
12*Wigan v. Manchester
13*St Helens Recs v. Manchester
14*Cheadle Hulme v. Manchester
15 Ashton-on-Mersey v. Flixton
15 Cheadle Hulme v. Bramhall
15 Brooklands v. Heaton Mersey

MANCHESTER ASSOCIATION—Continued

AUGUST
15 Monton v. Bury
15 Castleton v. Whalley Range
15 Middlewich v. Cheadle
15 Cheetham Hill v. Broughton
15*Bowdon v. Chorlton
15 Leigh v. Crosfield's Recs
15 Didsbury v. Urmston
15*Withington v. Earlestown
15 Bolton v. Lytham
15 Newton Heath v. Newton-le-W
15 Winnington Park v. Northwich
15*Winton v. Grappenhall
15 Warrington v. Prescot
15 Wigan v. St Helens
15 Sale v. Timperley
15 Weaste v. Worsley
19*Manchester v. Cheetham
20*Manchester v. Wigan
22 Cheadle v. Ashton-on-Mersey
22 Didsbury v. Bramhall
22 Timperley v. Brooklands
22 Weaste v. Bury
22 Castleton v. Heaton Mersey
22*Bowdon v. Cheetham Hill
22 Chorlton v. Wigan
22 Prescot v. Crosfield's Recs
22 Earlestown v. Winnington Park
22 Lytham v. Leigh
22 Newton Heath v. Middlewich
22 Warrington v. Monton
22 Newton-le-Willows v. St Helens
22 Whalley Range v. Northwich
22 Bolton v. Sale
22 S W Manchester v. Cheadle H
22 Urmston v. Worsley
22 Flixton v. Broughton
22*Wythenshawe v. Winton
25*Didsbury v. Manchester
29 Ashton-on-Mersey v. Northwich
29 Cheetham Hill v. Bramhall
29 Winnington P v. Brooklands
29 Bury v. Heaton Mersey
29 Worsley v. Castleton
29 Cheadle v. Lytham
29 Chorlton v. Bolton
29 Crosfield's Recs v. St Helens
29 Cheadle Hulme v. Didsbury
29 Earlestown v. S W Manchester
29 Leigh v. Prescot
29 Middlewich v. Newton-le-W
29 Monton v. Timperley
29*Withington v. Newton Heath
29 Sale v. Urmston

AUGUST
29*Colwyn Bay v. Warrington
29*Whalley Range v. Bowdon
29 Wigan v. Broughton
29 Flixton v. Weaste
29*Bowdon v. Winton

SEPTEMBER
5 Lytham v. Ashton-on-Mersey
5 Heaton Mersey v. Bramhall
5 Brooklands v. Middlewich
5 Castleton v. Bury
5 Didsbury v. Cheadle
5 Cheetham Hill v. Worsley
5 Chorlton v. Winnington Park
5 Bolton v. Crosfield's Recs
5 Wigan v. Earlestown
5 Northwich v. Leigh
5 Urmston v. Monton
5 Newton-le-Willows v. Prescot
5 St Helens v. Weaste
5 Whalley Range v. Sale
5 Broughton v. S W Manchester
5 Timperley v. Warrington
5 Cheadle Hulme v. Flixton
5*Winton v. Lancs S C
12 Weaste v. Ashton-on-Mersey
12 Bramhall v. Middlewich
12 Brooklands v. Winnington Park
12 Bury v. Newton Heath
12 Lytham v. Castleton
12 Cheadle v. Timperley
12 Cheetham Hill v. Wigan
12 Broughton v. Chorlton
12*Withington v. Crosfield's Recs
12 Whalley Range v. Didsbury
12 Earlestown v. Prescot
12 S W Manchester v. Heaton M
12 Bolton v. Leigh
12 Cheadle Hulme v. Monton
12 Northwich v. Newton-le-W
12 Worsley v. Urmston
12 Flixton v. Warrington
19 Heaton Mersey v. Ashton-on-M
19 Bramhall v. Cheetham Hill
19 Bury v. Worsley
19 Chorlton v. Cheadle
19 Earlestown v. Crosfield's Recs
19 Didsbury v. Timperley
19 Lytham v. Bolton
19 Monton v. Flixton
19 Whalley Range v. Urmston
19*Winton v. Withington
26 Ashton-on-Mersey v. Urmston
26 Cheetham Hill v. Didsbury

NORTHERN LEAGUE

APRIL
25 Darwen v. Lancaster
25 Kendal v. Chorley
25 Leyland Motors v. St. Annes
25 Morecambe v. Furness
25 Preston v. Leyland

MAY
2 Chorley v. Leyland Motors
2 Fleetwood v. Preston
2 Furness v. Darwen
2 Lancaster v. Kendal
2 Leyland v. Morecambe

NORTHERN LEAGUE—Continued

MAY

2 St. Annes v. Blackpool
9 Blackpool v. Chorley
9 Darwen v. Leyland
9 Furness v. Lancaster
9 Leyland Motors v. Kendal
9 Morecambe v. Fleetwood
9 Preston v. St. Annes
16 Chorley v. Preston
16 Fleetwood v. Darwen
16 Kendal v. Blackpool
16 Lancaster v. Leyland Motors
16 Leyland v. Furness
16 St. Annes v. Morecambe
23 Blackpool v. Leyland Motors
23 Darwen v. St. Annes
23 Furness v. Fleetwood
23 Leyland v. Lancaster
23 Morecambe v. Chorley
23 Preston v. Kendal
25 Chorley v. Darwen
25 Fleetwood v. Leyland
25 Kendal v. Morecambe
25 Lancaster v. Blackpool
25 Leyland Motors v. Preston
25 St. Annes v. Furness
30 Darwen v. Kendal
30 Fleetwood v. Lancaster
30 Furness v. Chorley
30 Leyland v. St. Annes
30 Morecambe v. Leyland Motors
30 Preston v. Blackpool

JUNE

2 Blackpool v. Fleetwood
2 Lancaster v. Morecambe
6 Blackpool v. Morecambe
6 Chorley v. Leyland
6 Kendal v. Furness
6 Lancaster v. Preston
6 Leyland Motors v. Darwen
6 St. Annes v. Fleetwood
13 Darwen v. Blackpool
13 Fleetwood v. Chorley
13 Furness v. Leyland Motors
13 Leyland v. Kendal
13 Morecambe v. Preston
13 St. Annes v. Lancaster
20 Blackpool v. Furness
20 Chorley v. St. Annes
20 Kendal v. Fleetwood
20 Leyland Motors v. Leyland
20 Morecambe v. Lancaster
20 Preston v Darwen
27 Darwen v. Morecambe
27 Fleetwood v. Leyland Motors
27 Furness v. Preston
27 Lancaster v. Chorley
27 Leyland v. Blackpool
27 St. Annes v. Kendal

JULY

4 Chorley v. Kendal
4 Fleetwood v. Blackpool
4 Furness v. Morecambe
4 Lancaster v. Darwen
4 Leyland v. Preston
4 St. Annes v. Leyland Motors
11 Blackpool v. St. Annes
11 Darwen v Furness
11 Kendal v. Lancaster
11 Leyland Motors v. Chorley
11 Morecambe v. Leyland
11 Preston v. Fleetwood
18 Chorley v. Blackpool
18 Fleetwood v. Morecambe
18 Kendal v. Leyland Motors
18 Lancaster v. Furness
18 Leyland v. Darwen
18 St. Annes v. Preston
25 Blackpool v. Kendal
25 Darwen v. Fleetwood
25 Furness v. Leyland
25 Leyland Motors v. Lancaster
25 Morecambe v. St. Annes
25 Preston v. Chorley

AUGUST

1 Chorley v. Morecambe
1 Fleetwood v. Furness
1 Kendal v. Preston
1 Lancaster v. Leyland
1 Leyland Motors v. Blackpool
1 St. Annes v. Darwen
3 Blackpool v. Lancaster
3 Furness v. St. Annes
3 Morecambe v. Kendal
3 Darwen v. Chorley
3 Preston v. Leyland Motors
8 Blackpool v. Preston
8 Chorley v. Furness
8 Kendal v. Darwen
8 Lancaster v. Fleetwood
8 Leyland Motors v. Morecambe
8 St. Annes v. Leyland
15 Darwen v. Leyland Motors
15 Fleetwood v. St. Annes
15 Furness v. Kendal
15 Leyland v. Chorley
15 Morecambe v. Blackpool
15 Preston v. Lancaster
22 Blackpool v. Darwen
22 Chorley v. Fleetwood
22 Kendal v. Leyland
22 Lancaster v. St. Annes
22 Leyland Motors v. Furness
22 Preston v. Morecambe
29 Darwen v. Preston
29 Fleetwood v. Kendal
29 Furness v. Blackpool
29 Leyland v. Leyland Motors
29 St. Annes v. Chorley

SEPTEMBER

5 Blackpool v. Leyland
5 Chorley v. Lancaster
5 Kendal v. St. Annes
5 Leyland Motors v. Fleetwood
5 Morecambe v. Darwen
5 Preston v. Furness
12 Leyland v. Fleetwood

NORTH LANCASHIRE LEAGUE

APRIL

25 Barrow v. Ulverston
25 Carnforth v. Millom
25 Haverigg v. Vickerstown
25 Lindal v. Whitehaven
25 Vickers Sports v. Dalton
25 Workington v. Netherfield

MAY

2 Dalton v. Barrow
2 Millom v. Haverigg
2 Netherfield v. Workington
2 Ulverston v. Vickers Sports
2 Vickerstown v. Carlisle
2 Whitehaven v. Carnforth
9 *Higson Cup (First Round)*
9 Vickerstown v. Netherfield
9 Lindal Moor v. Ulverston
9 Whitehaven v. Vickers Sports
9 Haverigg v. Carlisle
9 Barrow v. Dalton
9 Workington v. Windscale
16 Carlisle v. Netherfield
16 Carnforth v. Whitehaven
16 Dalton v. Ulverston
16 Haverigg v. Millom
16 Vickers Sports v. Lindal
16 Workington v. Vickerstown
23 Lindal v. Dalton
23 Millom v. Vickers Sports
23 Netherfield v. Carlisle
23 Ulverston v. Barrow
23 Vickerstown v. Haverigg
23 Whitehaven v. Workington
25 Barrow v. Lindal
25 Dalton v. Millom
25 Haverigg v. Carnforth
25 Ulverston v. Netherfield
25 Vickerstown v. Vickers Sports
25 Workington v. Carlisle
30 Carlisle v. Whitehaven
30 Haverigg v. Barrow
30 Lindal v. Millom
30 Netherfield v. Vickerstown
30 Vickers Sports v. Carnforth
30 Workington v. Ulverston

JUNE

6 Barrow v. Workington
6 Carnforth v. Netherfield
6 Dalton v. Vickers Sports
6 Millom v. Carlisle
6 Ulverston v. Haverigg
6 Whitehaven v. Lindal
13 Carlisle v. Millom
13 Haverigg v. Dalton
13 Lindal v. Barrow
13 Netherfield v. Carnforth
13 Vickers Sports v. Ulverston
13 Vickerstown v. Whitehaven
15-16 Dalton v. Lindal
20 Barrow v. Whitehaven
20 Carnforth v. Carlisle
20 Dalton v. Netherfield
20 Millom v. Lindal
20 Ulverston v. Vickerstown

JUNE

20 Workington v. Haverigg
23-24 Vickers S v. Vickerstown
27 Carlisle v. Carnforth
27 Haverigg v. Workington
27 Lindal v. Ulverston
27 Netherfield v. Barrow
27 Vickerstown v. Dalton
27 Whitehaven v. Millom
29-30 Barrow v. Vickers Sports

JULY

4 Carnforth v. Lindal
4 Dalton v. Vickerstown
4 Haverigg v. Carlisle
4 Netherfield v. Vickers Sports
4 Ulverston v. Millom
4 Workington v. Whitehaven
6-7 Vickerstown v. Barrow
11 Barrow v. Vickerstown
11 Carlisle v. Ulverston
11 Carnforth v. Dalton
11 Lindal v. Workington
11 Vickers Sports v. Haverigg
11 Whitehaven v. Netherfield
18 Barrow v. Carlisle
18 Dalton v. Whitehaven
18 Millom v. Carnforth
18 Ulverston v. Lindal
18 Vickerstown v. Netherfield
18 Workington v. Vickers Sports
25 Carlisle v. Dalton
25 Carnforth v. Barrow
25 Millom v. Vickerstown
25 Netherfield v. Ulverston
25 Vickers Sports v. Workington
25 Whitehaven v. Haverigg

AUGUST

1 Barrow v. Carnforth
1 Haverigg v. Lindal
1 Netherfield v. Millom
1 Ulverston v. Whitehaven
1 Vickers Sports v. Carlisle
1 Workington v. Dalton
3 Carlisle v. Workington
3 Dalton v. Haverigg
3 Lindal v. Vickers Sports
3 Millom v. Ulverston
3 Vickerstown v. Carnforth
3 Whitehaven v. Barrow
8 Barrow v. Millom
8 Carnforth v. Workington
8 Haverigg v. Ulverston
8 Lindal v. Vickerstown
8 Vickers Sports v. Netherfield
8 Whitehaven v. Carlisle
15 Carlisle v. Barrow
15 Millom v. Whitehaven
15 Netherfield v. Haverigg
15 Ulverston v. Dalton
15 Vickerstown v. Lindal
15 Workington v. Carnforth
22 Carnforth v. Haverigg
22 Dalton v. Workington
22 Carlisle v. Lindal

NORTH LANCASHIRE LEAGUE—Continued

AUGUST
22 Millom v. Netherfield
22 Vickerstown v. Ulverston
22 Whitehaven v. Vickers Sports
29 Lindal v. Carlisle
29 Haverigg v. Whitehaven
29 Netherfield v. Dalton
29 Ulverston v. Carnforth
29 Vickers Sports v. Barrow

AUGUST
29 Workington v. Millom

SEPTEMBER
5 Barrow v. Dalton
5 Carlisle v. Haverigg
5 Carnforth v. Vickers Sports
5 Lindal v. Netherfield
5 Millom v. Workington
5 Whitehaven v. Vickerstown

NORTH STAFFORDSHIRE LEAGUE

SENIOR "A" SECTION

APRIL
25 Longton v. Norton
25 Meakins v. Leek
25 Nantwich v. Burslem
25 Stone v. Hartshill
25 Porthill Park v. Bignall End
25 Knypersley v. Blythe Works

MAY
2 Norton v. Knypersley
2 Bignall End v. Longton
2 Hartshill v. Porthill Park
2 Burslem v. Stone
2 Leek v. Nantwich
2 Blythe Works v. Meakins
9 Longton v. Hartshill
9 Norton v. Bignall End
9 Nantwich v. Blythe Works
9 Stone v. Leek
9 Porthill Park v. Burslem
9 Knypersley v. Meakins
16 Bignall End v. Knypersley
16 Hartshill v. Norton
16 Burslem v. Longton
16 Leek v. Porthill Park
16 Blythe Works v. Stone
16 Meakins v. Nantwich
23 Longton v. Leek
23 Norton v. Burslem
23 Bignall End v. Hartshill
23 Stone v. Meakins
23 Porthill Park v. Blythe Works
23 Knypersley v. Nantwich
25 Hartshill v. Knypersley
25 Burslem v. Bignall End
25 Leek v. Norton
25 Blythe Works v. Longton
25 Meakins v. Porthill Park
25 Nantwich v. Stone
30 Longton v. Meakins
30 Norton v. Blythe Works
30 Bignall End v. Leek
30 Hartshill v. Burslem
30 Porthill Park v. Nantwich
30 Knypersley v. Stone

JUNE
6 Burslem v. Knypersley
6 Leek v. Hartshill
6 Blythe Works v. Bignall End
6 Meakins v. Norton
6 Nantwich v. Longton

JUNE
6 Stone v. Porthill Park
13 Longton v. Stone
13 Norton v. Nantwich
13 Bignall End v. Meakins
13 Hartshill v. Blythe Works
13 Burslem v. Leek
13 Knypersley v. Porthill Park
20 Blythe Works v. Burslem
20 Meakins v. Hartshill
20 Nantwich v. Bignall End
20 Stone v. Norton
20 Porthill Park v. Longton
20 Knypersley v. Leek
27 Longton v. Knypersley
27 Norton v. Porthill Park
27 Bignall End v. Stone
27 Hartshill v. Nantwich
27 Burslem v. Meakins
27 Leek v. Blythe Works

JULY
4 Norton v. Longton
4 Leek v. Meakins
4 Burslem v. Nantwich
4 Hartshill v. Stone
4 Bignall End v. Porthill Park
4 Blythe Works v. Knypersley
11 Knypersley v. Norton
11 Longton v. Bignall End
11 Porthill Park v. Hartshill
11 Stone v. Burslem
11 Nantwich v. Leek
11 Meakins v. Blythe Works
18 Hartshill v. Longton
18 Bignall End v. Norton
18 Blythe Works v. Nantwich
18 Leek v. Stone
18 Burslem v. Porthill Park
18 Meakins v. Knypersley
25 Knypersley v. Bignall End
25 Norton v. Hartshill
25 Longton v. Burslem
25 Porthill Park v. Leek
25 Stone v. Blythe Works
25 Nantwich v. Meakins

AUGUST
1 Leek v. Longton
1 Burslem v. Norton
1 Hartshill v. Bignall End
1 Meakins v. Stone
1 Blythe Works v. Porthill Park

NORTH STAFFORDSHIRE LEAGUE—Continued

AUGUST

1 Nantwich v. Knypersley
3 Knypersley v. Hartshill
3 Bignall End v. Burslem
3 Norton v. Leek
3 Longton v. Blythe Works
3 Porthill Park v. Meakins
3 Stone v. Nantwich
8 Meakins v. Longton
8 Blythe Works v. Norton
8 Leek v. Bignall End
8 Burslem v. Hartshill
8 Nantwich v. Porthill Park
8 Stone v. Knypersley
15 Knypersley v. Burslem
15 Hartshill v. Leek
15 Bignall End v. Blythe Works
15 Norton v. Meakins
15 Longton v. Nantwich
15 Porthill Park v. Stone
22 Stone v. Longton
22 Nantwich v. Norton
22 Meakins v. Bignall End
22 Blythe Works v. Hartshill
22 Leek v. Burslem
22 Porthill Park v. Knypersley
29 Burslem v. Blythe Works
29 Hartshill v. Meakins
29 Bignall End v. Nantwich
29 Norton v. Stone
29 Longton v. Porthill Park
29 Leek v. Knypersley

SEPTEMBER

5 Knypersley v. Longton
5 Porthill Park v. Norton
5 Stone v. Bignall End
5 Nantwich v. Hartshill
5 Meakins v. Burslem
5 Blythe Works v. Leek

SENIOR "B" SECTION

APRIL

18 Great Chell v. Crewe RR
18 Crewe LMR v. Cheadle
18 Congleton v. St Edward's H
18 Michelin v. Stoke MO
18 Sneyd Colliery v. Silverdale
18 Ashcombe Park v. Audley
18 Boltons v. Kidsgrove
25 Crewe RR v. Boltons
25 Audley v. Great Chell
25 Silverdale v. Ashcombe Park
25 Stoke MO v. Sneyd Colliery
25 St Edward's H v. Michelin
25 Cheadle v. Congleton
25 Kidsgrove v. Crewe LMR

MAY

2 Great Chell v. Silverdale
2 Crewe RR v. Audley
2 Congleton v. Kidsgrove
2 Michelin v. Cheadle
2 Sneyd Colliery v. St Edward's H
2 Ashcombe Park v. Stoke MO
2 Boltons v. Crewe LMR

MAY

9 Audley v. Boltons
9 Silverdale v. Crewe RR
9 Stoke MO v. Great Chell
9 St Edward's H v. Ashcombe Pk
9 Cheadle v. Sneyd Colliery
9 Kidsgrove v. Michelin
9 Crewe LMR v. Congleton
16 Great Chell v. St Edward's H
16 Crewe RR v. Stoke MO
16 Audley v. Silverdale
16 Michelin v. Crewe LMR
16 Sneyd Colliery v. Kidsgrove
16 Ashcombe Park v. Cheadle
16 Boltons v. Congleton
23 Silverdale v. Boltons
23 Stoke MO v. Audley
23 St Edward's H v. Crewe RR
23 Cheadle v. Great Chell
23 Kidsgrove v. Ashcombe Park
23 Crewe LMR v. Sneyd Colliery
23 Congleton v. Michelin
25 Great Chell v. Kidsgrove
25 Crewe RR v. Cheadle
25 Audley v. St Edward's H
25 Silverdale v. Stoke MO
25 Sneyd Colliery v. Congleton
25 Ashcombe Park v. Crewe LMR
25 Boltons v. Michelin
30 Stoke MO v. Boltons
30 St Edward's H v. Silverdale
30 Cheadle v. Audley
30 Kidsgrove v. Crewe RR
30 Crewe LMR v. Great Chell
30 Congleton v. Ashcombe Park
30 Michelin v. Sneyd Colliery

JUNE

6 Great Chell v. Congleton
6 Crewe RR v. Crewe LMR
6 Audley v. Kidsgrove
6 Silverdale v. Cheadle
6 Stoke MO v. St Edward's H
6 Ashcombe Park v. Michelin
6 Boltons v. Sneyd Colliery
13 St Edward's H v. Boltons
13 Cheadle v. Stoke MO
13 Kidsgrove v. Silverdale
13 Crewe LMR v. Audley
13 Congleton v. Crewe RR
13 Michelin v. Great Chell
13 Sneyd Colliery v. Ashcombe Pk
20 Great Chell v. Sneyd Colliery
20 Crewe RR v. Michelin
20 Audley v. Congleton
20 Silverdale v. Crewe LMR
20 Stoke MO v. Kidsgrove
20 St Edward's H v. Cheadle
20 Boltons v. Ashcombe Park
27 Kidsgrove v. St Edward's H
27 Crewe LMR v. Stoke MO
27 Congleton v. Silverdale
27 Michelin v. Audley
27 Sneyd Colliery v. Crewe RR
27 Ashcombe Park v. Great Chell

NORTH STAFFORDSHIRE LEAGUE—Continued

JUNE
27 Boltons v. Cheadle
JULY
4 Great Chell v. Boltons
4 Crewe RR v. Ashcombe Park
4 Audley v. Sneyd Colliery
4 Silverdale v. Michelin
4 Stoke MO v. Congleton
4 St Edward's H v. Crewe LMR
4 Cheadle v. Kidsgrove
11 Crewe RR v. Great Chell
11 Cheadle v. Crewe LMR
11 St Edward's H v. Congleton
11 Stoke MO v. Michelin
11 Silverdale v. Sneyd Colliery
11 Audley v. Ashcombe Park
11 Kidsgrove v. Boltons
18 Boltons v. Crewe RR
18 Great Chell v. Audley
18 Ashcombe Park v. Silverdale
18 Sneyd Colliery v. Stoke MO
18 Michelin v. St Edward's H
18 Congleton v. Cheadle
18 Crewe LMR v. Kidsgrove
25 Silverdale v. Great Chell
25 Audley v. Crewe RR
25 Kidsgrove v. Congleton
25 Cheadle v. Michelin
25 St Edward's H v. Sneyd Colliery
25 Stoke MO v. Ashcombe Park
25 Crewe LMR v. Boltons
AUGUST
1 Boltons v. Audley
1 Crewe RR v. Silverdale
1 Great Chell v. Stoke MO
1 Ashcombe Pk v. St Edward's H
1 Sneyd Colliery v. Cheadle
1 Michelin v. Kidsgrove
1 Congleton v. Crewe LMR
3 St Edward's H v. Great Chell
3 Stoke MO v. Crewe RR
3 Silverdale v. Audley
3 Crewe LMR v. Michelin
3 Kidsgrove v. Sneyd Colliery
3 Cheadle v. Ashcombe Park
3 Congleton v. Boltons
4 Boltons v. Great Chell
4 Ashcombe Park v. Crewe RR
4 Sneyd Colliery v. Audley
4 Michelin v. Silverdale
4 Congleton v. Stoke MO
4 Crewe LMR v. St Edward's H

AUGUST
4 Kidsgrove v. Cheadle
8 Boltons v. Silverdale
8 Audley v. Stoke MO
8 Crewe RR v. St Edward's H
8 Great Chell v. Cheadle
8 Ashcombe Park v. Kidsgrove
8 Sneyd Colliery v. Crewe LMR
8 Michelin v. Congleton
15 Kidsgrove v. Great Chell
15 Cheadle v. Crewe RR
15 St Edward's H v. Audley
15 Stoke MO v. Silverdale
15 Congleton v. Sneyd Colliery
15 Crewe LMR v. Ashcombe Park
15 Michelin v. Boltons
22 Boltons v. Stoke MO
22 Silverdale v. St Edward's H
22 Audley v. Cheadle
22 Crewe RR v. Kidsgrove
22 Great Chell v. Crewe LMR
22 Ashcombe Park v. Congleton
22 Sneyd Colliery v. Michelin
29 Congleton v. Great Chell
29 Crewe LMR v. Crewe RR
29 Kidsgrove v. Audley
29 Cheadle v. Silverdale
29 St Edward's H v. Stoke MO
29 Michelin v. Ashcombe Park
29 Sneyd Colliery v. Boltons
SEPTEMBER
5 Boltons v. St Edward's H
5 Stoke MO v. Cheadle
5 Silverdale v. Kidsgrove
5 Audley v. Crewe LMR
5 Crewe RR v. Congleton
5 Great Chell v. Michelin
5 Ashcombe Pk v. Sneyd Colliery
12 Sneyd Colliery v. Great Chell
12 Michelin v. Crewe RR
12 Congleton v. Audley
12 Crewe LMR v. Silverdale
12 Kidsgrove v. Stoke MO
12 Cheadle v. St Edward's H
12 Ashcombe Park v. Boltons
19 St Edward's H v. Kidsgrove
19 Stoke MO v. Crewe LMR
19 Silverdale v. Congleton
19 Audley v. Michelin
19 Crewe RR v. Sneyd Colliery
19 Great Chell v. Ashcombe Park
19 Cheadle v. Boltons

N. YORKSHIRE AND S. DURHAM LEAGUE

DIVISION "A"

MAY
2 Blackhall v. Guisborough
2 Darlington v. West Hartlepool
2 Norton v. Redcar
2 Middlesbro' v. Darlington R A
2 Saltburn v. Bishop Auckland
2 Synthonia v. Stockton
2 Thornaby v. Normanby Hall

MAY
9 Bishop Auckland v. Middlesbro'
9 Darlington R A v. Saltburn
9 Guisborough v. Thornaby
9 Normanby Hall v. Norton
9 Redcar v. Blackhall
9 Stockton v. Darlington
9 West Hartlepool v. Synthonia
16 Blackhall v. Darlington R A

N. YORKSHIRE & S. DURHAM LEAGUE—Continued

MAY

16 Darlington v. Bishop Auckland
16 Middlesbrough v. Redcar
16 Normanby Hall v. W Hartlepool
16 Saltburn v. Norton
16 Synthonia v. Guisborough
16 Thornaby v. Stockton
23 Bishop Auckland v. Blackhall
23 Darlington RA v. Synthonia
23 Guisborough v. Darlington
23 Norton v. Middlesbrough
23 Redcar v. Saltburn
23 Stockton v. Normanby Hall
23 West Hartlepool v. Thornaby
25 Blackhall v. Norton
25 Darlington v. Darlington R A
25 Normanby Hall v. Guisborough
25 Saltburn v. Middlesbrough
25 Stockton v. West Hartlepool
25 Synthonia v. Redcar
25 Thornaby v. Bishop Auckland
30 Bishop Auckland v. Synthonia
30 Darlington R A v. Thornaby
30 Guisborough v. Stockton
30 Middlesbrough v. Blackhall
30 Norton v. Darlington
30 Redcar v. Normanby Hall
30 Saltburn v. West Hartlepool

JUNE

6 Blackhall v. Saltburn
6 Darlington v. Redcar
6 Normanby H v. Darlington RA
6 Stockton v. Bishop Auckland
6 Synthonia v. Middlesbrough
6 Thornaby v. Norton
6 W Hartlepool v. Guisborough
13 B Auckland v. Guisborough
13 Blackhall v. Synthonia
13 Darlington R A v. Stockton
13 Middlesbrough v. Darlington
13 Norton v. West Hartlepool
13 Redcar v. Thornaby
13 Saltburn v. Normanby Hall
20 Darlington v. Blackhall
20 Guisborough v. Redcar
20 Normanby Hall v. B Auckland
20 Stockton v. Norton
20 Synthonia v. Saltburn
20 Thornaby v. Middlesbrough
20 W Hartlepool v. Darlington RA
27 B Auckland v. W Hartlepool
27 Blackhall v. Thornaby
27 Darlington RA v. Guisborough
27 Middlesbrough v. Normanby H
27 Norton v. Synthonia
27 Redcar v. Stockton
27 Saltburn v. Darlington

JULY

4 B Auckland v. Darlington R A
4 Darlington v. Synthonia
4 Guisborough v. Norton
4 Normanby Hall v. Blackhall
4 Stockton v. Middlesbrough
4 Thornaby v. Saltburn
4 West Hartlepool v. Redcar
11 Blackhall v. Stockton
11 Darlington v. Normanby Hall
11 Middlesbro' v. W Hartlepool
11 Redcar v. Darlington R A
11 Norton v. Bishop Auckland
11 Saltburn v. Guisborough
11 Synthonia v. Thornaby
18 Bishop Auckland v. Redcar
18 Darlington R A v. Norton
18 Guisborough v. Middlesbrough
18 Normanby Hall v. Synthonia
18 Stockton v. Saltburn
18 Thornaby v. Darlington
18 West Hartlepool v Blackhall
25 Bishop Auckland v. Darlington
25 Darlington R A v. Blackhall
25 Guisborough v. Synthonia
25 Norton v. Saltburn
25 Redcar v. Middlesbrough
25 Stockton v. Thornaby
25 W Hartlepool v. Normanby Hall

AUGUST

1 Blackhall v. Bishop Auckland
1 Darlington v. Guisborough
1 Middlesbrough v. Norton
1 Normanby Hall v. Stockton
1 Saltburn v. Redcar
1 Synthonia v. Darlington R A
1 Thornaby v. West Hartlepool
3 Bishop Auckland v. Thornaby
3 Darlington RA v. Darlington
3 Guisborough v. Normanby Hall
3 Middlesbrough v. Saltburn
3 Norton v. Blackhall
3 Redcar v. Synthonia
3 West Hartlepool v. Stockton
8 Blackhall v. Middlesbrough
8 Darlington v. Norton
8 Normanby Hall v. Redcar
8 Stockton v. Guisborough
8 Synthonia v. Bishop Auckland
8 Thornaby v. Darlington R A
8 West Hartlepool v. Saltburn
15 Bishop Auckland v. Stockton
15 Darlington RA v. Normanby H
15 Guisborough v. W Hartlepool
15 Middlesbrough v. Synthonia
15 Norton v. Thornaby
15 Redcar v. Darlington
15 Saltburn v. Blackhall
22 Darlington v. Middlesbrough
22 Guisborough v. B Auckland
22 Normanby Hall v. Saltburn
22 Stockton v. Darlington R A
22 Synthonia v. Blackhall
22 Thornaby v. Redcar
22 West Hartlepool v. Norton
29 B Auckland v. Normanby Hall
29 Blackhall v. Darlington
29 Darlington RA v. W Hartlepool
29 Middlesbrough v. Thornaby
29 Norton v. Stockton

N. YORKSHIRE & S. DURHAM LEAGUE—Continued

AUGUST

29 Redcar v. Guisborough
29 Saltburn v. Synthonia

SEPTEMBER

5 Darlington v. Saltburn
5 Guisborough v. Darlington RA
5 Normanby Hall v. Middlesbro'
5 Stockton v. Redcar
5 Synthonia v. Norton
5 Thornaby v. Blackhall
5 W Hartlepool v. B Auckland
12 Blackhall v. Normanby Hall
12 Darlington RA v. B Auckland
12 Middlesbrough v. Stockton
12 Norton v. Guisborough
12 Redcar v. West Hartlepool
12 Saltburn v. Thornaby
12 Synthonia v. Darlington

DIVISION "B"

MAY

2 Bishop Auckland v. Saltburn
2 Darlington RA v. Middlesbro'
2 Guisborough v. Blackhall
2 Marton v. Great Ayton
2 Normanby Hall v. Thornaby
2 Preston v. Yarm
2 Redcar v. Norton
2 Stockton v. Synthonia
2 West Hartlepool v. Darlington
9 Blackhall v. Redcar
9 Darlington v. Stockton
9 Great Ayton v. Preston
9 Middlesbro' v. Bishop Auckland
9 Norton v. Normanby Hall
9 Saltburn v. Darlington R A
9 Synthonia v. West Hartlepool
9 Thornaby v. Guisborough
9 Yarm v. Marton
16 Bishop Auckland v. Darlington
16 Darlington R A v. Yarm
16 Guisborough v. Great Ayton
16 Marton v. Synthonia
16 Norton v. Saltburn
16 Preston v. Blackhall
16 Redcar v. Middlesbrough
16 Stockton v. Thornaby
16 W Hartlepool v. Normanby H
23 Blackhall v. Bishop Auckland
23 Darlington v. Guisborough
23 Great Ayton v. W Hartlepool
23 Middlesbrough v. Norton
23 Normanby Hall v. Stockton
23 Saltburn v. Preston
23 Synthonia v. Darlington R A
23 Thornaby v. Marton
23 Yarm v. Redcar
25 Bishop Auckland v. Thornaby
25 Darlington RA v. Darlington
25 Guisborough v. Normanby Hall
25 Marton v. Saltburn
25 Middlesbrough v. Great Ayton
25 Norton v. Blackhall
25 Preston v. Stockton
25 Redcar v. Synthonia
25 West Hartlepool v. Yarm
30 Blackhall v. Middlesbrough
30 Darlington v. Preston
30 Great Ayton v. Redcar
30 Normanby Hall v. Marton
30 Stockton v. Guisborough
30 Synthonia v. Bishop Auckland
30 Thornaby v. Darlington R A
30 West Hartlepool v. Saltburn
30 Yarm v. Norton

JUNE

6 B Auckland v. Great Ayton
6 Darlington RA v. Normanby H
6 Guisborough v. W Hartlepool
6 Marton v. Stockton
6 Middlesbrough v. Yarm
6 Norton v. Thornaby
6 Preston v. Synthonia
6 Redcar v. Darlington
6 Saltburn v. Blackhall
13 Darlington v. Middlesbrough
13 Great Ayton v. Norton
13 Guisboro' v. Bishop Auckland
13 Normanby Hall v. Preston
13 Stockton v. Darlington R A
13 Synthonia v. Blackhall
13 Thornaby v. Redcar
13 West Hartlepool v. Marton
13 Yarm v. Saltburn
20 B Auckland v. Normanby Hall
20 Blackhall v. Yarm
20 Darlington RA v. Great Ayton
20 Marton v. Darlington
20 Middlesbrough v. Thornaby
20 Norton v. Stockton
20 Preston v. West Hartlepool
20 Redcar v. Guisborough
20 Saltburn v. Synthonia
27 Darlington v. Saltburn
27 Great Ayton v. Blackhall
27 Guisborough v. Yarm
27 Marton v. Darlington R A
27 Normanby Hall v. Middlesbro'
27 Stockton v. Redcar
27 Synthonia v. Norton
27 Thornaby v. Preston
27 W Hartlepool v. B Auckland

JULY

4 Blackhall v. Normanby Hall
4 Darlington RA v. B Auckland
4 Middlesbrough v. Stockton
4 Norton v. Marton
4 Preston v. Guisborough
4 Redcar v. Great Ayton
4 Saltburn v. Thornaby
4 Synthonia v. Darlington
4 Yarm v. West Hartlepool
11 Bishop Auckland v. Norton
11 Darlington R A v. Redcar
11 Great Ayton v. Yarm
11 Guisborough v. Saltburn
11 Marton v. Preston

N. YORKSHIRE & S. DURHAM LEAGUE—Continued

JULY

11 Normanby Hall v. Darlington
11 Stockton v. Blackhall
11 Thornaby v. Synthonia
11 W Hartlepool v. Middlesbrough
18 Blackhall v. Marton
18 Darlington v. Thornaby
18 Great Ayton v. Normanby Hall
18 Middlesbrough v. Guisborough
18 Norton v. Darlington R A
18 Redcar v. West Hartlepool
18 Saltburn v. Stockton
18 Synthonia v. Preston
18 Yarm v. Bishop Auckland
25 Blackhall v. Darlington R A
25 Darlington v. Bishop Auckland
25 Marton v. West Hartlepool
25 Middlesbrough v. Redcar
15 Normanby Hall v. Yarm
25 Preston v. Norton
25 Saltburn v. Great Ayton
25 Synthonia v. Guisborough
25 Thornaby v. Stockton

AUGUST

1 Bishop Auckland v. Blackhall
1 Darlington R A v. Preston
1 Great Ayton v. Darlington
1 Guisborough v. Marton
1 Norton v. Middlesbrough
1 Redcar v. Saltburn
1 Stockton v. Normanby Hall
1 West Hartlepool v. Thornaby
1 Yarm v. Synthonia
3 Blackhall v. Norton
3 Darlington v. Darlington R A
3 Marton v. Redcar
3 Normanby Hall v. Guisborough
3 Preston v. Bishop Auckland
3 Saltburn v. Middlesbrough
3 Stockton v. West Hartlepool
3 Synthonia v. Great Ayton
3 Thornaby v. Yarm
8 Bishop Auckland v. Synthonia
8 Darlington R A v. Marton
8 Great Ayton v. Thornaby
8 Guisborough v. Stockton
8 Middlesbrough v. Preston
8 Norton v. Darlington
8 Redcar v. Normanby Hall

AUGUST

8 Saltburn v. West Hartlepool
8 Yarm v. Blackhall
15 Blackhall v. Saltburn
15 Darlington v. Yarm
15 Marton v. Guisborough
15 Normanby H v. Darlington R A
15 Preston v. Redcar
15 Stockton v. Bishop Auckland
15 Synthonia v. Middlesbrough
15 Thornaby v. Norton
15 W Hartlepool v. Great Ayton
22 Bishop Auckland v. Marton
22 Blackhall v. Preston
22 Darlington R A v. Stockton
22 Great Ayton v. Synthonia
22 Middlesbrough v. Darlington
22 Norton v. West Hartlepool
22 Redcar v. Thornaby
22 Saltburn v. Normanby Hall
22 Yarm v. Guisborough
29 Darlington v. Blackhall
29 Guisborough v. Redcar
29 Marton v. Norton
29 Normanby Hall v. B Auckland
29 Preston v. Great Ayton
29 Stockton v. Yarm
29 Synthonia v. Saltburn
29 Thornaby v. Middlesbrough
29 W Hartlepool v. Darlington RA

SEPTEMBER

5 B Auckland v. W Hartlepool
5 Blackhall v. Thornaby
5 Darlington RA v. Guisborough
5 Great Ayton v. Stockton
5 Middlesbrough v. Marton
5 Norton v. Synthonia
5 Redcar v. Preston
5 Saltburn v. Darlington
5 Yarm v. Normanby Hall
12 Bishop Auckland v. Redcar
12 Darlington v. Great Ayton
12 Guisborough v. Norton
12 Normanby Hall v. Synthonia
12 Preston v. Darlington R A
12 Stockton v. Marton
12 Thornaby v. Saltburn
12 West Hartlepool v. Blackhall
12 Yarm v. Middlesbrough

RIBBLESDALE LEAGUE

APRIL

18 Gt Harwood v. Blackburn N
18 Ribblesdale W v. Earby
18 Read v. Settle
18 Baxenden v. Whalley
18 Skipton v. Padiham
18 Barnoldswick v. Clitheroe
25 Whalley v. Skipton
25 Clitheroe v. Blackburn N

APRIL

25 Read v. Barnoldswick
25 Baxenden v. Ribblesdale W
25 Settle v. Great Harwood
25 Earby v. Padiham

MAY

2 Great Harwood v. Read
2 Ribblesdale W v. Skipton
2 Padiham v. Whalley

RIBBLESDALE LEAGUE—Continued

May

2 Blackburn N v. Barnoldswick
2 Settle v. Clitheroe
2 Earby v. Baxenden
9 Whalley v. Ribblesdale W
9 Clitheroe v. Great Harwood
9 Read v. Blackburn Northern
9 Baxenden v. Padiham
9 Skipton v. Earby
9 Barnoldswick v. Settle
16 Whalley v. Read
16 Ribblesdale W v. Blackburn N
16 Padiham v. Settle
16 Baxenden v. Barnoldswick
16 Skipton v. Great Harwood
16 Earby v. Clitheroe
23 Great Harwood v. Padiham
23 Clitheroe v. Baxenden
23 Read v. Skipton
23 Blackburn N v. Earby
23 Settle v. Whalley
23 Barnoldswick v. Ribblesdale W
25 Whalley v. Great Harwood
25 Ribblesdale W v. Clitheroe
25 Padiham v. Read
25 Baxenden v. Blackburn N
25 Skipton v. Settle
25 Barnoldswick v. Earby
30 Great Harwood v. Baxenden
30 Clitheroe v. Skipton
30 Read v. Earby
30 Blackburn N v. Whalley
30 Settle v. Ribblesdale W
30 Barnoldswick v. Padiham

June

6 Whalley v. Clitheroe
6 Ribblesdale W v. Read
6 Padiham v. Blackburn N
6 Baxenden v. Settle
6 Skipton v. Barnoldswick
6 Earby v. Great Harwood
13 Gt Harwood v. Ribblesdale W
13 Clitheroe v. Padiham
13 Read v. Baxenden
13 Blackburn N v. Skipton
13 Settle v. Earby
13 Barnoldswick v. Whalley
20 Whalley v. Settle
20 Ribblesdale W v. Barnoldswick
20 Padiham v. Great Harwood
20 Baxenden v. Clitheroe
20 Skipton v. Read
20 Earby v. Blackburn Northern
27 Great Harwood v. Skipton
27 Clitheroe v. Earby
27 Read v. Whalley
27 Blackburn N v. Ribblesdale W
27 Settle v. Padiham
27 Barnoldswick v. Padiham

July

4 Whalley v. Blackburn N
4 Ribblesdale Wanderers v. Settle
4 Padiham v. Barnoldswick
4 Baxenden v. Great Harwood
4 Skipton v. Clitheroe
4 Earby v. Read
11 Great Harwood v. Whalley
11 Clitheroe v. Ribblesdale W
11 Read v. Padiham
11 Blackburn N v. Baxenden
11 Settle v. Skipton
11 Barnoldswick v. Earby
18 Whalley v. Barnoldswick
18 Ribblesdale W v. Gt Harwood
18 Padiham v. Clitheroe
18 Baxenden v. Read
18 Skipton v. Blackburn N
18 Earby v. Settle
25 Great Harwood v. Earby
25 Clitheroe v. Whalley
25 Read v. Ribblesdale W
25 Blackburn N v. Padiham
25 Settle v. Baxenden
25 Barnoldswick v. Skipton

August

1 Great Harwood v. Clitheroe
1 Ribblesdale W v. Whalley
1 Padiham v. Baxenden
1 Blackburn Northern v. Read
1 Settle v. Barnoldswick
1 Earby v. Skipton
8 Whalley v. Padiham
8 Clitheroe v. Settle
8 Read v. Great Harwood
8 Baxenden v. Earby
8 Skipton v. Ribblesdale W
8 Barnoldswick v. Blackburn N
15 Great Harwood v. Settle
15 Ribblesdale W v. Baxenden
15 Padiham v. Earby
15 Blackburn N v. Clitheroe
15 Skipton v. Whalley
15 Barnoldswick v. Read
22 Whalley v. Baxenden
22 Clitheroe v. Barnoldswick
22 Padiham v. Skipton
22 Blackburn N v. Gt Harwood
22 Settle v. Read
22 Earby v. Ribblesdale W
29 Great Harwood v. Barnoldswick
29 Ribblesdale W v. Padiham
29 Read v. Clitheroe
29 Baxenden v. Skipton
29 Settle v. Blackburn Northern
29 Earby v. Whalley

September

5 Whalley v. Earby
5 Clitheroe v. Read
5 Padiham v. Ribblesdale W
5 Blackburn Northern v. Settle
5 Skipton v. Baxenden
5 Barnoldswick v. Gt Harwood

SADDLEWORTH LEAGUE

APRIL

25 Moorside v. Uppermill
25 Flowery Field v. Greenfield
25 Austerlands v. Stayley
25 Friarmere v. English Steel
25 Micklehurst v. Saddleworth
25 Hollinwood v. Delph & D

MAY

2 Uppermill v. Flowery Field
2 Greenfield v. Austerlands
2 Stayley v. Friarmere
2 Delph v. Moorside
2 Saddleworth v. Hollinwood
2 English Steel v. Micklehurst
9 Austerlands v. Uppermill
9 Friarmere v. Greenfield
9 Stayley v. English Steel
9 Flowery Field v. Delph
9 Moorside v. Saddleworth
9 Hollinwood v. Micklehurst
12-13 Uppermill v. Friarmere
12-13 Greenfield v. Stayley
12-13 Delph v. Austerlands
12-13 Micklehurst v. Moorside
12-13 Saddleworth v. Flowery F
12-13 English Steel v. Hollinwood
16 Stayley v. Uppermill
16 Moorside v. Hollinwood
16 Flowery Field v. Micklehurst
16 Austerlands v. Saddleworth
16 Friarmere v. Delph
16 Greenfield v. English Steel
19-20 *H A Tanner Cup (First Round)*
19-20 Micklehurst v. English Steel
19-20, Greenfield v. Uppermill
19-20 Flowery F v. Austerlands
19-20 Delph v. Saddleworth
19-20 Friarmere v. Hollinwood
19-20 Stayley v. Moorside
23 Uppermill v. Greenfield
23 Delph v. Stayley
23 Saddleworth v. Friarmere
23 Micklehurst v. Austerlands
23 Hollinwood v. Flowery Field
23 English Steel v. Moorside
29 Delph v. Uppermill
29 Saddleworth v. Greenfield
29 Micklehurst v. Stayley
29 Friarmere v. Hollinwood
29 Austerlands v. Moorside
29 Flowery Field v. English Steel
30 Uppermill v. Delph
30 Greenfield v. Saddleworth
30 Stayley v. Micklehurst
30 Hollinwood v. Friarmere
30 Moorside v. Austerlands
30 English Steel v. Flowery Field

JUNE

2-3 *H A Tanner Cup (Second Round)*
6 English Steel v. Uppermill
6 Delph v. Greenfield
6 Saddleworth v. Stayley
6 Micklehurst v. Friarmere
6 Hollinwood v. Austerlands
6 Flowery Field v. Moorside
13 Uppermill v. Saddleworth
13 Greenfield v. Micklehurst
13 Stayley v. Hollinwood
13 Friarmere v. Moorside
13 Austerlands v. Flowery Field
13 English Steel v. Delph
20 Micklehurst v. Uppermill
20 Hollinwood v. Greenfield
20 Moorside v. Stayley
20 Flowery Field v. Friarmere
20 Saddleworth v. Delph
20 Austerlands v. English Steel
27 Uppermill v. Hollinwood
27 Greenfield v. Moorside
27 Stayley v. Flowery Field
27 Friarmere v. Austerlands
27 Delph v. Micklehurst
27 English Steel v. Saddleworth

JULY

4 Uppermill v. Moorside
4 Greenfield v. Flowery Field
4 Stayley v. Austerlands
4 English Steel v. Friarmere
4 Saddleworth v. Micklehurst
4 Delph v. Hollinwood
11 *H A Tanner Cup (Final)*
18 Flowery Field v. Uppermill
18 Austerlands v. Greenfield
18 Friarmere v. Stayley
18 Moorside v. Delph
18 Hollinwood v. Saddleworth
18 Micklehurst v. English Steel
25 Uppermill v. Austerlands
25 Greenfield v. Friarmere
25 English Steel v. Stayley
25 Delph v. Flowery Field
25 Saddleworth v. Moorside
25 Micklehurst v. Hollinwood

AUGUST

1 Greenfield v. Uppermill
1 Stayley v. Delph
1 Friarmere v. Saddleworth
1 Austerlands v. Micklehurst
1 Flowery Field v. Hollinwood
1 Moorside v. English Steel
4-5 Friarmere v. Uppermill
4-5 Austerlands v. Delph
4-5 Stayley v. Greenfield
4-5 Flowery Field v. Saddleworth
4-5 Moorside v. Micklehurst
4-5 Hollinwood v. English Steel
8 Uppermill v. Stayley
8 Hollinwood v. Moorside
8 Micklehurst v. Flowery Field
8 Saddleworth v. Austerlands
8 Delph v. Friarmere
8 English Steel v. Greenfield
15 Uppermill v. English Steel

SADDLEWORTH LEAGUE—Continued

AUGUST
15 Greenfield v. Delph
15 Stayley v. Saddleworth
15 Friarmere v. Micklehurst
15 Austerlands v. Hollinwood
15 Moorside v. Flowery Field
22 Saddleworth v. Uppermill
22 Micklehurst v. Greenfield
22 Hollinwood v. Stayley
22 Moorside v. Friarmere
22 Flowery Field v. Austerlands
22 Delph v. English Steel
29 Uppermill v. Micklehurst
29 Greenfield v. Hollinwood
29 Stayley v. Moorside

AUGUST
29 Friarmere v. Flowery Field
29 Delph v. Saddleworth
29 English Steel v. Austerlands

SEPTEMBER
5 Hollinwood v. Uppermill
5 Moorside v. Greenfield
5 Flowery Field v. Stayley
5 Austerlands v. Friarmere
5 Micklehurst v. Delph
5 Saddleworth v. English Steel

Second elevens *vice versa* in all cases, including First Round Cup-ties.

SOUTH LANCASHIRE LEAGUE

APRIL
25 Dunlops (R'dale) v. H Renold
25 Manchester E v. H Simon
25 Prestwich H v. Tweedale & S

MAY
2 Dunlops (Rochdale) v. C P A
2 Chadwicks v. C W S
2 Hans Renold v. H Simon
2 Manchester E v. Tweedale & S
2 Prestwich H v. Oldham Bat
9 Dunlops (Rochdale) v. C W S
9 Chadwicks v. Oldham Batteries
10 Tweedale & S v. Hans Renold
16 C W S v. Hans Renold
16 C P A v. Manchester Electricity
16 Prestwich H v. Chadwicks
16 H Simon v. Dunlops (R'dale)
16 Tweedale & S v. Oldham Bat
17 Dunlops (R'dale) v. Chadwicks
23 C W S v. Oldham Batteries
23 C P A v. H Simon
23 Chadwicks v. Tweedale & S
23 Prestwich H v. Dunlops (R)
23 Hans Renold v. Manchester E
24 Chadwicks v. Dunlops (R'dale)
30 Manchester Elec v. C W S
30 Oldham Batteries v. C P A
30 Chadwicks v. H Simon
30 Prestwich H v. Hans Renold
30 Tweedale & S v. Dunlops (R)

JUNE
6 H Simon v. C W S
6 Prestwich Hospital v. C P A
6 Manchester E v. Chadwicks
6 Dunlops (R'dale) v. Oldham B
6 Hans Renold v. Tweedale & S
7 C P A v. Chadwicks
13 Prestwich Hospital v. C W S
13 Tweedale & S v. C P A
13 Chadwicks v. Hans Renold
13 Dunlops (R) v. Manchester E
13 Oldham Batteries v. H Simon
20 C W S v. Tweedale & S

JUNE
20 Hans Renold v. Dunlops (R)
20 Manchester E v. Oldham Bat
20 Prestwich H v. H Simon
21 Hans Renold v. C P A
21 Oldham B v. Dunlops (R'dale)
27 C W S v. Dunlops (Rochdale)
27 Hans Renold v. Oldham B
27 Prestwich H v. Manchester E
27 Tweedale & S v. H Simon

JULY
4 C P A v. C W S
4 H Simon v. Manchester E
4 Prestwich H v. Tweedale & S
5 Oldham B v. Hans Renold
5 H Simon v. Tweedale & S
11 C W S v. Chadwicks
11 H Simon v. Hans Renold
11 Tweedale & S v. Manchester E
11 Prestwich H v. Oldham Bat
12 C P A v. Dunlops (Rochdale)
18 Hans Renold v. C W S
18 Manchester Electricity v. C P A
18 Prestwich H v. Chadwicks
18 Dunlops (Rochdale) v. H Simon
18 Oldham Bat v. Tweedale & S
19 Oldham Batteries v. Chadwicks
25 Oldham Batteries v. C W S
25 H Simon v. C P A
25 Tweedale & S v. Chadwicks
25 Prestwich H v. Dunlop (R'dale)
25 Manchester E v. Hans Renold
26 Tweedale & S v. C W S

AUGUST
1 C W S v. Manchester Electricity
1 C P A v. Oldham Batteries
1 H Simon v. Chadwicks
1 Dunlops (R) v. Tweedale & S
2 Manchester E v. Dunlops (R)
8 Chadwicks v. C P A
8 Prestwich H v. Manchester E
15 C W S v. C P A

SOUTH LANCASHIRE LEAGUE—Continued

AUGUST
15 Prestwich H v. Hans Renold
22 C W S v. H Simon
22 Prestwich Hospital v. C P A
22 Chadwicks v. Manchester E
23 C P A v. Hans Renold
29 Prestwich Hospital v. C W S
29 C P A v. Tweedale & S
29 Hans Renold v. Chadwicks
29 H Simon v. Oldham Batteries

SEPTEMBER
5 Oldham B v. Manchester E
5 Prestwich Hospital v. H Simon

YORKSHIRE COUNCIL

APRIL
18 King Cross v. Harrogate
25 Appleby-F S W v. Rotherham T
25 Ackworth v. English Electric
25 Askern v. Selby Olympia Recs
25 Atlas & Norfolk W v. Dd Brown Tractors
25 Bentley Colly v. Dearne Ath
25 British Ropes v. Scunthorpe T
25 Cleckheaton v. Dewsbury
25 Cortonwood Colly v. Swinton
25 Darfield v. Sowerby Bridge
25 Doncaster Town v. Castleford
25 Drighlington v. Chickenley
25 East Ardsley v. Hartshead M
25 Glasshoughton v. Wombwell M
25 Gomersal v. Mirfield
25 Goole Town v. Hull Y P I
25 Harrogate v. Hull
25 Heckmondwike v. Ossett
25 King Cross v. Barnsley
25 Laisterdyke v. Halifax
25 Liversedge v. Hanging Heaton
25 Maltby Main v. Steel Peech & T
25 Methley v. Leeds Zingari
25 Morley v. Batley
25 Rockingham C v. Brodsworth
25 Rossington v. Beighton
25 Scholes v. Thornhill
25 Staincliffe v. Birstall
25 Thackley v. Allerton Bywater
25 Thorne Colly v. Harworth Colly
25 Tong Park v. Knaresborough
25 Wakefield v. Huddersfield I C I
25 York v. Scarborough

MAY
2 Allerton Bywater v. Pontefract
2 Askern Main v. Ackworth
2 Aston Hall v. Sheffield C
2 Atlas & N W v. Eng Steel C
2 Batley v. Cleckheaton
2 Beighton v. Hallam
2 Bentley Colly v. Thorne Colly
2 Birstall v. Liversedge
2 Dd Brown T v. Selby O R
2 Castleford v. York
2 Chickenley v. Gomersal
2 Cortonwood Coll v. Maltby M
2 Dearne A v. Wombwell Main
2 Dewsbury v. Heckmondwike
2 Doncaster Town v. Sheffield U
2 Elsecar v. Bullcroft
2 English E v. Sowerby Bridge
2 Featherstone v. Altofts
2 Frickley Colly v. Shiregreen
2 Halifax v. Harrogate
2 Hanging Heaton v. Staincliffe
2 Hartshead Moor v. Wakefield
2 Harworth Coll v. Appleby-F S W
2 Hemsworth C v. Monk Bretton
2 Huddersfield I C I v. Scholes
2 Hull v. Scarborough
2 Laisterdyke v. Illingworth
2 Leeds v. Barnsley
2 Mexborough v. Firbeck
2 Mirfield v. East Ardsley
2 Mitchell Main v. Thorncliffe
2 Ossett v. Morley
2 Oulton v. Glasshoughton
2 Rossington v. Denaby & Cadeby
2 Rotherham Town v. King Cross
2 Scunthorpe T v. British Ropes
2 South Kirkby v. Knaresborough
2 Steel P & T v. Brodsworth
2 Swinton v. Rawmarsh
2 Thornhill v. Drighlington
2 Tong Park Leeds Zingari
2 Wath v. Rockingham
2 Whitwood Colly v. Methley
9 Ackworth v. Selby Olympia R
9 Altofts v. Whitwood Colliery
9 Atlas & N W v. Thorne Colly
9 Barnsley v. Rawmarsh
9 Beighton v. Thorncliffe
9 Bentley Colly v. Hemsworth C
9 British R v. Dd Brown T
9 Brodsworth v. Steel Peech & T
9 Bullcroft v. Aston Hall
9 Butterfields v. Tong Park
9 Cleckheaton v. Birstall
9 Darfield v. Leeds Zingari
9 Denaby & Cadeby v. Shiregreen
9 Doncaster Town v. Hull
9 Drighlington v. Hartshead M
9 East Ardsley v. Thornhill
9 Eng Steel C v. Dearne Ath
9 Glasshoughton v. Allerton B
9 Gomersal v. Huddersfield I C I
9 Goole Town v. Harrogate
9 Heckmondwike v. Batley
9 Hickleton v. Scarborough
9 Hull Y P I v. Scunthorpe T
9 Illingworth v. English E
9 King Cross v. Castleford

YORKSHIRE COUNCIL—Continued

MAY

9 Knaresborough v. Askern
9 Liversedge v. Dewsbury
9 Maltby Main v. Mexborough
9 Methley v. Featherstone
9 Mitchell Main v. Frickley Colly
9 Monk Bretton v. Harworth Coll
9 Morley v. Hanging Heaton
9 Pontefract v. Oulton
9 Rockingham v. Swinton
9 Rossington v. Elsecar
9 Rotherham T v. Appleby-F S W
9 Scholes v. Chickenley
9 Sheffield Coll v. Sheffield United
9 South Kirkby v. Hallam
9 Staincliffe v. Ossett
9 Steeton v. Laisterdyke
9 Thackley v. Sowerby Bridge
9 Wakefield v. Mirfield
9 Wath v. Firbeck
9 Wombwell Main v. Halifax
9 York v. Leeds
16 Allerton Bywater v. Methley
16 Appleby-F S W v. Eng Steel C
16 Askern Main v. Leeds Zingari
16 Aston Hall v. Maltby Main
16 Beighton v. Shiregreen
16 Birstall v. Drighlington
16 British Ropes v. Selby O R
76 Brodsworth v. Frickley Colly
16 Dd Brown Tractors v. Harrogate
16 Dearne Ath v. Monk Bretton
16 Dewsbury v. Thornhill
16 Doncaster Town v. King Cross
16 East Ardsley v. Knaresborough
16 Elsecar v. Denaby & Cadeby
16 English E v. Butterfields
16 Firbeck v. Wath
16 Glasshoughton v. Altofts
16 Halifax v. Atlas & Norfolk W
16 Hallam v. Rockingham
16 Hanging Heaton v. Chickenley
16 Hartshead Moor v. Scholes
16 Harworth Colly v. Bentley Colly
16 Hemsworth Colly v. Darfield
16 Hull v. Castleford
16 Hull Y P I v. Pontefract
16 Laisterdyke v. Ackworth
16 Liversedge v. Batley
16 Mexborough v. Thorncliffe
16 Mirfield v. Cleckheaton
16 Morley v. Leeds
16 Rotherham Town v. Barnsley
16 Scunthorpe Town v. York
16 Sheffield C Police v. Bullcroft
16 Sheffield Coll v. Scarborough
16 Sheffield United v. Rawmarsh
16 Sowerby Bridge v. Oultou
16 Staincliffe v., Wakefield
16 Steel Peech & T v. Mitchell M
16 Swinton v. South Kirkby
16 Thackley v. Illingworth
16 Thorne Colly v. Hickleton
16 Tong Park v. Steeton
16 Whitwood Colly v. Featherstone

MAY

16 Wombwell Main v. Goole
23 Ackworth v. Atlas & Norfolk W
23 Aston Hall v. Scunthorpe
23 Barnsley v. Scarborough
23 Batley v. Staincliffe
23 Dd Brown T v. British Ropes
23 Bullcroft v. Mexborough
23 Butterfields v. Allerton Bywater
23 Castleford v. Rotherham Town
23 Chickenley v. Mirfield
23 Cortonwood Coll v. Wombwell
23 Cleckheaton v. Heckmondwike
23 Elsecar v. Hallam
23 Eng Steel Corp v. Darfield
23 Featherstone v. Oulton
23 Frickley Coll v. Beighton
23 Halifax v. Askern
23 Hanging Heaton v. Dewsbury
23 Harrogate v. Appleby-F S W
23 Harworth C v. Dearne A
23 Hickleton v. Thorne Colly
23 Huddersfield I C I v. Hartshead
23 Illingworth v. Sowerby Bridge
23 King Cross v. Whitwood Colly
23 Knaresborough v. English E
23 Maltby Main v. Firbeck
23 Methley v. Hull Y P I
23 Mitchell Main v. Brodsworth
23 Monk Bretton v. Hemsworth C
23 Morley v. Birstall
23 Ossett v. Liversedge
23 Pontefract v. Goole Town
23 Rawmarsh v. Doncaster Town
23 Rockingham v. Denaby & C
23 Rossington v. South Kirkby
23 Scholes v. Drighlington
23 Selby O R v. Bentley Colly
23 Sheffield United v. Leeds
23 Steel P & T v. Sheffield C P
23 Steeton v. Thackley
23 Thorncliffe v. Shiregreen
23 Thornhill v. Gomersal
23 Tong Park v. Laisterdyke
23 Wakefield v. East Ardsley
23 Wath v. Swinton
23 York v. Hull
25 Altofts v. Allerton Bywater
25 Askern v. English Steel Cor.
25 Aston Hall v. Firbeck
25 Barnsley v. York
25 Beighton v. Elsecar
25 Bentley Colly v. Hickleton
25 Birstall v. Batley
25 British Ropes v. Illingworth
25 Dd Brown T v. Atlas & N W
25 Bullcroft v. Brodsworth
25 Castleford v. Rawmarsh
25 Darfield v. Wombwell Main
25 Dearne Ath v. Thorne Colly
25 Dewsbury v. Ossett
25 Drighlington v. Gomersal
25 East Ardsley v. Scholes
25 Featherstone v. Ackworth
25 Frickley Colly v. South Kirkby

YORKSHIRE COUNCIL—Continued

MAY

25 Glasshoughton v. Pontefract
25 Halifax v. Harworth Colly
25 Hallam v. Rossington
25 Hartshead Moor v. Thornhill
25 Heckmondwike v. Hanging H
25 Hull Y P I v. Monk Bretton
25 Knaresborough v. Steeton
25 Laisterdyke v. Hemsworth Coll
25 Leeds v. Doncaster Town
25 Liversedge v. Cleckheaton
25 Maltby Main v. Cortonwood C
25 Mexborough v. Denaby & C
25 Mirfield v. Huddersfield I C I
25 Oulton v. Methley
25 Rotherham Town v. Hull
25 Scunthorpe Tn v. Appleby-F S
25 Sheffield C Police v. Wath
25 Sheffield United v. King Cross
25 Shiregreen v. Steel Peech & T
25 Sowerby Bridge v. English E
25 Staincliffe v. Morley
25 Swinton v. Leeds Zingari
25 Thackley v. Tong Park
25 Thorncliffe v. Rockingham
25 Wakefield v. Chickenley
25 Whitwood Colly v. Butterfields
26 Batley v. Dewsbury
26 Brodsworth v. Sheffield C P
26 Dd Brown T v. Hickleton
26 Castleford v. Leeds
26 Chickenley v. Drighlington
26 Cleckheaton v. Staincliffe
26 Doncaster Town v. Barnsley
26 English E v. Laisterdyke
26 Eng Steel C v. Atlas & N W
26 Gomersal v. Hartshead Moor
26 Hallam v. Beighton
26 Hanging Heaton v. Liversedge
26 Harrogate v. Whitwood Colly
26 Hemsworth C v. South Kirkby
26 Huddersfield I C I v. E Ardsley
26 Hull v. Rawmarsh
26 Illingworth v. Butterfields
26 King Cross v. Sheffield United
26 Knaresborough v. Thackley
26 Monk Bretton v. Cortonwood C
26 Morley v. Heckmondwike
26 Ossett v. Birstall
26 Scholes v. Wakefield
26 Shiregreen v. Thorncliffe
26 Sowerby Bridge v. Tong Park
26 Swinton v. Halifax
26 Thornhill v. Mirfield
26 Wombwell Main v. Darfield
26 York v. Rotherham Town
30 Ackworth v. Bentley Colly
30 Appleby-F S W v. Allerton B
30 Askern Main v. Harworth Coll
30 Atlas & Norfolk W v. Monk B
30 Barnsley v. Leeds
30 Beighton v. Aston Hall
30 Brodsworth v. Mitchell Main
30 Butterfields v. Knaresborough
30 Cortonwood Coll v. Dearne Ath

MAY

30 Darfield v. Selby Olympia R
30 Denaby & Cadeby v. Swinton
30 Dewsbury v. Cleckheaton
30 Elsecar v. Thorncliffe
30 English Electric v. Steeton
30 Firbeck v. Sheffield C Police
30 Frickley Coll v. Steel P & T
30 Goole Town v. Methley
30 Harrogate v. D Brown Tractors
30 Hartshead Moor v. Chickenley
30 Heckmondwike v. Staincliffe
30 Hemsworth Colly v. Tong Park
30 Hickleton v. British Ropes
30 Hull v. Sheffield United
30 Hull Y P I v. Scarborough
30 Illingworth v. Thackley
30 Laisterdyke v. Sowerby Bridge
30 Mexborough v. Bullcroft
30 Mirfield v. Scholes
30 Ossett v. Hanging Heaton
30 Pontefract v. Featherstone
30 Rawmarsh v. King Cross
30 Rockingham v. Rossington
30 Rotherham Town v. Halifax
30 Scunthorpe Town v. Hallam
30 Shiregreen v. Eng. Steel Corpn
30 South Kirkby v. Leeds Zingari
30 Thorne Colly v. Glasshoughton
30 Thornhill v. Wakefield
30 Wath v. Maltby Main
30 Whitwood Colly v. Castleford
30 Wombwell Main v. Oulton
30 York v. Doncaster Town

JUNE

1 Elsecar v. Rockingham
1-2 Ossett v. Wakefield
2 Elsecar v. Cortonwood Colly
6 Allerton Bywater v. Oulton
6 Appleby-F S W v. Harworth C
6 Atlas & N W v. Askern Main
6 Bentley Colly v. Pontefract
6 Birstall v. Heckmondwike
6 Brodsworth v. Beighton
6 Bullcroft v. Firbeck
6 Castleford v. Barnsley
6 Cleckheaton v. Ossett
6 Dearne Ath v. D Brown T
6 Denaby & C v. Frickley Colly
6 Drighlington v. Scholes
6 East Ardsley v. Chickenley
6 Elsecar v. South Kirkby
6 English Electric v. Illingworth
6 Eng. Steel Corpn v. Ackworth
6 Glasshoughton v. Leeds Zingari
6 Halifax v. Whitwood Colly
6 Hanging Heaton v. Batley
6 Hemsworth Coll v. Featherstone
6 Hickleton v. Sheffield Collegte
6 Huddersfield I C I v. Thornhill
6 King Cross v. Doncaster Town
6 Knaresborough v. Harrogate
6 Leeds v. Rotherham Town
6 Liversedge v. Morley

YORKSHIRE COUNCIL—Continued

JUNE

6 Methley v. Altofts
6 Mexborough v. Wath
6 Mirfield v. Hartshead Moor
6 Mitchell M v. Hallam
6 Monk Bretton v. Darfield
6 Rawmarsh v. Scunthorpe Town
6 Rockingham v. Shiregreen
6 Rossington v. Swinton
6 Scarborough v. Hull
6 Selby Olympia R v. Hull Y P I
6 Sheffield C Police v. Aston Hall
6 Sheffield United v. York
6 Sowerby Bridge v. Steeton
6 Staincliffe v. Dewsbury
6 Thackley v. Laisterdyke
6 Thorncliffe v. Steel P & Tozer
6 Thorne Colly v. Goole Town
6 Tong Park v. Butterfields
6 Wakefield v. Gomersal
6 Wombwell M v. Cortonwood C
9-10 Sowerby Bridge v. King C
11 Sheffield Coll v. Brodsworth
13 Appleby-F S W v. Leeds Zingari
13 Aston Hall v. Bullcroft Colly
13 Atlas & Norfolk W v. Halifax
13 Barnsley v. Hull
13 Batley v. Hanging Heaton
13 Beighton v. Brodsworth
13 D Brown T v. Scarborough
13 Butterfields v. Sowerby Bridge
13 Chickenley v. Huddersfield I C I
13 Darfield v. Hemsworth Colly
13 Dewsbury v. Birstall
13 Drighlington v. Wakefield
13 Frickley Colly v. Mitchell Main
13 Glasshoughton v. Featherstone
13 Hallam v. Elsecar
13 Hartshead Moor v. Mirfield
13 Hickleton v. Dearne Ath
13 Hull Y P I v. Goole Town
13 King Cross v. York
13 Knaresborough v. Ackworth
13 Laisterdyke v. Tong Park
13 Leeds v. Rawmarsh
13 Maltby Main v. Rossington
13 Monk Bretton v Bentley Colly
13 Morley v. Cleckheaton
13 Ossett v. Heckmondwike
13 Oulton v. Altofts
13 Pontefract v. Methley
13 Rotherham T v. Doncaster T
13 Scholes v. Gomersal
13 Scunthorpe T v. Harworth Coll
13 Selby Olympia R v. Askern
13 Sheffield Coll v. Harrogate
13 Sheffield United v. Castleford
13 Shiregreen v. Denaby & Cadeby
13 South Kirkby v. Rockingham
13 Staincliffe v. Liversedge
13 Steeton v. Illingworth
13 Swinton v. Cortonwood Colly
13 Thackley v. English Electric
13 Thorncliffe v. Mexborough
13 Thorne Coll v. Eng Steel Corpn

JUNE

13 Thornhill v. East Ardsley
13 Wath v. Sheffield C Police
13 Wombwell Main v. Whitwood C
17-18 Halifax v. Sowerby Bridge
20 Altofts v. Pontefract
20 Atlas & N W v. British Ropes
20 Barnsley v. Sheffield Collegiate
20 Bentley Colly v. Darfield
20 Brodsworth v. Thorncliffe
20 Castleford v. King Cross
20 Cortonwood Coll v. Monk Bret
20 Dearne Ath v. Harworth Colly
20 Denaby & Cadeby v. Elsecar
20 Doncaster Town v. Hull Y P I
20 Featherstone v. Allerton By
20 Firbeck v. Rossington
20 Goole Town v. Whitwood Colly
20 Halifax v. Knaresborough
20 Hemsworth Colly v. Ackworth
20 Hull v. Leeds
20 Illingworth v. Tong Park
20 Laisterdyke v. Butterfields
20 Maltby Main v. Wath
20 Methley v. Glasshoughton
20 Mexborough v. Mitchell Main
20 Oulton v. Leeds Zingari
20 Rawmarsh v. Rotherham Town
20 Rockingham v. Hallam
20 Scarborough v. Hickleton
20 Scunthorpe T v. Aston Hall
20 Selby Olympia R v. Harrogate
20 Shiregreen v. Frickley Colly
20 South Kirkby v. Swinton
20 Sowerby Bridge v. Thackley
20 Steel Peech & T v. Beighton
20 Steeton v. English Electric
20 Thorne Colly v. Bullcroft
20 Wombwell Main v. Askern Main
20 York v. Sheffield United
23-24 Illingworth v. King Cross
25 Darfield v. Mitchell Main
27 Ackworth v. Laisterdyke
27 Allerton Bywater v. Halifax
27 Askern Main v. Wombwell M
27 Barnsley v. Leeds Zingari
27 Beighton v. South Kirkby
27 Birstall v. Staincliffe
27 British Ropes v. Harrogate
27 Brodsworth v. Shiregreen
27 D Brown T v. Appleby-F S W
27 Bullcroft v. Sheffield C Police
27 Butterfields v. English E
27 Castleford v. Sheffield United
27 Chickenley v. Hartshead Moor
27 Cortonwood C v. Featherstone
27 Darfield v. Goole Town
27 Dearne Ath v. Bentley Colly
27 Dewsbury v. Morley
27 East Ardsley v. Drighlington
27 Elsecar v. Swinton
27 Glasshoughton v. Doncaster T
27 Gomersal v. Wakefield
27 Hallam v. Denaby & Cadeby
27 Hanging Heaton v. Cleckheaton

YORKSHIRE COUNCIL—Continued

June

27 Harworth C v. Hemsworth C
27 Heckmondwike v. Liversedge
27 Hull Y P I v. Selby Olympia R
27 Illingworth v. Steeton
27 King Cross v. Hull
27 Methley v. Pontefract
27 Mexborough v. Maltby Main
27 Mirfield v. Thornhill
27 Mitchell M v. Steel Peech & T
27 Monk Bretton v. Frickley Colly
27 Ossett v. Batley
27 Rossington v. Rockingham
27 Rotherham T v. Scunthorpe T
27 Scarborough v. Leeds
27 Scholes v. Huddersfield I C I
27 Sheffield Collegiate v. Firbeck
27 Thackley v. Knaresborough
27 Thorne C v. Atlas & N W
27 Tong Park v. Sowerby Bridge
27 Wath v. Aston Hall
27 Whitwood Colly v. Oulton
27 York v. Rawmarsh

July

1-2 King Cross v. Sowerby Bridge
4 Ackworth v. English Steel C
4 Altofts v. Glasshoughton
4 Appleby-F S W v. D. Brown T
4 Askern Main v. Cortonwood C
4 Aston Hall v. Mexborough
4 Barnsley v. Castleford
4 British Ropes v. Hickleton
4 Brodsworth v. Sheffield C
4 Denaby & C v. Rockingham
4 Doncaster T v. Rotherham T
4 Elsecar v. Rossington
4 English Electric v. Thackley
4 Goole Town v. Atlas & N W
4 Halifax v. Illingworth
4 Harrogate v. Scarborough
4 Harworth Coll v. Monk Bretton
4 Knaresborough v. Laisterdyke
4 Leeds v. Hull
4 Methley v. Allerton Bywater
4 Mitchell Main v. Beighton
4 Oulton v. Featherstone
4 Pontefract v. Hull Y P I
4 Rawmarsh v. Sheffield United
4 Scunthorpe T v. Leeds Zingari
4 Selby Olympia R v. Darfield
4 Sheffield City P v. Maltby
4 Shiregreen v. South Kirkby
4 Sowerby Bridge v. Butterfields
4 Steel, P & T v. Thorncliffe
4 Steeton v. Tong Park
4 Swinton v. Hallam
4 Thorne Coll v. Bentley Coll
4 Wath v. Bullcroft Colliery
4 Whitwood C v. Hemsworth C
4 Wombwell Main v. Dearne Ath
4 York v. King Cross
7-8 King Cross v. Illingworth
7-8 Sowerby Bridge v. Halifax
11 Allerton B v. Glasshoughton

July

11 Aston Hall v. Wath
11 Barnsley v. King Cross
11 Batley v. Liversedge
11 Beighton v. Cortonwood Coll
11 British Ropes v. Appleby-FSW
11 D. Brown T v. Dearne Athletic
11 Bullcroft v. Thorne Colliery
11 Butterfields v. Steeton
11 Chickenley v. Hanging Heaton
11 Cleckheaton v. Mirfield
11 Denaby & Cadeby v. Rossington
11 Doncaster Town v. York
11 Drighlington v. Birstall
11 English S C v. Monk Bretton
11 Featherstone v. Methley
11 Firbeck v. Mexborough
11 Frickley Coll v. Brodsworth
11 Gomersal v. East Ardsley
11 Halifax v. Swinton
11 Hallam v. South Kirkby
11 Harrogate v. Knaresborough
11 Harworth Coll v. Askern Main
11 Hemsworth C v. Bentley C
11 Hull Y P I v. Leeds Zingari
11 Laisterdyke v. English Electric
11 Leeds v. Castleford
11 Maltby Main v. Sheffield City P
11 Oulton v. Pontefract
11 Rockingham v. Goole Town
11 Rotherham Town v. Rawmarsh
11 Scarborough v. Scunthorpe T
11 Scholes v. Hartshead Moor
11 Selby Olympia R v. Ackworth
11 Sheffield Collegiate v. Hickleton
11 Sheffield United v. Hull
11 Shiregreen v. Mitchell Main
11 Thorncliffe v. Elsecar
11 Thornhill v. Dewsbury
11 Tong Park v. Thackley
11 Wakefield v. Staincliffe
11 Whitwood Coll v. Altofts
13 Rockingham v. Elsecar
18 Ackworth v. Askern Main
18 Altofts v. Featherstone
18 Barnsley v. Doncaster Town
18 Beighton v. Mitchell Main
18 Bentley Coll v. Harworth Coll
18 Birstall v. Hanging Heaton
18 British Ropes v. Atlas & N S W
18 Castleford v. Hull
18 Cortonwood C v. Hemsworth C
18 Darfield v. English Steel C
18 Dewsbury v. Batley
18 Drighlington v. Thornhill
18 English Electric v. Tong Park
18 Frickley Coll v. Thorncliffe
18 Glasshoughton v. Oulton
18 Goole Town v. Wombwell Main
18 Halifax v. Laisterdyke
18 Harrogate v. Sheffield C
18 Hartshead Moor v. East Ardsley
18 Hickleton v. Leeds Zingari
18 Huddersfield ICI v. Gomersal
18 Illingworth v. Firbeck

YORKSHIRE COUNCIL—Continued

July

18 King Cross v. Leeds
18 Liversedge v. Heckmondwike
18 Maltby Main v. Aston Hall
18 Methley v. Knaresborough
18 Mirfield v. Chickenley
18 Monk Bretton v. Dearne Ath
18 Morley v. Ossett
18 Pontefract v Allerton Bywater
18 Rawmarsh v. York
18 Rockingham v. Bullcroft
18 Rossington v. Hallam
18 Scarborough v. D. Brown T
18 Scunthorpe Town v. Hull Y P I
18 Selby Olympia v. Thorne Coll
18 Sheffield C P v. Steel, P & T
18 Sheffield U v. Rotherham T
18 Shiregreen v. Brodsworth
18 South Kirkby v. Elsecar
18 Staincliffe v. Cleckheaton
18 Swinton v. Denaby & Cadeby
18 Thackley v. Butterfields
18 Wakefield v. Scholes
18 Wath v. Mexborough
25 Ackworth v. Goole Town
25 Altofts v. Harrogate
25 Aston Hall v. Sheffield City P
25 Batley v. Birstall
25 British Ropes v. Doncaster T
25 Brodsworth v. Rockingham
25 Bullcroft v. Wath
25 Butterfields v. Illingworth
25 Castleford v. Whitwood Coll
25 Cleckheaton v. Liversedge
25 Cortonwood Coll v. Hallam
25 Darfield v. Bentley Coll
25 Dearne Ath v. English Steel C
25 Denaby & C v. South Kirkby
25 East Ardsley v. Huddersf'd ICI
25 Firbeck Main v. Maltby Main
25 Frickley Coll v. Monk Bretton
25 Gomersal v. Scholes
25 Halifax v. Allerton Bywater
25 Hanging Heaton v. Morley
25 Heckmondwike v. Dewsbury
25 Hemsworth C v. Selby Olympia
25 Hickleton v. Appleby-F S W
25 Hull v. King Cross
25 Hull Y P I v. Methley
25 Knaresborough v. Leeds Z
25 Laisterdyke v. Thackley
25 Mirfield v. Drighlington
25 Mitchell Main v. Shiregreen
25 Ossett v. Staincliffe
25 Rossington v. Featherstone
25 Rotherham Town v. Leeds
25 Scarborough v. Sheffield C
25 Scunthorpe Town v. Rawmarsh
25 Sheffield United v. Barnsley
25 Steeton v. Sowerby Bridge
25 Swinton v. Mexborough
25 Thorncliffe v. Beighton
25 Thornhill v. Chickenley
25 Wakefield v. Hartshead Moor
25 Wombwell M v. Glasshoughton

July

25 York v. D. Brown Tractors
25 Oulton v. Atlas & N W

August

1 Allerton Bywater v. Leeds Z
1 Altofts v. Oulton
1 Appleby-FSW v. British Ropes
1 Askern Main v. Dearne Ath
1 Batley v. Heckmondwike
1 Beighton v. Frickley Colliery
1 Bentley Coll v. Ackworth
1 Birstall v. Cleckheaton
1 D. Brown T v. Thorne Colliery
1 Chickenley v. Thornhill
1 Darfield v. Hickleton
1 Denaby & Cadeby v. Hallam
1 Doncaster Town v. Rawmarsh
1 Drighlington v. East Ardsley
1 Featherstone v. Glasshoughton
1 Firbeck Main v. Bullcroft Coll
1 Harrogate v. Halifax
1 Hartshead Moor v. Gomersal
1 Hemsworth C v. Laisterdyke
1 Huddersf'd I C I v. Wakefield
1 Hull v. York
1 Knaresborough v. Methley
1 Leeds v. Sheffield United
1 Liversedge v. Ossett
1 Mitchell M v. Wombwell M
1 Monk Bretton v. Atlas & N W
1 Morley v. Dewsbury
1 Rockingham v. South Kirkby
1 Rossington v. Swinton
1 Rotherham T v. Castleford
1 Scarborough v. Barnsley
1 Scholes v. Mirfield
1 Selby Olympia v. Pontefract
1 Sheffield City P v. Mexboro
1 Sheffield C v. Aston Hall
1 Shiregreen v. Elsecar
1 Sowerby Bridge v. Illingworth
1 Staincliffe v. Hanging Heaton
1 Steel, Peech & T v. Maltby
1 Steeton v. Butterfields
1 Thorncliffe v. Brodsworth
1 Thorne Colliery v. Thackley
1 Wath v. Scunthorpe Town
1 Whitwood Coll v. King Cross
3 Ackworth v. Featherstone
3 Allerton Bywater v. Altofts
3 Appleby-FSW v. Scunthorpe T
3 Denaby & C v. Mexborough
3 Doncaster Town v. Leeds
3 Elsecar v. Beighton
3 English Steel C v. Askern Main
3 Firbeck Main v. Aston Hall
3 Hallam v. Mitchell Main
3 Harrogate v. Selby Olympia R
3 Hemsworth C v. Whitwood C
3 Hickleton v. Bentley Coll
3 Knaresborough v. East Ardsley
3 Hull v. Rotherham Town
3 Methley v. Oulton
3 Pontefract v. Glasshoughton

YORKSHIRE COUNCIL—Continued

AUGUST

3 Rawmarsh v. Castleford
3 Rockingham v. Thorncliffe
3 Rossington v. Maltby Main
3 Scarborough v. Sheffield United
3 Sheffield C P v. Brodsworth
3 South Kirkby v. Frickley Coll
3 Steel, P & T v. Shiregreen
3 Swinton v. Wath
3 Thorne Coll v. Dearne Athletic
3 Wakefield v. British Ropes
3 York v. Barnsley
4 Bullcroft v. Rockingham
4 Cortonwood Coll v. Beighton
4 Doncaster T v. British Ropes
4 Hallam v. Swinton
4 Methley v. Leeds Zingari
4 Mitchell Main v. Darfield
4 Rawmarsh v. Hull
4 Rotherham Town v. York
4 South Kirkby v. Hemsworth C
4 Wakefield v. Ossett
4 Whitwood Coll v. Harrogate
8 Askern Main v. Atlas & N W
8 Barnsley v. Rotherham Town
8 Birstall v. Ossett
8 Butterfields v. Thackley
8 Castleford v. Ackworth
8 Chickenley v. Wakefield
8 Cleckheaton v. Hanging Heaton
8 Darfield v. Monk Bretton
8 Dearne Athletic v. Hickleton
8 Denaby & C v. Cortonwood Coll
8 Dewsbury v. Liversedge
8 East Ardsley v. Mirfield
8 English E v. Knaresborough
8 English Steel C v. Appleby-F S W
8 Featherstone v. Hemsworth C
8 Gomersal v. Drighlington
8 Goole Town v. Rockingham
8 Halifax v. Wombwell Main
8 Hartshead M v. Huddersf'd I C I
8 Harworth Coll v. Thorne Coll
8 Heckmondwike v. Morley
8 Hull v. Harrogate
8 King Cross v. Rawmarsh
8 Laisterdyke v. Steeton
8 Leeds v. York
8 Maltby Main v. Bullcroft
8 Methley v. Whitwood Colliery
8 Mexborough v. Aston Hall
8 Pontefract v. Leeds Zingari
8 Scarborough v. Hull Y P I
8 Scunthorpe T v. Sheffield C
8 Selby Olympia v. British Ropes
8 Sheffield City P v. Firbeck
8 Sheffield U v. Doncaster T
8 Shiregreen v. Beighton
8 South Kirkby v. Rossington
8 Staincliffe v. Batley
8 Steel, Peech & T v. Frickley C
8 Swinton v. Elsecar
8 Thorncliffe v. Mitchell Main
8 Thornhill v. Scholes
8 Tong Park v. Bentley Colliery

AUGUST

8 Wath v. Hallam
15 Allerton B v. Featherstone
15 Atlas & N W v. Goole Town
15 Batley v. Morley
15 Beighton v. Steel, Peech & T
15 British Ropes v. Leeds Zingari
15 Brodsworth v. Firbeck
15 Bullcroft v. Maltby Main
15 Dearne Athletic v. Askern Main
15 Dewsbury v. Staincliffe
15 Elsecar v. Shiregreen
15 Glasshoughton v. Methley
15 Hallam v. Aston Hall
15 Hanging H v. Heckmondwike
15 Hartshead M v. Drighlington
15 Hemsworth C v. Harworth C
15 Hickleton v. Darfield
15 Huddersf'd ICI v. Chickenley
15 Hull v. Doncaster Town
15 Hull Y P I v. Ackworth
15 Illingworth v. Halifax
15 King Cross v. Leeds
15 Knaresborough v. Butterfields
15 Liversedge v. Birstall
15 Mexborough v. Sheffield City P
15 Mirfield v. Gomersal
15 Monk Bretton v. English S C
15 Ossett v. Cleckheaton
15 Oulton v. Whitwood Colliery
15 Pontefract v. Altofts
15 Rawmarsh v. Barnsley
15 Rotherham T v. Sheffield U
15 Scarborough v. Harrogate
15 Scholes v. East Ardsley
15 Scunthorpe T v. Rossington
15 Sheffield Collegiate v. Bentley C
15 South Kirkby v. Denaby & C
15 Sowerby Bridge v. Laisterdyke
15 Swinton v. Rockingham
15 Thorncliffe v. Frickley Colliery
15 Thorne Coll v. Selby Olympia R
15 Tong Park v. English Electric
15 Wakefield v. Thornhill
15 Wombwell M v. Mitchell M
15 York v. Castleford
22 Ackworth v. English Electric
22 Altofts v. Methley
22 Appleby-F S W v. Hickleton
22 Aston Hall v. Steel, Peech & T
22 Atlas & N W v. Dearne Ath
22 Barnsley v. Sheffield United
22 Beighton v. Rossington
22 Bentley Coll v. Monk Bretton
22 Birstall v. Dewsbury
22 Brodsworth v. Bullcroft
22 D. Brown T v. Leeds Zingari
22 Butterfields v. Laisterdyke
22 Castleford v. Doncaster Town
22 Chickenley v. Scholes
22 Cleckheaton v. Batley
22 Cortonwood Coll v. Elsecar
22 Darfield v. Askern Main
22 Drighlington v. Huddersf'd ICI
22 East Ardsley v. Gomersal

YORKSHIRE COUNCIL—Continued

AUGUST

22 English Steel C v. Wombwell M
22 Featherstone v. Pontefract
22 Firbeck v. Sheffield Collegiate
22 Frickley C v. Denaby & Cadeby
22 Goole Town v. Thorne Coll
22 Hallam v. Wath
22 Hanging Heaton v. Ossett
22 Harrogate v. British Ropes
22 Harworth C v. Scunthorpe T
22 Hull v. Hull Y P I
22 King Cross v. Rotherham Town
22 Knaresborough v. Halifax
22 Mexborough v. Swinton
22 Mirfield v. Wakefield
22 Morley v. Liversedge
22 Oulton v. Allerton Bywater
22 Rawmarsh v. Leeds
22 Scarborough v. York
22 Selby Olympia v. Hemsworth C
22 Shiregreen v. Rockingham
22 South Kirkby v. Beighton
22 Staincliffe v. Heckmondwike
22 Thackley v. Steeton
22 Thornhill v. Hartshead Moor
22 Tong Park v. Illingworth
22 Whitwood C v. Glasshoughton
24 Barnsley v. Hull
29 Ackworth v. Castleford
29 Allerton Bywater v. Thackley
29 Appleby-F S W v. Harrogate
29 Askern Main v. Darfield
29 Aston Hall v. Beighton
29 Atlas & N W v. Shiregreen
29 Batley v. Ossett
29 Bentley C v. Selby Olympia R
29 Bullcroft v. Elsecar
29 Butterfields v. Whitwood Coll
29 Chickenley v. East Ardsley
29 Cleckheaton v. Morley
29 Dearne Ath v. English Electric
29 Dewsbury v. Hanging Heaton
29 Doncaster T v. Glasshoughton
29 English Steel C v. Thorne Coll
29 Featherstone v. King Cross
29 Firbeck M v. Brodsworth
29 Gomersal v. Thornhill
29 Halifax v. Rotherham Town

AUGUST

29 Hallam v. Cortonwood Coll
29 Heckmondwike v. Birstall
29 Hickleton v. D. Brown T
29 Huddersf'd I C I v. Mirfield
29 Hull Y P I v. Hull
29 Illingworth v. British Ropes
29 Laisterdyke v. Knaresborough
29 Leeds v. Scarborough
29 Liversedge v. Staincliffe
29 Methley v. Goole Town
29 Mitchell M v. Mexborough
29 Oulton v. Sowerby Bridge
29 Rawmarsh v. Swinton
29 Rockingham v. Wath
29 Sheffield Collegiate v. Barnsley
29 Steeton v. Leeds Zingari
29 Tong Park v. Hemsworth Coll
29 Wakefield v. Drighlington
29 Wombwell M v. Pontefract
29 York v. Scunthorpe Town

SEPTEMBER

5 Allerton B v. Appleby-F S W
5 Bentley C v. Sheffield Collegiate
5 D. Brown Tractors v. York
5 Darfield v. Atlas & N W
5 Drighlington v. Mirfield
5 East Ardsley v. Wakefield
5 English Electric v. Dearne Ath
5 English Steel v. Scunthorpe T
5 Firbeck v. Beighton
5 Gomersal v. Chickenley
5 Goole Town v. Ackworth
5 Hanging Heaton v. Birstall
5 Harrogate v. King Cross
5 Heckmondwike v. Cleckheaton
5 Hull v. Leeds Zingari
5 Hull Y P I v. Doncaster Town
5 Illingworth v. Laisterdyke
5 Knaresborough v. Tong Park
5 Morley v. Staincliffe
5 Ossett v. Dewsbury
5 Pontefract v. Wombwell Main
5 Sowerby Bridge v. Swinton
5 Thackley v. Thorne Colliery
5 Thornhill v. Huddersf'd I C I
5 Whitwood Colliery v. Halifax
12 Huddersf'd ICI v. Drighlington

HUDDERSFIELD AND DISTRICT LEAGUE

SECTION "A"

APRIL

18 Almondbury v. Lascelles Hall
18 Bradley Mills v. Broad Oak
18 Elland v. Thongsbridge
18 Meltham v. Golcar
18 Primrose Hill v. Honley
18 Rastrick v. Huddersfield
25 Broad Oak v. Elland
25 Golcar v. Almondbury
25 Honley v. Meltham
25 Huddersfield v. Primrose Hill

APRIL

25 Lascelles Hall v. Bradley Mill
25 Thongsbridge v. Rastrick

MAY

2 Almondbury v. Honley
2 Bradley Mills v. Golcar
2 Elland v. Lascelles Hall
2 Meltham v. Huddersfield
2 Rastrick v. Primrose Hill
2 Thongsbridge v. Broad Oak
9 Broad Oak v. Rastrick
9 Golcar v. Elland

HUDDERSFIELD & DISTRICT LEAGUE—Continued

MAY

9 Honley v. Bradley Mills
9 Huddersfield v. Almondbury
9 Lascelles Hall v. Thongsbridge
9 Primrose Hill v. Meltham
16 *Sykes Cup (1st Round)*
16 Bradley Mills v. Shepley
16 Broad Oak v. Armitage Br
16 Elland v. Linthwaite
16 Hall Bower v. Dalton
16 Holmfirth v. Slaithwaite
16 Huddersfield v. Thongsbridge
16 Kirkburton v. Meltham
16 Kirkheaton v. Rastrick
16 Lascelles Hall v. Primrose Hill
16 Marsden v. Almondbury
16 Paddock v. Honley
16 Lockwood v. Golcar
23 Almondbury v. Primrose Hill
23 Bradley Mills v. Huddersfield
23 Broad Oak v. Lascelles Hall
23 Elland v. Honley
23 Rastrick v. Meltham
23 Thongsbridge v. Golcar
25 Elland v. Huddersfield
25 Golcar v. Broad Oak
25 Honley v. Thongsbridge
25 Lascelles Hall v. Rastrick
25 Meltham v. Almondbury
25 Primrose Hill v. Bradley Mills
26 Almondbury v. Meltham
26 Bradley Mills v. Primrose Hill
26 Broad Oak v. Golcar
26 Huddersfield v. Elland
26 Rastrick v. Lascelles Hall
26 Thongsbridge v. Honley
30 Golcar v. Lascelles Hall
30 Honley v. Broad Oak
30 Huddersfield v. Thongsbridge
30 Meltham v. Bradley Mills
30 Primrose Hill v. Elland
30 Rastrick v. Almondbury

JUNE

6 Bradley Mills v. Almondbury
6 Broad Oak v. Huddersfield
6 Elland v. Meltham
6 Golcar v. Rastrick
6 Lascelles Hall v. Honley
6 Thongsbridge v. Primrose Hill
13 Almondbury v. Elland
13 Honley v. Golcar
13 Huddersfield v. Lascelles Hall
13 Meltham v. Thongsbridge
13 Pr mrose Hill v. Broad Oak
13 Rastrick v. Bradley Mills
20 Broad Oak v. Meltham
20 Elland v. Bradley Mills
20 Golcar v. Huddersfield
20 Honley v. Rastrick
20 Lascelles Hall v. Primrose Hill
20 Thongsbridge v. Almondbury
27 Almondbury v. Broad Oak
27 Bradley Mills v. Thongsbridge
27 Huddersfield v. Honley
27 Meltham v. Lascelles Hall
27 Primrose Hill v. Golçar
27 Rastrick v. Elland

JULY

4 Broad Oak v. Bradley Mills
4 Golcar v. Meltham
4 Honley v. Primrose Hill
4 Huddersfield v. Rastrick
4 Lascelles Hall v. Almondbury
4 Thongsbridge v. Elland
11 Almondbury v. Golcar
11 Bradley Mills v. Lascelles Hall
11 Elland v. Broad Oak
11 Meltham v. Honley
11 Primrose Hill v. Huddersfield
11 Rastrick v. Thongsbridge
18 Broad Oak v. Thongsbridge
18 Golcar v. Bradley Mills
18 Honley v. Almondbury
18 Huddersfield v. Meltham
18 Lascelles Hall v. Elland
18 Primrose Hill v. Rastrick
25 Almondbury v. Huddersfield
25 Bradley Mills v. Honley
25 Elland v. Golcar
25 Meltham v. Primrose Hill
25 Rastrick v. Broad Oak
25 Thongsbridge v. Lascelles Hall

AUGUST

8 Golcar v. Thongsbridge
8 Honley v. Elland
8 Huddersfield v. Bradley Mills
8 Lascelles Hall v. Broad Oak
8 Meltham v. Rastrick
8 Primrose Hill v. Almondbury
15 Almondbury v. Rastrick
15 Bradley Mills v. Meltham
15 Broad Oak v. Honley
15 Elland v. Primrose Hill
15 Lascelles Hall v. Golcar
15 Thongsbridge v. Huddersfield
22 Almondbury v. Bradley Mills
22 Honley v. Lascelles Hall
22 Huddersfield v. Broad Oak
22 Meltham v. Elland
22 Primrose Hill v. Thongsbridge
22 Rastrick v. Golcar
29 Bradley Mills v. Rastrick
29 Broad Oak v. Primrose Hill
29 Elland v. Almondbury
29 Golcar v. Honley
29 Lascelles Hall v. Huddersfield
29 Thongsbridge v. Meltham

SEPTEMBER

5 Almondbury v. Thongsbridge
5 Bradley Mills v. Elland
5 Huddersfield v. Golcar
5 Meltham v. Broad Oak
5 Primrose Hill v. Lascelles Hall
5 Rastrick v. Honley
12 Broad Oak v. Almondbury
12 Elland v. Rastrick

HUDDERSFIELD & DISTRICT LEAGUE—Continued

SEPTEMBER

12 Golcar v. Primrose Hill
12 Honley v. Huddersfield
12 Lascelles Hall v. Meltham
12 Thongsbridge v. Bradley Mills

SECTION "B"

APRIL

18 Armitage Bridge v. Dalton
18 Hall Bower v. Shepley
18 Holmfirth v. Lockwood
18 Kirkheaton v. Paddock
18 Linthwaite v. Kirkburton
18 Marsden v. Slaithwaite
25 Dalton v. Holmfirth
25 Kirkburton v. Kirkheaton
25 Lockwood v. Linthwaite
25 Paddock v. Marsden
25 Shepley v. Armitage Bridge
25 Slaithwaite v. Hall Bower

MAY

2 Armitage Bridge v. Slaithwaite
2 Hall Bower v. Paddock
2 Kirkheaton v. Lockwood
2 Linthwaite v. Holmfirth
2 Marsden v. Kirkburton
2 Shepley v. Dalton
9 Dalton v. Linthwaite
9 Holmfirth v. Kirkheaton
9 Kirkburton v. Hall Bower
9 Lockwood v. Marsden
9 Paddock v. Armitage Bridge
9 Slaithwaite v. Shepley
23 Armitage Bridge v. Kirkburton
23 Hall Bower v. Lockwood
23 Kirkheaton v. Linthwaite
23 Marsden v. Holmfirth
23 Shepley v. Paddock
23 Slaithwaite v. Dalton
25 Holmfirth v. Hall Bower
25 Kirkburton v. Shepley
25 Kirkheaton v. Dalton
25 Linthwaite v. Marsden
25 Lockwood v. Armitage Bridge
25 Paddock v. Slaithwaite
26 Armitage Bridge v. Lockwood
26 Dalton v. Kirkheaton
26 Hall Bower v. Holmfirth
26 Marsden v. Linthwaite
26 Shepley v. Kirkburton
26 Slaithwaite v. Paddock
30 Holmfirth v. Armitage Bridge
30 Kirkburton v. Slaithwaite
30 Kirkheaton v. Marsden
30 Linthwaite v. Hall Bower
30 Lockwood v. Shepley
30 Paddock v. Dalton

JUNE

6 Armitage Bridge v. Linthwaite
6 Dalton v. Marsden
6 Hall Bower v. Kirkheaton
6 Paddock v. Kirkburton
6 Shepley v. Holmfirth
6 Slaithwaite v. Lockwood
13 Holmfirth v. Slaithwaite
13 Kirkburton v. Dalton
13 Kirkheaton v. Armitage Bridge
13 Linthwaite v. Shepley
13 Lockwood v. Paddock
13 Marsden v. Hall Bower
20 Armitage Bridge v. Marsden
20 Dalton v. Hall Bower
20 Kirkburton v. Lockwood
20 Paddock v. Holmfirth
20 Shepley v. Kirkheaton
20 Slaithwaite v. Linthwaite
27 Hall Bower v. Armitage Bridge
27 Holmfirth v. Kirkburton
27 Kirkheaton v. Slaithwaite
27 Linthwaite v. Paddock
27 Lockwood v. Dalton
27 Marsden v. Shepley

JULY

4 Dalton v. Armitage Bridge
4 Kirkburton v. Linthwaite
4 Lockwood v. Holmfirth
4 Paddock v. Kirkheaton
4 Shepley v. Hall Bower
4 Slaithwaite v. Marsden
11 Armitage Bridge v. Shepley
11 Hall Bower v. Slaithwaite
11 Holmfirth v. Dalton
11 Kirkheaton v. Kirkburton
11 Linthwaite v. Lockwood
11 Marsden v. Paddock
18 Dalton v. Shepley
18 Holmfirth v. Linthwaite
18 Kirkburton v. Marsden
18 Lockwood v. Kirkheaton
18 Paddock v. Hall Bower
18 Slaithwaite v. Armitage Bridge
25 Armitage Bridge v. Paddock
25 Hall Bower v. Kirkburton
25 Kirkheaton v. Holmfirth
25 Linthwaite v. Dalton
25 Marsden v. Lockwood
25 Shepley v. Slaithwaite

AUGUST

8 Dalton v. Slaithwaite
8 Holmfirth v. Marsden
8 Kirkburton v. Armitage Bridge
8 Linthwaite v. Kirkheaton
8 Lockwood v. Hall Bower
8 Paddock v. Shepley
15 Armitage Bridge v. Holmfirth
15 Dalton v. Paddock
15 Hall Bower v. Linthwaite
15 Marsden v. Kirkheaton
15 Shepley v. Lockwood
15 Slaithwaite v. Kirkburton
22 Holmfirth v. Shepley
22 Kirkburton v. Paddock
22 Kirkheaton v. Hall Bower

HUDDERSFIELD & DISTRICT LEAGUE—Continued

AUGUST

22 Linthwaite v. Armitage Bridge
22 Lockwood v. Slaithwaite
22 Marsden v. Dalton
29 Armitage Bridge v. Kirkheaton
29 Dalton v. Kirkburton
29 Hall Bower v. Marsden
29 Paddock v. Lockwood
29 Shepley v. Linthwaite
29 Slaithwaite v. Holmfirth

SEPTEMBER

5 Hall Bower v. Dalton
5 Holmfirth v. Paddock
5 Kirkheaton v. Shepley
5 Linthwaite v. Slaithwaite
5 Lockwood v. Kirkburton
5 Marsden v. Armitage Bridge
12 Armitage Bridge v. Hall Bower
12 Dalton v. Lockwood
12 Kirkburton v. Holmfirth
12 Paddock v. Linthwaite
12 Shepley v. Marsden
12 Slaithwaite v. Kirkheaton

CUP TIE DATES

JUNE

8 *Sykes Cup (2nd Round)*
15 *Paddock Shield (2nd Round)*
22 *Sykes Cup (3rd Round)*
29 *Paddock Shield (3rd Round)*

JULY

6 *Sykes Cup (First Semi-Final)*
13 *Sykes Cup (Second Semi-Final)*
20 *Paddock Shield (Semi-Final)*
27 *Paddock Shield (Final Tie)*

AUGUST

1 *Sykes Cup (Final Tie)*

TICKETS! TICKETS! TICKETS!

M.C.C. have sent a letter to members of Middlesex C.C.C., the club that shares the use of Lord's, telling why the county members get only about 500 stand tickets a day out of more than 7,000 for the second Test against Australia.

There have been many complaints by Middlesex members who consider the allocation unfair.

M.C.C. state that of the tickets available more than 3,000 go to the general public. About 1,000 go to first-class and minor counties, members of the teams and overseas visitors.

Of the rest, M.C.C. members, many times more than those of Middlesex, get about 2,300.

FIRST SHEFFIELD SHIELD WIN FOR 14 SEASONS

South Australia won the Sheffield Shield for the first time since the 1938-39 season when they beat Western Australia by an innings and 20 runs.

The match was a triumph for Geoff Noblet, the medium-fast bowler who was rejected in selecting the side to tour England.

He took 10 wickets for 109 in the match. In Western Australia's second innings he took four for 18 in eight overs.

LEAGUE AVERAGES

BOLTON ASSOCIATION

(Including League and Cup)

BATTING	No. of inns.	Total runs	Highest score	Not out	Avge.
Woodruff, Adlington	22	720	69*	11	65.45
Riley, Astley and Tyldesley	22	733	78	7	48.86
E. Spencer, Adlington	10	284	67	4	47.33
Hough, Taylor Brothers	23	703	105	4	37.00
B. Holt, Atherton	9	220	74	1	27.50
Peters, Atherton	22	479	74	4	26.61
J. H. Davies, Little Hulton	23	551	81*	1	25.04
R. Harrop, Walkden M.M.	17	349	70*	3	24.92
K. Dagnall, Walker Institute	13	296	57	1	24.66
G. M. Blakey, Farnworth S.C.	22	468	52*	2	23.40
A. Blinkhorn, Walker Institute	14	256	74*	3	23.27

*Not out

BOWLING	O.	M.	R.	W.	Avge.
G. T. Seddon, Walkden M.M.	160.2	34	390	56	6.98
Walmsley, Walker Institute	244.6	42	771	92	8.35
D. Hallsworth, Taylor Bros.	69.5	8	258	30	8.60
Elliott, Farnworth S.C.	264	40	795	91	8.73
Riley, Astley & Tyldesley	129.7	15	456	51	8.93
J. T. Seddon, Walkden M.M.	92.1	10	369	41	9.00
K. Taylor, Walkden M.M.	55.6	4	212	23	9.21
Wr. Mather, Edgworth R.	193.1	44	515	55	9.36
Greenhalgh, Tootals S.C.	238.2	14	846	89	9.50
G. M. Blakey, Farnworth S.C.	98.3	10	349	36	9.69

HUDDERSFIELD LEAGUE

BATTING	No. of inns.	Total runs	Highest score	Not out	Avge.
T. Thornton, Elland	16	671	92*	3	51.61
G. K. Chadwick, Golcar	20	734	102	4	45.87
†E. Needham, Elland	18	590	81	4	42.14
E. Gill, Paddock	23	805	107	3	40.25
L. H. Haigh, Lascelles Hall	20	551	100*	5	36.73
D. Parker, Huddersfield	24	764	71*	3	36.38
†F. Molyneux, Kirkburton	22	714	83	2	35.70
C. Sykes, Honley	24	739	96*	3	35.19
R. C. Codd, Meltham	18	447	91*	5	34.38
†J. Wood, Honley	25	651	189	6	34.26
W. Bedford, Almondbury	22	547	73*	6	34.19
F. N. Riding, Lockwood	18	477	106*	4	34.00

BOWLING	O.	M.	R.	W.	Avge.
G. Blackburn, Shepley	237	50	593	63	9.41
†R. B. Rae, Huddersfield	461.4	95	1076	108	9.96
H. Horner, Dalton	189	43	426	39	10.92
†H. Sills, Holmfirth	269	73	592	54	10.96
L. Green, Honley	367.1	78	812	74	10.97
†G. Boothroyd, Broad Oak	219	46	478	40	11.09
J. Barker, Meltham	272.1	66	664	59	11.25
R. Lisle, Bradley Mills	167.2	21	575	50	11.50
B. Shaw, Lascelles Hall	274	77	630	53	11.88
E. H. Hill, Rastrick	232.2	41	600	50	12.00
†A. Topp, Meltham	364.4	97	902	74	12.19
†J. Wood, Honley	306.5	87	646	53	12.19

† Denotes Professional. * Not out

BRADFORD LEAGUE

BATTING	No. of inns.	Total runs	Highest score	Not out	Avge.
W. Horner, Idle	19	927	139*	5	66.21
R. Illingworth, Farsley	16	844	162*	3	64.92
R. Booth, Lightcliffe	16	516	86*	8	64.50
D. Dobson, Baildon	20	980	124*	3	57.65
E. S. Barraclough, Bradford	20	853	109*	4	53.31
K. Warnett, Windhill	18	629	90*	6	52.41
J. C. Rigg, Bingley	20	780	112*	4	48.75
D. E. V. Padgett, Bowling O. Lane	17	696	137*	2	46.40
D. Bateson, Saltaire	22	783	85	4	43.50
G. F. H. Phillips, Idle	19	725	113	2	42.64
L. Horsman, Idle	13	411	73*	3	41.10
J. H. Chatburn, Queensbury	19	607	100*	4	40.46
J. R. Burnet, Baildon	16	395	75	6	39.50
A. L. Taylor, Spen Victoria	18	628	97	2	39.25
J. A. Claughton, Farsley	20	578	103*	5	38.53
A. G. Padgett Lidget Green	20	611	90	4	38.19
R. Ferguson, Bankfoot	17	598	126	1	37.37
B. J. Thompson, Pudsey St. L'rence	20	684	74*	1	36.00
R. Barker, Yeadon	15	381	81*	4	34.63
J. M. Cownley, Salts	20	550	85*	4	34.37
A. E. Chapman, Undercliffe	19	512	68*	4	34.13
H. Morton, Great Horton	17	406	100*	5	33.83
G. Bottomley, Lightcliffe	12	169	37*	7	33.80
B. Henry, Bowling Old Lane	16	505	101*	1	33.66
D. Graham, Lidget Green	13	234	45*	6	33.43
N. O. Robson, Baildon	19	533	59*	3	33.31
E. Grant, East Bierley	20	556	105	3	32.70
J. A. Swift, Bowling Old Lane	18	544	102	1	32.00
A. Hartley, Lightcliffe	16	352	60	5	32.00
J. P. Whitehead, Pudsey St. L.	17	412	75	4	31.69
R. K. Claughton, Yeadon	20	560	96*	2	31.11
R. H. Sykes, Windhill	22	635	73	1	30.24
M. S. Woodcock, Bankfoot	20	481	58	4	30.06
J. Van Gelovan, Lidget Green	18	480	58	2	30.00

BOWLING	O.	M.	R.	W.	Avge.
W. H. Copson, Lidget Green	257.5	55	699	71	9.84
H. Hoyle, Spen Victoria	84	13	370	30	12.33
T. Tetley, Baildon	185.3	20	697	52	13.40
F. Clayforth, Keighley	217.2	40	758	55	13.78
A. Hartley, Lightcliffe	203.7	22	831	60	13.85
L. Baxter, Great Horton	152.6	22	505	36	14.03
J. W. Hastings, Farsley	248.7	21	942	67	14.06
W. A. Gossopp, Queensbury	180.1	17	605	43	14.07
D. Rhodes, Saltaire	134.4	17	481	34	14.14
W. Burkenshaw, Baildon	265.2	53	811	57	14.23
G. E. Govier, Undercliffe	239.1	46	667	44	15.15
R. Illingworth, Farsley	130.7	17	559	36	15.53
A. Vickers, Bingley	304	35	1207	77	15.67
J. P. Whitehead, Pudsey St. L.	247	34	989	63	15.69
S. Gibson, Eccleshill	160.4	16	591	37	15.99
B. Hall, East Bierley	202.2	12	897	53	16.92
G. Carter, Pudsey St. Law.	222.1	40	856	49	17.46
N. Kitson, Idle	201.1	23	710	40	17.75
T. Falkingham, Yeadon	185	33	629	35	17.97
A. Exley, Great Horton	174	13	684	37	18.48
N. Clarke, Queensbury	122	8	576	31	18.58
F. Wharton, Yeadon	208.5	23	719	37	19.43
B. Moore, Spen Victoria	147.3	14	626	32	19.56
J. Walker, Bowling Old Lane	201.3	34	649	33	19.66
G. Clough, Undercliffe	164.5	27	671	34	19.73
J. R. Ashman, Idle	174.2	24	751	38	19.76
J. H. Burton, Bingley	238.2	32	836	42	19.90

LANCASHIRE LEAGUE

BATTING	No. of inns.	Total runs	Not out	Avge.
Weekes, Bacup	23	1292	7	80.74
Walcott, Enfield	20	955	8	79.58
B. H. Pair'deau, Burnley	11	384	5	64.00
Alley, Colne	23	1055	6	62.05
Carrigan, Church	20	719	6	51.35
Marshall, Lowerhouse	23	969	3	48.45
Mankad, Haslingden	21	725	6	48.33
P. Wight, Burnley	22	453	12	45.30
Mohamed, Ramsbottom	22	841	2	42.05
Dooland, East Lancashire	22	496	10	41.33
M. Gibson, East Lancashire	19	481	7	40.08
R. Pickles, Nelson	8	160	4	40.00
Madden, Rawtenstall	24	678	7	39.88
J. Chew, Rishton	11	346	2	38.44
Raymer, Accrington	23	686	5	38.11
Denison, Todmorden	25	760	5	38.00
Pepper, Burnley	23	793	2	37.76
T. Incles, Rawtenstall	24	772	3	36.76
Lindwall, Nelson	19	480	5	34.28
Sohoni, Rishton	20	614	2	34.11
J. J. Reid, East Lancashire	24	682	2	31.00
C. Duerden, Nelson	19	339	8	30.81
S. Entwistle, Bacup	22	595	1	28.33
C. Hawkwood, Nelson	14	252	5	28.00
R. Warburton, Nelson	17	419	2	27.93
J. Haworth, Church	23	580	2	27.61
H. Dawson, Todmorden	21	522	2	27.42
F. Hopwood, East Lancashire	22	587	0	26.67
H. Pilkington, Church	22	440	5	25.88

BOWLING	O.	R.	W.	Avge.
Dooland, East Lancashire	254.6	709	98	7.23
Lindwall, Nelson	294	804	96	8.37
P. White, Rawtenstall	19.4	96	10	9.60
T. Dickinson, East Lancashire	148.3	401	35	11.45
F. Houlker, Enfield	88.1	293	25	11.72
J. Brunton, Burnley	95	302	25	12.08
Pepper, Burnley	314.6	1107	86	12.87
R. Pickles, Nelson	40	275	21	13.09
R. Banks, Rawtenstall	299.7	937	70	13.38
J. H. Chadwick, East Lancashire	115.1	430	32	13.43
Sohoni, Rishton	364	1076	80	13.45
Raymer, Accrington	262.3	946	65	14.55
A. Ramsbottom, Rishton	140.4	398	27	14.74
J. Kenyon, Rishton	144.9	429	29	14.79
Denison, Todmorden	302.6	1002	62	16.16

NORTH LANCASHIRE LEAGUE

BATTING	No. of inns.	Total runs	Highest score	Not out	Avge.
E. Miller, Ulverston	14	334	62*	7	47.71
I. Stephens, Millom	18	488	72	5	37.54
P. Judge, Carlisle	12	340	81	2	34.00
H. Stretch, Lindal	12	347	85	1	31.54
H. Nutton, V.S.C.	19	486	83	3	30.37

BOWLING	O.	M.	R.	W.	Avge.
F. P. Deallott, Ulverston	191.5	44	461	54	8.53
K. Reid, Carnforth	311.5	105	518	57	9.09
E. St. Hill, Vickerstown	332.5	101	646	70	9.23
K. Brothwood, Netherfield	249.1	60	562	59	9.52
J. McEwan, Ulverston	220.3	67	453	47	9.64
R. Coulson, Lindal	307.3	81	646	66	9.78

CENTRAL LANCASHIRE LEAGUE

BATTING	No. of inns.	Total runs	Highest score	Not out	Avge.
F. M. Worrell, Radcliffe	24	1082	152*	10	77.28
E. R. Conradi, Heywood	6	185	87*	2	46.25
J. Pettiford, Oldham	25	855	100*	6	45.00
J. R. Reid, Heywood	26	982	131*	4	44.63
P. Fawkes, Middleton	9	202	61*	4	40.40
W. Walmsley, Oldham	19	627	114*	3	39.18
C. J. Barnett, Rochdale	26	901	116	2	37.53
J. Oakes, Werneth	23	685	95	3	34.20
G. Holland, Rochdale	20	503	76	5	33.51

BOWLING	O.	M.	R.	W.	Avge.
S. Ramadhin, Crompton	392.1	101	991	128	7.74
F. Moore, Rochdale	48	9	143	17	8.41
J. Dyson, Werneth	80.2	12	279	32	8.71
W. F. Cockburn, Milnrow	312.2	61	899	92	9.77
J. R. Reid, Heywood	361.3	45	1168	114	10.24
C. J. Barnett, Rochdale	383.4	78	982	94	10.44
A. Alker, Werneth	50.4	5	174	16	10.87

LANCASHIRE AND CHESHIRE LEAGUE

Qualifications 200 runs: 12 innings

BATTING	No. of inns.	Total runs	Highest score	Not out	Avge.
F. W. Millett, Macclesfield	22	703	145	6	43.93
K. Morgan, Swinton	13	400	98	3	40.00
A. Siddall, Unsworth	19	467	81	2	27.47
R. Ainsworth, Denton S. L.	17	356	57*	4	27.38
R. Carlisle, Bollington	17	406	70	1	25.37
G. B. Edge, Prestwich	21	504	59	1	25.20

BOWLING	O.	M.	R.	W.	Avge.
R. Collins, Longsight	112.4	21	324	40	8.10
R. Hart, Dukinfield	179	40	436	49	8.89
J. G. Collins, Levenshulme	202	37	583	52	11.20
R. Ainsworth, Denton S.L.	181.7	22	551	48	11.48
A. Brown, East Levenshulme	225	38	703	61	11.52

WEST LANCASHIRE LEAGUE

DIVISION "A"

BATTING	No. of inns.	Total runs	Highest score	Not out	Avge.
†R. Southworth, Highfield	20	574	66	6	41.00
†W. McKittrick, Standish	20	476	94	5	31.74
J. Heaton, Highfield	18	391	83	5	30.08
W. Cave, Orrell R.T.	18	455	79*	2	28.44
J. Simm, Spring View	13	241	69	3	24.10
W. Miller, Eccleston	15	234	57*	5	23.40

BOWLING	O.	M.	R.	W.	Avge.
†W. McKittrick, Standish	207	38	611	96	6.36
G. Brown, Spring View	166	38	427	60	7.12
R. Seddon, Standish	98	16	290	39	7.44
J. Dearden, Highfield	234	44	689	89	7.74
F. Pearson, Orrell R.T.	114	14	326	42	7.76
J. Pennington, Norley Hall	155	27	412	49	8.41
†P. Charles, Poolstock	208	41	604	70	8.62
G. Melling, Orrell R.T.	154	33	426	49	8.69

† Denotes Professional. * Denotes not out

THE LEAGUES, 1952

BOLTON ASSOCIATION

	Played	Won	Lost	Drawn	Pts.
Astley and Tyldesley Colls.	22	11	1	10	43
Farnworth S.C.	22	12	5	5	41
Taylor Brothers	22	11	4	7	40
Tootal's S.C.	22	11	6	5	38
Walkden Moor Meths	22	11	7	4	37
Little Hulton	22	7	7	8	29
Walker Institute	22	8	9	5	29
Atherton Collieries	22	7	9	6	27
Adlington	22	6	8	8	26
Edgworth Rees	22	4	12	6	18
Clifton	22	3	12	7	16
Barton Hall	22	3	14	5	14

BRADFORD LEAGUE

Division I

	Played	Won	Lost	Drawn	Pts.
Baildon	22	13	2	7	59
Lightcliffe	22	10	4	8	48
Pudsey St. Lawrence	22	10	6	6	46
Idle	22	8	4	10	42
Salts	22	8	7	7	39
Bingley	22	8	8	6	38
Great Horton	22	7	9	6	34
Yeadon	22	6	8	8	32
Queensbury	22	5	8	9	29
Bradford	22	4	11	7	23
Keighley	22	3	10	9	21

Division II

	Played	Won	Lost	Drawn	Pts.
Lidget Green	22	11	1	10	54
Farsley	22	11	2	9	53
Windhill	22	9	7	6	42
Undercliffe	22	8	7	7	39
East Bierley	22	8	7	7	39
Saltaire	22	8	8	6	38
Bowling Old Lane	22	4	6	12	28
Bankfoot	22	4	6	12	28
Spen Victoria	22	5	10	7	27
Eccleshill	22	4	12	6	22
Brighouse	22	1	12	9	13

LANCASHIRE LEAGUE

	Played	Won	Lost	Drawn	Pts.
East Lancashire	26	15	2	9	54
Burnley	26	13	5	8	47
Nelson	26	11	1	14	47
Rawtenstall	26	8	4	14	38
Haslingden	26	7	5	14	35
Lowerhouse	26	5	6	15	30
Enfield	26	5	7	14	29
Rishton	26	5	8	13	28
Bacup	26	4	7	15	27
Todmorden	26	4	7	15	27
Colne	26	4	9	13	25
Church	26	3	8	15	24
Accrington	26	3	9	14	23
Ramsbottom	26	1	10	15	18

HUDDERSFIELD LEAGUE

SECTION "A"

	Played	Won	Lost	Drawn	Pts.
Rastrick	22	12	5	5	41
Huddersfield	22	10	4	8	38
Lascelles Hall	22	11	6	5	38
Almondbury	22	10	6	6	36
Golcar	22	8	7	7	31
Bradley Mills	22	8	10	4	28
Thongsbridge	22	7	8	7	28
Broad Oak	22	6	9	7	25
Elland	22	6	9	7	25
Primrose Hill	22	6	9	7	25
Slaithwaite	22	5	10	7	22
Lockwood	22	4	10	8	20

SECTION "B"

	Played	Won	Lost	Drawn	Pts.
Honley	22	14	3	5	47
Meltham	22	12	4	6	42
Shepley	22	11	7	4	37
*Kirkburton	22	9	5	8	36
Paddock	22	8	6	8	32
Kirkheaton	22	9	9	4	31
Holmfirth	22	8	8	6	30
Dalton	22	8	10	4	28
*Marsden	22	7	9	6	28
Hall Bower	22	5	9	8	23
*Linthwaite	22	4	12	6	19
*Armitage Bridge	22	1	14	7	11

* Two points for a tie

LANCASHIRE AND CHESHIRE LEAGUE

	Played	Won	Lost	Drawn	Pts
Macclesfield	26	12	4	10	46
Unsworth	26	10	5	11	41
Stalybridge	26	10	7	9	39
Denton St. Lawrence	26	9	6	11	38
Longsight	26	9	6	11	38
Stand	26	9	6	11	38
Swinton	26	8	5	13	37
Dukinfield	26	8	9	9	33
Bollington	26	7	9	10	31
Glossop	26	7	9	10	31
Levenshulme	26	7	9	10	31
East Levenshulme	26	6	10	10	28
Prestwich	26	4	12	10	22
Cheetham	26	4	13	9	21

NORTHERN LEAGUE

	Played	Won	Lost	Drawn	Pts.
St. Annes	20	9	0	11	38
Chorley	20	10	4	6	36
Fleetwood	20	7	2	11*	33
Blackpool	20	6	3	11	29
Leyland	20	6	5	9	27
Furness	20	4	5	11	23
Lancaster	20	4	9	7	19
Morecambe	20	2	6	12*	19
Darwen	20	3	8	9	18
Kendal	20	2	6	12	18
Leyland Motors	20	2	7	11	17

* Includes two points for a tie

NORTH LANCASHIRE LEAGUE

	Played	Won	Lost	Drawn 2	Drawn 1	Pts.
Vickerstown	20	10	2	*3	5	40½
Carlisle	20	9	4	2	5	36
Barrow	20	9	3	*1	7	35½
Netherfield	20	8	6	0	6	30
Millom	20	7	4	0	9	30
Ulverston	20	8	7	0	5	29
Dalton	20	7	7	0	6	27
Whitehaven	20	6	7	1	6	26
Carnforth	20	7	9	0	4	25
Haverigg	20	5	8	0	7	22
Lindal Moor	20	3	9	2	6	19
Workington	20	4	9	0	7	19
Vickers Sports Club	20	2	10	2	6	16

* Includes 1½pts. each for tied game

BIRMINGHAM LEAGUE

	Played	Won	Lost	Drawn	Pts.
Dudley	18	7	1	10	31
Smethwick	18	7	2	9	30
Stourbridge	18	7	3	8	29
Walsall	18	7	5	6	27
West Bromwich Dartmouth	18	5	6	7	22
Moseley	18	4	5	9	21
Old Hill	18	4	5	9	21
Kidderminster	18	4	6	8	20
Aston Unity	18	3	8	7	16
Mitchells & Butlers	18	2	9	7	13

WEST LANCASHIRE LEAGUE

Division A

	Played	Won	Lost	Drawn	Pts.
Highfield	22	15	2	5	50
Standish	22	13	3	6	45
Orrell Red Triangle	22	10	4	8	38
Eccleston	22	10	6	6	36
Blackrod	22	9	7	6	33
Spring View	22	9	8	5	32
Bedford Methodists	22	6	8	8	26
Poolstock	22	6	8	8	26
Winstanley Park	22	7	11	4	25
Norley Hall	22	5	11	6	21
R.O.F. Chorley	22	4	13	5	17
Bickershaw Collieries	22	3	16	3	12

BOLTON LEAGUE

	Played	Won	Lost	Drawn	Pts.
Walkden	22	11	1	10	43
Kearsley	22	10	3	9	39
Heaton	22	8	3	11	36
Tonge	22	8	5	9	33
Astley Bridge	22	5	4	13	28
Horwich R.M.I.	22	6	7	9	27
Westhoughton	22	6	8	8	26
*Bradshaw	22	5	8	9	25
Eagley	22	4	7	11	23
Farnworth	22	4	9	9	21
Little Lever	22	4	9	9	21
Egerton	22	4	11	7	19

* Two points for tie

CENTRAL LANCASHIRE LEAGUE

	Played	Won	Lost	Drawn	Pts.
Rochdale	26	13	3	10	49
Heywood	26	13	5	8	47
Crompton	26	10	5	11	41
Milnrow	26	10	5	11	41
Radcliffe	26	10	5	11	41
Oldham	26	10	8	8	38
Middleton	26	8	5	13	37
Littleborough	26	7	8	11	32
Royton	26	6	7	13	31
Ashton	26	7	10	9	30
Werneth	26	6	9	11	29
Stockport	26	6	11	9	27
Castleton Moor	26	2	14	10	16
Walsden	26	3	16	7	16

NORTH STAFFORDSHIRE LEAGUE

Section "A"

	Played	Won	Lost	Drawn	Pts.
Burslem	22	13	3	6	45
Blythe Works	22	11	3	8	41
Leek	22	11	6	5	38
Norton	22	9	4	9	36
Knypersley	22	7	6	9	30
Longton	22	6	6	10	28
Nantwich	22	5	4	13	28
Porthill Park	22	5	5	12	27
Stone	22	5	8	9	24
Bignall End	22	3	9	10	19
Meakins	22	4	11	7	19
Sneyd Colliery	22	0	14	8	8

Section "B"

	Played	Won	Lost	Drawn	Pts.
Hartshill	22	12	4	6	42
Crewe L.M.R.	22	11	5	6	39
Audley	22	11	7	4	37
Great Chell	22	10	5	7	37
St. Edward's H.	22	8	6	8	32
Crewe Rolls Royce	22	8	8	6	30
Silverdale	22	6	6	10	28
Kidsgrove	22	7	9	6	27
Boltons	22	7	11	4	25
Stoke M.O.	22	6	10	6	24
Michelin	22	5	12	5	20
Ashcombe Park	22	3	11	8	17

NORTH YORKSHIRE AND SOUTH DURHAM LEAGUE

Division A

	Played	Won	Lost	Drawn	Pts.
Redcar	22	13	3	6	45
Darlington	22	10	1	11	41
Middlesbrough	22	12	6	4	40
Norton	22	10	7	5	35
Thornaby	22	9	7	6	33
Bishop Auckland	22	7	8	7	28
West Hartlepool	22	6	8	8	26
Synthonia	22	5	6	11	26
Stockton	22	6	10	6	24
Darlington R. A.	22	5	8	9	24
Blackhall	22	5	9	8	23
Saltburn	22	3	7	12	21
Normanby Hall	22	5	11	6	21
Guisborough	22	4	9	9	21

RYDER CUP VENUE

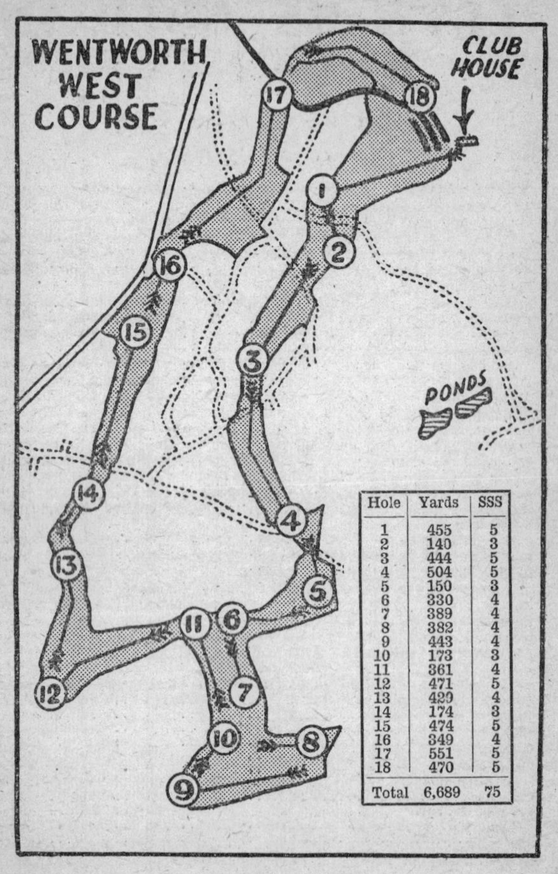

Hole	Yards	SSS
1	455	5
2	140	3
3	444	5
4	504	5
5	150	3
6	330	4
7	389	4
8	382	4
9	443	4
10	173	3
11	361	4
12	471	5
13	429	4
14	174	3
15	474	5
16	349	4
17	551	5
18	470	5
Total	6,689	75

GOLF IN 1953

LET'S BE BOLD IN RYDER CUP

Playing at the Flag

By ST. ANDREWS

WENTWORTH Golf Club, Virginia Water, Surrey, are planning to make the tenth Ryder Cup International match over the famous West Course next October a memorable occasion.

Although it will be the first time the official Ryder Cup battle has been played there—or in the south of England, for that matter—it was at Wentworth that the first clash of American and British professionals took place in 1926.

This friendly match between the leading exponents of the game in the two countries gave birth to the idea of the biennial match, started in America the following year, for which the late Samuel Ryder, the St. Albans seed merchant, gave the gold trophy bearing his name.

In that unofficial test, Great Britain did better than they have ever done since, winning by 13 games to one, with one halved, in a 10-aside match against an American team including stars like Walter Hagen, Tommy Armour, Al Watrous, Jim Barnes and Joe Kirkwood.

In the 26 years the trophy has been played for nine times and only twice have our men been successful, first in 1929 at Moortown, Leeds, and then four years later at Southport and Ainsdale.

During the win at Moortown the temperature was more akin to January than May, and George Duncan, then captain of the British team, scored the biggest singles victory in the whole series by beating Walter Hagen by 10 and 8.

Our last grip of the Cup, as holders, was in 1933, when, with the last putt of the last match at Ainsdale, Syd Easterbrook beat Densmore Shute to give Britain a victory by 6 matches to 5.

A great effort in 1949 at Ganton, Yorkshire, where the home team only lost by 7 to 5, was followed by a further disastrous defeat in 1951 at Pinehurst, North Carolina. And now to Wentworth and its alluring woodland. Virginia Water is one of the most attractive settings around London.

NO LET-UP

The selection of the West Course, known with respect and affection by professionals as " The Burma Road ", is recognition for one of the stiffest tests of golf in the country. With a total length of 6,689 yards and a par of 75, its exacting quality lies in the fact that the " cracks," striving by extra length to knock strokes off the par total, are allowed no margin for latitude in direction.

At almost every hole they have to place the tee-shot, which, for big hitters, means taking a shade of risk to cash-in on their greater length.

Long, narrow fairways, trees, gorse, heather and formidable bunkers add to difficulties, and a finish of 5, 4, 5, 5, including the longest hole on the course, means that from first to last there can be no let-up.

(Continued overleaf)

More Match-Play Practice Needed

From past results the prospects of a British victory do not appear to be very bright and, if form is maintained this summer, it would seem that the backbone of the team will consist of D. J. Rees, F. Daly, C. H. Ward and Max Faulkner, all past members of defeated sides.

Harry Weetman, the British " Power Golfer " and John Panton, quiet, phlegmatic, and rated one of the finest long iron-players Britain has produced for years, will both have benefited by their baptism in Ryder Cup games at Pinehurst in 1951, and Arthur Lees is by no means a spent force, as witness his solitary victory on that same occasion.

Eric Brown is regarded by many as almost a certainty ; his record and age, plus his fighting qualities in match-play, all enhance his claim for recognition.

Tom Haliburton, on his home course, will also be a force to be reckoned with, and the young assistants, Peter Alliss, son of a famous father, and Tony Harmon, who staggered the big-wigs with his golf in the 1952 Match Play Championship, will bring the dash and zest of youth into a team which sadly needs young blood.

Henry Cotton was selected for the 1929 match as a stripling of 22 to contribute to our first victory, and the door is now wide open for the young professional to make his mark.

If our players are to win back the Cup one fact emerges clearly: they must have more match-play practice. What better than in challenge matches, of which we have so few these days ?

The surfeit of stroke-play events develops a stroke-play complex. Our men cling to the old tactics of pitching for the middle of the green and rolling their first putt up to the side of the hole, at least for the first few holes, and in consequence are late starters.

PLAYING AT THE FLAG

Boldness in playing at the flag, as practised by the Americans, is essential to get in the first blow . . . then fight all the way to win, not merely to reduce a deficit due to a careful start.

The British Selection Committee can be relied upon to pick the best available side, and if this is done early enough, the players will have time to settle down and, placed under the captaincy of Henry Cotton, either in a playing or non-playing capacity, will have the advantage of his unrivalled experience in these matches, coupled with home advantages.

The Americans select their team on the performances of their players in the Championships and big tournaments, and for that reason quite a few of the men of the victorious 1951 team may be omitted.

Ben Hogan, regarded by many as one of the greatest-of-all-time, should be an automatic selection as captain and, if he makes the trip in a playing capacity, we shall see him in action for the first time on British turf.

Sam Snead and Lloyd Mangrum are virtual certainties, and Jack Burke and Ed. Oliver were also members of the 1951 team. Other possibles are Julius Boro, Jim Turnesa, Carey Middlecoff, Ted Kroll, Dave Douglas, Johnny Palmer and Fred Haas, all players with high reputations and tournament experience.

These men command respect but they can be beaten, and our prospects will be all the brighter if our men will forget the reputation of their opponents and play to kill from the first tee.

STORY OF RYDER CUP

THE Ryder Cup was presented by Mr. Samuel Ryder, of St. Albans, for competition between teams of British and American professionals. The trophy was first competed for in 1927, and the contest takes place in alternate years, each country being visited in turn. Results to date :—

At Worcester, Mass., U.S.A., 1927, U.S.A. won by 9 matches to 2 matches.

At Moortown, Leeds, 1929, Great Britain won by 6 matches to 4 matches.

At Scioto Columbus, Ohio, U.S.A. 1931, U.S.A. won by 9 matches to 3 matches.

At Southport and Ainsdale, Southport, 1933, Great Britain won by 6 matches to 5 matches.

At Ridgewood, New Jersey, 1935, U.S.A. won by 8 matches to 2 matches.

At Southport and Ainsdale, Southport, 1937, U.S.A. won by 7 matches to 3 matches.

At Portland, Oregon, 1947, U.S.A. won by 11 matches to 1 match.

At Ganton, Yorkshire, 1949, U.S.A. won by 7 matches to 5 matches.

At Pinehurst, North Carolina, 1951, U.S.A. won by 9 matches to 2, with one match halved. Details :—

SINGLES

United States		Great Britain	
Jack Burke (4 & 3)	1	James Adams	0
Lloyd Mangrum (6 & 5)	1	Harry Weetman	0
Jimmy Demaret (2 up)	1	Dai Rees	0
Clayton Heafner (half)	0	Fred Daly (half)	0
Skip Alexander (8 & 7)	1	John Panton	0
Ed. Oliver	0	Arthur Lees (2 up)	1
Ben Hogan (3 & 2)	1	Charles Ward	0
Sam Snead (4 & 3)	1	Max Faulkner	0
Total	6	Total	1

One match halved.

FOURSOMES

United States		Great Britain	
Clayton Heafner and Jack Burke (5 & 3)	1	Max Faulkner and Dai Rees	0
Ed. Oliver and Henry Ransom	0	Charles Ward and Arthur Lees (2 & 1)	1
Lloyd Mangrum and Sam Snead (5 & 4)	1	James Adams and John Panton	0
Ben Hogan and Jimmy Demaret (5 & 4)	1	Fred Daly and Ken Bousfield	0
Total	3	Total	1

Aggregate: United States 9, Great Britain 2, with one match halved.

CARNOUSTIE: A CHAMPIONS' COURSE

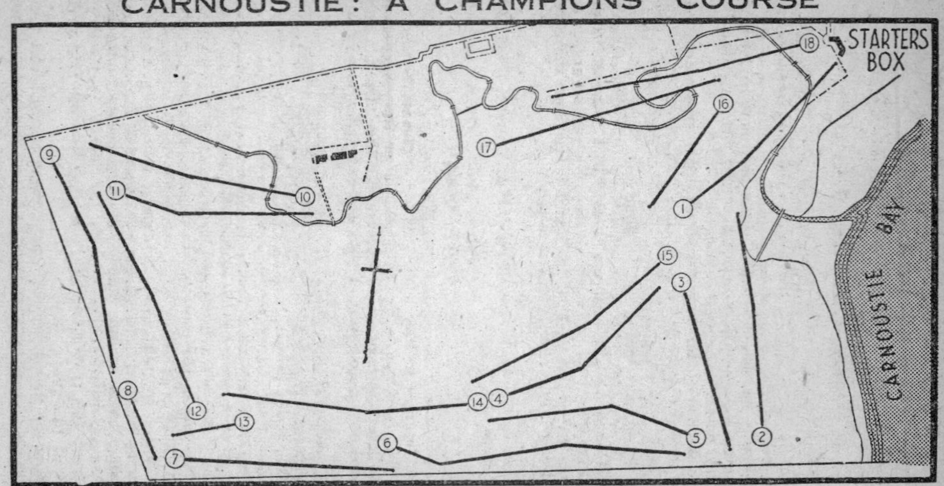

Plan of Carnoustie (Angus) venue of the Coronation Year Open Championship.

CARNOUSTIE

Charms of 1953 Open Course: Beware the Burn!

AFTER an interval of 15 years, Carnoustie, on the east coast of Scotland, is to be the venue of the 1953 Open Championship beginning Monday, July 6.

When it was played there for the first time in 1931, T. D. Armour, the Scottish-American, scored his sensational one-stroke victory over José Jurado.

At the end of the third round, the little Argentinian led the field by 5 strokes from Armour, but a final round of 77 " opened the door " for Tommy Armour to slip through with a brilliant 71 and win the title by one shot.

In 1937, the links staged its second Championship, and Henry Cotton won the second of his three " Open " victories, on this occasion against the full strength entry of the American Ryder Cup Team fresh from their defeat of the British team at Southport.

The final day's play was affected by so much casual water on the course that the officials were in some doubt about cancelling the Championship.

70 STILL BEST

Although Carnoustie has not the Championship traditions of St. Andrews or Prestwick, it was a celebrated course before the championships were begun and, after the remodelling of three holes, its baptism as a venue for the " Open " in 1931 showed it to possess one of the hardest finishes on any British links.

In neither championship was 70 " broken."

Carnoustie is natural golf, and it has variety. No two holes on this sandy terrain bear any similarity to each other, nor do more than two consective holes run in the same direction. Hence, with any wind about, it is necessary to know how to play all the different kinds of shots which this element creates.

The " Barry Burn " and " Jockie's Burn," to be crossed several times throughout the round, plus other natural hazards of plantation and dunes, provide a tough proposition. In fact, the fearsome finish in which the " Barry " plays the leading role is one of the most nerve-racking tests on any Championship course. Its width at the point where it guards the home green is fully 25 feet, and it is generally running full for the greater part of the year.

Shots are demanded requiring judgment, skill and courage above the ordinary, and it is, in truth, a " Champion's Course."

Length of Holes—See Next Page

Professional Champions, 1952

British Open .. .. A. D. Locke
American Open .. .. Julius Boros
Australian Open .. .. N. Von Nida
Argentine Open .. .. Roberto De Vicenzo
French Open.. .. .. A. D. Locke
Belgian Open .. .. A. Cerda
Dutch Open .. .. C. S. Denny
German Open .. .. A. Cerda
Spanish Open .. .. Max Faulkner
Swiss Open .. .. U. Grappassonni
Italian Open .. .. E. Brown
Canadian Open .. .. Johnny Palmer
Egyptian Open .. .. Hassan Hassanein
Irish Championship .. .. F. Daly
Ulster Championship .. .. W. J. Clarke
American P.G.A. Championship .. .. .. J. Turnesa
Welsh Championship .. .. W. S. Collins
Scottish Championship .. .. J. Campbell
Belgian Championship.. .. .. F. Van Donck
Swedish Open .. .. Arne Werkell

CARNOUSTIE : 1953 "Open" Venue

LENGTH OF HOLES

No. of Holes	Name	Yards	Scratch Score	No. of Holes	Name	Yards	Scratch Score
1	Cup	401	4	10	South America	406	4
2	Gulley	418	5	11	Dyke	352	4
3	Jockie's Burn	321	4	12	Southward Ho !	467	5
4	Hillocks	365	4	13	Whins	135	3
5	Brae	363	4	14	Spectacles	473	5
6	Long	521	5	15	Luckyslap	424	4
7	Plantation	376	4	16	Barry Burn	235	3
8	Short	146	3	17	Island	428	5
9	Railway	417	4	18	Home	453	5
					In	3373	38
					Out	3328	37
	Out	3328	37			6701	75

GOLF MILESTONES

1413 Golf became popular game in Scotland

1553 Archbishop of St. Andrews approved the rights of the community to the St. Andrews links

1603 Golf course laid out on Blackheath Common

1754 Royal and Ancient Golf Club of St. Andrews founded

1860 Open Championship instituted

1875 Death of Young Tom Morris

1886 Amateur Championship instituted

1891 Term "bogey" first used

1893 Ladies' Championship instituted

1901 P.G.A. founded

1902 Amateur International, England v. Scotland, started

1902 Alex Herd, first professional to win Open Championship with rubber-cored ball

1904 First overseas player won Amateur Championship (W. Travis)

1907 First overseas player won Open Championship (A. Massy)

1908 Death of Old Tom Morris

1912 John Ball won his 8th Amateur Championship—a record.

1914 Harry Vardon won his sixth Open Championship—a record

1919 R. and A. took over control of Open and Amateur Championships

1919 Girls' Championship instituted

1920 The "limited" golf ball introduced

1921 Boys' Championship instituted

1921 Use of grooved clubs prohibited

1922 Walker Cup match (Great Britain v. America) instituted

1923 "Yorkshire Evening News" tournament

1927 Ryder Cup match (Great Britain v. America) instituted

1929 Steel-shafted golf clubs approved

1930 Bobby Jones won Open, Amateur, also American Open and Amateur Championships in the same year—a record

1932 Curtis Cup match (Great Britain v. U.S.A.) instituted

1933 Miss Poppy Wingate competed in the "Yorkshire Evening News" tournament (first time a woman competed in a professional tournament)

1934 After 10 successive victories by Americans, Henry Cotton won Open Championship

1935 Lawson Little won British and American Amateur Championships for second successive year—a record

1937 Death of Harry Vardon

1937 European Golf Association formed

1938 Great Britain won Walker Cup match for the first time

1938 Limitation of number of clubs (fourteen)

1946 Open Championship Prize Fund increased to £1,000

1947 Fred Daly—first Irishman to win "Open"

1949 Bobby Locke—first South African to win "Open"

1950 Death of James Braid

1952 Uniform golf rules throughout world became operative from January 1

1952 Great Britain won Curtis Cup for first time

IS WALKER CUP WORTH WHILE?

THIS YEAR'S TEST AT MERION

By a Special Correspondent

THE United States Golf Association Challenge Trophy accrued from an informal conversation some thirty-two years ago while George H. Walker, President of the U.S. Golf Association at the time, and W. N. Boase, Chairman of the Championship Committee of the R. and A., were playing a friendly round.

Quite casually Mr. Walker said he would like to present a trophy for an international golf competition, and Mr. Boase replied " Why not ? " Nothing more was thought of the conversation, at least by the Royal and Ancient, until in 1921 a massive silver trophy was presented for this purpose by Mr. Walker. Now it is generally known as the " Walker Cup."

There was an informal match for the trophy at Hoylake in 1921, but it was not until 1922 that the matches really became organised to be played each year, alternately in Britain and America. In 1924 it was agreed to play the match every two years, and this was carried out until the Hitler war caused a break from 1938 to 1947.

Britain broke through American domination in 1938 but, since, has continued to meet defeat. Are the results too one-sided to justify continuance ? If the result is all-important such a decision might be justified, but it can reasonably be claimed that no other international event has been so free from discordant note.

The competition has always been fought in the spirit of friendly rivalry visualised by its inaugurator, and has done much to strengthen the sporting ties between the two nations. The answer, then, is obvious.

On September 4 and 5, Great Britain takes up the struggle again at Merion, Massachusetts, with the odds once more favouring the Americans. We have never won over there but a team can be chosen with a real hope, on form, provided our men shed the inferiority complex.

LIKELY PLAYERS

HERE are thumb-nail sketches of probable players :

R. J. WHITE : Played in the 1947-49-51 matches and is unbeaten in six games. No. 1 amateur in the British Isles and regarded by many as a match for the best anywhere.

J. B. CARR : Came through the 1947-49-51 matches with a very good record. Powerful. Revels in the cut-and-thrust of match-play.

BLENDING YOUTH AND VIGOUR

J. D. A. LANGLEY (1936 and '51) has a classical style and ideal temperament for the big occasion.

J. L. MORGAN (1951) learned a lot from this Walker Cup experience. Professional for four years, now re-instated as an amateur. A thoughtful but powerful golfer, and fine match-player.

A. A. DUNCAN has a first-class record in British match-play. Determined and confident. Not likely to be over-awed by the occasion.

IAN CALDWELL (1951) halved his singles match. Talented young golfer with a brilliant future. A natural choice on form.

F. W. G. DEIGHTON was selected in 1951 but unable to play. Young, strong and capable. A brilliant player.

D. A. BLAIR is a sound, powerful Scottish golfer with a natural flair for rising to the occasion.

P. F. SCRUTTON, a much-discussed young golfer of great experience, is capable almost of beating the lot when in the mood.

Other candidates include A. H. Perowne, M. Lees, S. Brough, D. Rawlinson, A. Turner, J. W. Jones and J. Glover.

Clearly, then, a British team blending youth, vigour and experience can be formed. Power is the first essential and another need is hard practice with first-class professionals.

PREVIOUS WALKER CUP TESTS

THE Walker Cup was presented by Mr. George H. Walker, President of the U.S.A. Golf Association. The Cup is not intended for competition solely between Great Britain and U.S.A. France, Canada, Australia, the Argentine, or any other nation could submit a challenge which might be accepted. Results to date :—

At National Links, U.S.A., 1922, U.S.A. won by 8 matches to 4 matches.

At St. Andrews, 1923, U.S.A. won by 6 matches to 5 matches.

At Garden City, New York, 1924, U.S.A. won by 9 matches to 3 matches.

At St. Andrews, 1926, U.S.A. won by 6 matches to 5 matches.

At Chicago, U.S.A., 1928, U.S.A. won by 11 matches to 1 match.

At Royal St. George's, 1930, U.S.A. won by 10 matches to 2 matches.

At Brooklyn, Mass., 1932, U.S.A. won by 8 matches to 1 match.

At St. Andrews, 1934, U.S.A. won by 9 matches to 2 matches.

At Pine Valley, 1936, U.S.A. won by 9 matches to nil (3 halved).

At St. Andrews, 1938, Great Britain won by 7 matches to 4 matches.

At St. Andrews, 1947, U.S.A. won by 8 matches to 4 matches.

At Winged Foot, New York, 1949, U.S.A. won by 10 matches to 2 matches.

At Birkdale, 1951, U.S.A. won by 6 matches to 3 matches (3 halved).

STARS' RECORDS

HENRY COTTON—Born January 26, 1907. Club: Monte Carlo. Tournament record: British Open, 1934-37-48, 3rd, 1936-38; Belgian Open, 1930-34-38; French Open, 1946-47; Czech Open, 1937-38; German Open, 1937-38-39; Match-play champion, 1932-39-46; Dunlop Southport, 1931-32; Silver King, 1937; "Yorkshire Evening News," 1935; Spalding, 1947; Vardon Trophy, 1938. Member Ryder Cup team, 1929-37-47.

CHARLES WARD—Born September 16, 1911. Club: Little Aston. Major tournament record: Midland Championship, 1933-34; West of England, 1935; "Daily Mail," 1945 and 1950; Tied Silver King, 1948; Runner-up, Brand-Lochryn, 1946; Runner-up, Dunlop, Southport, 1947; "Yorkshire Evening News," 1948; Vardon Trophy, 1948 and 1949; Dunlop & Lotus, 1951. Member Ryder Cup team, 1947, 1949, 1951.

DAI REES—Born March 31, 1913. Club: South Herts. Major tournament record: "News of the World," 1936-38-49-50; Silver King, 1946; Spalding, 1946; "Yorkshire Evening News," 1939, 1950, 1951; "Daily Mail," 1947; Irish Open, 1948; "News Chronicle," 1947 and 1950; Dunlop Masters, 1950. Member Ryder Cup team, 1937, 1947, 1949, 1951.

SAM KING—Born March 27, 1911. Club: Knowle Park, Kent. Major tournament record: Kent Professional, 1932-33-34-35-36-37-46-47-51; "Daily Mail," 1937; Harry Hunter Memorial Cup, 1936; "Yorkshire Evening News," 1944, 1949; Runner-up, "Daily Mail," 1936; Runner-up, "News Chronicle," 1937; Runner-up, Silver King, 1947. Member Ryder Cup team, 1937-47-49.

JAMES ADAMS—Born October 21, 1910. Club: Royal Mid-Surrey. Major tournament record: Irish Professional, 1933; Penfold, 1936; Joint winner, Dunlop Masters, 1947; Runner-up, Open, 1936-38; Runner-up, Match Play Championship, 1937-1947, 1951; Joint winner, Silver King, 1948; Runner-up, Irish Open, 1937. Member Ryder Cup team, 1947, 1949, 1951.

FRED DALY—Born October 11, 1911. Club: Balmoral, Belfast. Major tournament record: Manchester "Evening Chronicle," 1949; Ulster Championship, 1936-40-41-43-44-46; Irish Professional, 1940-46-52; Irish Open, 1946; Open Championship, 1947; Dunlop, 1948; Penfold, 1948; Match-Play Championship, 1947-48-52; Willie Nolan Cup, 1940-45-46; Lotus, 1950. Member Ryder Cup team, 1947, 1949, 1951. Won Daks Tourney, 1952.

ARTHUR LEES—Born February 21, 1908. Club: Sunningdale. Major tournament record: Yorkshire Open, 1935-39-46; Yorkshire Professional, 1935; 2nd place, German and Czecho-Slovak. Open, 1937; Penfold, 1951; Runner-up, Dunlop Southport, 1938; 5th place, Open, 1947; Dunlop Masters, 1947. Member Ryder Cup team, 1947, 1949, 1951.

KEN BOUSFIELD—Born Marston Moor, Yorkshire, 1919. Selected with Fred Daly, John Panton and Harry Bradshaw to represent British professionals on South African tour 1950-1. Won Assistants' Championship, 1948; Won "News Chronicle," 1951; second Penfold tournament, 1948; Semi-finalist "Y. E. News," 1949. Played for Great Britain v. U.S.A. in 1949-51 Ryder Cup matches.

REGINALD HORNE.—Born July 19, 1909. Major tournament record: Hampshire Champion, 1936-38; "News of the World," 1945; Winner, Silver King, 1952; Runner-up, British Open, 1947. Member Ryder Cup team, 1947.

Men to Watch

ARTHUR D'ARCY (BOBBY) LOCKE—Born Germiston, Transvaal, South Africa, 1917. Holder of the British Open Championship 1949-50. When 14 won South African Boys' Championship. Won Amateur and Open Championships of South Africa, 1935-1937. Turned professional 1938 and won South African Open, 1938, 1939, 1946. South African professional championship winner 1938, 1939; Irish Open, 1938; New Zealand Open, 1938. During the second world war served in the Royal Air Force as a bomber pilot. Won £6,500 prize-money in U.S. tour in 1947. Won Tam o' Shanter tournament, 1950.

MAX FAULKNER—Born July 29, 1916. Club: Blackmoor. Major tournament record: Berks and Bucks Championship, 1937; 3rd place, Irish Open, 1937, 1947; Midland Open, 1938; 2nd place, Belgian Open, 1939, 1947; Dunlop Southport, 1946; 2nd place, "Daily Mail," 1945; 2nd place, Dunlop Masters, 1946; 2nd place, Brand-Lochryn, 1947; Dunlop & Lotus, 1949, Open Championship, 1951; Dunlop Masters, 1951. Member Ryder Cup team, 1947, 1949, 1951.

NORMAN VON NIDA—Born Sydney, Australia. Visited Great Britain in 1947-48, 1950-51. In 1947 was the biggest money winner in British tournaments and in 1948 captured the Vardon Trophy. Made his first steps in golf as a caddie in Queensland at the age of 11.

FLORY VAN DONCK—Born Brussels, 1912. Another frequent and popular visitor from Belgium. Won Belgian Professional Championship, 1935-38; Belgian Open, 1939; Dutch Open, 1936-37; Italian Open, 1938; "Evening Chronicle," 1947; Silver King, 1951: North British, Harrogate, 1951.

JOHN PANTON—Born Pitlochry, 1916. Semi-finalist, Boys' Championship, 1934; Won Scottish Professional Championship, 1948-49-50-51; Northern Open, 1948; Silver King, 1950; Daks, 1951. Member of 1951 Ryder Cup team. Present Harry Vardon Trophy-holder.

ERIC CHALMERS BROWN—Born Edinburgh, 1925. Club: Hartsbourne. Won Scottish Amateur Championship, 1946; turned professional, 1946. Won Northern Open Championship, 1950, and Swiss Open Championship, 1951. Won Italian Open Championship, 1952; Runner-up, 1951. Won Cameron-Kinghorn Tournament, 1950, Penfold Tournament, 1952.

JACK HARGREAVES—Born 1914. Club: Sutton Coldfield. Won Northern Assistants' Championship, 1936. Third in Open, 1948. Won Warwickshire Open, 1948. Warwickshire Professional Champion, 1949-51. Won Spalding Tournament, 1951; Joint Runner-up, Silver King and "News Chronicle" Tournament, 1951. Member of Ryder Cup Team, 1951.

HARRY WEETMAN—Born 1920. Club: Croham Hurst. Won Assistants' Championship, 1949-50; Herts. Open Champion, 1948; Match Play Championship, 1951; Dunlop Masters' Tournament, Vardon Trophy winner, 1952. Member of Ryder Cup team, 1951.

PETER ALLISS—Born 1930. Played for English v. Scottish Boys, 1946. Turned professional, 1949. Won Long-Driving Competition 1949. Joint-second Assistants' Championship, 1949. Won Assistants Championship, 1952.

PETER THOMSON—Born Melbourne, Australia, 1929. Leading amateur in Australian Open Championship, 1948. Turned professional, 1949. Runner-up Australian Open Championship, 1950; won in 1951. Won New Zealand Championship, 1950-51. Runner-up North British Harrogate Tournament, 1951. Runner-up British Open Championship, 1952.

Do You Know the Rules?

QUESTIONS GOING THE ROUNDS

Limit of Clubs in Bag

Q.—How many clubs may a golfer carry in his bag ?

A.—They must not exceed 14.

Practice on Competition Day

Q.—May a player practise on the putting greens before playing a **match** or a **medal** round?

A.—The rule forbidding practice on a putting green applies only to events decided by **medal** play.

Courtesy when Driving

Q.—You are one of four players on the tee and it is your turn to drive. What courtesy do you expect to receive ?

A.—(1) No bags on the teeing ground.
(2) All players stand on the right of the teeing ground.
(3) No other ball is teed up before you have driven.
(4) There is complete silence and absence of movement.
(5) No shadows should be cast by any player near the spot from where you are striking.

Addressing the Ball

Q.—While in the act of addressing his ball on the putting-green a player—in the "waggle" of his putter before making his stroke—tapped the ball with his club-head. The ball turned half-over but returned to its original position. Was this a stroke ?

A.—The distance this ball moved cannot be considered as merely oscillation, and therefore, the movement counts as a stroke.

Q.—Addressing the ball in heather a player lightly grounds his club. Any penalty ?

A.—No. Heather is not a hazard.

Q.—May a player when playing through the green and addressing a ball, ground the club in front of the ball ? What, if any, is the penalty in (1) match play, and (2) medal play ?

A.—The player may ground his club, provided he does not improve the position of the ball.

YOUR RIGHTS ON THE TEE

Moving the Tee-Box

Q.—A player tees a ball within three inches of the tee-box and claims he can remove the box as it might interfere with sighting the ball. Right or wrong?

A.—A sand-box is a loose impediment and may be removed. It is usual to mark the limits of the teeing-ground with discs, and to place the sand-box in a position which does not interfere with a stroke played from the edge of the teeing-ground.

Practice Swings

Q.—On the teeing-ground a player took a practice swing, struck the ground near his teed ball, and caused the ball to fall off the tee. Any penalty?

A.—No. The practice swing was not a stroke, and the teed ball was not in play.

Q.—Any penalty if the **club** had touched the ball?

A.—Yes. Any contact between the head of the club and the ball, resulting in movement of the ball, constitutes a stroke.

Teeing Ground Limits

Q.—May a player stand outside the limits of the teeing-ground to play a ball teed within limits ?

A.—Yes.

Honour on Tee

Q.—**Match Play.** You stand 2 up on the 17th tee where your opponent has the honour. The 17th hole is halved. Who takes the honour on the 18th tee ?

A.—You do ; as the winner of the match by 2 and 1, you are entitled to the honour on the 18th tee.

Tee-shot Out of Bounds

Q.—If a player hits his tee-shot out of bounds, can he play his next shot from another spot on the tee ?

A.—Yes.

TEASERS ABOUT THE BALL—

Teeing Ground

Q.—The ball is driven from a spot in front of the teeing-ground limits.

A.—**Match play:** The ball may be at once recalled by the opposing side and re-teed without penalty. **Medal play:** The player must count that stroke, tee a ball, and play a second stroke from within the limits.

Q.—What is the penalty if you tee your ball more than two club lengths behind the front limits of the teeing ground?

A.—Count that stroke and re-tee the ball within the limits of the teeing ground.

Looking for Lost Ball

Q.—A player loses his ball. How long may he search for it? What is the lost-ball penalty?

A.—The search may last five minutes. If it is found after that time, he may not play it. Lost-ball penalty is loss of stroke and distance.

Ball Lost and Found

Q.—A player considers a ball to be lost and is walking back to play another when the ball is found.

A.—By walking back the player has given up the ball and he must therefore play another ball from the original spot under penalty of stroke and distance.

Ball Strikes Player

Q.—If your ball hits yourself, your partner (in a foursome) or one of the caddies, what is the penalty?

A.—Loss of hole in match play, 2 strokes in medal play.

Identifying the Ball

Q.—You wish to identify a ball to make sure it is your own. What should you do?

A.—Inform your opponent that you wish to lift it for identification, and afterwards replace it on the same spot.

IMPEDIMENTS: UNPLAYABLE

Dropping a Ball

Q.—What is the correct way to drop a ball ?

A.—Face the hole, stand erect, and drop the ball behind you over your shoulder.

Q.—What is the penalty for dropping a ball incorrectly ?

A.—One stroke.

Unplayable Ball

Q.—Who decides whether a ball is unplayable ?

A.—The player. The decision rests entirely with him.

Ball Hits Opponent's Ball

Q.—In a **medal** competition, your ball hits your opponent's ball on the putting green.

A.—The penalty is two strokes, but if played from a hazard no penalty is incurred.

Ball Knocked into Hole

Q.—What happens in a **match** when one ball strikes the other and knocks it into the hole ?

A.—The player whose ball is knocked into the hole is deemed to have holed out at his last stroke.

Impediment on Ball

Q.—You find that your ball, in playing through the green, has a lump of mud adhering to it. What does the rule entitle you to do ?

A.—Nothing, just play the ball as it is.

Damaged Ball

Q.—You top an iron shot very badly and when you reach the ball you find it to be damaged and quite unfit for play. May you change your ball, if so will there be a penalty attached ?

A.—Yes, you may change the ball if you intimate your intention to do so to your fellow competitor or marker. Do this and no penalty is attached.

CASUAL WATER QUERIES

Hits Opponent's Ball

Q.—In a match A's ball, played from beyond the limits of the putting-green, hits B's (opponent's) ball, and knocks it further from the hole. Can B replace his ball?

A.—Yes, if he chooses.

Ball in Casual Water

Q.—What is meant by the term "casual water"? Should it be of sufficient depth to cover the ball, partly cover the ball, interfere with the lie of the ball?

A.—If the water interferes with the lie of the ball or the stance of the player on any part of the course, except in hazards, it may be deemed "casual water."

Q.—What may you do if your ball is in casual water in a hazard, or is lost therein?

A.—You may drop a ball either:
(*a*) in the hazard without penalty not nearer hole or
(*b*) behind the hazard, keeping the spot at which the ball enters the water between yourself and the hole.
Penalty, one stroke.

Water in the Hole

Q.—Playing in a **medal** competition a player putted to within six inches of the hole. He placed his hand into the hole, and putted the ball into his hand. He did this because the hole was partly filled with muddy water. Is this allowable?

A.—No.

Frozen Water

Q.—Is casual water, in a frozen state, treated as casual water even if frozen solid?

A.—Yes. This is the usual custom both on the putting-green and "through the green."

Drives Out of Turn

Q.—In a **match** a player has the honour but his opponent drives out of turn.

A.—The ball may be at once recalled by the opponent, and re-teed without penalty.

BUNKERED! WAY OUT

Striking the Flag-Stick

Q.—If a player, taking part in a **match** strikes an unattended flag from a distance within 20 yards of the hole, what is the penalty ?

A.—There is no penalty.

Q.—If, in a **medal round,** the player strikes the flag from within 20 yards, should he be penalised ?

A.—Yes. In **medal play** the penalty for striking the flag-stick with a shot played from within 20 yards of the hole is two strokes.

Loose Impediments

Q.—Before taking his shot on the fairway a player removed a divot lying two feet in front of the ball.

A.—No penalty.

Loose Impediments, etc., on the Green

Q.—Loose impediments on the line of the putt may be removed. How?

A.—The club must not be laid with more than its own weight upon the ground, nor must the player press anything down either with the club or in any other way.

Bag in the Bunker

Q.—Before playing a shot out of a bunker, a player placed his bag of clubs in the bunker about three yards behind the ball. Should he be penalised ?

A.—No. Provided the action of the player did not facilitate his shot.

Playing Out of Bunker

Q.—When playing out of a bunker your club touches the sand behind the ball in the back-swing.

A.—The penalty is one stroke.

Q.—When a ball lies in or touches a hazard, may a player remove any loose impediment in the hazard ?

A.—No.

SIX ERRORS TO AVOID

Bogey . . . Leaving out Holes

Q.—In a **bogey** competition a player leaves out a hole (or holes) to save time, and counts it a loss.

A.—This breaks no rule, but such an action is not in accordance with the spirit of the game.

Line to the Hole

Q.—You ask your caddie for a line to the hole. This he gives you and rests on the ground at that point to be sure you remember the line.

A.—This is wrong. Your caddie should give you the line and then move away.

Rub of the Green

Q.—What happens if an outside agency:
(*a*) stops your ball while in motion.
(*b*) displaces your ball when at rest.

A.—In the first case (a) you would do nothing, it is a rub of the green. In the second case you would drop a ball as nearly as possible to the place where it lay, without penalty.

Six Breaches

Q.—Can you give six breaches of the Rules of Golf which would result in your disqualification in Stroke Play ?

A.—(*a*) Before starting, playing on or to any putting green.
(*b*) For returning a score lower than that actually done.
(*c*) For not playing the stipulated round.
(*d*) For seeking, or willingly receiving advice.
(*e*) Failing to hole out at every hole with your own ball.
(*f*) For agreeing to exclude the operation of a rule, or waive a penalty.

Bunker Footmarks

Q.—In a **match** a player fails to get out of a bunker. Then, prior to playing his next shot, he removes the marks made by his feet.

A.—This is permissible so long as his action does not improv the lie of the ball or help him in subsequent shots.

Standing Out of Bounds

Q.—May a player stand out of bounds, to play a ball lying within bounds ?

A.—Yes.

OPEN CHAMPION

A. D. LOCKE, South Africa, who regained the Open Championship at Royal Lytham

AMATEUR CHAMPION

HARVIE WARD, who retained the British Amateur championship trophy for America with a 6 and 5 victory over his fellow countryman, Frank Stranahan, at Troon

MATCH-PLAY CHAMPION

FRED DALY, Balmoral, Belfast, won the Match-play championship with a great victory over the Belgian, Flory van Donck, in the final at Walton Heath

RYDER CUP CAPTAIN

HENRY COTTON, recalled to lead Britain's Coronation Year Challenge for the Ryder Cup against the United States at Wentworth

WOMEN'S CHAMPION

Miss MOIRA PATERSON, 29-year-old Curtis Cup player, regained the British women's championship for Scotland after a great game in the final with Miss Frances Stephens

GIRLS' CHAMPION

ANN PHILLIPS, Whitefield, Lancashire, won the British Girls' Championship for the North with an easy victory in the final at Stoke Poges

BOYS' CHAMPION

M. F. BONNALACK, of Thorpe Hall, Essex, is the new British boy champion golfer

SCOTTISH STAR

JOHN PANTON, Glenbervie, was one of Scotland's leading lights in the 1952 tournament series

GOLF RECORDS

Chief Feats at a Glance

OPEN CHAMPIONSHIP WINS

HARRY VARDON won the Open Championship on six occasions, namely: 1896, 1898, 1899, 1903, 1911 and 1914—a world record.

Young Tom Morris won the Open Championship four times in succession.

AMATEUR HONOURS

JOHN BALL created a record in Amateur Golf by winning the Amateur Championship on eight occasions, namely: 1888, 1890, 1892, 1894, 1899, 1907, 1910 and 1912. He won the Open Championship in 1890, being the first amateur to accomplish this feat.

ALL FOUR IN ONE YEAR

BOBBY JONES achieved the unparalleled performance in 1930 of winning the Open and Amateur Championships of Great Britain and America.

Lawson Little won the British and American Amateur Championships in 1934 and 1935.

LOWEST OPEN AGGREGATE

BOBBY LOCKE holds the lowest aggregate record in the Open Championship—279 over 72 holes, and three others—Alfred Perry, Henry Cotton and Gene Sarazen—previously accomplished an aggregate of 283.

HAGEN'S WINS

WALTER HAGEN won the Open Championship, 1922, 1924, 1928 and 1929, the greatest number of victories by an overseas competitor.

Walter Hagen and Joe Kirkwood in about twenty-five years each have played on over 2,500 golf courses.

RECORD TOURNAMENT ROUND

TOM HALIBURTON broke the record for a single round in any British Tournament by returning a 61 in the Spalding Tournament at Worthing, 1952.

LOWEST ROUND IN OPEN

HENRY COTTON, in the Open Championship at Sandwich, 1934, with a score of 65, broke his own record of the course and established a new record for any round ever played in the Open Championship. His aggregate of 204 for three consecutive rounds established still another record.

CHAMPIONSHIP COURSES

Record Scores

OLD COURSE, ST. ANDREWS.—*A. Dowie (71); D. J. Rees, F. Bullock (67).
CARNOUSTIE.—*Hector Thomson, *A. E. McLeod (70); R. A. Whitcombe, C. Lacey, E. Dudley, H. Picard (70).
DEAL.—*R. Sweeny, jun., *P. F. Scrutton (69); P. Alliss, J. Adams (67).
HOYLAKE.—*R. T. Jones (70); N. von Nida, Henry Cotton, L. B. Ayton (69).
MUIRFIELD.—*W. Lawson Little, *E. C. Kingsley (69); Henry Cotton (66).
PRESTWICK.—*R. D. R. Walker, *H. C. B. Davies (72); Macdonald Smith (69).
ROYAL LYTHAM & ST. ANNES. *J. W. Jones (71).
ROYAL SANDWICH (ST. GEORGE'S.—*E. Martin Smith, *Douglas Grant, *C. J. H. Tolley, *J. G. Blackwell (68); Henry Cotton (65).
TROON.—*F. Stranahan (66); F. Van Donck (65).
WESTWARD HO!—*Hon. M. Scott (68); C. H. Ward (70).

* Denotes Amateur

9 HOLES IN 29

LEO. DIEGEL, in the Ryder Cup match at Moortown, Leeds, in 1929, playing against Abe Mitchell, did the first nine holes in 29.

Charles B. Macfarlane, playing in the fourth round of the Amateur Championship at Sandwich, in 1914, against "Chick" Evans, the American, did the first nine holes in 31, the lowest known for nine holes in the Amateur Championship.

Percy Alliss, playing in the Italian Open Championship at San Remo in 1935, returned rounds of 67, 66, 66, 63=262.

BIG MARGINS

LAWSON LITTLE scored a record victory in the Amateur Championship by defeating James Wallace, in the final by 14 and 13 in 1934.

Archie Compston beat Walter Hagen in a 72 holes challenge match for £500 by 18 up and 17 to play.

In the Amateur Championship at Muirfield, 1920, Captain Carter defeated his American opponent by 10 and 8.

CHAMPION AT 19

IN his twentieth year, A. Gordon Barry won the Amateur Championship at Prestwick in 1905.

In his fifty-fourth year, the Hon. Michael Scott won the Amateur Championship at Hoylake in 1933.

Arthur Havers, at the age of fifteen, survived the qualifying stages of the Open Championship at Troon in 1914.

HOLES IN ONE

ALEX. HERD holed out in one at nineteen holes. This is the greatest number of holes done in one by a single individual.

CARD FOR 1953

Championship and Stroke Tournaments

(All stroke competitions, unless otherwise stated)

March 25-27.—Sunningdale Amateur-Professional Foursomes, Sunningdale.

April 8-9.—Goodwin (Sheffield) Foursomes, Southern qualifying tournament.

April 21-23.—Assistant Professionals' tournament, Coombe Hill.

April 29.—Midland Professional championship, Harborne.

May 5-8.—Dunlop tournament, Wentworth.

May 12-14.—Gor-ray Assistant Professionals' championship, Hartsbourne (match-play).

May 13-14.—" News of the World " West of England section qualifying competition and West of England championship, Teignmouth.

May 14.—" News of the World " East Anglian section qualifying competition, Eaton.

May 19-22.—Penfold tournament.

May 27.—Goodwin (Sheffield) Foursomes, Midlands qualifying tournament, Hollinwell, Notts.

May 27-28.—Goodwin (Sheffield) Foursomes, Northern qualifying tournament, Starbeck (Harrogate).

June 10-12.—Daks tournament, Wentworth.

June 17-18.—Welsh professional championship, Tenby.

June 17-19.—" Yorkshire Evening News " tournament, Sand Moor.

June 25.—" Eastern Daily Press " tournament, Royal Norwich

July 6-10.—Open Championship, Carnoustie.

July 14-18.—Coronation open tournament, Braid Hills, Edinburgh.

July 21-25.—Swallow-Harrogate Two Thousand Guineas tournament, Harrogate.

July 29-31.—Irish Open (£3,000 championship), Belvoir Park, Belfast.

August 12-13.—" News of the World," Northern section qualifying competition.

August 12-14.—" Spalding " tournament, Worthing.

August 19.—" News of the World " Midland qualifying competition, Sherwood Forest.

August 19-20.—" News of the World " Southern qualifying competition, Mill Hill.

August 26-28.—" Lotus " tournament.

September 3-5.—" Goodwin " Sheffield tournament finals (foursomes), Lindrick.

September 15-19.—" News of the World " match-play championship finals, Ganton.

October 2-3.—Ryder Cup match (Britain v. U.S.A.), Wentworth.

October 7-8.—Dunlop Masters' tournament.

October 14-15.—Palace Hotel Short Course tournament, Torquay.

October 19-23.—Gleneagles—Saxone Professional-Amateur foursomes tournament, Gleneagles.

AMATEUR TESTS

March 20-21.—Oxford v. Cambridge, Rye.
March 25-27.—Sunningdale Amateur-Professional Foursomes, Sunningdale.

April 4-7.—West of Ireland Open Amateur Championship, Rosses Point Co. Sligo.
April 16-19.—Halford Hewitt Cup, Deal and Sandwich.
April 27—**May 2.—English Amateur Championship Royal Birkdale.**

May 6.—Royal and Ancient Spring Medal, St. Andrews.
May 15.—Scottish Women's medal tournament and Glover Cup, Carnoustie.
May 16.—Royal St. George's Grand Challenge Cup, Sandwich.
May 18-21.—Scottish Women's championship, Carnoustie.
May 18-21.—Irish Women's championship, Rosslare.
May 23-26.—East of Ireland open championship, Baltray, Co. Louth.
May 25-30.—**Amateur Championship, Royal Liverpool (Hoylake).**

June 10-13.—South-West Counties' Amateur championship, Royal North Devon.
June 10-13.—North Wales championship, Llandudno (West Shore).
June 10-12.—**Amateur International matches and Walker Cup trials, Killarney.**
June 12.—Women's International, Wales v. New Zealand, at Prestatyn.
June 13.—Women's International, Wales v. Canada, at Llandudno (Maesdu)
June 14.—"Golf Illustrated" Gold Vase, Sunningdale.
June 15-19.—**Irish Open Amateur championship, Killarney.**
June 18-19.—Women's International matches, Royal Porthcawl.
June 22-26.—**British Women's championship, Royal Porthcawl.**
June 29-July 3.—L.G.U. Commonwealth Tournament, Formby.

July 6-10.—Open Championship, Carnoustie.
July 11.—"Silver Tassie" Competition, Gleneagles.
July 13-15.—North of Ireland Open Amateur championship, Royal Portrush.
July 16.—Women's Coronation Tournament Finals, Royal Mid-Surrey.
July 20-25.—**Scottish Amateur Championship, Western Gailes.**
July 29-Aug. 1.—"Glasgow Evening News" Foursomes tournament.

August 10-15.—Eden Tournament, St. Andrews.
August 10 (commencing).—South of Ireland Amateur open championship, Lahinch (Co. Clare).
August 11-14.—Amateur Open tournament, Nairn.
August 24-25.—Artisans' Association tournament, Berkshire.
August 24-29.—**Boys' International and Championship, Dunbar.**

September 1-6.—R. & A. Calcutta Cup, St. Andrews.
September 4-5.—**Walker Cup (U.S.A. v. Britain), at Kittansett, Marion (Mass., U.S.A.).**
September 7.—R. & A. Jubilee Vase, St. Andrews.
September 8-11.—Girls' International and Championship, Woodhall Spa.
September 9.—(commencing date) Irish Amateur championship, Rosses Point, Co. Sligo.
September 9-19.—Welsh Amateur championship, Prestatyn.
September 10-12.—**English Golf Union Brabazon Trophy competition, Sunningdale.**
September 16.—Royal & Ancient Club's Amateur medal, St. Andrews.
September 17-19.—"Scottish Daily Mail" Amateur Mixed Foursomes Finals, Gleneagles.
September 17-18.—English Women's County Finals, Princes, Sandwich.
September 21-25.—English Women's Close championship, Princes, Sandwich.

October 7.—International, Belgium v. Britain (Women), in Belgium.
October 12-15.—Open Scratch Mixed Foursomes, Worplesdon.
October 19-23.—**Gleneagles—Saxone Amateur-Professional foursomes, Glenagles.**

YOU MUST HAVE THE BEST COMMENT TO GO WITH THE CRICKET SCORE

It's extra-important this year because

THE AUSTRALIANS ARE HERE

for a Test series of intense interest.

ARCHIE LEDBROOKE

is the writer to follow for news and views

The Tests will be viewed also "through Australian eyes" by

JACK FINGLETON

famous Australian critic and former Test batsman.

TESTS AND ALL THE OTHER CRICKET ARE BEST COVERED IN THE

DAILY DISPATCH

THE CURTIS CUP

THE Curtis Cup was presented by the sisters Harriet and Margaret Curtis, of Boston, Massachusetts, in 1932 to "stimulate the friendly rivalry among women golfers in many lands." Play is by foursomes and singles over 18 holes.

RESULTS :

At Wentworth, Surrey, 1932, U.S.A. won by 5 matches to 3 matches (1 halved).

At Chevy Chase, 1934, U.S.A. won by 6 matches to 2 matches (1 halved).

At Gleneagles, Perthshire, 1936, the tournament was drawn at 4 matches each (1 halved).

At the Essex County Club, U.S.A., 1938, U.S.A. won by 5 matches to 3 matches (1 halved).

At Birkdale, Southport, Lancs., 1948, U.S.A. won by 6 matches to 2 matches (1 halved).

At Buffalo, New York, 1950, U.S.A. won by 7 matches to 1 match (1 halved).

At Muirfield, Scotland, 1952, Britain won by 5 matches to 4. Results (British players named first) :

FOURSOMES

Miss J. Donald and Miss Elizabeth Price beat Miss D. Kirby and Miss G. de Moss 3 and 2.

Miss F. Stephens and Mrs. G. Valentine lost to Miss C. Doran and Miss M. Lindsay 6 and 4.

Miss M. Paterson and Miss P. Garvey beat Miss P. Riley and Miss P. O'Sullivan 2 and 1.

SINGLES

Miss J. Donald lost to Miss D. Kirby 1 up.
Miss F. Stephens beat Miss M. Lindsay 2 and 1.
Miss M. Paterson lost to Miss P. Riley 6 and 4.
Miss J. Bisgood beat Miss M. Murray 6 and 5.
Miss P. Garvey lost to Miss P. Doran 3 and 2.
Miss E. Price beat Miss G. de Moss 3 and 2.

NEW AMATEUR-PRO. TOURNEY

A new amateur-professional partnership tournament enters the l'st of big money golf events this year with the inauguration of the Gleneagles-Saxone £3,000 competition.

It will take the form of a match-play handicap foursomes on the Gleneagles Hotel King's Course between October 19 and 23.

The competition will be on a knock-out basis, with 32 professionals partnering amateurs of up to six handicap.

A

SPORTING CHRONICLE SERVICE

CRICKET

You must read the informative match reports by

EDGAR TURNER, who toured with the 1951-52 M.C.C. team in India and Pakistan,

and

BASIL EASTERBROOK, who during the summer will follow the fortunes of the Australian team.

Full reports and full scores of all matches every day.

GOLF

EDGAR TURNER and **DERRICK COLLIER** will combine in a comprehensive coverage, including detailed scores, of all the major tournaments.

If it's sport you'll find it all in the

SPORTING CHRONICLE

AND ATHLETIC NEWS,

the only all-sports daily.

Leading Tournament Scores, 1952

SILVER KING

	Rounds 1st	2nd	3rd	4th	Ttl.
R. W. Horne (Hendon)	67	68	68	73	276
A. Lees (Sunningdale)	73	65	69	70	277
C. H. Ward (Little Aston)	69	68	72	70	279
H. Weetman (Croham Hurst)	67	69	73	71	280
R. Burton (Coombe Hill)	71	68	73	69	281
C. S. Denny (North Middlesex)	70	66	72	74	282

DUNLOP

	Rounds 1st	2nd	3rd	4th	5th	Ttl.
M. Faulkner (Hindhead)	68	73	67	65	72	345
T. Haliburton (Wentworth)	74	70	68	68	72	352
P. W. Thomson (Australia)	73	71	71	71	69	355
N. Sutton (Leigh)	72	71	72	69	71	355
J. Panton (Glenbervie)	72	71	74	69	69	355
F. Bullock (Glasgow)	70	76	70	71	71	358

SPALDING

	Rounds 1st	2nd	3rd	4th	Ttl.
H. Weetman (Croham Hurst)	66	67	68	70	271
A. Cerda (Argentine)	69	65	70	67	271
W. Shankland (Potter's Bar)	67	66	70	69	272
T. B. Haliburton (Wentworth)	61	65	75	72	273
S. L. King (Knole Park)	68	71	73	66	278
M. Faulkner (St. George's Hill)	71	69	68	72	280

YORKSHIRE EVENING NEWS

	Rounds 1st	2nd	3rd	4th	Ttl.
D. J. Rees (South Herts)	72	67	73	71	283
T. H. Cotton (Royal Mid-Surrey)	70	70	72	72	284
S. S. Scott (Carlisle City)	67	73	73	71	284
M. Faulkner (St. George's Hill)	73	68	70	74	285
F. Bullock (Glasgow)	72	70	74	70	286
A. Cerda (Argentine)	69	74	73	72	287

DAKS

	Rounds 1st	2nd	3rd	4th	Ttl.
F. Daly (Balmoral)	67	72	69	72	280
J. Hargreaves (Sutton Coldfield)	74	70	72	66	282
H. Bradshaw (Portmarnock)	72	71	75	65	283
A. Lees (Sunningdale)	66	74	74	69	283
S. L. King (Knole Park)	75	65	68	76	284
N. G. von Nida (Australia)	71	74	69	70	284

THE OPEN CHAMPIONSHIP

	Rounds 1st	2nd	3rd	4th	Ttl.
A. D. Locke (South Africa)	69	71	74	73	287
P. W. Thomson (Australia)	68	73	77	70	288
F. Daly (Balmoral)	67	69	77	76	289
T. H. Cotton (Royal Mid-Surrey)	75	74	74	71	294
A. Cerda (Argentine)	73	73	76	73	295
S. L. King (Knole Park)	71	74	74	76	295

NORTH BRITISH HARROGATE

	Rounds 1st	2nd	3rd	4th	5th	Ttl.
J. Panton (Glenbervie)	74	67	68	67	67	343
H. Weetman (Croham Hurst)	69	72	69	67	72	349
F. Van Donck (Belgium)	67	71	75	71	66	350
H. Bradshaw (Portmarnock)	67	69	73	70	72	351
D. J. Rees (South Herts)	69	67	71	73	72	352
P. W. Thomson (Australia)	74	68	70	70	70	352

LOTUS

	Rounds 1st	2nd	3rd	4th	Ttl.
A. D. Locke (South Africa)	63	67	70	66	266
H. Bradshaw (Portmarnock)	68	65	70	71	274
A. Lees (Sunningdale)	69	63	71	73	276
J. Panton (Glenbervie)	73	66	67	71	277
E. E. Whitcombe (Chigwell)	75	63	67	72	277
E. C. Brown (Sandy Lodge)	72	66	67	73	278
S. L. King (Knole Park)	68	70	70	70	278

IRISH PROFESSIONAL

	Rounds 1st	2nd	3rd	4th	Ttl.
F. Daly (Balmoral)	73	70	71	71	284
H. Bradshaw (Portmarnock)	73	71	72	70	286
R. Hayden (Woodbrook)	82	74	71	68	295

NEWS OF WORLD MATCH PLAY

In the final, at Walton Heath, **F. Daly** (Balmoral, Belfast) beat **F. Van Donck** (Waterloo, Belgium) by **4** and **3.**

GOODWIN PROFESSIONAL FOURSOMES

In the final, at Abbeydale, Sheffield, **J. Panton** (Glenbervie) and **N. Roffe** (Coventry) beat **A. Poulton** (Burhill) and **R. Kemp** (St. Mellons) by **6** and **5.**

DUNLOP MASTERS

	Rounds 1st	2nd	3rd	4th	Ttl.
H. Weetman (Croham Hurst)	71	72	66	72	281
A. Lees (Sunningdale)	75	69	70	71	285
M. Faulkner (St. George's Hill)	74	73	71	69	287
N. Sutton (Exeter)	73	71	75	69	288
J. Hargreaves (Sutton Coldfield)	70	69	73	77	289

SECRETARIES

ROYAL AND ANCIENT GOLF CLUB OF ST. ANDREWS: The Secretary, St. Andrews, Fife

ENGLISH GOLF UNION: Major A. Whitley Lavarack, M.C., "Greenways," Hill View Road, Claygate, Esher, Surrey

SCOTTISH GOLF UNION: W. M. Berrie, C.A., 20, Atholl Crescent, Edinburgh

IRELAND, GOLFING UNION OF: William A. Menton, Phœnix Chambers, 12, Trinity Street, Dublin

WELSH GOLFING UNION: F. E. Perry, 35, West Bute Street, Cardiff

PROFESSIONAL GOLFERS' ASSOCIATION OF AMERICA: Thomas W. Crane, 134, North La Salle Street, Chicago, 2, Ill., U.S.A.

OPEN GOLF CHAMPIONSHIP: The Secretary, Royal and Ancient Golf Club, St. Andrews, Fife

UNITED STATES GOLF ASSOCIATION: Joseph C. Dey, Jnr., Golf House, 40, East 38th Street, New York 16, U.S.A.

PROFESSIONAL GOLFERS' ASSOCIATION: Comdr. R. C. T. Roe, R.N. (ret'd). Ethelburga House, 91 and 93, Bishopsgate, London, E.C.2

SCOTTISH PROFESSIONAL GOLFERS' ASSOCIATION: Robert Brown, C.A., 157, West George Street, Glasgow, C.2

IRISH PROFESSIONAL GOLFERS' ASSOCIATION: W. Kinsella, Skerries Golf Club, Dublin

AMATEUR GOLF CHAMPIONSHIP: The Secretary, Royal and Ancient Golf Club, St. Andrews, Fife

ARTISAN GOLFERS' ASSOCIATION: W. J. Gardner, The Moor, Wooburn Green, near High Wycombe, Bucks.

BOYS' AMATEUR CHAMPIONSHIP: The Secretary, Royal and Ancient Golf Club, St. Andrews, Fife

DERBYSHIRE UNION OF GOLF CLUBS: R. E. Fryer, 18, City Road, Derby

GIRLS' CHAMPIONSHIP: Miss B. Hale, Ladies' Golf Union, 39, Eccleston Square, Victoria, London, S.W.1

GOLF GREENKEEPERS' ASSOCIATION (BRITISH): D. V. D. Moss, 56, Avondale Road, South Croydon, Surrey.

KENT GOLF UNION: Geoffrey Simpson, Stapleden, The Drive, Sevenoaks, Kent

LADIES' GOLF UNION: Miss B. Hale, 39, Eccleston Square, Victoria, London, S.W.1

MIDLAND COUNTIES' GOLF ASSOCIATION: C. E. Cowney, F.C.A., 55, Temple Row, Birmingham 2

NORFOLK COUNTY GOLF UNION: H. R. Craske, Sheringham Golf Club, Sheringham, Norfolk

NOTTINGHAMSHIRE UNION OF GOLF CLUBS: T. Dexter Hall, Albion Chambers, King Street, Nottingham

SHEFFIELD UNION OF GOLF CLUBS: Fred Bye, 21, Edale Road, Ecclesall, Sheffield

SOUTH WALES GOLFERS' ALLIANCE H. T. Hinchcliffe, 5, Ty-Wern Road, Rhiwbina, Cardiff.

STAFFORDSHIRE UNION OF GOLF CLUBS: F. W. G. Church, The Green, Darlaston, Staffs.

SURREY COUNTY GOLF UNION: Lt.-Col. J. N. Fenton, Seventeenth, Knightsbridge Road, Camberley, Surrey

WARWICKSHIRE UNION OF GOLF CLUBS: W. N. Dudley Evans, A.C.A. c/o E. Stokes & Co., 1-3, Old Bank Place, High Street, Sutton Coldfield, and Queen's College Chambers Paradise Street, Birmingham.

YORKSHIRE UNION OF PROFESSIONAL GOLFERS: A. G. Weldon, Lightcliffe Golf Club, Halifax, Yorks.

YORKSHIRE UNION OF GOLF CLUBS: Gordon Wright, c/o Ganton G. C., Nr. Scarborough.

TOURNAMENTS

"NEWS OF THE WORLD" TOURNAMENT

1903 J. Braid
1904 J. H. Taylor
1905 J. Braid
1906 A. Herd
1907 J. Braid
1908 J. H. Taylor
1909 T. Ball
1910 Sherlock
1911 J. Braid
1912 H. Vardon
1913 G. Duncan
1914-18 War interval
1919 A. Mitchell
1920 A. Mitchell
1921 A. Seymour
1922 G. Gadd
1923 R. G. Wilson
1924 E. R. Whitcombe
1925 A. Compston
1926 A. Herd
1927 A. Compston
1928 C. A. Whitcombe
1929 A. Mitchell
1930 C. A. Whitcombe
1931 A. H. Padgham
1932 T. H. Cotton
1933 P. Alliss
1934 J. J. Busson
1935 A. H. Padgham
1936 D. J. Rees
1937 P. Alliss
1938 D. J. Rees
1939 No Competition
1940 T. H. Cotton
1946 T. H. Cotton
1947 F. Daly
1948 F. Daly
1949 D. J. Rees
1950 D. J. Rees
1951 H. Weetman
1952 F. Daly

"DAILY MAIL" TOURNAMENT

1919 Abe Mitchell
1920 George Duncan
1921 A. E. Hallam
1922 George Duncan
1923 E. Ray
1924 C. A. Whitcombe
1925 C. Johns
1926 A. Boomer
1927 Abe Mitchell
1928-35 No tournament
1936 A. H. Padgham
1937 S. L. King
1938 A. Perry
1939 T. H. Cotton
1940 R. Burton
1945 C. H. Ward
1946 A. H. Padgham
1947 D. J. Rees
1948 N. G. Von Nida
1949 T. Haliburton
1950 C. H. Ward
1951 No Competition
1951-52 No Competition

"YORKSHIRE EVENING NEWS" TOURNAMENT

1923 H. C. Jolly
1924 R. Robson
1925 Len Holland
1926 C. A. Whitcombe
1927 E. R. Whitcombe
1928 C. A. Whitcombe
1929 J. Turnesa
1930 H. C. Jolly
1931 E. R. Whitcombe
1932 B. Hodson
1933 A. J. Lacey
1934 A. H. Padgham
1935 T. H. Cotton
1936 R. Burton
1937 A. J. Lacey
1938 A. Perry
1939 D. J. Rees
1944 S. L. King
1945 A. Compston
1946 A. D. Locke
1947 { T. H. Cotton / N. G. Von Nida
1948 C. H. Ward
1949 S. L. King
1950 D. J. Rees
1951 { D. J. Rees / N. G. Von Nida
1952 D. J. Rees

GOODWIN FOURSOMES

1952 J. Panton and N. Roffe

Post-War Results

SILVER KING

1946 D. J. Rees
1947 A. H. Padgham
1948 J. Adams & C. H. Ward
1949 R. Burton
1950 J. Panton
1951 F. van Donck
1952 R. W. Horne

BRAND-LOCHRYN

1946 A. D. Locke
1947 N. G. Von Nida
1948 C. H. Ward
1949-50-51-52 No Competition

SPALDING

1946 D. J. Rees
1947 T. H. Cotton
1948 N. G. Von Nida
1949 C. H. Ward
1950 A. D. Locke
1951 J. Hargreaves
1952 { H. Weetman / A. Cerda }

STAR

1946 T. H. Cotton
1947 N. G. Von Nida
1948-49-50-51-52 No Competition

EVENING CHRONICLE

1947 F. van Donck
1948 N. G. Von Nida
1949 F. Daly
1950-51-52 No Competition

IRISH OPEN

1946 F. Daly
1947 H. Bradshaw
1948 D. J. Rees
1949 H. Bradshaw
1950 O. Pickworth
1951-52 Not played

NORTH BRITISH-HARROGATE

1947 N. G. Von Nida
1948 R. de Vicenzo
1949 C. H. Ward
1950 A. D. Locke
1951 F. van Donck
1952 J. Panton

LOTUS

1946 R. A. Whitcombe
1947 N. G. Von Nida
1948 N. G. Von Nida
1949 M. Faulkner
1950 F. Daly
1951 C. H. Ward
1952 A. D. Locke

NEWS-CHRONICLE

1946 N. G. Von Nida
1947 D. J. Rees
1948 R. Horne & A. Dailey
1949 R. Burton
1950 D. J. Rees
1951 K. Bousfield
1952 No Contest

PENFOLD

1946 N. Sutton
1947 { N. G. Von Nida / D. J. Rees / R. A. Whitcombe }
1948 F. Daly
1949 J. Burton & M. Faulkner
1950 N. Sutton & Mrs. A. Gee
1951 A. Lees
1952 E. C. Brown

DAILY TELEGRAPH

1947 R. J. White & C. H. Ward
1948 G. H. Micklem & C. H. Ward
1949 R. J. White & R. Horne
1950 J. Bruen & W. Smithers
1951 W. S. McLeod & W. J. Cox
1952 No Contest

DAKS

1951 J. Panton
1952 F. Daly

DUNLOP

1951 (Little Aston), C. H. Ward
1952 M. Faulkner

DUNLOP MASTERS

1946 A. D. Locke & J. Adams
1947 A. Lees
1948 N. G. Von Nida
1949 C. H. Ward
1950 A. D. Locke
1951 M. Faulkner
1952 H. Weetman

Major Professional Tournaments

Leading Averages of 1952

Name	Club	Pts	T'rna-ments	Avge	Strokes	R'nds	St'ke Avge
H. Weetman	Croham Hurst	79	9	8.77	2711	38	71.34
M. Faulkner	St. Georges Hill	54	6	9.0	1648	23	71.65
A. Lees	Sunningdale	72	8	9.0	2421	34	71.20
H. Bradshaw	Portmarnock	66	7	9.42	2144	30	71.46
J. Panton	Glenbervie	91	9	10.11	2723	38	71.65
N. G. von Nida	Australia	74	7	10.57	2159	30	71.96
A. Cerda	Argentina	53	5	10.60	1517	21	72.23
T. B. Haliburton	Wentworth	96	8	12.00	2445	34	71.91
N. Sutton	Exeter	85	7	12.14	2180	30	72.66
F. Daly	Balmoral	99	8	12.37	2445	34	71.91
S. L. King	Knole Park	100	8	12.50	2449	34	72.02
J. Hargreaves	Sutton Coldfield	88	7	12.57	2171	30	72.36
S. S. Scott	Carlisle	105	8	13.12	2466	34	72.52
E. C. Brown	Sandy Lodge	95	7	13.57	2108	29	72.68
D. J. Rees	South Herts	138	9	15.33	2620	36	72.77
K. Bousfield	Coombe Hill (A)	138	9	15.33	2770	38	72.89
F. Van Donck	Royal Waterloo	112	7	16.00	1973	27	73.07
A. Poulton	Burhill (A)	113	7	16 14	2119	29	73.06
W. D. Smithers	Long Ashton	100	6	16.66	1840	25	73.60
C. H. Ward	Little Aston	120	7	17.14	2020	28	72.14
A. S. Waters	Worplesdon	139	8	17.37	2484	34	73.05
E. G. Lester	Bristol & Clifton	110	6	18.33	1736	24	72.33
R. W. Horne	Hendon	130	7	18.57	1901	26	73.11
C. S. Denny	North Middlesex	98	5	19.60	1385	19	72.89
B. J. Hunt	Atherstone (A)	139	7	19.85	2053	28	73.32
E. E. Whitcombe	Chigwell	108	5	21.60	1321	18	73.38
F. Bullock	Glasgow	174	8	21.75	2052	28	73.28
W. Shankland	Potters Bar	131	6	21.83	1379	19	72.57
J. R. M. Jacobs	Unattached	177	8	22.12	2214	30	73.80
K. W. C. Adwick	Letchworth	134	6	22 33	1758	24	73.25
R. Burton	Coombe Hill	135	6	22.50	1533	21	73.00
R. G. French	West Surrey	161	7	23 00	1993	27	73.81
P. Alliss	Ferndown (A)	165	7	23.57	1784	24	74.33
T. W. Allen	Richmond Park	144	6	24.00	1598	22	72.72
A. J. Harman	R. Wimbledon (A)	145	6	24 16	1540	21	73.33
A. F. Stickley	Ealing	170	7	24.28	1696	23	73.30
L. B. Ayton	Worthing	174	7	24.85	1917	26	73.73
H. A. J. Young	Sonning	152	6	25.33	1568	21	74.66
W. J. Cox	Fulwell	127	5	25.40	1094	15	72.93
F. G. Allott	Enfield	128	5	25 60	1269	17	74.64
R. A. Knight	Wanstead	154	6	25.66	1395	19	73.42
G. W. McIntosh	Unattached	182	7	25.99	1862	25	74.45
W. C. A. Hancock	Stockport	210	8	26.25	2077	28	74.17
E. W. Ward	Tyrrells Wood	162	6	27.00	1253	17	73.70
J. H. Hawkins	Maidenhead	138	5	27.60	1132	15	75.46
A. G. Harrison	Hill Barn	166	6	27.66	1259	17	74.05
T. H. T. Fairbairn	Reddish Vale	196	7	28.00	1633	22	74.22
R. P. Mills	Wentworth (A)	196	7	28.00	1931	26	74.26
K. H. Redford	Stanmore	177	6	29.50	1412	19	74.31
A. Perry	Leatherhead	149	5	29.80	971	13	74.69

CHAMPIONSHIPS: OPEN WINNERS

1860 W. Park, Musselburgh
1861 Tom Morris, sen., Prestwick
1862 Tom Morris, sen., Prestwick
1863 W. Park, Musselburgh
1864 Tom Morris, sen., Prestwick
1865 A. Strath, St. Andrews
1866 W. Park, Musselburgh
1867 Tom Morris, sen., St. Andrews
1868 Tom Morris, jun., St. Andrews
1869 Tom Morris, jun., St. Andrews
1870 Tom Morris, jun., St. Andrews
1872 Tom Morris, jun., St. Andrews
1873 Tom Kidd, St. Andrews
1874 Mungo Park, Musselburgh
1875 Willie Park, Musselburgh
1876 Bob Martin, St. Andrews
1877 Jamie Anderson, St. Andrews
1878 Jamie Anderson, St. Andrews
1879 Jamie Anderson, St. Andrews
1880 Bob Ferguson, Musselburgh
1881 Bob Ferguson, Musselburgh
1882 Bob Ferguson, Musselburgh
1883 W. Fernie, Dumfries
1884 Jack Simpson, Carnoustie
1885 Bob Martin, St. Andrews
1886 D. Brown, Musselburgh
1887 W. Park, jun., Musselburgh
1888 Jack Burns, Warwick
1889 W. Park, jun., Musselburgh
1890*John Ball, Rgyal Liverpool
1891 Hugh Kirkaldy, St. Andrews
1892*H. H. Hilton, Royal Liverpool
1893 W. Auchterlonie, St. Andrews
1894 J. H. Taylor, Winchester
1895 J. H. Taylor, Winchester
1896 H. Vardon, Ganton
1897*H. H. Hilton, Royal Liverpool
1898 H. Vardon, Ganton
1899 H. Vardon, Ganton
1900 J. H. Taylor, Mid-Surrey
1901 James Braid, Romford
1902 Alex. Herd, Huddersfield
1903 H. Vardon, Totteridge
1904 Jack White, Sunningdale
1905 James Braid, Walton Heath
1906 James Braid, Walton Heath
1907 Arnaud Massy, La Boulie
1908 James Braid, Walton Heath
1909 J. H. Taylor, Mid-Surrey
1910 James Braid, Walton Heath
1911 Harry Vardon, Totteridge
1912 E. Ray, Oxhey
1913 J. H. Taylor, Mid-Surrey
1914 Harry Vardon, Totteridge
1915-19 War interval
1920 George Duncan, Hanger Hill
1921 Jock Hutchison, U.S.A.
1922 Walter Hagen, U.S.A.
1923 A. G. Havers, Coombe Hill
1924 Walter Hagen, U.S.A.
1925 Jim Barnes, U.S.A.
1926*R. T. Jones, U.S.A.
1927*R. T. Jones, U.S.A.
1928 Walter Hagen, U.S.A.
1929 Walter Hagen, U.S.A.
1930*R. T. Jones, U.S.A.
1931 T. D. Armour, U.S.A.
1932 G. Sarazen, U.S.A.
1933 D. Shute, U.S.A.
1934 T. H. Cotton, Waterloo, Belgium
1935 A. Perry, Leatherhead
1936 A. H. Padgham, Sundridge Park
1937 T. H. Cotton, Ashridge
1938 R. A. Whitcombe, Parkstone
1939 R. Burton, Sale
1940-45 War interval
1946 S. Snead, U.S.A., 1
A. D. Locke, South Africa
J. Bulla, U.S.A., joint 2nd
D. J. Rees, Hindhead
T. H. Cotton, Royal Mid-Surrey
C. H. Ward, Little Aston
N. Von Nida, Australia, joint 3rd
1947 F. Daly, Balmoral, 1
*F. Stranahan, U.S.A.
R. W. Horne, Hendon, joint 2nd
W. Shankland, Templenewsam, 3
1948 T. H. Cotton, Royal Mid-Surrey, 1
F. Daly, Balmoral, 2
R. de Vicenzo, Argentina
N. G. Von Nida, Australia
C. H. Ward, Little Aston
J. Hargreaves, Sutton Coldfield, joint 3rd
1949 A. D. Locke, South Africa, 1
H. Bradshaw, Kilcroney, 2
R. de Vicenzo, Argentina, 3
1950 A. D. Locke, South Africa, 1
R. de Vicenzo, Argentina, 2
F. Daly, Balmoral
D. J. Rees, S. Herts, joint 3rd
1951 M. Faulkner, unattached, 1
A. Cerda, Argentine, 2
C. H. Ward, Little Aston, 3
1952 A. D. Locke, South Africa, 1
P. W. Thomson, Australia, 2
F. Daly, Balmoral, 3

* Amateur

AMATEUR GOLF TITLE WINS

1885 A. F. MacFie
1886 H. G. Hutchinson
1887 H. G. Hutchinson
1888 John Ball
1889 J. E. Laidlay
1890 John Ball
1891 J. E. Laidlay
1892 John Ball
1893 Peter Anderson
1894 John Ball
1895 L. M. B. Melville
1896 F. G. Tait
1897 A. J. T. Allan
1898 F. G. Tait
1899 John Ball
1900 H. H. Hilton
1901 H. H. Hilton
1902 C. Hutchings
1903 R. Maxwell
1904 W. J. Travis
1905 A. G. Barry
1906 James Robb
1907 John Ball
1908 E. A. Lassen
1909 R. Maxwell
1910 John Ball
1911 H. H. Hilton
1912 John Ball
1913 H. H. Hilton
1914 J. L. C. Jenkins
1915-19 War interval
1920 Cyril J. H. Tolley
1921 W. I. Hunter
1922 E. W. E. Holderness
1923 R. H. Wethered
1924 E. W. E. Holderness
1925 Robert Harris
1926 Jesse Sweetser
1927 Dr. W. Tweddell
1928 T. P. Perkins
1929 C. J. H. Tolley
1930 R. T. Jones
1931 E. Martin Smith
1932 J. De Forest
1933 Hon. M. Scott
1934 Lawson Little
1935 Lawson Little
1936 H. Thomson
1937 R. Sweeney, jun.
1938 C. R. Yates, U.S.A.
1939 A. T. Kyle
1940-45 War interval
1946 J. Bruen, Cork, beat R. F. Sweeney, U.S.A.
1947 W. P. Turnesa, U.S.A., beat R. D. Chapman, U.S.A.
1948 F. R. Stranahan, U.S.A., beat C. Stowe, Penn.
1949 S. M. McCready, Sunningdale, beat W. P. Turnesa, U.S.A.
1950 F. R. Stranahan, U.S.A., beat R. D. Chapman, U.S.A.
1951 R. D. Chapman, U.S.A., beat C. R. Coe, U.S.A.
1952 J. Harvie Ward, jun., U.S.A., beat F. Stranahan, U.S.A.

TOURNAMENT AVERAGES: OTHER RECORDS

Name	Club	Pts	T'rna-ments	Avge	Strokes	R'nds	St'ke Avge
A. D. Locke	South Africa	5	3	1.66	838	12	69.83
T. H. Cotton	Unattached	33	4	8.25	1154	16	72.12
B. Wilkes	South Africa (A)	97	3	32.33	666	9	74.00
J. B. Ado	France	223	7	31.85	1499	20	74.95
P. W. Thomson	Australia	Picked up in 2 tournaments					

STARS OF U.S.

AMERICAN OPEN

1894 Willie Dunn
1895 H. J. Rawlins
1896 J. Foulis
1897 J. Lloyd
1898 Fred Herd
1899 W. Smith
1900 Harry Vardon
1901 W. Anderson
1902 L. Auchterlonie
1903 W. Anderson
1904 W. Anderson
1905 W. Anderson
1906 Alex. Smith
1907 Alex. Ross
1908 Fred M'Leod
1909 Geo. Sargent
1910 Alex. Smith
1911 J. J. M'Dermott
1912 J. J. M'Dermott
1913*F. Ouimet
1914 Walter Hagen
1915*J. D. Travers
1916*Charles Evans
1917-18 War interval
1919 Walter Hagen
1920 E. Ray
1921 Jim Barnes
1922 G. Sarazen
1923*R. T. Jones
1924 Cyril Walker
1925 Wm. MacFarlane
1926*R. T. Jones
1927 T. D. Armour
1928 J. Farrell
1929*R. T. Jones
1930*R. T. Jones
1931 B. Burke
1932 G. Sarazen
1933*J. Goodman
1934 O. Dutra
1935 S. Parks
1936 T. Manero
1937 R. Guldahl
1938 R. Guldahl
1939 Byron Nelson
1940 J. Lawson Little
1941 Craig Wood
1946 Lloyd Mangrum
1947 L. Worsham
1948 B. Hogan
1949 C. Middlecoff
1950 B. Hogan
1951 B. Hogan
1952 J. Boros

* *Amateur*

AMERICAN AMATEUR

1893 W. G. Lawrence
1894 L. B. Stoddart
1895 C. B. Macdonald
1896 H. J. Whigham
1897 H. J. Whigham
1898 Finlay S. Douglas
1899 H. M. Harriman
1900 W. J. Travis
1901 W. J. Travis
1902 Louis N. James
1903 W. J. Travis
1904 H. Chandler Egan
1905 H. Chandler Egan
1906 E. M. Byers
1907 Jerome D. Travers
1908 Jerome D. Travers
1909 R. Gardner
1910 W. C. Fownes, Jun.
1911 H. H. Hilton
1912 Jerome D. Travers
1913 Jerome D. Travers
1914 F. Ouimet
1915 R. A. Gardner
1916 Chas. Evans
1917-18 War interval
1919 D. Herron
1920 C. Evans
1921 J. Guildford
1922 J. Sweetser
1923 Max Marston
1924 R. T. Jones
1925 R. T. Jones
1926 Geo. Von Elm
1927 R. T. Jones
1928 R. T. Jones
1929 H. R. Johnston
1930 R. T. Jones
1931 F. Ouimet
1932 C. R. Somerville
1933 G. T. Dunlap
1934 W. Lawson Little
1935 W. Lawson Little
1936 J. Fischer
1937 J. Goodman
1938 W. Turnesa
1939 G. Yates
1940 R. Chapman
1941 M. Ward
1946 E. Bishop
1947 S. Rigel
1948 W. Turnesa
1949 C. R. Coe
1950 S. Urzetta
1951 W. Maxwell
1952 J. Westlands

Amateur Champions

Winners of English, Scottish and Welsh Titles

ENGLISH AMATEUR CHAMPIONSHIP

1925 T. F. Ellison
1926 T. F. Ellison
1927 T. P. Perkins
1928 J. A. Stout
1929 W. Sutton
1930 T. A. Bourn
1931 L. G. Crawley
1932 E. W. Fiddian
1933 J. Woollam
1934 S. Lunt
1935 J. Woollam
1936 H. Bentley
1937 J. J. Pennink
1938 J. J. Pennink
1939 A. L. Bentley
1946 I. R. Patey
1947 G. Micklem
1948 A. G. B. Helm
1949 R. White
1950 J. D. A. Langley
1951 G. Roberts
1952 E. B. Millward

SCOTTISH AMATEUR CHAMPIONSHIP

1922 J. Wilson
1923 T. M. Burrell
1924 W. W. Mackenzie
1925 J. T. Dobson
1926 W. J. Guild
1927 A. Jamieson, jun.
1928 W. W. Mackenzie
1929 J. T. Bookless
1930 K. Greig
1931 J. Wilson
1932 J. M'Lean
1933 J. M'Lean
1934 J. M'Lean
1935 H. Thomson
1936 E. D. Hamilton
1937 H. McInally
1938 E. D. Hamilton
1939 H. McInally
1946 E. Brown
1947 H. McInally
1948 A. S. Flockhart
1949 R. Wight
1950 W. C. Gibson
1951 J. M. Dykes
1952 J. Dewar

WELSH Amateur Native Championship

1900 T. M. Barlow
1901 Major Green
1902 James Hunter
1903 James Hunter
1904 Hal. Ludlow
1905 J. Duncan, jun.
1906 George Renwick
1907 L. A. Phillips
1908 George Renwick
1909 John Duncan, jun.
1910 George Renwick
1911 H. M. Lloyd
1912 L. A. Phillips
1913 H. N. Atkinson
1914-19 War interval
1920 H. R. Howell
1921 C. E. L. Fairchild
1922 H. R. Howell
1923 H. R. Howell
1924 H. R. Howell
1925 C. E. L. Fairchild
1926 D. R. Lewis
1927 D. R. Lewis
1928 C. C. Marston
1929 H. R. Howell
1930 H. R. Howell
1931 H. R. Howell
1932 H. R. Howell
1933 J. L. Black
1934 S. B. Roberts
1935 R. Chapman
1936 R. M. de Lloyd
1937 D. H. Lewis
1938 A. A. Duncan
1939-45 War interval
1946 J. V. Moody
1947 S. B. Roberts
1948 A. A. Duncan
1949 A. Evans
1950 J. L. Morgan
1951 J. L. Morgan
1952 A. A. Duncan

Irish and Girls' Events

IRISH AMATEUR CHAMPIONSHIP

1893 Thos. Dickson
1894 R. Magill, jun.
1895 W. H. Webb
1896 J. Stewart-Moore, jun
1897 H. E. Reade
1898 W. H. Webb
1899 H. E. Reade
1900 R. G. N. Henry
1901 W. H. Boyd
1902 F. B. Newett
1903 H. E. Reade
1904 H. A. Boyd
1905 F. B. Newett
1906 H. A. Boyd
1907 H. M. Cairnes
1908 Lionel Munn
1909 A. H. Patterson
1910 J. F. Jameson
1911 L. O. Munn
1912 A. H. Craig
1913 L. O. Munn
1914 L. O. Munn
1915-18 War interval
1919 E. Carter
1920 C. O. Hexlet
1921 E. Carter
1922 Ector Munn
1923 Dr. J. D. M'Cormack
1924 Dr. J. D. M'Cormack
1925 C. Robertson
1926 A. C. Allison
1927 Dr. J. D. M'Cormack
1928 D. E. B. Soulby
1929 D. E. B. Soulby
1930 J. Burke
1931 J. Burke
1932 J. Burke
1933 J. Burke
1934 J. C. Brown
1935 Roy McConnell
1936 J. Burke
1937 J. Bruen, jun.
1938 J. Bruen, jun.
1939 G. H. Owens
1940 J. Burke
1941-45 War interval
1946 J. Burke
1947 J. Burke
1948 C. Ewing
1949 J. Carroll
1950 B. Herlihy
1951 C. Ewing
1952 N. Drew

GIRLS' CHAMPIONSHIP

1919 Miss Audrey Croft
1920 Miss C. Clark
1921 Miss W. Sarson
1922 Miss M. Wickenden
1923 Miss M. Mackay
1924 Mlle. Thion de la Chaume
1925 Miss Enid Wilson
1926 Miss Diana Esmond
1927 Miss Diana Fishwick
1928 Miss Diana Fishwick
1929 Miss Nan Baird
1930 Miss Pauline Doran
1931 Miss Pauline Doran
1932 Miss Pauline Doran
1933 Miss J. Anderson
1934 Miss N. Jupp
1935 Miss P. Falkner
1936 Miss P. Edwards
1937 Mlle. L. Vagliano
1938 Miss S. Stroyan
1939-48 No competition
1949 Miss P. Davies
1950 Miss J. Robertson
1951 Miss J. Redgate
1952 Miss A. Phillips

WOMEN'S AND BOYS' TESTS

LADIES' CHAMPIONSHIP

1893 Lady Margaret Scott
1894 Lady Margaret Scott
1895 Lady Margaret Scott
1896 Miss Pascoe
1897 Miss E. C. Orr
1898 Miss L. Thomson
1899 Miss M. Hexlet
1900 Miss Adair
1901 Miss Graham
1902 Miss M. Hexlet
1903 Miss Adair
1904 Miss L. Dod
1905 Miss B. Thompson
1906 Mrs. Kennion
1907 Miss M. Hexlet
1908 Miss M. Titterton
1909 Miss D. Campbell
1910 Miss Grant Suttie
1911 Miss D. Campbell
1912 Miss G. Ravenscroft
1913 Miss M. Dodd
1914 Miss C. Leitch
1915-19 War interval
1920 Miss C. Leitch
1921 Miss C. Leitch
1922 Miss J. Wethered
1923 Miss D. Chambers
1924 Miss J. Wethered
1925 Miss J. Wethered
1926 Miss C. Leitch
1927 Mlle. Thion de la Chaume
1928 Mlle. Nanette Le Blan
1929 Miss J. Wethered
1930 Miss D. Fishwick
1931 Miss E. Wilson
1932 Miss E. Wilson
1933 Miss E. Wilson
1934 Mrs. A. M. Holm
1935 Miss W. Morgan
1936 Miss P. Barton
1937 Miss J. Anderson
1938 Mrs. A. M. Holm
1939 Miss P. Barton
1946 Mrs. G. W. Hetherington
1947 Mrs. M. Zaharias
1948 Miss L. Suggs
1949 Miss F. Stephens
1950 Vicomtesse de Saint Sauveur
1951 Mrs. P. G. McCann
1952 Miss M. Paterson

BOYS' CHAMPIONSHIP

Winner	*Year*	*Runner-up*
A. D. D. Mathieson	1921	G. H. Lintott
H. S. Mitchell	1922	W. Greenfield
A. D. D. Mathieson	1923	H. S. Mitchell
R. W. Peattie	1924	P. Manuevrier
R. W. Peattie	1925	A. M'Nair
E. A. M'Ruvie	1926	C. W. Timmis
E. W. Fiddian	1927	K. Forbes
S. Scheftel	1928	A. Dobbie
J. Lindsay	1929	J. Scott-Riddell
J. Lindsay	1930	J. Todd
H. Thomson	1931	F. McGloin
J. S. Macdonald	1932	L. A. Hardie
P. B. Lucas	1933	W. M'Lachlan
R. S. Burles	1934	F. B. Allpass
J. D. Langley	1935	R. Norris
J. Bruen	1936	W. Innes
I. M. Roberts	1937	J. Stewart
W. Smeaton	1938	T. Snowball
S. B. Williamson	1939	K. G. Thom
A. F. D. MacGregor	1946	D. F. Dunstan
J. Armour	1947	I. Caldwell
J. Pritchett	1948	D. Reid
H. MacAnespie	1949	N. Drew
J. Glover	1950	I. Young
N. Dunn	1951	M. Lunt
M. Bonallack	1952	A. Shepperson

COUNTY CHAMPIONSHIPS

CHESHIRE AMATEUR CHAMPIONSHIP

1921 G. Tweedale
1922 G. Tweedale
1923 I. Sidebottom
1924 M. S. Walker
1925 D. Eadie
1926 W. Sutton
1927 W. Sutton
1928 N. Sutton
1929 J. Braid, jun.
1930 H. W. Heslop
1931 E. Coventry
1932 H. D. Porter
1933 H. M. N. Fogg
1934 C. W. Timmis
1935 J. Abraham
1936 W. Sutton
1937 H. E. Walker
1938 E. Davenport
1939 M. W. Budd
1940-45 War interval
1946 C. W. Timmis
1947 P. Clark
1948 C. W. Timmis
1949 S. Mettam
1950 H. Humphreys
1951 H. Humphreys
1952 D. H. L. Shone

DERBYSHIRE AMATEUR CHAMPIONSHIP

1913 Dr. H. Barber
1914-20 War interval
1921 G. Nutt
1922 E. P. W. Davis
1923 B. W. Maltby
1924 T. G. M. Ward
1925 J. C. Harrison
1926 C. Thorpe
1927 C. Thorpe
1928 T. B. Farrington
1929 C. Thorpe
1930 C. Thorpe
1931 C. Thorpe
1932 C. Thorpe
1933 J. Long
1934 C. Thorpe
1935 A. Robinson
1936 E. Ashmore
1937 A. Robinson
1938 J. Armitt
1939 H. Bennett
1940-45 War interval
1946 J. Armitt
1947 R. Pattinson
1948 R. Pattinson
1949 R. Pattinson
1950 J. Armitt
1951 R. Pattinson
1952 H. Bennett

KENT AMATEUR CHAMPIONSHIP

1925 L. Schon
1926 T. Chilton
1927 W. C. Wright
1928 A. J. Evans
1929 F. Parry
1930 E. R. Tipple
1931 J. C. V. Moberley
1932 F. McGloin
1933 H. S. Mitchell
1934 O. Austreng
1935 F. McGloin
1936 O. Austreng
1937 O. Austreng
1938 A. T. Wilson
1939 Dr. J. Slaherty
1940-45 War interval
1946 T. D. Page
1947 M. Hough
1948 A. G. S. Penman
1949 A. G. S. Penman
1950 A. G. S. Penman
1951 A. G. S. Penman
1952 M. D. Asprey

NEXT UNION SECRETARY

Major A. J. Whitley Lavarack, who retires as secretary of the English Golf Union on March 31, 1954, will be succeeded by Captain W. G. L. Folkard, secretary of Mill Hill Golf Club, London.

Captain Folkard will assist Major Lavarack from July 1 this year until he takes over.

ALWAYS FIRST

Covering up?

I suppose, however, there'll still be more wrangling about that than there'll be at Lord's this week over the Australian request that all Test wickets here and in Australia should be covered.

Although it's being pressed hard I think the final decision will be that they shall be covered in Australia, where weather conditions can have a far greater effect on the result than they can here—shades of Brisbane—and that conditions at present prevailing at home will be allowed to remain.

HAROLD MAYES: Talking sport in the "Empire News," Oct. 5, 1952.

WITH WHAT IS NEWS IN SPORT

THE PAPER ?

SUNDAY
EMPIRE
NEWS

OF COURSE

COUNTY TITLES

LANCASHIRE AMATEUR CHAMPIONSHIP

1910 G. F. Smith
1911 R. W. Crummack
1912 R. W. Crummack
1913 R. Jennison
1914 S. Robinson
1915-19 War interval
1920 R. W. Crummack
1921 A. T. Dixon
1922 T. L. C. Heald
1923 R. H. Hardman
1924 D. E. B. Soulby
1925 S. Robinson
1926 S. Robinson
1927 R. H. Hardman
1928 S. Robinson
1929 S. Robinson
1930 R. H. Hardman
1931 H. G. Bentley
1932 H. G. Bentley
1933 J. Kennedy, jun.
1934 A. R. Walton
1935 E. Halliwell
1936 D. S. Coates
1937 I. W. Calder
1938 I. W. Calder
1939 H. G. Bentley
1940-45 War interval
1946 R. K. Bell
1947 W. K. Hargreaves
1948 R. J. White
1949 J. W. Jones
1950 I. W. Calder
1951 J R. Wroe
1952 D. T. Stevenson

LIVERPOOL CHAMPIONSHIP (*Amateur and Professional*)

1923 R. D. Vickers
1924 R. D. Vickers
1925 J. Bond
1926 W. H. Davies
1927 W. Robertson
1928 R. D. Vickers
1929 W. H. Davies
1930 E. W. Kenyon
1931 W. H. Davies
1932 W. H. Davies
1933 W. H. Davies
1934 E. W Kenyon
1935 C. Fryer
1936 R. Halsall
1937 W. H. Davies
1938 J. H. Busson
1939 John Burton
1940-45 War interval
1946 John Burton
1947 John Burton
1948 J. W. Jones
1949 E. Green
1950 R. S. Jarman
1951 John Burton
1952 E. Large

Manchester and District Professional Championship

1920 Peter Rainford
1921 W. R. Bourne
1922 A. E. Hallam
1923 No Championship
1924 J. Scarth
1925 T. G. Renouf
1926 T. Barber
1927 D. C. Jones
1928 G. Good
1929 F. Taggart
1930 J. Burton
1931 D. C. Jones
1932 P. H. Rodgers
1933 T. Pierpont
1934 F. E. Dennis
1935 A. J. Isherwood
1936 A. J. Isherwood
1937 F. E. Dennis
1938 R. Burton
1939 R. Burton
1946 A. J Isherwood
1947 A. Perry
1948 T. Gardner
1949 N. Sutton
1950 T. Fairbairn
1951 G. Howard
1952 E. W. H. Kenyon

AMATEUR TESTS

Manchester and District Open Championship

1936 D. C. Jones
1937 A. Walker
1938 A. J. Isherwood
1939 N. Sutton
1940-45 War interval
1946 A. J. Isherwood
1947 A. Perry
1948 T. Gardner
1949 N. Sutton
1950 T. Fairbairn
1951 G. Howard
1952 E. W. H. Kenyon

Midland Counties Amateur Competition

1895 C. S. Hayward
1896 C. S. Hayward
1897 A. M. Chance
1898 E. F. Chance
1899 T. Fitzherbert
1900 F. W. Clive
1901 C. A. Palmer
1902 S. C. Healing
1903 F. M. Lindner
1904 C. A. Palmer
1905 E. Blackwell
1906 E. Blackwell
1907 C. A. Palmer
1908 F. A. Woolley
1909 F. A. Woolley
1910 J. Humphries
1911 F. A. Woolley
1912 E. Blackwell
1913 F. A. Woolley
1914 F. A. Woolley
1915-18 War interval
1919 J. B. Beddard
1920 C. Bretherton
1921 C. Bretherton
1922 J. B. Beddard
1923 I. S. Sidebottom
1924 W. H. Priest
1925 R. P. Humphries
1926 R. P. Humphries
1927 T. P. Perkins
1928 D. S. Bruce
1929 H. Arnold
1930 D. A. Fiddian
1931 E. W. Fiddian
1932 S. T. Matthews
1933 Dr. A. R. M'Callum
1934 S. Lunt
1935 C. Stowe
1936 D. M. Sutherland
1937 Dr. W. Anderson
1938 J. S. Mitchley
1939 Dr. W. M. Robb
1940-46 War interval
1947 H. J. Roberts
1948 C. Stowe
1949 J. L. Morgan
1950 J. L. Morgan
1951 J. M. Urry
1952 J. L. Morgan

STAFFS AMATEUR CHAMPIONSHIP

1924 J. B. Beddard
1925 J. B. Beddard
1926 J. B. Beddard
1927 Abandoned
1928 J. B. Beddard
1929 J. B. Beddard
1930 Dr. G. J. Moore
1931 R. M. W. Pritchard
1932 G. S. Beharrell
1933 R. B. Bayliss
1934 C. Stowe
1935 T. R. Deighton
1936 T. R. Deighton
1937 K. W. Chaundy
1938 G. Mills
1939 C. Stowe
1940-45 War interval
1946 C. Stowe
1947 E. Perry
1948 C. Stowe
1949 P. Squire
1950 M. D. Morgan
1951 S. M. Sangster
1952 J. Beales

COUNTY TESTS

YORKSHIRE AMATEUR CHAMPIONSHIP

1894 F. E. Woodhead
1895 F. E. Woodhead
1896 G. H. Peacock
1897 H. B. M'Carthy
1898 F. E. Woodhead
1899 F. E. Woodhead
1900 E. A. Lassen
1901 H. B. M'Carthy
1902 W. P. Wightman
1903 H. D. Gaunt
1904 H. H. Barker
1905 J. S. Roddam
1906 H. H. Barker
1907 C. Hodgson
1908 E. A. Lassen
1909 E. A. Lassen
1910 L. Butler Smith
1911 H. D. Gaunt
1912 J. L. Crowther
1913 E. A. Lassen
1914 E. A. Lassen
1915-18 War interval
1919 D. M. Smith
1920 C. Hodgson
1921 B. Wragg
1922 C. Hodgson
1923 W. C. Macfarlane
1924 B. Wragg
1925 J. Robinson
1926 N. W. Dunn
1927 J. Robinson
1928 J. Robinson
1929 J. Gent
1930 J. Robinson
1931 A. Fell
1932 T. J. Thirsk
1933 G. Marwood
1934 J. Robinson
1935 A. T. Kyle
1936 A. T. Kyle
1937 J. E. Gent
1938 J. E. Gent
1939 S. E. Banks
1940-45 War interval
1946 W. V. Hembry
1947 J. E. Gent
1948 Dr. J. R. Acfield
1949 M. Lee
1950 M. Lee
1951 R. Arend
1952 M. Lee

Index to Advertisements

Printed by Withy Grove Press Ltd., Manchester 4, and published by Kemsley Newspapers Ltd., Manchester and London.